✔ KT-486-401

FAMILY LAW AND FAMILY VALUES

ONE WEEK L

Oñati International Series in Law and Society

A SERIES PUBLISHED FOR THE OÑATI INSTITUTE FOR THE SOCIOLOGY OF LAW

General Editors

William L F Felstiner   Johannes Feest

Board of General Editors

Rosemary Hunter, Griffiths University, Australia
Carlos Lugo, Hostos Law School, Puerto Rico
David Nelken, Macerata University, Italy
Jacek Kurczewski, Warsaw University, Poland
Marie Claire Foblets, Leuven University, Belgium
Roderick Macdonald, McGill University, Canada

Titles in this Series

Social Dynamics of Crime and Control: New Theories for a World in Transition edited by Susannah Karstedt and Kai Bussmann

Criminal Policy in Transition edited by Andrew Rutherford and Penny Green

Making Law for Families edited by Mavis Maclean

Poverty and the Law edited by Peter Robson and Asbjørn Kjønstad

Adapting Legal Cultures edited by Johannes Feest and David Nelken

Rethinking Law Society and Governance: Foucault's Bequest edited by Gary Wickham and George Pavlich

Rules and Networks edited by Richard Appelbaum, Bill Felstiner and Volkmar Gessner

Women in the World's Legal Professions edited by Ulrike Schultz and Gisela Shaw

Healing the Wounds edited by Marie-Claire Foblets and Trutz von Trotha

Imaginary Boundaries of Justice edited by Ronnie Lippens

Family Law and Family Values

Edited by

Mavis Maclean

Oñati International Series in Law and Society

A SERIES PUBLISHED FOR THE OÑATI INSTITUTE
FOR THE SOCIOLOGY OF LAW

·HART·
PUBLISHING

OXFORD AND PORTLAND, OREGON
2005

Published in North America (US and Canada) by
Hart Publishing
c/o International Specialized Book Services
5804 NE Hassalo Street
Portland, Oregon
97213–3644
USA

Hart Publishing is a specialist legal publisher based in Oxford, England. To order further copies
of this book or to request a list of other publications please write to:

Hart Publishing, Salter's Boatyard, Folly Bridge,
Abingdon Road, Oxford OX1 4LB
Telephone: +44 (0)1865 245533 or Fax: +44 (0)1865 794882

WEBSITE: http://www.hartpub.co.uk

British Library Cataloguing in Publication Data
Data Available

ISBN 1–84113–547–X (cloth)
ISBN 1–84113–548–8 (paper)

Typeset by Compuscript Ltd, Shannon
Printed and bound in Great Britain by
Biddles Ltd, www.biddles.co.uk

ACKNOWLEDGEMENTS

The International Institute for the Sociology of Law in Oñati has enabled this group of scholars who share an interest in family law and family policy, but come from a variety of academic disciplines and countries, to meet, to argue and to develop their ideas over almost a decade. We are grateful for this opportunity and proud to present our third volume of essays. This follows on from our first volume, *Family Law and Family Policy in the New Europe*, published in 1997, which looked at the development of family law in a period of rapid transition in Eastern Europe when norms and values were re-examined and a great deal of legislative activity was taking place. This led us in our second volume, *Making Law for Families*, published in 2000, to look closely at the law-making process, with which some of us had become closely involved. Looking at this process and at the struggle of law reformers to respond to changing family forms has brought us full circle to look again at the purposes and values underlying family law, and at the relationship between 'Family Law and Family Values'.

We are particularly grateful to Malen Gordoa for her impeccable organisation of the meeting and to Jenny Dix for her editing skills.

CONTENTS

CONTRIBUTORS

Masha Antokolskaia taught private law at the Moscow State Law Academy from 1989 to 1998 and from 1993 to 1995 was a member of the drafting team elaborating the New Russian Family Code (in force since 1996). From 1998, Dr Antokolskaia was a research fellow at the Molengraaff Institute of Private Law, University of Utrecht, studying Perspectives for the Harmonisation of Family Law in Europe. She is now Professor of Family Law at the Vrije University, Amsterdam and is a member of the Commission on European Family Law.

Benoit Bastard is Directeur de Recherche at the Centre de Sociologie des Organisations, Centre National de la Recherche Scientifique, Paris.

Jef Breda assists Professor van Houtte at the University of Antwerp (Universitaire Faculteiten Sint-Ignatius Antwerpen).

Laura Cardia Vonèche is a Senior Researcher at the Institute for Public Health, University of Geneva.

Michelle Cottier is a research assistant and PhD student at the Faculty of Law at the University of Basel, Switzerland. She is a former student of the Oñati Masters Programme in the Sociology of Law. Her current research interests are transsexualism and the law, same-sex partnerships, secrecy in adoption, child protection and juvenile penal law.

John Eekelaar FBA is a Fellow of Pembroke College, Oxford, and Reader in Law at the University of Oxford.

Malgorzata Fuszara teaches at the Institute for Applied Social Studies at the University of Warsaw. She is a Board Member of the IISL, Oñati.

Lisa Glennon is a Lecturer in Law at Queen's University, Belfast. Her main research interest is family law, in particular the legal definition of the family in the light of contemporary societal trends, the legal regulation of gender and sexuality, and the distribution of property and income on relationship breakdown.

Jacek Kurczewski is Professor of Sociology of Custom and Law at the University of Warsaw. From 1991 to 1993 he was Deputy Speaker and member of the Polish Parliament, and from 1997 to 1998 he was Director of the International Institute for Sociology of Law in Oñati, Spain. He is the author of *Conflict and 'Solidarność'* (Warsaw, 1981), *Resurrection of Rights in Poland* (Oxford, 1993), *Deputies and Public Opinion* (Warsaw, 1999) and co-editor of *Corruption in Social Life* (Warsaw, 2000).

Jane Lewis is Professor of Social Policy at the London School of Economics. Her most recent book is *The End of Marriage? Individualism and Intimate Relations* (Cheltenham, Edward Elgar, 2001).

Mavis Maclean CBE is Director of the Oxford Centre for Family Law and Policy in the Department of Social Policy and Social Work, University of Oxford, and a Senior Research Fellow in the Faculty of Law. She is former President of the RCSL, a Fellow of the IISL, and Academic Adviser to the Department for Constitutional Affairs.

Valeria Mazzotta is a lawyer practising in civil and family law, and assistant to Professor Sesta in the Department of Private and Family Law, University of Bologna. She is a co-founding member of the Observatory on Family Law, District of Treviso. Her special interests are 'extra legal' relationships and new trends in family law.

Katrin Mueller-Johnson is a graduate of the Free University of Berlin and Oxford University. She is currently a PhD student at the Department of Human Development at Cornell University and an international associate of the Oxford Centre for Family Law and Policy. Her current research focuses on two distinct areas: the facilitation of post-divorce parental contact through child contact centres, and the suggestibility of vulnerable witnesses, such as children and the elderly. On completion of her PhD she will be taking up a post at the Institute of Criminology, Cambridge University.

Stefka Naoumova is a Professor of Law at the Institute for State and Law, University of Sofia.

Teresa Picontó Novales teaches at the University of Zaragoza in Spain. She has published a number of books about family law and family policies. These include *La Protección de la Infancia: Aspectos Sociales y Juridicos* (Zaragoza, Egido, 1996) and *En las Fronteras del Derecho: Estudio de Casos y Reflexiones Generales* (Madrid, Dykinson, 2000).

Johanna Schiratzki is an Associate Professor in the Faculty of Law, Stockholm University. She was a visiting fellow of the Centre for Socio-Legal Studies, Wolfson College, Oxford in 2000 and is now Director of the Stockholm University Institute of Social Civil Law. Her publications address the best interests of the child in relation to such things as custody issues, artificial reproduction, human rights, migration law and Muslim law.

Julie Shapiro is Professor of Law in the School of Law, University of Seattle.

Carol Smart is Professor of Sociology and Director of the Centre for Research on Family Kinship and Childhood at the University of Leeds. She is also Deputy Director of the ESRC research group on Care, Values and the Future of Welfare (CAVA). She is currently researching the influence of divorce on wider kin relationships, transnational kinship and contact and residence disputes concerning children. Research publications include *The Changing Experience of Childhood: Families and Divorce* (with B Neale and A Wade, Cambridge, Polity, 2001), *Family Fragments?* (with B Neale, Cambridge, Polity, 1999) and *The New Family?* (edited with EB Silva, London, Routledge, 1999).

Velina Todorova currently teaches Family and Inheritance Law at the Plovdiv University and works for the Bulgarian State Agency for Child Protection. She has been a member of the International Society for Family Law since 1997. Her research interests include family law, children, parent–child relationships, state intervention, public care for children, and personal obligations deriving from family relations.

Jean van Houtte is Emeritus Professor of Sociology and Sociology of Law at the University of Antwerp (UFSIA). He is the founding director of its Centre for Sociology of Law, and an honorary Rector of the same university. He is a past president of the Research Committee on the Sociology of Law and one of the founding fathers of the International Institute for Sociology of Law in Oñati. His research interests and publications relate to the administration of (civil) justice, family law, and legal professions in Belgium and Europe.

Maria João Romão Carreiro Vaz Tomé teaches at the Portuguese Catholic University School of Law in Porto and works as a legal adviser to the Portuguese Central Bank. Her research interests include family law, social security law and financial law.

Wolfgang Voegeli is Professor of Civil and Economic Law at HWP-Hamburg University of Economics and Politics. He has conducted a number of interdisciplinary socio-legal studies in the field of family law, and is currently programme director of the Master of European Studies at HWP.

Introduction

MAVIS MACLEAN

P UBLIC CONCERN AND political debate have been dominated to a surprising degree throughout Western and Central Europe, Australia,
North America and the Far East since the late 1980s by concerns
about the structure of family life, as a more fluid and dynamic pattern of
personal relationships has been developing and making demands upon
those responsible for shaping the policy landscape.

Each individual experiences obligations arising from personal relationships. These are often difficult to meet due to lack of resources whether of
time or money, and give rise to conflicting obligations involving not only
tension between the demands of various relationships or between meeting
current or future needs, but also between private norms and the demands
of a public regulatory system. At a time of increasing complexity, diversity
and change in living arrangements we wish to explore how obligations as
perceived by the individual sit alongside those put in place as part of a system of legal rules. We have used the term 'personal relationships' as we wish
to move beyond ideas of family based on legal status or household composition to explore the obligations which arise from new forms of relationship
such as same-sex couples, serial parenting relationships, obligations across
generations and obligations arising from friendships which may be based
on geographical proximity or shared experience in work or leisure.

The questions addressed in this volume are concerned firstly with the
nature of family law. What is this entity known as the family? How does it
differ from other groups such as colleagues, neighbours, or friends? Are
there new kinds of relationship which we might seek to regulate, such as
same-sex relationships or the responsibilities of adult children to older parents? What do we seek from such a regulatory framework? Risk management? Protection of weaker parties? The promotion of a set of common social
or moral values, or protection of the public interest from the demands of
those in difficulty as a result of relationship breakdown? What are the macro
level norms concerning the nature of the obligation to care or to earn? Finally,
we ask whether there is a continuing role for family law at a time when individual choice is widely held to be the dominant mode of social organisation.

In our focus on the nature of the obligations which arise from personal
relationships we distinguish these from the obligations which arise in the

market place or in the context of work. These personal relationships may be based in a variety of contexts, either a legally defined relationship such as marriage, or a de facto relationship based on sharing a common household over time such as cohabitation, or on biology either as parent or child where there will be dependency at both ends of the age range, or in wider kin networks, or with social relationships based purely on personal choice. Recent work in the UK by the editor with John Eekelaar with young couples indicates that although there is a reliance on the language of individual choice rather than that of rights or duties, nevertheless this individualism is based very firmly within a context of social, familial or normative factors. For example, when we asked why a couple had married rather than lived together we would often hear, 'I thought about this and this is what I wanted to do', but this would often be swiftly followed by 'my parents really wanted us to marry' or 'I am Catholic/Muslim and this is what we do'. We are as yet unclear as to how the law fits into this contextualised individualism.

The volume has four parts. Part I is concerned with the framing of Family Law and Family Values. The first chapter by John Eekelaar questions the debate on the apparent breakdown of family values described by American and British writers, and the growth of self-seeking behaviour. This has been countered by Etzioni in the call for a new communitarianism and an embargo on new rights. Eekelaar sees instead the development of a new individualism based on autonomy requiring negotiation with others holding similar values. The question for family lawyers is how far this negotiation takes place within the context of shared understandings, and how the concept of justice is invoked where there are competing claims. With increasing diversity, and perhaps reduced common understandings, the role of law may need to go beyond individual conflict-solving to providing the basis for social cohesion. It is hoped that the new research in Oxford into discovering what people think their personal obligations are will be an important step in the process of evaluating legal frameworks. Wolfgang Voegeli in chapter 2 describes how in Germany the Federal Court, in judgments related to family matters, has moved away from social ordering towards social protection, with a weakening interest in marriage and a growing concern to protect those affected by relationship breakdown.

In chapter 3 Malgorzata Fuszara and Jacek Kurczewski address the question of the complexity of the boundary between family values and the values of friendship in determining the obligations which arise from personal relationships. They point to the place of family in the Polish Constitution where it is associated with procreation and the protection of children. But friendship too has been historically regulated by law and at one time assumed a family-like form through blood brotherhood. This relationship overrode the duty of a soldier, who, if he were to come across his 'brother' on the field of battle, was required to pass by without action. Furthermore, friendship may or may not exist within a sexual or legally married relationship, and a sexual relationship and the procreation of children may or may not occur between friends. In Europe, they suggest the boundary between kin and friends is becoming more open, as household partnership may not involve any formal relationship, and may be temporary, and that as households change a continuing relationship can change a family tie into a friendship. They quote Martha Finemans's suggestion that in order to avoid preferring one mode over another, the legal privileges of family status could be taken away, or alternatively that preferential treatment should be extended to all who are close and practise the traditional family values of support and care.

The final chapter (4) in this first part from Jane Lewis explores the changing context for the family obligation to care and to earn at the macro level from a social policy perspective. The traditional two-parent family, in which the man went out to work and the woman took care of the home, has eroded in respect of family change and labour market change towards a model where all adults earn. But this shift towards individual economic responsibility has not been accompanied by a parallel change in the acceptance of responsibility by all adults for the unpaid work of caring for dependant family members.

The second part of the volume is concerned with the new kinds of relationship between parents and children, and the role of law in supporting and controlling various developments. In chapter 5 Julie Shapiro addresses the devaluation of the genetic connection to children through assisted reproduction, and points out how market values have affected family formation with the development of the new technologies which may in the United States involve the purchase of gametes (see also Sterrett, 2002). This marketisation brings to the fore the issue of the rights of those adults who have entered into contracts, and may make it harder to keep the welfare of the child centre stage. Laura Cardia Vonèche and Benoit Bastard discuss in chapter 6 how new forms of co-parenting after separation are being supported by the state where there is a political will for each child to have continuing relationships with both parents, but the authors raise doubts as to whether this can be achieved in practice. Even where both parents have internalised such a view there may still be a need for professional help in achieving these goals. Katrin Mueller-Johnson (chapter 7) agrees that even where parents have internalised the message that continuing parenting is desirable, they may need a great deal of professional help in achieving this in conflicted families. But what kind of help? Johanna Schiratzka describes in chapter 8 how, where there is conflict in Swedish families, the law is no longer seen as the appropriate mechanism for intervention. Finally in this section (chapter 9), Carol Smart discusses the social habits and etiquette that develop after separation and divorce among the wider kin group, and in particular the nature of the relationships that do continue after household disruption. The needs of the children are an important determinant, but so is the degree of friendship between the adults involved.

Part III of the volume looks at relationships between adults. What kinds of relationship, like marriage, currently rest within a legal framework and which lie outside? Do we wish to change this balance? What are the implications of doing so either for same-sex couples or for heterosexual couples with a common household? Lisa Glennon opens this section of the book with a discussion (chapter 10) of the evolutionary development of same-sex union rights in Canada, where the statutory schemes containing reference to spousal status have been held up for scrutiny before the equality framework of the Canadian Charter of Rights and Freedoms. She finds the location of same-sex issues within the equality agenda, rather than within the family change agenda, as helpful not only in normalising same-sex relationships but also because once full relational equality has been achieved, taking the pro-equality approach rather than awaiting change in the institution of marriage could enable more fundamental questions about the nature of relational rights and obligations for all couples to be raised. The section ends with three chapters (11 to 13) describing recent approaches to legislative change in three European countries. Michelle Cottier looks at the new draft law to regularise same-sex unions put out for public consultation in Switzerland in November 2001. Matrimonial law was taken as the starting point, and tested to see if the detail would fit same-sex unions rather than following the equality route, and the focus has been on same-sex 'marriage' rather than the regulation of de facto relationships regard-less of gender. The main impact of the debate, however, has been to open up demands for the circle of relationships regulated by law to be expanded. Valeria Mazzotta has addressed the very recent consideration of unions other than marriage by Italian jurists and family policy experts. The law in Italy ignores homosexuality, but will in the near future need to listen to the European Parliament's calls for equality of treatment (eg the Paper on Fundamental Rights signed in Nice in December 2000). Hopes for normalisation in Italy are pinned to the process of Europeanisation and to the acceptance, under natural law, of the need to protect the place of the affections, but the hand of tradition rests heavily on the legislature. Teresa Picontó Novales addresses the situation in Spain, where marriage is no longer the only means of entry into conjugal life, and where first the courts and more recently the legislators have begun to address the injustices resulting from the present lack of protection for de facto couples. The autonomous communities have taken the lead here (Roca, 2000). But if the welfare of children is the key issue in approaching the regulation of couple relationships, the debate on the adoption of minors by same-sex couples remains heated and unresolved. The issues arising from these chapters are closely linked to our previous volume, and indicate the plurality of debates which impact on the development of this kind of regulatory change and particularly the tension between case law and legislative change. In the civil law countries where legislative change is linked to the democratic process, it may take longer for 'Progressive' legal change to take place than in common law jurisdictions, where jurists can argue equality issues and move forward case by case, to be followed later by law reform for the community as a whole.

Finally, in Part IV we deal with two sets of issues emerging to new prominence: first that of the obligations of adult children to their elderly parents, and secondly the tensions between increasing diversity in ethnicity, language and custom within societies and attempts to build harmonisation of family law in Europe. The volume closes with a contribution addressing the overall topic of the book, the relationship between Family Law and Family Values today.

In the first part of this section (chapter 14) Jean van Houtte and Jef Breda raise the question of where responsibility lies for the maintenance of older people in need: with the family or with the state? Elderly people in residential care cannot themselves meet the costs this entails, and the state is now in difficulty as both the numbers involved and the unit costs have rapidly increased, and though the state has a right to call upon the younger generation to contribute to the financial burden it is in practice unacceptable to seek cash transfers between the younger generation and the responsible public authority. The most that can be achieved seems to be the acceptance of the need for younger people to organise the necessary care, despite the more stringent requirements of the law. There is a clear divergence between what is thought acceptable practice and what could be required by law. In chapter 15 Velina Todorova describes a very different situation in Bulgaria where it is only recently that the responsibility of the younger for the older generation has been questioned with marketisation and individualism since transition. But the traditional dependance of adult children on their parents and reciprocal care for the dependant elderly has been buttressed by recent legal reforms, despite the popular preference for voluntary arrangements.

Finally, we come to issues of diversity and harmonisation. Continuing with material from Bulgaria, Stefka Naoumova notes in chapter 16 that ethnic differences are now recognised as central to the processes of democratisation and marketisation. But there are also serious problems associated with the special status, economic welfare and employment for the different ethnic groups due to substantial differences in their educational and qualification levels. The key values for Bulgarian society remain the protection of children, family honour and preservation of health, and moral and human dignity. Finally, Masha Antokolskaia brings to our attention in chapter 17 the question of family values and the harmonisation of family law. She raises the question of whether there are pan-European values in existence because, if so, these appear to range from divorce on demand in the United Kingdom to the total absence of full divorce in Malta. There is no right to divorce in the European Charter, because the Charter reflects the lowest common denominator within the range of opinion involved. If minorities feel that law is based on the more conservative values, then inevitably they will regard their rights as being infringed. But if law is based on more progressive values, it will always be more permissive, but nevertheless the conservative majority may arrange their lives as they wish without hindrance. So Antokolskaia argues for a more permissive base for family law, in that those of a more conservative disposition can always restrain their activities, whereas if the law is more conservative, those of a more progressive tendency will be unable to live as they choose.

The closing chapter from Maria Vaz Tomé—on 'Family Law and Family Values on Portugal'—looks across at the pre-eminence of the family as an institution enshrined in the constitution, and affected by both canon and civil laws. But the concept of the family underlying the legal norms is far more homogeneous than the diversity of social reality. She argues persuasively for the rethinking of family law in terms of the functions we want the family to perform and, while accepting the limitation of the power of law, at the same time avoiding unduly minimising its potential to influence social tends.

REFERENCES

Roca, E (2000) 'Catalunia' in M Maclean (ed), *Making Law for Families* (Oxford, Hart Publishing).

Sterrett, S (2002) Introductory Essay, *Law and Society Review* 30/2: 209–17 (Special Issue on *Nonbiological Parenting*).

PART I

Framing Family Law

1

Personal Obligations

JOHN EEKELAAR

INTRODUCTION

I T IS WIDELY accepted that significant changes occurred in family behaviour in Western societies during the last quarter of the twentieth century; so much so that the well known American contemporary historian, Fukuyama (1999) has called this event 'The Great Disruption'. In Britain, the main characteristics associated with the event have been the following:[1]

— a decline in fertility (down by one third between 1961 and 1997);
— an increase in extra marital births (from 5 per cent of all live births in 1961 to 37 per cent in 1997);
— an increase in divorce: a five-fold increase in the divorce rate between 1971 and 1996;
— a doubling of the number of lone parent families between 1971 and 1991;
— a decline in marriage rates, such that while 5 per cent of girls who were 16 in 1974 are projected to be single at the age of 50, it is projected that 26 per cent who were 16 in 1991 will not have married by the age of 50;
— a doubling of the number of women cohabiting outside marriage between 1981 and 1996;
— an increase in the number of brides who had lived with their future husband before marriage from 5 per cent in the mid 1960s to 70 per cent of those marrying in the early 1990s;
— a decline in the proportion of households made up of adults with dependent children from 38 per cent of all households in 1961 to 23 per cent in 1998, and an increase in single person households from 11 to 28 per cent over the same period;
— a perception of a massive rise in crime over this period.

These events are said to be linked to attitudinal changes, and commentators in the United States and Britain have ascribed what they see as the breakdown

---

[1] This is taken from Gibson (2000).

in family values to a growth in more self-seeking behaviour by women and men. The literature is fully reviewed by Jane Lewis (2001a). Thus when Amitai Etzioni launched a populist communitarian manifesto, calling for a restoration of a sense of responsibility to communities, he demanded an embargo on the creation of new rights.[2] This communitarian counter-attack was part of a general reaction to the perceived over-liberalisation of the law during the 1970 and 1980s. The Divorce Reform Act 1969 moved away from the matrimonial offence doctrine and the procedure was effec- tively de-judicialised in 1977 when the 'special procedure' was fully estab- lished. Legitimacy became legally almost irrelevant after the Family Law Reform Acts of 1969 and1987. The legally dominant position of the hus- band during marriage and divorce was removed and it is at least arguable that a culture of financial dependency of former wives on their former hus- bands has diminished, to be replaced by a desire to achieve 'clean breaks'. In short, law seems to be walking in step with broad social changes which suggest a weakening of associative ties. Some said it encouraged increasing amorality (Morgan, 1995).

Yet policy did not always move in that direction. It has frequently been remarked that the emphasis in legal policy has shifted from focus on the relationship between the adults to their responsibilities to the children (Children Act 1989, Child Support Acts 1991, 1995). This emphasis on parental responsibility might be said to be intended to act as a counterpoise to the pursuit of individual rights and interests. It could even be argued that the distribution of assets between divorcing parties might be moving away from a welfarist mode of division designed to alleviate need towards an assessment of entitlement derived from contributions to a joint enterprise in which efforts in the market place and in the domestic arena are to be accorded equal worth,[3] reinforcing the responsibilities spouses owe to one another. However, this has now to be seen within the context of the added boost given to individual rights by the Human Rights Act 1998. Of course, the rights most relevant to family law, those to respect for private and fam- ily life, are qualified by references to the rights of others, but their express protection once again gives renewed scope for delineation of individualist interests. Yet, the renewed emphasis on rights does not necessarily imply a reduction of responsibilities, for, on the whole, one person's rights are another person's duties.

What all this amounts to is a confused picture of the framework within which personal relationships are conducted. People may doubt whether such relationships give rise to obligations, whether legal or moral. Yet it is still surely the case that people say of others in personal relationships: 'he ought to have done this' or 'she ought not to have done that'. Perhaps they sometimes speak in terms of rights and entitlements (for example, a right to

---

[2] Etzioni (1995), discussed by Eekelaar (2001).
[3] *White v White* [2001] 1 All ER 1.

receive a share in marital assets), or even (though probably on the promptings of lawyers) of their human rights. It might be contended that the very idea of 'family' is synonymous with the existence of a sense of obligation, even if sometimes only in small matters. So, the assumption of such obligations is one way in which individuals can absorb others into the family, such as the way in which an adult can be held to have treated a child as a 'child of the family', or cohabitants of the same sex can be held to become members of a 'family'.[4] But how can this idea of obligation survive in an environment in which individual rights prevail over associative obligations and in which self-interest dominates personal relationships?

NEGOTIATION AND BEYOND

It seems necessary to try to obtain a balanced picture of the present state of personal obligations. The issue was seriously debated in the United States after the publication in 1985 by Robert Bellah and colleagues of *Habits of the Heart: Individualism and Commitment in American Life*. This identified 'individualism' as 'the first language in which Americans tend to think about their lives', leading them to value 'independence' and 'self-reliance' above all else (Bellah *et al*, 1985: viii). This was a very broad-brush analysis. It was based on four separate research programmes, some involving discussions with private individuals, others with psychotherapists, voluntary associations and political organisations, involving (together) 'over' 200 interviewees. Much of the discussion on values in the private sphere centres around four individuals chosen as paradigms, who speak in very general terms about their 'philosophies of life'. The authors found that they had difficulty in 'justifying the goals of a morally good life'; they were confused about defining 'the nature of success, the meaning of freedom and the requirements of justice' (*ibid* 1985: 21). Since these are issues with which philosophers and theologians have wrestled for centuries, the problems of the respondents are very understandable. Similarly, their observation that

> Americans are … torn between love as an expression of spontaneous inner, freedom, a deeply personal, but necessarily somewhat arbitrary, choice, and the image of love as a firmly planted, permanent commitment, embodying obligations   (Bellah *et al*, 1985: 93)

does nothing other than take up an age-old theme, whether expressed in terms of conflict between individual passion and obligations to wider family (*Romeo and Juliet*), country (a standard operatic theme: see *Norma*, *Aida* and many others), or spouse (see Pushkin, *Eugene Onegin*, or, for those preferring classic cinema, *Casablanca*).

---

[4] See *Fitzpatrick v Sterling Housing Association* [1999] 4 All ER 705.

I do not dismiss the perception the authors hold of a certain indulgent self-centredness in contemporary American behaviour, but the generality of the discussion and the nature of the evidence on which it is based suggests that considerable caution should be exercised regarding their conclusions. There seems to be confusion about the central idea of 'individualism' or 'individualisation'. For Bellah *et al* this seems to denote a kind of self-centred indulgence; to be contrasted with a disposition towards 'commitment' and recognition of 'obligations'. But it is not so simple. In 1992 Anthony Giddens drew attention to the growth of the ideal of romantic love from the late eighteenth century and its displacement, in post-modernity, by forms of relationship referred to variously as 'confluent' love, 'pure' relationships or the democratisation of intimacy (Giddens, 1992). Romantic love involves 'projection identification' which creates a 'feeling of wholeness with the other' (*ibid* ch 3 and 61–2). The achievement of identification with the other was an end in itself, allowing no room for adaptation and change. If I may expand a little on Giddens's picture, the ethos of nineteenth-century romanticism can be seen as an extreme version of forms of communitarianism, where the self becomes totally immersed in the other in an ultimate act of self-sacrifice. There is truly no space for adaptation and change, which is why the romantic ideal was always unattainable, or if attained, extinguished in death, as in the *Liebestod*, or, in more modest versions, banished in the timeless and non-worldly formula: 'They lived happily ever after.' So was this, then, the antithesis of modern individualistic self-indulgence? Not at all, because, for all his or her identification with the 'other', the romantic lover is totally self-absorbed. No allowance whatever is made for the self-identity of the 'other', who is pursued with the intensity of addiction.

But these are images, abstractions born of idealisations of basic human wants and desires. Real life for people during the age of romanticism was a very different matter, as Giddens (1992: 62) points out, and I suspect it may be very different today from the self-indulgent portrait of individualism painted by Bellah *et al*. Elisabeth Beck-Gernsheim had earlier illuminated social reality more tellingly when in 1983 she explained how women's lives were beginning to change from one devoted to 'living for others' to 'a bit of a life of our own'.[5] In describing this, she drew mostly upon macro demographic data concerning changes in female education and work-patterns, so little could be said about the way norms were perceived. Was the 'living for others' an aspect of romantic love? Partly, no doubt, the myths of romantic love fed into it, but more importantly it reflected the social norms which were imposed in the post-Enlightenment era. They imposed a role to be lived by women, especially married women. Enough has been written about that. What is of concern here is the nature of the dispensation which is emerging from their decline. What is the content of this new 'individualisation'?

[5] 'From "Living for Others" to "A Life of One's Own": Individualisation and Women', first published in 1983, reprinted in Beck and Beck-Gernsheim (2001) ch 5.

The answer to this question sketched by Giddens in 1992 and by Beck and Beck-Gernsheim in 1995, both of whom drew on a wide range of contemporary literature (in Giddens's case, especially psychoanalytical discourses), is very similar. 'Confluent love', wrote Giddens, 'is not necessarily monogamous ... What holds the pure relationship together is the acceptance of each partner "until further notice", that each gains sufficient benefit from the relationship to make its continuation worthwhile.'[6] Central to this is the role of 'negotiation'. The rights and obligations arising from the relationship are subject to negotiation.[7] Even sexuality is a matter of negotiation, whether it be the matter of sexual exclusivity, or even the nature of the sexuality itself.[8] Beck and Beck-Gernsheim describe the same phenomenon. They call it creating a 'do-it-yourself life history' (Beck and Beck-Gernsheim, 2001: ch 6 and 88). In daily life, 'more and more things have to be negotiated, planned, personally brought about' (*ibid* 91). The organisation of life after divorce 'has to be negotiated, often fought over' (*ibid* 94).

So here we have a glimpse of the new individualisation. It is hardly a world of 'do as I please'. Autonomy may have become a newly important value, but it is restrained by the necessity of co-existing with other people who are exercising the same value. Co-existence is made possible through negotiation. But this analysis throws up new problems. What is meant by negotiation? Does it occur within a socially unregulated market place? The concept of negotiation was central to Finch and Mason's account of family responsibilities published in 1993. This remains a pioneering and seminal study of the role of 'responsibility' in family relationships. Yet it must be remembered that Finch and Mason were primarily concerned with wider kin networks. They argued that responsibilities were not seen to be derived from 'rules' or pre-existing obligations, but 'the course of action which a person takes emerges out of his or her interaction with other people' (Finch and Mason, 1993: 62). In an earlier book, *Family Obligations and Social Change* (Finch, 1989), Finch made an important analysis of what negotiation might mean in this context. It was not equivalent to conscious bargaining, but referred to an *understanding* which emerged over time 'that there are certain things which they would do for each other if necessary' (*ibid* 181). But Finch was clear that such 'negotiation' did not take place in a vacuum, but within 'external structures'. It is these structures which create 'shared understandings' absorbed through membership of society that underlie the negotiations, for example (as Finch explains) that 'most people, both sons and daughters, acknowledge some responsibility for their parents in old age; daughters are commonly thought to be the people most suited to provide nursing care, for their mothers especially; men do not give up their jobs to care for a parent' (*ibid* 183). This reference acknowledges

[6] Giddens 1992: 63.
[7] *Ibid* 191.
[8] *Ibid* 63 and 96.

the role of 'social rules', which Finch describes as not being so much 'moral' rules 'concerned with determining how someone "ought" to behave, as common perceptions of "how the world works"' (*ibid*). This acknowledgement of norms is underlined by Finch's view that 'negotiation' is conducted according to normative guidelines, which require consideration of the person with whom the negotiation takes place, the state of the relationship with that person, the pattern of exchanges with that person, the effects of the outcome of the negotiation on that person's other family relationships and whether the issue being negotiated is appropriate for both parties at this point it time (*ibid* 178). As stated by Finch, these guidelines are reminiscent of those 'considerations' family courts are required to pay regard to when making decisions about children or financial resource-allocation. And just as is the case with those considerations, so these guidelines, and the 'negotiations', take place within some kind of normative framework. It has probably always been thus, though for the reasons mentioned by Beck-Gersheim, and other reasons, the nature of the 'shared understandings' (that is, the normative framework), and therefore of the outcomes 'negotiated' within them, has changed. Simply to refer to negotiation or reflexivity as the new model does not indicate what these shared understandings are. One needs to go further.

Carol Smart and Bren Neale did indeed do that in *Family Fragments?* (published in 1999). This was essentially a study of post-separation parenting. During 1994–6 31 women and 29 men were interviewed twice, at 12 and 18 months after their separation; 48 had previously been married. The sample was not 'representative', for it had been reached largely through support groups and by advertisement. But that did not matter as the purpose was to detect whether there were 'newly emergent forms of responsibilities, caring patterns and ethical codes' (Smart and Neale, 1999: 40). Smart and Neale concluded that indeed there were. These people were not acting amorally, in the sense that they reflected on their decisions and weighed up their consequences. Drawing heavily on Gilligan (1982) and on Bauman (1995), they argued that the mothers exhibited an ethic of care. As I understand it, this means that, for them, their decisions about what 'should be done' were solutions to specific problems in which their primary guideline was the practical manifestation of 'care' for another, in this case, the children. The fathers, by contrast, tended to proclaim an 'ethic of justice', which was abstract and rights-based, and they used the rhetoric of equality. Smart and Neale considered these two 'ethics' to be antithetical (Smart and Neale, 1999: 170–1).

This study is an important affirmation that the diminution of prescribed family and social roles has not necessarily resulted in a society devoid of ethical principle. But the authors' presentation of the two contrasting ethics suggests that we may be some distance from the 'shared understandings' referred to by Finch. Yet is this so? It may be that the division between the mothers' and fathers' ethical positions is not as gender-based, nor as anti-thetical, as it may appear. Smart and Neale's subjects were exclusively concerned with childcare. Mavis Maclean and I found something like the reverse of their findings when we considered mothers' and fathers' attitudes to financial support (Maclean and Eekelaar, 1997). In this context we found that the mothers tended to use more abstract concepts of justice in holding that men were obliged to put their obligations to their biological children above competing claims by new sets of children with whom the men were living, whereas the men, while recognising their obligation towards their first set of biological children, were keener to qualify it on account of their competing social obligations to new children or stepchildren. So the explanation for Smart and Neale's finding may simply be that mothers spoke the language of care because they were usually taking day-to-day care of the children. They did not need to use the language of justice because their interests coincided with maintaining their care for the children. By contrast, the only way the men could advance their claim was to appeal to a principle of justice that they should be entitled to exercise part of that care and reconcile it with competing claims of the workplace and of new family circumstances. In fact, Smart and Neale refer to occasions when the mothers wished to distance themselves from the fathers by recapturing their own 'space' (Smart and Neale, 1999: 141). It seems that they were trying to reconcile the children's interests, and thus the caring ethic, with their own newly emerging interests. Although the authors do not express it in this way, the resolution of such conflicts involves principles of justice. In short, it seems that both the ethic of care and the ethic of justice can be explained, should one choose to do so, by reference to some shared 'abstract' principle which demands due attention to be paid to the interests of all the actors, that the care of children is one of the most significant of these interests, but is not necessarily the only relevant one.

The circumstances of post-separation parenting is of course a good context in which to examine the norms to which people have reference when determining what their personal obligations are. But it is a very special context, which arises only after shared living has finished. We still need to know more about the norms to which shared living may give rise. Jane Lewis has made an important contribution to this knowledge in her 2001 book, *The End of Marriage?*. Lewis accepts that the advent of individualism 'does not mean that there will be no consciousness of "ought", but it is no longer imposed but has to be negotiated' (Lewis, 2001b: 126). To discover more about such negotiation, she interviewed 17 married couples with children and 17 unmarried couples with children, aged between 27 and 50, recruited by advertisement in nursing, teaching and social work publications. In order to provide a generational perspective, 72 of their parents were also interviewed. This was clearly not a 'representative' sample of the general population, and was not intended to be because one of the main objectives was to explore areas 'likely to reveal the balance between attention to self, as opposed to attention to other and to the relationship' (*ibid* 128), and the sample was designed to further that objective. However, some further questions (but not interviews) were posed to 777 people drawn from an Omnibus Survey by the Office for National Statistics, which was representative. Lewis describes the central issue as revolving around the idea of 'commitment'. The unmarried had tended to 'drift' into long-term unmarried cohabitation. They had lived together for so long they saw little point in marrying (*ibid* 135–6). They saw their 'commitment' as being 'private' rather than 'public'. Half of the unmarried and one-quarter of the married said they had no obligations to one another, or had not thought about them; but for the rest, they saw the obligation as coming from 'within' and not externally imposed.

> The crucial thing ... was seen to be the existence of commitment rather than its manifestation. Given that ... it is not surprising that most people in the sample also felt that it was proper to treat married and cohabiting parents the same.   (Lewis, 2001b: 145)

The nature of this 'commitment' is explored. It seems to consist in a willingness to apply the balance between work and family responsibilities in a 'fair' way, given the continued emphasis on the provision of childcare by the mother. Each should devote time to the family and respect the other's 'personal' time. Issues should be discussed, so communication is an important element. But in conclusion Lewis says: 'when the sense of social obligations is so fluid, it is undoubtedly difficult to find principles to underpin legal obligations' (Lewis, 2001b: 190). The picture is one of pragmatic compromise, and, although Lewis herself does not emphasise the concept, a sense of the importance of mutual *respect*. The idea of 'respect' is an important feature of autonomy and of rights discourse: one remembers Ronald Dworkin's 'right to equal concern and respect'. Yet is this enough to explain inter-personal behaviour? I will return to this point later; I will only say here that, even if this turns out to be an important explanatory factor, it is unlikely to tell the whole story because one may respect someone, and yet disagree with their viewpoint, or have to decide between the interests of a number of people whom one respects.

THE ROLE OF THE LAW

Has the law played a role in the construction of a new 'ethic' of interpersonal relations? So far, I have referred only to the fact that legal changes seem to have dismantled an earlier era of prescription through concepts such as fault-based divorce, illegitimacy and male dominance. But has it played a more positive role in promoting a different set of values? I suggested that it has done so in an unpublished paper given in 1983 which I called 'The Democratisation of Family Law', and which appeared in a revised form in 1987 (Eekelaar, 1987). There, drawing on Foucault, I tried to distinguish between the situations where law attempted to influence social behaviour through coercion and where it tried to achieve the same results through what I called 'normative' law. By that I referred to circumstances where the law, assuming a certain mode of inter-personal behaviour as being desirable, did not punish people for non-compliance, but promoted the desired consequences through various techniques, such as giving a surviving spouse a claim against the estate of a deceased testator, or safeguarding the occupation of the matrimonial home, or, after divorce, re-allocating assets in the way the court thinks just. More recently we have seen this technique operate through the Child Support Agency, which will work out the sums that absent fathers should be paying for their children. This raises the question as to how far the norms that lie behind the 'pragmatic compromises' observed by Lewis (if there are any) might be influenced by these legal developments; or whether, perhaps, these legal developments follow social behaviour. Mavis Maclean *et al* (2002) have remarked that data uncovered by the National Centre for Social Research have shown that the arrangements made between married people who separate look different from those made by the unmarried, although their circumstances are very similar. In particular, unlike the married, unmarried mothers make no bid to remain in occupation of the home or to acquire a share in the value of capital assets. She wonders whether this might follow from the fact that the law operates in a different way when married people separate than when unmarried people separate, leading, perhaps, to different expectations when similar circumstances arise.

A FURTHER INVESTIGATION

We can see that the important work that has been done in this area has established that a simple picture of a 'breakdown' of any sense of restraint on individual self-interest in personal relationships is far too simple. Yet the picture remains confused. *Do* people have a sense of obligation? Finch and Mason do not think people see themselves as following rules, yet Finch draws attention to 'shared understandings' about 'how the world works'. Lewis noted a rejection of 'externally imposed' obligations, and a reluctance to prescribe for others, yet the presence of internally generated commitment and a sense of 'fairness'. Smart and Neale emphasised a strong ethic of caring, at least among separated mothers. It seems, therefore, that one should hold open the possibility that people may still believe that personal obligations exist. But to gain a fuller understanding of them, we may need to conduct a more systematic exploration of the way people behave in their personal lives.

It is the intention of myself and my colleague, Mavis Maclean, at the Oxford Centre for Family Law and Policy (OXFLAP), to attempt this. We wish first of all to tap into that generation which experienced its childhood during the years when the 'great disruption' began first to make its impact on family life. These would be people born in the late 1960s, who are now in their early thirties. They would be drawn from an Omnibus Sample obtained from the Office for National Statistics, and would therefore be more reflective of the general population than the other studies. The reason for concentrating on this generation is to obtain a sample in which it is possible to separate those whose childhood was affected by family disruption and those whose childhood was not so disrupted, so that we can judge the extent (if any) to which the sense of obligation (if any) that they hold concerning personal relationships is affected by childhood experience. We want to ask them about how they responded to certain key events in what is often called the family life cycle, but which, in more individualist mode, might be called their personal lives, and, above all, *why* they responded as they did. The key events are forming a co-residential unit, becoming a parent, leaving a co-residential unit, experiencing the departure of children from home and feeling the first effects of the dependency of elderly parents. Not every respondent will have experienced all these events; we will not confine ourselves to parents.

The respondents will be asked about both the effect of such events on their actual behaviour and the reasons for such behaviour. This is likely to be a very difficult undertaking. The question *why* individuals acted as they did is an extraordinarily difficult one to answer. Is it answerable at all? Could one contemplate that people might claim that they acted in a certain way simply because that is what they wanted to do, or 'felt like' doing, at the time? To this the answer must be: whatever people may say, they must act for a reason. For, while at some level we can talk about acting on one's desires (eating when hungry; sleeping when tired), this turns out to be a very limited way of accounting for behaviour. It is not simply that there are many occasions when we do not in fact act on our desires, crudely conceived. It assumes that the only way we can decide between conflicting desires is to choose the strongest desire (although the expression 'choose' seems inappropriate, for the image seems closer to the stronger desire dictating the choice). In such a scenario, you would not need to, perhaps could not, weigh up all your desires. Your action would just 'happen', flowing from the desire. But that seems a strange way to explain behaviour. While people sometimes do lose control and act on urges alone, those are generally considered to be pathological cases (Raz, 1999b: 51–6).[9] You can also sometimes want things, but have no reason to have them (you already have enough, for example). In such cases acquiring them can be some form of

---

[9] Scanlon (1998) 41–9 argues that even when quenching 'brute' wants, satisfaction of the desires are not reasons for action but the future pleasures which the desires point towards. See also Dancy (2000) 35–8.

addiction. It therefore seems more plausible to say that in the standard case the action you choose you choose for a reason.

So we must assume that, at least normally, behaviour is undertaken for reasons, even if these may sometimes be hidden from the actors themselves. Respondents should be given the opportunity to articulate reasons, and if an outline of some reasons emerges, further elucidation of confirmation could be sought. Uncovering the reasons for action has not only an explanatory purpose. A reason must refer to something that is of value to the actor. To act for a reason which holds no value for the actor is to act for no reason at all. As Raz has put it: 'reasons are rooted in values' (Raz, 1999a: 252).[10] This is of particular importance in this context, for by reflecting on people's reasons for acting, we may access the values they hold.[11] One important goal of the empirical work will be to gain an insight into the values people hold in conducting their personal lives.

A TAXONOMY OF TYPES OF REASONS

Before engaging in the empirical work, it is important to hypothesise the possible ways in which the data might be analysed. To assist in this, I will use the following hypothetical case. Suppose a couple, Adam and Eve, begin to live together. They might or might not be married. They live in a house which is owned by Adam. After five years, Adam decides to raise a loan to purchase a rival company. He secures the loan by a charge on the house, and immediately makes the purchase. He tells Eve nothing about this, though he is counting on Eve's earnings to help him to repay the loan. Within days, however, the rival company collapses and the money is lost. Eve, meanwhile, has become pregnant, also without telling Adam that this had been her intention, knowing him to be reluctant to have children. When the truth is out, Adam wants Eve to terminate the pregnancy. Eve wants the child, but she knows that if she has the child, it is likely that the loan will not be repaid, and the house will be sold. Perhaps this couple does not have a future together. No matter. What is of interest is to examine what went wrong. It is likely that each will accuse the other of having acted wrongly in some way: that, had they acted differently, the problem could have been avoided. But what kinds of reasons could underlie such normative claims?

[10] See also p 261: 'one can only want something because of a good one believes the thing to have'.

[11] Raz (1986) ch 12 seems to make the stronger claim that if the thing one wants (or, perhaps more strictly, has a reason to want) is good for the agent, it is good in itself. This is consistent with his view that reasons are objective: only good reasons are reasons, and good reasons are those which promote the agent's well-being. Hence he concludes (p 318) that 'conflicts between morality and the agent's well-being, albeit inevitable, are only accidental and occasional'. I am doubtful whether Raz's concept of well-being is sufficiently robust to give helpful guidance in many circumstances: for example, to answer the question whether Adam or Eve had a (good) reason for not communicating with each other in the scenario spelt out below.

1 Rule-Based Duties

One type of reason could refer to compliance with rule-based duties, although the studies mentioned earlier tended to dismiss these as reasons for the actions investigated. But one can imagine that it could be said that, had Adam and Eve complied with their duties to one another, they could have avoided the mess they got into. Adam, it could be said, ought not to have taken out the loan on the house without first telling Eve, thereby giving her a chance to argue against it (or perhaps even to legally block it), or at least to alter her plans regarding conceiving the child. Similarly for Eve: she should not have allowed herself to become pregnant without telling Adam of her intention. This of course is to some extent wisdom after the event. Adam had no reason to believe Eve was planning to become pregnant. Perhaps he believed she would have approved his plans, or at least have shown indifference to them. Perhaps Eve believed that, when confronted with the reality of her pregnancy, Adam would have softened his opposition to having a child. But if they were under a duty to tell each other of their actions, that would have held whatever the outcome. Could such duties be reasons for action? If so, what could be the source of these duties?

It would be (relatively) easy to answer this in the case of Adam if there was some legal principle demanding consultation between partners before one of them entered a significant transaction concerning their common dwelling. But, while some laws might state this, at least in the case of married partners, not all do. English law does not. So, if there is no legal duty, on what basis might an English Adam be held to have failed in his duty? One possibility is to appeal to social norms. In the community in which he lives, it may be understood that people should not act as he acted. As we have seen, Janet Finch's analysis is compatible with a belief that such social norms can inform our understanding about what is the right thing to do. On the other hand, is it right to consider people bound by the standards of others? Perhaps Adam thinks he is bound in this way, taking as his standard for action the precepts which others around him hold. Although he broke one of those norms, he may now think that he acted wrongly, and even feel some guilt. Perhaps this is the way most of us judge our actions. I don't think we know the answer to this, and I think it is important that we find out more about it. The question will be: if people in Adam's position normally tell their partners such things, is the reason why they do it their belief that this is what other people think everyone should do?[12] If Adam was aware of this, then he has consciously broken a social rule.

But even if there was a legal or social rule requiring Adam to consult Eve, Adam might have taken the view that he was not bound by it. He might say:

---

[12] The norm would be a reason for Adam's action. According to Raz's analysis, the norm (wither legal or social) would provide an 'exclusionary' reason. That is, it would provide a ground for action which precluded consideration of other, competing, reasons: Raz (1999b) 80–1.

'I must follow what my conscience tells, and I am not morally bound by what the law says or by what others think I should do.' As GEM Anscombe (1997: 38–9) remarked,

> one cannot be impressed by this idea (that moral obligations derive from the norms of society) if one reflects what the 'norms' of a society can be like.

The same could be said of legal norms. Still, Adam is not necessarily saying that he believes he is always free to do just as he pleases. He is only saying that he does not see social or legal norms as providing a reason why he should have consulted with Eve. But might there be some other reason that put him under a duty to do so?

But what kind of reasons must people have in order to put them under what they would consider to be a moral duty?[13] We have seen that Adam might have rejected 'following the law', or 'following social norms' as sufficient to do this. It might be argued that following legal or social norms could normally be taken to provide the basis for a moral duty unless some moral principle was clearly contravened. The argument would be that legal or social norms perform an important co-ordinating function and promote social stability, and this provides a good moral reason in itself to compel their acceptance, unless in a particular case following them would lead to a greater moral harm. This reasoning gives a certain moral status to the law or social norms in themselves.[14] On the other hand, it might be argued that legal or social norms merely provide good proxies for indicating what is the moral thing to do, since they often embody good moral principle, but that they themselves command no moral respect. People would need to decide in every individual case whether the values they represented constituted sufficient moral reasons for action.[15] It is of course very common to refer to religious teachings or precepts as reasons for action, and this is often taken as providing a sufficient moral warrant for such action on the assumption that religion is a source of morality. Some may prefer to treat religious teachings and precepts as proxies for moral justifications in the same way as it has just been argued might be done for secular law and social norms.

But are there 'moral justifications', independent of legal, social or religious norms, from which duties can be derived? Moral philosophers have advanced various formulations to distinguish reasons which have moral content as distinct from those which are self-interested or self-serving. They usually tend to require the reasons to be derivable from maxims or principles of a generalisable kind. Scanlon (1998) brackets these ideas under the term 'contractualism'. His version is that 'what we owe each other' can be

---

[13] This is the issue raised by Dancy (2000) 1–2 when he speaks of 'normative' (as opposed to motivating) reasons: these are the reasons we cite 'in favour of' an action.

[14] This in brief is the view taken by Finnis (1984).

[15] This in a nutshell represents the approach taken by Raz (1995) ch 15. It is well expressed by Wasserstrom (1968) 278–9.

identified from maxims which others, with the same aim, could not reasonably reject.[16] This is clearly related to the Golden Rule ('act towards to others as you would expect others to act towards you'). To a large extent Scanlon's formulation would be satisfied by direct reference to actually held social norms, at least if they were held by almost everybody, for if others could not reasonably reject a maxim, they probably hold it too. If they do not hold it, the problem arises of knowing whether their rejection is unreasonable. This method may require us to consider whether whole populations, or segments of them, might be acting unreasonably, a difficult issue. In fact, people are unlikely to accept maxims that damage their interests, so if one's obligations are determined by maxims which *all* others accept, general fairness seems assured.[17] So Eve could not claim that Adam was under a duty to inform her of his transaction on the basis of a maxim that only men owe this duty to women, because Adam, and most men, could reasonably reject this, and are likely to do so. But if the basis was that all partners should provide this information, the maxim is more likely to be accepted by Adam. However, whether *everyone* would accept it is unclear: some partners may believe that no one should be under such a duty. Whether this is reasonable or unreasonable seems essentially contestable, and the nature of Adam's duty remains unresolved.

2 Duties Associated with Virtue, Care and Particularism

Alternative avenues might be open. One could appeal to the virtues of co-operation, trust and caring within relationships. These can be seen as aspects of a conception of morality which is rooted not in rules or maxims but in ideas about what it is to be a good person. Exercising benevolence is an important way of being a good person, and one way of doing that is caring for others, in particular, those close to you.[18] This, I take it, is at the root of the 'care' ethic detected by Smart and Neale. A related approach is to adopt what Raz calls the 'moral point of view' (Raz, 1999a: ch 11). Adam, it could be said, has reason to inform Eve of his actions because this promotes the values associated with respect and friendship. Such behaviour, it can be said, contributes to Adam's well-being as much as to Eve's (Raz, 1995: ch 2). I referred earlier to the idea of respect which seemed to appear in Jane Lewis's data on interpersonal behaviour. However, it is important

---

[16] 'an act is wrong if it would be disallowed by any *principle* that no one could reasonably reject' (Scanlon, 1998: 197, original emphasis).

[17] This would not hold for maxims which are not self-regarding. Take the principle: 'do not indulge in pastimes which injure animals'. It is unclear whether it would be reasonable or unreasonable for others to reject this. But if they did, they would suffer no detriment, so it is less likely to form a social rule than one which stated: 'do not indulge in pastimes which seriously injure other people'. Nor would it hold if the maxim, held by a majority, discriminated against a minority.

[18] See the discussion by Slote (1997).

not to shut out the possibility of altruistic behaviour. A significant, perhaps *the most* significant, component of much religious teaching is promotion of the notion of sacrifice. That God sacrificed Himself for humankind is the cornerstone of Christian belief, and Christians are supposed to be willing to make sacrifices for the benefit of others. Self-sacrifice in one form or another is indeed central to most forms of communitarian thinking, for individuals are held to be required, ultimately, to subordinate (sacrifice) their interests to that of the community. Self-sacrifice may of course be conceived of as a duty laid down by a rule. On the other hand, it may be thought of as arising from the requirements of virtue.

But while these strategies are useful in indicating what moral behaviour is, they are less successful in determining people's responses to particular circumstances. Adam may think he cares greatly for Eve, yet consider business matters to be for him, not for her. Indeed, Adam might resist the claim that he (morally) 'ought' to have told Eve by arguing that the element of trust in their relationship would be undermined by referring such matters to her. So his acceptance of the virtues of love, trust, respect and even sacrifice could co-exist with a belief that he should not, or need not, have informed Eve of his plans. *That* decision will be determined by the social rules he accepts.

There is another possible option to social rules as determinants of decisions. The idea that it is the facts themselves which determine decisions, or, at least strongly influence them, has been advanced by particularists, exemplified by Jonathan Dancy (1993). It is indeed possible for the achievement of a specific circumstance, or the avoidance of a specific circumstance (say, by pulling a child out of the path of an oncoming vehicle) to count as a reason for someone's action. It may be that further reflection would show that the actor is following some more abstract principle, and this could perhaps be detected by observing the actor's decisions in other, similar, cases. But I do not think it necessary for the actor to articulate such general principles, or even reflect on them, though others may do so and thereby discover a deeper motivation. It is also possible that deeper reflection will fail to yield an abstract principle, so that the decisions could seem arbitrary, for they reflect confused values. But that does not prevent the actors' appreciation of the facts from constituting reasons. Dancy's point seems to be a stronger one that one and the same set of facts can constitute a reason both for and against an action because of the context in which they arise. But Raz has argued that this effects an arbitrary distinction between the 'facts' and the 'context': it assumes the context does not form part of the reason, whereas, if the reason is seen in its completeness, it will do (Raz, 1999a: ch 10). The message of this debate seems to be that people's judgements must be seen fully in the context in which they are made, for knowledge of the surrounding context is likely to be necessary properly to comprehend the reason given, and thereby reveal the underlying values.

3 Prudential Reasons

James Griffin has been said to have articulated a 'prudential' theory of well-being (Griffin, 1986; Sumner, 2000). I do not wish to develop any discussion on the nature of prudential reasons. I will note only that it is conceivable that the kinds of reasons people may offer for their actions could be *entirely* self-serving, in the sense that the sole objective may be conceived of as being improving the circumstances of the respondent. It is of course not impossible for prudential reasons to be compatible with other-regarding action (Raz, 2000).

4 Appealing to their Rights?

It is an interesting speculation whether, if asked to comment on their situation, Adam or Eve would refer to the 'rights' that either of them might have. We do not know whether people in such situations characteristically do this, or whether they might more usually use the language of duty, and it is important to have more information about this.

CONCLUSIONS

Discovering what people think their personal obligations are, and why, seems to be an important step in evaluating legal frameworks, whether it be the structure of legal obligations to wider kin (as described by van Houtte and Breda in ch 14), or the role of grandparents (Smart in ch 9) or the role of marriage (see Picontó Novales in ch 13). We might be able to explore the relationship between the values people see in family relationships and in relationships of friendship (discussed by Fuszara and Kurczewski in ch 3) and throw some light on ethnic or other differences (see Naoumova in ch 16). These preparatory thoughts are intended to set the scene for such an exploration.

REFERENCES

Anscombe, GEM (1997) *Modern Moral Philosophy*, reprinted in R Crisp and M Slote (eds), *Virtue Ethics* (Oxford, Oxford University Press).
Bauman, Z (1995) *Life in Fragments* (Oxford, Blackwell).
Beck, U and Beck-Gernsheim, E (1995) *The Normal Chaos of Love* (Cambridge, Cambridge University Press).
—— (2001) *Individualization* (London, Sage).
Bellah, RE, Madsen, R, Sullivan, WM, Swidler, A and Tipton, SM (1985, updated 1996) *Habits of the Heart: Individualism and Commitment in American Life* (California, University of California Press).
Dancy, J (1993) *Moral Reasons* (Oxford, Blackwell).
—— (2000) *Practical Reality* (Oxford, Oxford University Press).

Eekelaar, J (1987) 'Family Law and Social Control' in J Eekelaar and J Bell (eds), *Oxford Essays in Jurisprudence (Third Series)* (Oxford, Oxford University Press).

—— (2001) 'Family Law: The Communitarian Message' *Oxford Journal of Legal Studies* 21: 181.

Etzioni, A (1995) *The Spirit of Community: Rights, Responsibilities and the Communitarian Agenda* (London, Fontana).

Finch, J (1989) *Family Obligations and Social Change* (Cambridge, Polity Press).

Finch, J and Mason J (1993) *Negotiating Family Responsibilities* (London, Routledge).

Finnis, J (1984) 'The Authority of Law in the Predicament of Contemporary Social Theory' *Journal of Law, Ethics and Public Policy* 1: 115.

Fukuyama, F (1999) *The Great Disruption* (London, Profile Books).

Gibson, C (2000) 'Changing Family Patterns in England and Wales over the Last Fifty Years' in SN Katz, J Eekelaar and M Maclean (eds), *Cross Currents: Family Law and Policy in the US and England* (Oxford, Oxford University Press).

Giddens, A (1992) *The Transformation of Intimacy: Sexuality, Love and Eroticism in Modern Societies* (Cambridge, Polity Press).

Gilligan, C (1982) *In Different Voice* (Cambridge, Mass, Harvard University Press).

Griffin, J (1986) *Well-Being: Its Meaning, Measurement, and Moral Importance* (Oxford, Oxford University Press).

Lewis, J (2001a) 'Debates and Issues Regarding Marriage and Cohabitation in the British and American Literature' *International Journal of Law, Policy and the Family* 15: 169.

—— (2001b) *The End of Marriage? Individualism and Intimate Relationships* (London, Edward Elgar).

Maclean, M and Eekelaar J (1997) *The Parental Obligation: A Study of Parenthood across Households* (Oxford, Hart Publishing).

Maclean, M, Eekelaar J, Arthur S, Finch S, Fitzgerald R and Pearson, P (2002) 'When Cohabiting Parents Separate—Law and Expectations' *Family Law* 32: 373–380.

Morgan, P (1995) *Farewell to the Family* (London, Institute of Economic Affairs).

Raz, J (1986) *The Morality of Freedom* (Oxford, Oxford University Press).

—— (1995) *Ethics in the Public Domain* (Oxford, Oxford University Press).

—— (1999a) *Engaging Reason: On the Theory of Value and Action* (Oxford, Oxford University Press).

—— (ed) (1999b) *Practical Reason and Norms* (Oxford, Oxford University Press).

—— (2000) 'The Central Conflict: Morality and Self-Interest' in R Crisp and B Hooker (eds), *Well-Being and Morality: Essays in Honour of James Griffin* (Oxford, Oxford University Press).

Scanlon, M (1998) *What We Owe to Each Other* (Cambridge, Mass, Harvard University Press).

Slote, M (1997) 'Agent-based Virtue Ethics' in R Crisp and M Slote (eds), *Virtue Ethics* (Oxford, Oxford University Press).

Smart, C and Neale, B (1999) *Family Fragments?* (Cambridge, Polity Press).

Sumner, LW (2000) 'Something in Between' in R Crisp and B Hooker (eds), *Well-Being and Morality: Essays in Honour of James Griffin* (Oxford, Oxford University Press).

Wasserstrom, RA (1968) 'The Obligation to Obey the Law' in RS Summers (ed), *Essays in Legal Philosophy* (Oxford, Basil Blackwell).

2

Basic Values and Family Law in Recent Judgments of the Federal Constitutional Court of Germany

WOLFGANG VOEGELI

INTRODUCTION

F AMILY LAW IS undergoing a secular process of individualisation. The law is progressively taking note of, and giving effect to, individual personal arrangements which complement and are substituted for the traditional family founded on marriage. Recent legislative changes in Germany include the Registered Partnership Act of 2001[1] and complex reform of the children's law, in effect since 1998,[2] which deals with parenthood, children's inheritance rights, and child custody and child maintenance.

The latter assimilated the rights of non-marital children to those of marital children, recognising unmarried parents and their children as a family. It also takes account of the complex arrangements that follow divorce and remarriage. Parents with whom the child is living and even step-parents can take binding decisions in matters of everyday life while the parent with whom the child is not living retains his or her say in fundamental issues. In questions of succession and child maintenance the former distinction between marital children and non-marital children is also eliminated.

The new Registered Partnership Act provides for a marriage-like legal relationship for same-sex partners, which can be officially recorded by a public authority, usually the registrar. Partners incur obligations of care and maintenance, receive inheritance rights, and their relationship can only be dissolved by court order. Such a partnership, though, has as yet no consequences with respect to taxes and social security insurance benefits. This form of legal relationship is not available for partners of the opposite sex.

---

[1] *Gesetz über die eingetragene Lebenspartnerschaft* of 16 February 2001, Bundesgesetzblatt I, 2001, 266.

[2] Mainly *Gesetz zur Reform des Kindschaftsrechts* of 16 December 1997, Bundesgesetzblatt I, 1997, 2942.

Here the strong value attached to marriage by the German constitution still prevails and has so far prevented any legislation offering protection to partners in de facto unions like that which the New South Wales De Facto Relationships Act has been offering for over fifteen years.

At the same time the law increasingly takes note of the financial burdens of families in tax and social insurance law. Traditionally, such burdens were only given marginal consideration, and benefits for families depended on the fact of marriage rather than the actual cost of rearing children. It took several decisions by the Federal Constitutional Court (FCC) to force the legislator to acknowledge the burdens of child rearing irrespective of whether the parents were married or not.

In this chapter these developments will be considered in the context of the historical process of the functional change of family law. Judgments by the FCC[3] from 1998 onwards on family law and related areas in which the interpretation of Article 6 *Grundgesetz*[4] was an issue, except for those concerned with tax and social insurance, have been analysed to note how:

— the law takes note of individual moral obligations and social developments
— individual rights and obligations are being construed
— the public interest is expressed in the ordering of family relations.

HISTORICAL BACKGROUND

Over 20 years ago I published an essay on functional change in German family law over time (Voegeli, 1982). The main proposition was that a shift had taken place from public to private ordering, and from defining the public interest behind public ordering as an element of social ordering, to defining it as an element of social protection. Family law has always been a mixture of contract and status related norms. The concept of regulating individual family relations by contract has a long tradition with regard to family property. But it is a modern concept with respect to entry into and exit from formal personal relationships. Whereas the act of entering into a marriage has been seen as a contract since the Enlightenment, the terms and conditions of marital life and the conditions of exit were more or less under state control and not a matter of individual choice. There was a brief period in the first half of the nineteenth century when the conditions for exit were rather liberal in Prussia and the concept of contract was given considerable room in contrast to later in the nineteenth century, when state control of the institution of marriage tightened. But it is only in recent years that the law has honoured private contracts regulating cohabitation outside marriage, and

---

[3] All judgments of the FCC analysed in this chapter are to be found online under www.bverfg.de. They are cited by file-number and date.

[4] Basic Law—the constitution of the Federal Republic of Germany.

private ordering of the conditions of living together inside marriage. On the other hand, where there is no formal contract, private exchanges of goods and services in cohabitation are seen as strictly voluntary, and not giving rise to any compensation claims at breakdown, although there are exceptions where the courts construct an implied partnership in relation to specific items of property.

Public ordering of family relations was originally based on a concept of public interest that focuses on upholding a certain order of society. In modern times this focus has slowly shifted towards protection of the weak. The concept of marriage as an institution served to assert the moral superiority of the bourgeois classes over the nobility and to domesticate the working class. Marriage in this sense is an element of what may be called *Disziplinargesellschaft* in the sense of Max Weber. The family based on marriage was instrumental in the 'fabrication of dependable man' (Treiber and Steinert, 1980). Men and women had to be pressed into an institution which would generate responsibility under state control. Although in a capitalist society the individual as an abstract legal person has almost unlimited competence to make everything the object of legally relevant dispositions, the family had to be excluded, in the interests of stability.

In modern times the need to discipline citizens directly is reduced. The whole structure of society is such that it automatically disciplines its members. Socialisation and education is organised by society under legal regulation. And the working life of the individual is regulated by strong social expectations, work patterns and a social security system. A disciplined cultural motivation and the requisite social infrastructure make external discipline superfluous, as far as the institutions of marriage and the family are concerned. Where discipline is seen as necessary it is enforced by state agencies directly. Furthermore, access to the workforce and provisions of the welfare state make all women economically independent to such an extent that exit decisions by women have become much easier.

The consequence has been a shift in the interpretation of the public interest that is still strong in family law from upholding a specific order of society to a focus on social protection. This shift is also supported by modern acknowledgement of the individual as being at the centre of constitutional theory. To curb individual freedom requires a definition of public interest that is legitimate in constitutional terms. It is rather difficult to argue that marriage represents a moral value that ranks higher than individual freedom. But social protection of the weak, ie children, or a spouse who has partially relinquished employment for the sake of child rearing and housekeeping, is such a legitimate public interest. In Germany it ranks as a constitutionally protected value. Moreover, the needs of these weaker parties for protection have arisen out of joint family decisions. But protection is still linked to marriage. With the exception of children and parents, outside marriage there is almost no social protection for the weak through family law.

RECENT JUDGMENTS BY THE
BUNDESVERFASSUNGSGERICHT (FCC)

1 Cohabitation Outside Marriage

(a) Registered Partnerships For Homosexual Couples—1 Bvf 1/01 of 17 July 2002

The Registered Partnerships Act[5] 2001 has been very controversial in the *Bundestag* (German Parliament) and the bill was divided into two, the first containing the substantive law which needed no consent by the *Bundesrat* (second chamber) and a second containing tax provisions and administrative procedure which did need such consent and which was subsequently defeated. The consequence was that it was up to the *Länder* individually to regulate administrative procedures.

Mainstream conservative opinion on the constitutional protection of marriage derives from article 6 of the German *Grundgesetz* which obliges the state not to replicate the legal regulation of marriage in other legally ordered partnerships. The basis of this opinion is Article 6: (a) an individual *liberal right* to freely enter into a marriage; (b) an *institutional guarantee* binding the state to offer a comprehensive set of rules setting up marriage as a traditional form of partnership; and (c) a *constitutional fundamental value judgment* binding the state to protect marriage against legal infringements of any sort.

The plaintiffs challenging the constitutionality of the new Registered Partnerships Act argued that the special protection afforded to marriage by the constitution includes protection of the exclusivity of marriage as an institution. In their view the constitution requires an order to differentiate between marriage and other partnerships and prevents the legislator from providing for other partnerships similar to marriage.

The FCC reiterated its case law by which the elements of marriage protected by the constitution are that it is a union of infinite duration, includes one man with one woman, is founded on a mutual and free decision with the participation of state authorities, with equal rights for both spouses, and freedom for spouses to decide their communal living arrangements.

The FCC declared that the Registered Partnerships Act does not violate the freedom to enter into a marriage. The legislator left open what is to happen when a partner in a registered partnership wants to marry. But persons already married or in a registered partnership may not enter into a new registered partnership. Technically, any member of a registered partnership may enter into a marriage freely with the effect, as prevailing opinion would have it, that the registered partnership would cease to exist *ipso iure*. This

---

[5] Registered Partnerships Act 2001: *Gesetz zu Beendigung der Diskriminierung gleichgeschlechtlicher Gemeinschaften*, Bundesgesetzblatt I, 2001, 266.

is not an omission by the legislator. Instead, it is the result of the legislator's anticipation that otherwise the FCC might see the freedom to marry as infringed. The court declared, however, that the legislator was free to make an existing registered partnership an impediment to marriage as such a rule would serve to protect the institution of marriage. Indeed, it is hard to imagine that the FCC could have ruled that an existing partnership would be an infringement of the freedom to marry since such partnerships are terminable upon either mutual consent after one year or individual choice after three.

With respect to institutional guarantee the court has always ruled that within the structure formed by the elements outlined above, the legislator is free to regulate marriage. In the present case the court is of the opinion that the Registered Partnerships Act does not affect the institutional guarantee because this only protects marriage and does not prohibit other unions that are not marriages.

Regarding the constitutional value judgment the court has constantly held that the state must desist from any actions that harm the institution of marriage, and must promote marriage. The main rule derived from the reform is that the state may not put married couples at a disadvantage compared to other couples. This clearly is not the case with the registered partnerships of same-sex couples. Moreover, the court argued against two of its members with dissenting opinions who derive from Article 6 *Grundgesetz* a duty to discriminate against other forms of unions. While the court generally argues that Article 6 contains no such duty, it does limit this ruling to same-sex partnerships and other unions that cannot compete with marriage. It expressly states that it would be different if the legislator were to introduce a legally ordered form of partnership available to different sex couples as that would produce incentives not to marry. The court gives the example of a partnership where couples have the same rights as married couples but fewer obligations. The legislator is barred only from creating an institution that would be interchangeable with marriage. The court explicitly holds that the legislator may set up rules for unmarried couples that fall short of creating a de facto marriage.

The striking feature of this judgment is that in two dissenting opinions the institutional guarantee is construed to have much more scope. The present president of the court, Papier, objected to the narrow construction of the majority and especially the acceptance by the majority of the changing character of marriage as an empirical social institution. He argued that Article 6 *Grundgesetz* incorporates material normative standards, which the legislator has to abide by. In his reasoning the institutional guarantee bars the legislator from setting up marriage-like unions under a different name. By that reasoning, and it is widely represented in legal literature, marriage as an institution becomes exclusive in the sense that it effectively bars the legislator from setting up marriage-like unions. Papier expressly stated that the constitution puts marriage as a heterosexual union under the protection of the state. And this means in his reasoning that the state has to guarantee that personal unions of adults are to be heterosexual and are to be marriages.

The judgment marks another step in the direction of legal acceptance of social change in family life. It acknowledges individual choice and, while there is no constitutional right for members of non-marriage unions to be protected by the law, the legislator is free to offer such protection, with a reservation by the court regarding heterosexual couples if such unions produce incentives not to marry.

Regarding homosexual couples the underlying moral argument of the majority is that society profits from individuals taking responsibility for one another in legally protected unions, while the president argued along the lines of traditional family law, seeing marriage as a form of social ordering. Marriage by this argument is seen not only as offering the necessary protection to family members unable to protect themselves, but also as an institution incorporating a public interest in a specific order of society. But even according to the majority opinion the scope for the regulation of cohabitation of heterosexual couples is not clear. Whether formal regulation of cohabitation is feasible is at least debatable. It seems that the court still upholds elements of the old concept of public interest in the regulation of marriage. But the obiter dicta are flexible enough to allow anything short of a union copying marriage to be enacted for de facto couples.

(b) Residence Rights for Fathers of Foreign Nationality—2 BvR 231/100 of 30 January 2002

In a case concerning the granting of a residence permit to a father, who did not have German nationality, of a child who was of German nationality, the FCC took occasion to set standards both in an injunction (2 BvR 1523/99 of 31 August 1999) and in the final decision following a series of decisions (on the protection by Article 6 *Grundgesetz* against measures ending the residence of foreigners—BVerfGE[6] 76, p 1 (41ff); 80, p 1 (90ff); extension of the protection of Article 6 *Grundgesetz* to non-marital fathers—BVerfGE 92, p 58 (176ff); protection of fathers with visiting rights—BVerfGE 64, p 180 (187ff)).

In this case the mother was of German nationality and the parents were not married. The authorities wished to extradite the father on the grounds that he had been residing illegally in Germany and was in hiding, trying to avoid extradition. Several applications by the father to be awarded formal refugee status had been declined. The court made it quite clear that when deciding on extradition the authorities would have to consider the constitutional protection of the family including non-marital families, and that the

---

[6] *Entscheidungen des Bundesverfassungsgerichts*—Reports of the FCC, cited by volume and page.

legislator had accepted this view when introducing the new children's law equalising the status of marital and non-marital children. It then went on to state that the constitution protects the obligation of the state to protect the family, which in itself is a public interest, and that this takes precedence over any public interest in the extradition of a foreigner. It would have to be shown in each individual case that there is a constitutionally relevant value that should take precedence over the protection of the family. The enforcement of the residence law for foreigners is not seen as such a value by the court. Hence, the fact that the father had been living illegally in Germany and that he had been evading the authorities through hiding were judged as irrelevant by the court.

The decision has two important aspects: (1) the valuation of family relations as against other public interests and (2) the high value attached to non-marital family relationships. The first aspect is important because for a long time the courts had held that a married German mother could be expected to follow her husband to his native country together with her child, who is also a German citizen. The courts were of the opinion that the protection of the family could take place anywhere in the world and they would not stop the extradition of a foreigner to protect the family.[7] The decision clearly shows that the protection of the family no longer has the connotation of establishing a specific order of society by repressive means. But rather it signifies the duty of the welfare state to offer practical protection to families who would otherwise be in jeopardy through actions of state authorities.

The second aspect is closely connected. The equal valuation given to non-marital families shows that the FCC is of the opinion that family relations outside marriage are a social fact to be considered, and that where protection of the weak is at issue the family form is of no importance. The court, though, does place importance on the fact that the parents have registered joint custody. Where no family ties have been established in everyday life there is nothing to protect. The court has consistently not held that formal legal family obligations are essential but rather—in the case of parents—the factual discharge of parental duties. In an obiter dictum the court makes it quite clear that it considers actively used visiting rights as family relations protected under Article 6 para 1 *Grundgesetz*.

(c) Conclusion

Family forms outside of marriage are protected by the FCC, especially as far as children are concerned. The children's law of 1998 has changed not only the immediate family obligations but has an effect on other sectors of the law, too. The court takes the rights and obligations of non-marital

---

[7] The author, while doing his practical stages for the second state law exam in Germany at a public authority handling complaints in matters of residence permits, got bad marks on his work for building his reasoning on the arguments that the FCC nowadays uses.

fathers seriously and protects them if the rights are actively used and the obligations honoured. The FCC still sees marriage as an institution carrying moral value in itself, representing a public interest to be asserted against individual ordering of life styles. But while individual agreements between unmarried couples in questions of property, maintenance and child custody are honoured by the law it will not give protection where such agreements are not in place. Whereas same-sex couples now enjoy quasi-marital rights, and the FCC has upheld that law, it remains unclear as to how much protection the legislator might afford unmarried couples should he choose to regulate unmarried cohabitation in the way laid down by the New South Wales De Facto Relationships Act. For the cases decided by the court, though, the trend is clearly towards further recognition by the law of the empirical individualisation of family forms. At the same time the transformation of hitherto only moral obligations into legal ones, as in the case of same-sex partnerships, is seen as a positive move.

2 Protection of the Weak

(a) Unconscionable Marriage Contracts 1 BvR 12/92 of 6 February 2001, 1 BvR 1766/92 of 29 March 2001

In the first case, in 1976 a 26-year-old pregnant woman signed a marriage contract with the father of the child, who had been opposed to marriage and wary of the new maintenance law about to come into effect in 1977, waiving all maternal maintenance claims and indemnifying the father against all maintenance claims for the child above DM 150 per month. They then married before the birth of the child. The wife was earning an income, though substantially less than the husband's. Both assumed that it would be the wife's responsibility to rear the child and that in the case of divorce she would be awarded custody. The couple divorced in 1989 and in 1990 the child sued the father for maintenance. The lower court granted the claim, arguing that the marriage contract of 1976 was *contra bones mores*. The father then sued the mother to indemnify him. The lower court dismissed the action. The Court of Appeals (*Oberlandesgericht*) ruled in favour of the father. The plaintiff was not given leave to appeal to the Federal Supreme Court on a point of law.

The courts have held marriage contracts to be void where the waiving of maintenance claims necessarily led to the spouse having to claim welfare benefits from the state (BGH,[8] FamRZ[9] 1983, p 137; NJW[10] 1991, p 913; NJW 1992, p 3164). To waive a maintenance claim thus forcing the custodial parent of a small child to enter the labour market is not seen as being

---

[8] *Bundesgerichtshof*—Federal Supreme Court.
[9] *Zeitschrift für das gesamte Familienrecht*—Journal of Family Law, cited by year and page.
[10] *Neue Juristische Wochenschrift*—New Weekly Law Journal, cited by year and page.

contra bones mores (BGH, FamRZ 1985, p 788). Only in special cases of unforeseen future developments have the courts held such contracts to be void in accordance with the principle of good faith, and in view of the necessary protection of the interest of the child (BGH, FamRZ 1985, p 788; FamRZ 1987, p 46; FamRZ 1991, p 306ff). A marriage contract was upheld by the Federal Supreme Court where before entering into a marriage a pregnant woman had waived her claim to maintenance after divorce. The spouse allegedly had exercised duress as he could have declined to marry and only be responsible as the father of a child born out of wedlock (BGH, FamRZ 1992, p 1403; FamRZ 1996, p 1536; FamRZ 1997, p 156). Moreover, compared to the situation of a single mother with only a limited claim to maintenance after the birth of a child (one year old at the time the contract was signed; para 1615 l BGB) her rights as a married woman were considerably better even with the waiver of post-divorce maintenance. The interest of the child is already served if the custodial parent may adequately devote herself to the necessary care of the child. The lower court of appeal had granted a substantially higher amount (BGH, FamRZ 1995, p 291; FamRZ 1997, p 873).

Indemnifying the non-custodial parent against maintenance claims from a child is generally seen as a valid contract wherein a person obliges him or herself to pay the debt of another person without becoming a debtor of the original creditor (para 329 BGB). Such a contract has been held to be unconscionable where an indemnification was granted in return for a waiver of visiting rights. This was seen as an improper commercialisation of child custody (BGH, FamRZ 1984, p 778). In a different case where in the contract the non-custodial parent agreed not to claim custody and was granted an indemnification the Federal Supreme Court held the contract to be valid as the granting of custody to the indemnifying parent was in the best interest of the child (BGH, FamRZ 1986, p 444).

Statute law is quite inconsistent regarding the standard of protection against the signing away of rights. While no waiver is possible in the case of maintenance claims in the ascending and descending line (para 1614, sub-para 1 BGB) as well as in the case of spouse maintenance during marriage or separation (para 1360a, sub-para 3 and para 1361, sub-para 4 BGB), a waiver of spouse maintenance after divorce may be freely agreed. There is not even a requirement that this contract should be in writing (para 1585c BGB). Marriage contracts altering the matrimonial property regime are valid but need to be signed before a notary public who has the duty to inform both spouses of the consequences of their contract (para 1408, sub-para 1, 1410 BGB). Contracts concerning individual items of marital property are valid without any form except for landed property where the contract has to be notarised. A contract altering the statutory system of pension splitting upon divorce is void if divorce proceedings begin within one year (para 1408, sub-para 2 BGB). If entered into in connection with divorce proceedings it needs to be approved by the Family Court (para 1587, sub-para 2 BGB).

The FCC held the judgment by the appellate court in this case to be unconstitutional, violating Article 6 para 1 *Grundgesetz*. The protection awarded therein to marriage and the family obliges the state to set limits to private autonomous contractual ordering where a contract is an expression or result not of a marital partnership based on equality, but rather of the dominant position of one spouse. In such cases of structural imbalance it is the duty of the courts to control and correct the contents of a contract (at para 31).

The FCC invokes article 6 para 4 *Grundgesetz* which offers special protection to mothers. From that clause it derives a duty of the courts to offer protection to a pregnant woman against pressure being exerted on her from her social surroundings and by the father of the child, especially if such pressure results in terms of a contract that massively militates against her interest (at para 33). In such a case the necessary basis for private autonomous decisions is no longer given.

According to the FCC structural inequality is assumed, if an unmarried pregnant woman has put before her the alternative either to care for the child alone or accept inadequate conditions in a marriage contract. While the appellate court had argued normatively, citing the right of the father not to enter into a marriage and finding that even under the unfavourable conditions of the marriage contract the mother still acquired a better legal position than she would have had as a single mother, the FCC argues empirically. It looks at the factual social situation of unmarried mothers. Its main arguments are:

1   Pregnancy is a situation in which women are under pressure. They have to radically change their life plan and accept responsibility for the child. The FCC then cites empirical studies that have shown that during pregnancy the partnership with the father of the child breaks down at a significantly higher rate than normal (Vaskovics, Rost and Rupp, 1997: 59ff). At the same time pregnancy bears health risks for mother and child (at para 34).

2   At the time the contract was signed unmarried mothers were still stigmatised to a considerable degree. Thus a pregnant woman experienced social pressure to marry and to justify not marrying to her family and friends, and later to her child. Single mothers suffer more psychological stress than married mothers. This fact has been related to the higher death rates of small children of unmarried mothers (Anthes, 1979: 162ff, at para 35).

3   The economic situation of unmarried mothers is significantly worse than that of married mothers. In the worst case an unmarried mother carries responsibility for the child alone, has a limited maintenance claim for herself (in 1976, one year if she was unable to be

employed; today, three years), while her income generally is halved because of the time she needs to devote to rearing the child. This leads to one-third of households of single mothers having an income below the welfare threshold, whereas only 15 per cent of children of married couples live under such conditions (Vaskovics, Rost and Rupp, 1997: 126). Moreover, the compliance of fathers of children born out of wedlock, with maintenance obligations is considerably lower than where the parents were married (Bundesministerium, 2000: 139ff, at paras 36, 37).

The FCC takes these socio-legal empirical studies to construct a situation of structural imbalance which typically applies to pregnant women. Hence pregnant single women become a category of persons just like workers and tenants who need the protection of the state because of their inherent weakness. This special protection is mandated by the constitution and the FCC sets out to spell it out where the legislator has failed to do so. The court acknowledges that in the individual case the waiving of maintenance rights might be justified, especially where spouses conceive of their union as a partnership in which both spouses actually take equal responsibility for the rearing of children. But where a more traditional set-up prevails in which women give up employment to some extent, the structural imbalance is assumed. The mere promise of marriage is not seen as a sufficient counter-balance as in marriage men do not just give up rights and acquire obligations but also acquire rights.

The court then went on to look at the facts of the case and came to the conclusion that the appellate court had not given due consideration to the extent of the constitutional protection of mothers in construing the unconscionability provision of the German Civil Code, the gross imbalance of obligations being such that the woman even took over part of the man's obligation to pay child maintenance which he would have had as a father of a child born out of wedlock.

Furthermore, the FCC saw Article 6 para 2 *Grundgesetz* violated which gives a constitutional basic right to parents to care for and rear their children and defines this right as an obligation towards the child, too. The FCC has always construed this right as being in the interest of the child, obliging the parents to consider the best interest of the child (BVerfGE 59, 360 (382); 75, 201 (218)). Consequently, parents are not protected if they use this right irresponsibly. If the interest of the child is endangered the state is called upon to take protective measures. So far the FCC has dealt with cases of state intervention in parents' custodial rights. It now extends its case law to child maintenance. It is the duty of the parents, set by the constitution, to afford the child adequate maintenance. They are free to decide how they discharge themselves of this duty. Their decision, though, has to secure the maintenance of the child appropriately with respect to the financial situation of both parents. Anything less would be a violation of the child's constitutional rights (at para 48).

Where one parent indemnifies the other against maintenance claims by the child this can only be upheld if that parent can cover his or her own living expenses and adequate maintenance for the child (calculated with respect to the income of the non-custodial parent) out of his or her own income. If that is only possible if the custodial parent is employed full time, then the necessary costs of childcare have to be covered, too (at paras 52–4). In the present case the mother's income clearly was totally inadequate to cover these expenses.

The cases show that the FCC protects private ordering of family relations only within the boundaries formed by the need for social protection of the weaker party. The court uses Article 6 *Grundgesetz* for this. This article was originally designed to protect parental rights against state intervention in the light of experience during the Nazi era. It is now used to set guidelines for state intervention into private ordering. This is relevant not only for marriage contracts as in the present case. It touches upon all instances where legal financial obligations are waived within personal relations. These judgments are a clear indication that the constitution is being used to formulate a public interest focused on the need for social protection and includes all forms of family relations.

(b) Construction of Post-Divorce Maintenance Claims—1 BvR 105/95 of 5 February 2002

In this case the FCC looked at the case law regarding spouse maintenance after divorce. The court combined three cases of the 1990s where divorced spouses claimed that the case law of the Federal Supreme Court on post divorce spouse maintenance violated Article 6 para 2 *Grundgesetz*. Until 2001 the latter had consistently held that spouse maintenance was to be calculated in two different ways depending on whether the spouse claiming maintenance had been employed during marriage or not. Where a spouse had been employed and stayed employed to the same extent after divorce, maintenance was calculated by subtracting the income of the claimant— usually the wife—from the adjusted income (adjusted for maintenance payments to children, necessary expenses for earning an income etc) of the debtor—usually the husband—and awarding three sevenths of the difference as maintenance to the wife, this method being called the difference method. Where a spouse had not been employed during marriage but took up employment after divorce the maintenance needs of the wife were set at three sevenths of the adjusted income of the husband. Her maintenance claim was calculated by subtracting her income from the maintenance need thus established, this method being called the deduction method.

The reason for this difference in calculation methods was that the law stated in para 1578 BGB that the level of maintenance was set according

to the conditions of the marital life of the couple. In the former case law of
the Federal Supreme Court the latter was defined by the marital standard
of living, ie the income of the couple during marriage. Thus, had both
spouses earned an income, then the conditions of the marital life of the
couple were defined by their joint income. Had only one spouse earned an
income and the other tended to the household and to the rearing of children
then the conditions of the marital life of the couple were determined by the
employed spouse's income.

This case law ignored the value of the work of wives in keeping house
and rearing children. Furthermore, it had an element of arbitrariness to it.
Depending on which phase the marriage was in, the wife's income after
divorce was counted as having defined the conditions of the marital life
of the couple or not. If divorce occurred during the phase when children
had to be tended to, the mother would earn little or nothing. When the
phase of child rearing was over the wife would be fully employed. But to
prove that full employment of the wife had been part of a joint life plan of
the couple for that period was difficult. Such decisions often are not taken
well in advance, but as the situation changes.

The deduction method was abandoned by the Federal Supreme Court
in a judgment dated 13 June 2001 (FamRZ 2001, p 986). The Federal
Supreme Court now argues that the value of the housework by the wife
has to be taken into account. It contributes to setting the conditions of
the marital life of the couple and is substituted for by earned income
after divorce. Thus the difference method now prevails. The FCC gives a
constitutional reasoning for this change in the case law of the Federal
Supreme Court. The old construction of the maintenance obligation violated Articles 6 para 1 and 3 para 2 *Grundgesetz*, the former putting
marriage and the family under the protection of the state, the latter setting equal rights for men and women. The court argues that spouses are
free to decide on the division of labour in their marriage. If one of the
spouses gives up earning in favour of homemaking and child rearing then
this is a decision that both spouses are responsible for. This responsibility extends until after divorce. The constitutional protection of marriage
and the family, informed by the constitutional equal rights clause, mandates a construction of maintenance rights that is in keeping with joint
responsibility for marital decisions affecting income. It is then not possible to let only one of the spouses bear the burden alone after divorce.
Moreover, Article 6 para 1 together with Article 3 para 2 *Grundgesetz*
normatively set the contribution of both spouses during marriage as
being equal. This is not to say that household work is valued in money
terms as being equal to earned income, however large that may be. But
it does say that the law includes all contributions, be they in money or in
kind, without valuing them in money and then deems the total contribution of each spouse as being equal. According to the FCC this normative

equality is being violated by the former construction of spouse maintenance claims after divorce.

Furthermore, the court argues, the challenged construction of the maintenance claim presupposes that the decisions taken by the spouses on the allocation of the tasks of keeping house and rearing children have a final quality. Behind such a concept stands the assumption that the breadwinner–homemaker model of marriages still prevails. The court then draws on empirical research in family sociology to confront this assumption with the reality of modern family formation. The average age of women at marriage rose from 23 (1975) to 28 (1998). Furthermore, the rate of employment of married mothers has risen considerably. In 2000 74 per cent of mothers whose youngest child was aged 15–18 were employed and 61 per cent of all mothers with at least one minor child were in part-time employment. The FCC draws the conclusion that there is enough empirical evidence to support the hypothesis that the traditional breadwinner–homemaker model has been superseded by a model of dual career marriages with partial withdrawal of mothers from the work force during child rearing (at para 36). Marital living conditions are hence generally characterised by an initial dual income, a partial abstention from gainful employment by mothers during child rearing and a resumption of employment after the children have grown up. The construction of marital living conditions based on what the arrangements were at a certain point in time is seen as inadmissible by the court as such a method does not consider the changes over time, and thus results in discrimination against mothers (at para 35).

(c) Conclusion

In the decisions analysed in this section the court has given a new meaning to the constitutional protection of the family. In line with concepts of consumer protection and inalienable labour rights the court developed a substantive concept of individual autonomy as a prerequisite for the validity of contracts. Thus, family law obligations become mandatory in many cases where up to now private ordering has often led to women signing themselves off to destitution. The irony of the old law had been that private ordering was not tolerated regarding the conditions of marital life and the exit from marriage, but was tolerated regarding the conditions after divorce. Thus the actual protection of the law was linked to the couple staying married. The new construction gives protection where it is most needed: after divorce.

A similar conclusion may be drawn from the last decision. Although it does not set new standards of state intervention into private ordering it does give a new meaning to family law rights. The original normative concept behind spouse maintenance was that in the breadwinner–homemaker marriage the woman had to be protected and had to be given a maintenance claim that would secure her economic standard of living according to the standard she had enjoyed during marriage. This had always been a normative concept with little relevance to reality, as we all know. As soon as women no longer conformed to this model they tended to be looked upon as no longer in need of protection. But in real life there was no alternative to becoming self-sufficient, which meant that under the old construction of maintenance rights the protection of the law was largely symbolic, especially in cases where the need was the greatest, ie where minor children had to be cared for.

The court has brought the normative concepts of spouse maintenance law in line with social reality. Two households after divorce could not generally be financed on one income. And it is generally the mother who will have limited employment opportunities because of caring for children. These facts had been ignored for a long time in the construction of maintenance claims. Furthermore, the law now no longer turns a blind eye to situations of duress in which pregnant women sign away their rights. The court has thus consistently defined the public interest as social protection and redefined the limits of private ordering.

3 Ongoing Family Relations after Divorce—Visiting Rights and Spousal Co-Operation—1 BvR 2029/00 of 5 February 2002

In this case a divorced father now living far away from his children had requested his ex-wife to bring the children to the airport and put them on the plane so that he could exercise his visiting rights. She had declined and the family courts backed her view. The family courts' main argument was that the custodial parent is not obliged to use her time and money to alleviate the financial burden of the non-custodial parent that he incurs when exercising his visiting rights.

The FCC held that both parents had constitutional rights regarding the care and rearing of their children and that these rights are to be exercised in the best interest of the children. In the case of conflicting constitutional rights the favourite approach of the FCC is a *practical concord* to be struck between these rights, optimising their efficacy. In this case the constitutional rights of the child also have to be considered. If, as in this case it might very well be, the construction of the visiting rights of the father led to his practically not being able to exercise them or only to a considerably lesser degree, then this is seen by the FCC as a violation of the father's rights emanating from Article 6 para 2 *Grundgesetz*. The court also considers this as an infringement on the rights of the child to having contact with his or her father. The parents then are obliged to co-operate. While this case is not in any way a spectacular move in a new direction, it does underline the preoccupation of the court with questions of defining individual rights in complex family arrangements that still necessitate basic co-operation in the interest of the children. The new children's law of 1997 has been a move in that direction, trying to strike a new balance between the rights of children and the legal position of married parents, divorced parents and unmarried parents. For the first time the rights of the child have become the focus of the law and the status of the parents is reduced to a mere accessory fact. In this case the same pattern may be observed. The decision hinges on the rights of the child to have a visiting parent; also, of course, on the rights of the visiting parent. But it is doubtful whether the latter alone would have sufficed. Thus, family relations are defined from the point of view of the child and to a much lesser degree by marital status.

CONCLUSION

In the judgments of the FCC analysed here, an increasing recognition of factual social developments is to be found. The court has become very sensitive to social change and refers to empirical socio-legal studies to underline its argumentation. It takes note of the social and legal recognition of same-sex partnerships and does not try to construe the constitution in such a way as to set a monopoly for marriage as the only possible legal form of a partnership which constitutional theory would have allowed. But it does not give a clear indication as to how much legal ordering of heterosexual cohabitation it would allow.

The court furthermore acknowledges the diversity of family forms and tries to give equal chances to parent–child relationships irrespective of marital status. It does so in a subtle way, at times not deciding in favour of the plaintiffs but referring the lower courts to the new children's law as guidance for argument in other legal contexts. Most importantly, the court acknowledges the situations of need that mostly women face after divorce and construes the constitution in such a way as to give maximum recognition to them in family law.

Individual rights and obligations are being construed in accordance with social need and are transferred into normative guidelines but also with taking a functional approach to complex family situations. Freedom of contract is curbed and inalienable rights are introduced to protect the weak through a bold construction of the unconscionability clause of the civil code. The court thereby strengthens the legal approach that focuses on constitutional values when interpreting general clauses in statutes.

The change of focus of the public interest in legal regulation of the family from social ordering to social protection has been extended. Generally, in all economically relevant cases social protection now ranks first. The focus of legal protection is now on situations where protection is really needed, especially in post-divorce relationships. The focus is rightly moving away from the ongoing marriage, which generally offers protection without legal rights having to be enforced. Marriage as an element of social order still figures where the legal recognition of other heterosexual unions is the issue, although the boundaries are softening.

All in all, the FCC has unequivocally demonstrated a sensitive and sensible reaction to social change, allowing sweeping changes of the law where the legislator has reacted to social change, and putting constraints on the law where such a reaction was not forthcoming. The persistent though weaker stress on marriage as an element of social ordering may be interpreted as a concession to the value structure prevailing in society.

REFERENCES

Anthes (1979) 'Vorurteile gegenüber ledigen Müttern' in LF Neumann (ed), *Sozialforschung und Soziale Demokratie, Festschrift für Otto Blume* (Bonn, Verl, Neue Gesellschaft).

Bundesministerium (2000) Bundesministerium für Familie, Senioren, Frauen und Jugend (ed), *Die wirtschaftlichen Folgen von Trennung und Scheidung*, S. 139ff.

Treiber, H and Steinert, H (1980) *Die Fabrikation des zuverlässigen Menschen: über die "Wahlverwandtschaft" von Kloster-und Fabrikdisziplin* (Munich, Moos).

Vaskovics, LA, Rost, H and Rupp, M (1997) *Lebenslage nichtehelicher Kinder: Rechtstatsaechliche Untersuchung zu Lebenslagen und Entwicklungsverlaeufen nichtehelicher* (Cologne, Bundesanzeiger).

Voegeli, W (1982) 'Funktionswandel des Scheidungsrechts', in *Kritische Justiz* 132–155.

3

Family Values, Friendship Values: Opposition or Continuity?

MALGORZATA FUSZARA and JACEK KURCZEWSKI

> There is something about friendship that appears to be quintessentially post-modern. Overwhelmingly friendship has connotations of freedom, choice, individuality and, crucially, subversion. (Pahl, 2000: 166)

S IGNS OF CHANGE in the way personal relationships are arranged are manifest throughout Western culture. Marriage, if it happens at all, is delayed. Motherhood is often single, and single status is often chosen as a permanent way of life. Assisted procreation and artificial reproduction are available on request; homosexual unions are legalised and have a right to adoption. The desacralisation of marriage is evident. From time to time there are reports of a return to the monogamous parenting family ideal, suggesting the possibility of cyclic oscillation in cultural patterns. However, it seems that the change is deeper, wider and more decisive. Legislators are under pressure to act in order to adjust to the growing demand for change, and it seems that they might do worse than to assume that the whole process is reversible. The law which fits the old forms of family life is still with us, and it would be easy to revive in the case of a return to the old ways. But if the law is to help with the pressing needs of a society undergoing change, then a more long term perspective is needed. This is where the social scientist enters the picture, trying to redefine cultural patterns in ways that best express the manifest as well as the still hidden aspects of social transformation. Our contribution in this chapter is located within this framework. Its aim is modest, that is, to suggest that conceptual re-adjustment may support this transformation better than obdurate adhesion to the old concepts that can blindfold the legislator or politician to the actual challenge of change.

The purpose of this volume is to discuss 'family values' in law. The first task is to reconsider the meaning of 'family values', and the consensus, or lack of it, concerning this concept. Are these 'family values' common across cultures or are they culture dependent; are they permanent or do they change over time? We start therefore with consideration of what belongs within the term 'family values' and what does not. In Poland to mention 'family values' almost automatically locates the debate within the traditional Roman Catholic view of the family as those—and in Poland only those (and they are a majority not a minority)—who share such a perspective speak about the need to cultivate 'family values'.

This traditional meaning of 'family values' centres around *procreation*. In the traditional interpretation of marriage and family the aim of marriage is procreation, which both legitimates sexual cohabitation and constitutes the role of women. But even if we use this simple interpretation whereby perpetuation of the human species is the obvious goal of family life, the matter is not so clear in our cultural circle. Law has been used for centuries to distinguish between procreation within culturally acceptable limits, and the biological act of procreation outside marriage. But, it should be recalled, this was not so in every culture. The division of children into legitimate and illegitimate, and the subsequent discrimination against the rights of the latter is of quite recent origin in some legal systems. As late as the 1970s Belgium was sued concerning the injustice of giving different legal status to children born inside and outside of marriage. It is therefore not the act of procreation per se that matters, but its special forms which have been accorded differential ranking through privileges prescribed in law.

Thus, despite the apparent simplicity and clarity of procreation as a value, culture imposes its own set of meanings in determining what is 'appropriate procreation' and what is not. This can be seen particularly clearly when Western European and Northern American culture is compared with cultures that include in the 'offspring' all children irrespective of whether they are born within marriage or outside, particularly in cultures where the majority of children are born outside registered marriages.

In addition, among other family values one also finds that of the care and upbringing of children a more contemporary formulation is the wider obligation of *protection*, both of the young by elders and of the elderly by the younger generation. This protection, however, especially the personal protection of offspring, is a relatively new invention in Europe. Traditionally it includes proper upbringing, education and providing a start in adult life. One need not look at recent reproductive technologies to observe that the legal construction of the duty of protection within the family is dependent on the closeness of the persons counted as family. One might illustrate this issue through discussion of a range of obligations of a foster child towards a non-biological parent.

Protective obligations within a family are, however, much wider than parent and child, and cover not only ascendants and descendants but also the wider family, and are linked with *loyalty* and *trust*. Traditional family values are also characterised by *permanence* and *indissolubility*. While this remains uncontested between parents, children and kin it becomes more complicated in the case of marriage. The traditional concept of 'family values' assumes without discussion that marriage is an indissoluble union for life, unless in exceptional circumstances some other value is violated such as the right to procreation. Other reasons, even violence, may legitimate temporary separation but not divorce or the dissolution of marriage.

We turn now to the question of which of the above 'family values' can be translated into law. We mentioned the way in which the principle of legitimacy, which only included children born within marriage, had been translated into the law. Other non-marital and extra-marital forms of procreation had for centuries excluded those born illegitimately from the full rights associated with 'legitimate' offspring. Across the centuries the law also enforced—though we do not discuss here its effectiveness—the permanence and indissolubility of the marital union, though we note here the longstanding discrepancy between the law of the state and the law of the church (depending on the denomination).

This last point brings us to consideration of the curious similarities between the family law of secular states and the expectations of Canon Law from a Polish perspective. Several similarities could have been observed in Poland which had experienced both the political monopoly of socialist doctrine and the de facto dominance of the Roman Catholic religion. Though both were in opposition to each other, there were points common to the cognitive and normative absolutism of the two opposing doctrines. In the area of the family, both sets of doctrine agreed on the subordination of the individual to the collective good, though in Catholic doctrine the continuation of family, nation and the reproduction of the human species are the goals, while in Communist doctrine it was the good of the family, society and the historical progress of mankind which took precedence. Convergence was not a reality, however, as proved by the freedom to divorce and access to abortion introduced under Communism after the Second World War, while the church supported political and civil rights against the overpowering will of the party-state.

To explain the low rate of divorce in Poland solely by traditional Catholicism is insufficient, though the pressure of the social milieu on the individual is beyond doubt. In Poland and indeed throughout Central and Eastern Europe in the post-Second World War period research into the economy of insufficiency used to show how important it was, for securing a 'civilised life', or even to secure the basic goods of everyday life, to have access to a network of relationships, primarily between people linked by family bonds. Interactions were taking place on the border between legality and illegality, that is activities forbidden by the authorities but not necessarily morally culpable, such as illegal butchery. Keeping such activities secret within a circle of persons on whose loyalty and discretion one could unconditionally rely was of the utmost importance. One could not have survived without such a network of persons in whom one had a special trust. That this was also the 'own zone' into which political authority could not enter was also important. After all, police and politicians were also members of this zone in which everybody had a sense of reality and freedom, including the political freedom to express their own views. The high importance attached at that time to family life by Poles of both genders is best explained in this way.

But in the past, the language of kinship was used historically not only in relation to biological kin, but also to denote particular forms of friendship, for example, in adoption rites and in substitute brotherhood. A special rite was used to set up this brotherhood among unrelated men, regardless of nationality or faith. More importantly, such bonds seem to have superseded hostility between nations at war. 'Brethren' who met on the battlefield were obliged to pass by without fighting each other, and if one was taken prisoner the duty of the other was to come to his aid. Such bonds were established in the seventeenth century between Christian Poles and Muslim Tartars, helping many to survive the numerous wars in the border countries separating Crimean Khanat and the Polish Respublica. According to historical records, in 1652 after the Poles lost the battle of Batoh, 'only the several thousand Polish prisoners of war who had brothers' among the victorious Crimean Tartars survived. The rite was secular in character and consisted of pouring water over sables (furs). In the nineteenth century under the influence of Islam, the bond was made sacred at a time when the borders were being pacified by Russia. Amongst the so-called Lithuanian Tartars—prisoners of war settled with families as an auxiliary military force in today's Byelorus, Lithuania and Poland—the bond was called 'akhret' and was established at home in the presence of a mullah. 'Akhret' brothers were obliged to respect and aid each other and their offspring were forbidden to intermarry. Though domestic in setting, the rite remained highly symbolic and any abuse of the resulting duties was regarded as repugnant (Borawski and Dubiñski, 1986: 198–9).

The Polish nobility often used symbols of brotherhood in their relationships. Community and equality within the nobility were stressed by using the greeting 'Sir Brother!' ('Panie Bracie!') as the standard form of mutual address between all men, not only actual brothers (Tazbir, 1978: 53ff). Status differences within the noble population of the old Polish Respublics, which accounted for about 10 per cent of the whole population, were also expressed by reference to the terminology of 'brotherhood'. 'Elder brothers' and 'younger brothers' were the official expressions used to distinguish between members of the Senate and of the lower nobility (Maciszewski, 1969: 54ff). 'Brotherhood' was based on equality of rights and duties, and, most importantly, in the right to elect the kings of Poland and the right to be elected. Interestingly, the distinctions within the otherwise internally equal estate of the nobility were expressed through the metaphor of the different rights and the status of brothers within the family, where the position of elder and younger brothers were actually different.

Pahl's (2000) book, *On Friendship*, includes lengthy reference to the role of friendship in former Soviet society. This has been subject to the attention of both insiders and outside observers under totalitarian rule. An American anthropologist who wrote a book on Polish society in the 1980s observed:

> The family can be defined narrowly or broadly, and people often conceive of it in operational terms. Those who have no living close family members and the few who have little contact with family often consider przyjaciele (close friends) as family. Close friends become 'just like in the family'. ... 'The family' is not necessarily derived from a blood group. What is important is that an individual has a defined circle of people around him who perform the duties of family members. ... Exchanges within the family are long-term, implicit and carry with them moral obligations, a promise of reciprocated support. (Wedel, 1986: 103)

Writing after Communism, the Polish authors Smigielska and Czynczyk could not separate family and friends when describing the way 'families' survived the Old System and adjusted to transformation. Their document is full of statements like the following:

> Family members and friends often performed the role of therapists, and were expected to give advice or just to listen to another person's complaints and to sympathise or share happiness. ...
>
> Engagement in the problems of one's family and friends was a matter of course: 'I'm looking for a specialist for a sick child of my friends'. ...
>
> Participation in family life was inseparably connected with joint celebrations, occasional meetings of the family and friends to celebrate weddings, name days, birthdays, or first Communions. ...
>
> Between family members and among friends, borrowing and lending money is quite natural. 'We borrowed money from our friends to finish the repairs in our flat'. The debts are usually paid back without interest or extra sums for inflation: (Smigielska and Czynczyk, 1994: 83–5)

The frequency of this 'family and friends' conjunction is symptomatic as the paper was written for a book dealing with family law and life. The authors struggled unconsciously with social reality as is witnessed by the statement that 'The discussion so far has been concerned directly with a narrow view of family, that is the relationship between husband, wife, and children' (Smigielska and Czynczyk, 1994: 85). We query whether it really did, and for how long the authors were able to focus on a 'narrow view of family' without resisting such a distorted perspective. After describing the rather demanding attitude of a husband towards a wife they comment:

> Our observations show that the husband is not the person for many women with whom they could talk as they talk with friends. The conversations with

friends are the wife's sphere of privacy within the family: 'Some days, as soon as he's back from work, I just serve him dinner and hurry to my friend or she visits me. We have coffee in the kitchen and talk about our own matters. I'm entitled to this: dinner's cooked, the flat's tidied up—what else should I do?' ... While the wives have privacy in the form of conversations with their female friends, the husbands satisfy the same need by meeting their male friends 'for a beer' [... or on their own with TV or a particular hobby]:

(Smigielska and Czynczyk, 1994: 86)

So, towards the end of the twentieth century the Polish family consisted ideally not of Husband, Wife, Daughter and Son, but of Husband's Friend and Wife's Friend as well. This was the real extended family—a fact left unnoticed, as often happens with things that are part of everyday 'normality'. In fact, the family extended into the webs of friendship covering the whole of society. In what is considered as the old and outdated climate of mutual gender relations, Husband and Wife have separate zones of intimacy shared with their same-sex friends; the same occurs with the adolescent offspring as well as with the older generation:

Friendship	Friendship
Husband's Male Friend	Wife
Husband	Wife's Female Friend

Family

It would be an exaggeration to suggest, however, that intimacy is nurtured only within friendship circles which cut across marital ties. A fairer way to describe the situation is to present the success of two different intimacies which are defended against each other. Each member of the family has his or her wall of intimacy against another partner but each may at least have the right, if not the obligation, to share family intimacy against the friends as well. This has been unexpectedly confirmed by the new Polish Constitution of 1997 which in article 47 explicitly makes a distinction between the family life and the private life of an individual, and promises protection for both.[1]

It is within this context, perhaps, that it may be helpful to refer to another Polish study on friendship within the family, and specifically about the concept of friendship within marriage (Bielko, 2001). The author studied 100 couples who remained together for at least three years. They were asked about the meaning of marital friendship. The answers given gave priority (in decreasing order) to: sexual and erotic experience (64 per cent of

[1] 'Everyone shall have the right to legal protection of his private and family life, of his honour and good reputation and to make decisions about his personal life' (art 47, Constitution of Republic of Poland of 1997 (1999)). Polish original is gender-neutral.

all respondents), love (51 per cent), permanence and indissolubility (32 per cent), family relationships (19 per cent), and economic community (7 per cent). The order was the same for men and women, though some differences appeared. The husbands were more likely to stress sex and eroticism, and the wives more likely to emphasise permanence and indissolubility. The differences were more apparent with respect to length of marital history: those married for at least 26 years were less likely to point to sex and eroticism and more likely to stress feelings of love as the essence of marital friendship than those married for four to nine years.

The exclusive and permanent erotic—to use the word that mediates between sex and love—bond most strongly characterises marital friendship in these definitions. This is reinforced by the fact that almost half the respondents point to sexual loyalty as the basic proof of marital friendship. Nevertheless there are other indicators: these include support in crisis; solidarity in the case of external conflict; support in everyday life; assistance with individual development; and surrender of one's own ambitions for the partner's good. Bielko argued 'They attempt to implement the ideal of the erotic union of mutually attached friends', adding that in this way marital friendship differs from other forms of friendship. One may observe in this context, firstly, that friendship between husband and wife was also assumed as an ideal by St Thomas Aquinas (*Summa Contra Gentiles* III.123), who observed that 'friendship is founded in some equality'.

We do not think that it is an accident that to study friendship in marriage Bielko decided to sample couples from the metropolitan intelligentsia. The importance of friendship in Polish society increases with social position and education.

> Among workers and peasants, family usually plays the most important role in economy and exchange; among the intelligentsia, close friends are often more important in problem solving. (Wedel, 1986: 103)

But what is friendship? A mysterious and awesome ambiguous veil has long concealed the concept. Aristotle writes on *philia* and *philein*. Classical *philia* covers all possible unions of love and friendship, not discriminating between any of these. Aristotle writes of *philia* and *philein* and translators struggle to render these terms in modern languages as 'like', 'love' or 'befriend', depending on the context and convention. Should we read the famous line in his *Rhetoric* (II.1380: 35) as 'Our friend is he whom we like and who likes us' or 'whom we love and who loves us'? Classical authors like Cicero describe a *coup de foudre* when the flame of friendship falls upon two statesmen; but it is anachronistic to categorise these feelings as heterosexual or sexual love and 'Platonic' love or non-erotic friendship. One may suspect that there is no *philia* without Eros, and that Eros is many-faceted and of varying intensity. Not surprisingly French students of friendship point to the 'problem' that is created for a married partner by a heterosexual friendship of his or her marital partner, as happened in 40 per cent of the cases studied (Maissonneuve and Lamy, 1993).

For Aquinas 'amicitia virtus' as a social pattern of inter-relationship still derives from friendship proper, 'amicitia amor', the union of two souls (Biełko, 2001: 35). Throughout the centuries the ideal of friendship continues as the paradigm for disinterested intimacy and mutual devotion. According to Aristotle one wishes the friend good for the other's sake and makes all efforts to fulfil this wish. 'What is a friend?', Boswell asks Dr Johnson on Saturday 24 April 1779. The latter answers provocatively, 'One who supports you and comforts you, while others do not.' Johnson, however, stresses different aspects pointing to the need for an 'intimate friend, with whom one might compare thoughts and cherish private virtues' (Boswell, 1903: 368). While Boswell pointed to the egocentric value of friendship, Dr Johnson defined it as a specific social field where certain virtues could be practised. Neverthe-less, loyalty remains for him inseparable from this field, as well as mutual confidence: 'It is a breach of confidence not to tell a friend he is marrying "a whore"' (Boswell, 1903: 358). In this bold remark he comes back to the clas- sical concept of 'wishing him the best' at the risk of this news being un-welcome to the impassioned friend. Let us observe also that disinterestedness and reciprocity, loyalty and unconditional trust as friendship values are also stressed during socialisation and through school as adolescent friendships develop to enter the realm of adult rights and obligations.

The ethnography of kinship-based societies describes how with social distance a relationship gradually becomes depersonalised. Victor Turner summarised the structural context within which the opposition between Family and Friendship appears, in his description of patrilineal societies:

> In these societies, as numerous scholars have shown, the mother's brother, who has weak jural authority over his nephew, nevertheless may have a close personal tie of friendship with him, may give him sanctuary from paternal harshness, and, very often, has mystical powers of blessing and cursing over him. Here weak legal authority in a corporate group setting is countered by strong personal and mystical influences.   (Turner, 1969: 119)

For all readers of the impressive story of the conflict between fatherly love and avuncular rule in the matrilineal society of the Trobriand Islands, this statement sounds like an inversion of the situation there as described by Bronislaw Malinowski. The 'hard kin' relations in societies that make formalistic distinctions when classifying people into exclusive and total kin groups are counterbalanced by 'soft' affective friendship relations with outsiders across the generational lines.

As European societies are generally based upon double descent through male and female lines and extend to non-kin groups, this gradual depersonalisation is a defining characteristic, usually covered by household co-existence. Previous research has shown that the more distant the relationship, the more substantial the interest at stake needs to be in order to mobilise a sense of obligation. However, on the other hand, when the stakes become so high that they mobilise the total stranger, generalised charity becomes the only available response. A stranger by definition is someone outside the personal knowledge bank of the individual. The question then arises as to how the individual may be able to utilise his own social capital data bank, and when it will be necessary to switch to the anonymous list of helping strangers.

Two concepts that have been enshrined since the beginning in European culture as the foundation of personal relations are 'family' and 'friendship'.[1a] Of these two concepts, the first has been prominent as an area of public interest, while the second was relegated to the private sphere where there is no political or policy interest. This is reflected in the abundance of research on family-type relations and the under-development of research on friendship-type relations. In the meantime, the interpretation and social function of both cultural institutions has changed. *Families* are defined as closed social territories of exclusive loyalties and total in character, while some *friendships* became institutionalised in, for example, mutual benefit associations. The European concept of friendship has in the modern era been characterised by ambiguity, as it covers crosscutting areas of voluntary and mutual trust. On the other hand, friendship is referred to as the basis for social support that may at least in part substitute for traditional family roles. The ambiguity of friendship is linked with the ambiguity of family, the subversiveness of the first in competition with the second.

The conventional perspective assumes that social relations may be divided into those that derive from marriage and others. Though marriage is voluntary, it involves the involuntary mutual status transition for the *kin* of both partners, who thus acquire (and lose) social capital whether they like it or not. The recognised offspring inherit the social capital of their parents. Under this traditional model, marriages were broken, offspring were being born out of wedlock, and non-'related' friends were of more social use sometimes than 'proper' relatives. The meaning of reproductive partnership has changed in recent decades in Europe and it may come to be individually regulated in personalised contracts between partners.

In Europe the border between kin and friends is becoming more open as household partnership *may not involve formalisation of relations, and inter-kin relations may be temporary.* So, for instance, the continuation of social relations after a divorce can change a family tie into friendship.

[1a] This is also more widely Mediterranean, as in Arabic one says 'habiba' both for a beloved one and for a friend.

The very development of the modern technology of human reproduction may
lead to the point at which sex becomes irrelevant for parenthood. This is quite
rightly disquieting for moral philosophers. Social parenthood is nothing more
than friendship if performed at its best. One can imagine human beings reproduced with the help of surrogate fathers and artificial wombs, but all the
experiments with early socialisation prove that one cannot imagine normal
human beings brought up without the atmosphere of trust and care. But this
is simply another way to define friendship. The reproductive independence of
the individuals together with economic independence might add up to the
same freedom of choice that renders the family contract fragile. The same
might be said of sexual freedom and permissiveness. Altogether, the family
may remain forever the crosscutting of gender and age even if friendship will
remain the only bond within it on which to count. After all, the life to be
reproduced needs to be one of dignity.   (Kurczewski, 1990: 16–17)

Recent attitudinal research carried out in Poland but extending coverage
into Central Europe throws some light on how these processes are unfold-
ing in an area which for many years existed under a totalitarian regime that
necessitated reliance on family and friendship for survival. Taylor Nelson
Sofres OBOP, who continues to carry out surveys on marital values provided figures in 2002 for representative surveys made in Poland, the Czech
Republic, Slovakia and Hungary (about 4000 respondents altogether).[2] For
the majority marital union does not mean the ending of romantic love nor
loss of freedom. 'Mutual respect and trust' came first in the list of important factors for marital happiness in all the countries studied except
Slovakia, where marital fidelity predominates. In Poland mutual openness
and confidence ranks highest (third), as well as happy sex (fourth), equality in household tasks (sixth) and religious similarity (tenth). In Slovakia
marital loyalty predominates, while good sex (as in the Czech Republic) is
less important than a good income. Hungarians, like Poles and Czechs, put
mutual respect and trust before fidelity, and like Poles rate good sex as
more important than good money. Poles stress religious homogeneity, and
they also stress social class similarity more than other Central European
nations. On the whole, Poles stress good sex and sharing household duties
most often, and Czechs the least.

    The variation in national cultures with respect to marriage and the fam-
ily in the region is shown in Table 3.1.

    Surprisingly, despite the well-known Catholic affiliation of Poles, they
show the most liberal attitude to marriage. Czechs and Slovaks seem to
cherish the traditional concept of marriage, which may force them to decide
to avoid it. Poles above all see so many practical nuances in marital life that
they may be more able to maintain the formal institution with the help of
all these liberal adjustments. Wives may be older than husbands, a couple
need not marry at all, they may have children without formal marriage or

[2] Internet release from 17 September 2002 by Taylor Nelson Sofres OBOP, http:
//www.obop.pl.

Table 3.1 Attitudes to Marriage in Four Central-Eastern
European Countries in 2002

	% agreeing with the statement			
	Czech Republic	Slovakia	Poland	Hungary
Doesn't matter if wife is older than her husband	62	50	82	62
Doesn't matter if man and woman live together without marriage	55	37	59	52
Doesn't matter if one has out of wedlock children	24	40	53	49
Doesn't matter if a couple does not wish to have the children	26	24	59	27
Women should stop working when they begot the children	20	15	24	25
Marriage means surrender of freedom	27	19	14	13
Marriage is the end of love	19	11	4	9

may not have children at all—all this makes marriage resemble a union based on friendship.

These pragmatic attitudes are on the increase in Poland. In our own earlier surveys this process has been documented since 1988, when, in the national sample, cohabitation was acceptable to 32 per cent, rising to 43 per cent in 1992, and 45 per cent in 1996. In the same period the characterisation of cohabitation as 'sinful' decreased from 81 per cent to 61 per cent (cf Kurczewski, 1997: 20). With these processes gradually the opposition between gender-based models of the family, a female model putting stress on mutual rights and obligations and a male model with a more relaxed approach to duties, may disappear in order to 'elaborate a more consensual model that would be acceptable for both women and men that would more equally distribute the burden between the mother and father' (Fuszara, 1994: 320–1).

Our socio-legal perspective on personal relations understands these as comprising a network of mutual rights and obligations, but the ways in which they are defined may differ either between the individuals concerned, or between individuals and a group such as the state or the church that regulates them. The degree of harmonisation of mutual normative expectations is held to be indicative of social integration. Historically, it was assumed that at the end of industrial transformation a new integration would be achieved, but the concept of private autonomy helped to preserve national, ethnic, religious and other cultural specificities, thus facilitating variation and the continued co-existence of private moral orders at the margins of state regulation. Post-modern developments led to the deprivatisation of personal relations. These became increasingly subject to public scrutiny, while at the same time legitimisation of cultural and individual variation has been achieved with the help of the principle of tolerance that lies at heart of post-modern society. New forms of previously private relationships, such as cohabitation which is not based in legal status, are beginning to be the subject of public regulation, while the traditional legal forms, such as marriage, are coming under pressure. The effect is thus of normative pluralism recognised at the public—official regulation—level. This strengthens the dominant perspective recognising a possible plurality of perspectives held by the individual. Our working assumption is that the societies of Europe differ as to the degree or stage which this process has reached. Research is needed to provide baseline data mapping of the sets of expectations held by individuals at various stages in their family life. This knowledge could facilitate moves towards harmonisation of the official law which regulates personal relations within Europe.

Personal relations are not defined exclusively in family terms, though members of kinship networks remain the paradigm. The household may or may not be the starting point for the networks which the individual takes part in, but, nevertheless, it remains of central concern to the state, as it is obliged to provide services depending on the ability of individuals to satisfy the needs that were previously secured through the co-operation of household members functioning as a unit. Some of these ties remain though move outside the household in practice. For example, partnership in reproduction still remains the identifier for primary responsibility for the dependant child. Dr Samuel Johnson praised the virtue of friendship that could convey unpleasant truth to a man about his partner's sexual licence for practical reasons as 'to prevent the consequences of imposition'. Dr Johnson might have answered that having the male property rights to the offspring removed would not remove the duty to inform from the friend, but would make the fact of little significance as to the friend's well-being.

In his discussion of democratising intimacy Anthony Giddens sets eroticism against sex: 'Eroticism is sexuality reintegrated within a wider range of emotional purposes, paramount among which is communication' (Giddens, 1992: 204). Thinking about the 'subversive ambiguity' of friendship with all the shades of mutual *philia* involved, one may see friendship as the cultural form within which people 'might compare minds and cherish private virtues' on the basis of an emotional bond guarded by trust, reciprocity and altruism. New family forms are travelling in this direction and a new friendship law could recognise the reality and help to provide the appropriate instruments of recognition, protection and assistance. Those who fear this kind of development should be reminded that all this means is simply making family meet with friendship as in the ancient classical ideal.

If the notion of friendship remains unclear, it is not surprising that the relationship between family and friendship is even less clear. A recent British study of friendship sees the picture in a following way:

A 'modern' family-like style of friendship could be based on former lovers or partners. ... Heterosexual friendships, couple friendships and the whole gamut of friendship styles pioneered and publicised by the Bloomsbury group are all part of the great range of possible relationships in the contemporary world of friendship. The topic deserves a longer and more extensive discussion than is possible here. (Pahl, 2000: 21)

If 'family values' are at the centre of the family debate and one observes change in families, does it mean that values are changing? It would seem a hazardous and unsubstantiated claim. After all, access to and participation in a network of loyal persons, present and immutable, whom one may trust, on whose aid and protection one may count and whom one should protect seems to be of too great permanent and elementary value to undergo change. It is not the change in 'family values' that is the problem, but rather the fact that it is no longer necessarily the family within which we practise these values. Procreation is no longer (and in truth never was) entirely linked with marriage. Protection and mutual aid are practised by people who are close but not necessarily linked by 'blood', that is genetically or through sacramental and registered marriage. In this way friendship—free, voluntary, and more flexible though loyal—serves the function that was once monopolised by the family. Here we arrive at the recently manifested paradox: relaxing regulation of the family is being compensated for by increasing the regulation of other relationships. Legal privileges were given to the family as it was involved in the fulfilment of socially significant values. We therefore have two options: first, as suggested by Martha Fineman (1995), to take away the 'privileges' of the family and leave it as undifferentiated legally, or—as we prefer—to extend the preferential treatment to all those in 'close' relationships who practise family values. The state needs some evidence to prove that, for example, a friend has the right to carry out a banking operation on his or her friend's account, or agree to surgery when his or her friend is in a coma, etc. All this necessitates the formalisation of friendship. The law developed over the centuries to help the family could be extended in some form now to cover all our close relationships both to improve the legal framework and to enable people to cohabit peacefully.

REFERENCES

Aquinas, *Summa Contra Gentiles*, III.123 (Manchester, NH, Sophia Institute Press, 2002).

Aristotle, *Rhetoric*.

Biełko, M (2001) *Przyjał Małłeska (Marital Friendship)* (Warsaw, Łak).

Borawski, P and Dubiński, A (1986) *Tatarzy Polscy. Dzieje, Obrzłdy, Legendy, Tradycje (Polish Tartars. History, Rites, Legends, Traditions)* (Warsaw, Iskry).

Boswell, J (1903) *The Life of Samuel Johnson* (London, Routledge).

Poland, A and Caldwell, A (trs) (1999) *The Constitution of the Republic of Poland as Adopted by the National Assembly on 2 April 1997*, in M Wyrzykowski (ed), *Constitutional Essays* (Warsaw, Institute of Public Affairs).

Fineman, M (1995) *The Neutered Mother, the Sexual Family and Other Twentieth Century Tragedies* (London, Routledge).

Fuszara, M (1994) *Rodzina w sądzie (Family in the Court)* (Warsaw, Sociology of Custom and Law Department, ISNS University of Warsaw).

Giddens, A (1992) *The Transformation of Intimacy*: Sexuality, Love and Eroticism in Modern Societies (Cambridge, Polity Press).

Kurczewski, J (1990) 'The Last Argument of Aquinas: Instead of an Introduction' in J Kurczewski and A Czynczyk (eds), *Family, Gender and Body in Law and Society Today* (Warsaw, Sociology of Custom and Law Department, ISNS University of Warsaw).

——(1997) '"Family" in Politics and Law: In Search of a Theory' in J Kurczewski and M Maclean (eds), *Family Law and Family Policy in the New Europe* (Dartmouth, Aldershot).

——(2001) Preface to M Biełko, *Przyjał Malleska (Marital Friendship)*. (Warsaw, Łak).

Maciszewski, J (1969) *Szlachta Polska i jej Palstwo (Polish Nobility and Its State)* (Warsaw, WP).

Maissonneuve, J and Lamy, L (1993) *La Psycho-Sociologie de l'Amitie (Psycho-Sociology of Friendship)* (Paris, Presses Universitaires de France).

Pahl, R (2000) *On Friendship* (Cambridge, Polity).

Smigielska, J and Czynczyk, A (1994) 'What do Family Members and Friends Expect from One Another at the Transition to Democracy?' in M Maclean and J Kurczewski (eds), *Families, Politics and the Law* (Oxford; Oxford University Press).

Tazbir, J (1978) *Kultura Szlachecka w Polsce (Nobility Culture in Poland)* (Warsaw, WP).

Turner, V (1969) *The Ritual Process: Structure and Anti-Structure* (Ithaca, New York, Cornell University Press).

Wedel, J (1986) *The Private Poland* (New York, Facts on File Publications).

4

The Changing Context for the Obligation to Care and to Earn

JANE LEWIS

THERE ARE MACRO-LEVEL expectations regarding the way in which families should 'look' and 'work'. The 'traditional', two parent family in which the man went 'out to work' and the woman stayed at home full- or part-time constituted a particular pattern of gendered contributions and supports. The erosion of this model has taken place in respect of family change and labour market change. The way in which these behavioural changes interact with the shifts in normative prescriptions and legislative activity is extremely complex and can only be hinted at in this chapter, which focuses more on the nature of the shift away from a male breadwinner model towards an adult worker model family. This shift assumes a much greater degree of individualisation, in the sense of economic independence, which raises issues about the valuing and sharing of care work.

THE MALE BREADWINNER MODEL FAMILY

The traditional male breadwinner model family, in which the husband/ father took primary responsibility for earning, and the wife/mother primary responsibility for the unpaid work of care and for housework, became the norm for people as well as policymakers during the first part of the twentieth century. Indeed there is considerable evidence to suggest that this family form and gendered pattern of contributions was internalised as an ideal, even among working people, whose daily practices were often very different (Lewis, 1986). After all, Tilly and Scott (1975) have shown how working class women were likely to engage in casual employment as and when the family economy demanded it, and John Gillis (1997) has pointed out that cohabitation was much more common in early twentieth-century England, following informal separation or widowhood, than it was in the middle of the century. Nevertheless, the ideal of a male breadwinner family model provided the crucial underpinning for the male trades unionists' claim to a family wage (Horrell and Humphries, 1997; Seccombe, 1993).

The traditional male breadwinner model family was also firmly embedded in private law and public policy. The law of marriage and divorce not only regulated entry into marriage and exit from it, but also effectively prescribed a particular idea of marriage. First and foremost, sex was to be kept inside marriage. Second, family law underpinned traditional notions of obligation between men and women. The idea that marriage involves male financial support for women and children, and female performance of domestic and caring duties—the essence of the traditional male breadwinner model—was reflected in what happened when marriage ended under the rules of the old fault-based divorce (Weitzman, 1981, 1985). Blame was allocated by the courts and decisions made about children (who invariably went with their mothers), property (which for most part stayed with the husband), and alimony (for the dependent wife).

Public policy also embedded the assumptions of the male breadwinner model into the systems of social support that grew up in virtually all Western countries during the early part of the twentieth century. Modern states are by definition also welfare states, although the extent to which collective provision has been institutionalised varies considerably. The settlement at the heart of the modern welfare state is that between capital and labour. But it has increasingly been recognised that this settlement entailed a particular kind of gender regime (Lewis, 1992; Orloff, 1993; Esping Andersen, 1999; Crouch, 1999). The old labour contract, hammered out in the early part of the twentieth century through restrictions on the hours of work, minimum wage regulations, pension entitlements, sickness and unemployment insurance and paid holidays, was designed first and foremost for the regularly employed male breadwinner and provision had to be made for women and children, again classified as dependants.

The gender settlement meant that those marginal to the labour market got cash cover via dependants' benefits. Alain Supiot (1999) has described the labour/capital settlement in terms of security traded for dependence. A similar set of arrangements can be said to have marked the gender settlement. The male breadwinner model was based on a set of assumptions about male and female contributions at the household level that prescribed a particular kind of interdependence and family solidarity. In particular, female economic dependence was inscribed in the model. Sir William Beveridge's blueprint for the post-war welfare state in the UK (Cmd 6404, 1942) gave an enthusiastic welcome to the equal-but-different parts to be played by men and women in the family. He insisted on using the term 'partnership' to describe marriage and drew attention to the importance of women's role in reproduction, at a time when low birth rates were a particular cause for concern. In the post-war welfare settlement, married women were to pay less by way of social insurance contributions and receive less by way of benefits. To this day, tax/benefit systems are rarely fully 'individualised'; the unit of assessment is often the couple or the household.

By mid century, then, the male breadwinner model was built into the fabric of society, and the post-war welfare settlement in particular assumed regular and full male employment *and* stable families in which women would be provided for largely via their husbands' earnings and their husbands' social contributions. When this is understood, the amount of material as well as psychological investment in the traditional family model becomes clearer and the anxiety over its apparent demise easier to understand. The traditional two-parent, nuclear family was understood as fundamental to the success of Western economies. The classic sociology of the family published in the immediate post-war decades tried to understand family change in the context of societal change, and together with neo-classical economic theory, concluded that the stable, traditionally organised two-parent nuclear family was supremely well suited to producing individuals able to function in a liberal individualist market economy (Parsons and Bales, 1955).

The male breadwinner model family worked in practice for a majority of families for only a very short period in the years following the Second World War. But as a set of normative prescriptions, accepted in large measure by people as well as policymakers, the model proved to be powerful and very long-lasting in some Western European countries. While Scandinavian governments took explicit decisions in the 1970s to move away from this set of assumptions and, in particular, to pull women into the labour market (through the imposition of individual taxation, and the provision of both parental leaves and child care services), a shift away from the principles of the male breadwinner model has only become explicit in countries such as the UK, Ireland, Germany and The Netherlands as part of much broader welfare state restructuring in the 1990s (Lewis, 1992, 2001, 2002). The way in which the male breadwinner family model gave rise to a set of normative expectations about the roles of men and women in the family is examined in the next section.

NORMATIVE PRESCRIPTION AND THE MALE BREADWINNER MODEL

Rational choice theorists such as Jon Elster (1991) may acknowledge the existence of norms, but use them only as a residual form of explanation, to be invoked to explain the awkward bits that are left when the rational choice analysis is complete. Sophisticated economic approaches, such as that using the idea of the 'convention', interpreted by Sugden (1998: 454) in terms of tacit agreements or common understandings giving rise to shared expectations, acknowledge the importance of the cultural variable, but stop short at the idea that norms are internalised. Thus Sugden (1998) has argued that conventional practices can generate normative expectations, which may in turn be significant for the stability of conventions.

Others, however, insist that norms and values are *embedded* in society and are part of the framework within which choices are made. After all, norms by definition are not chosen, and a decision to abide by them may be made consciously or seemingly without any conscious interrogation of alternatives.[1] Thus Sunstein (1997) has insisted that individual choices are a function of norms, meanings and roles, and that individuals may therefore have little control over them. Puzzles of rationality, he argues, are the product of social norms and moral judgements.

In the case of the male breadwinner model, its use has firstly been descriptive of a pattern of economic activity in the family. Inevitably it tended to underplay the amount of female labour market activity, but it was not inaccurate in its portrayal of a society in which men took primary responsibility for earning and women for caring. Secondly, the model was internalised by a majority of people, certainly in the years following the Second World War, and this served to condition expectations within marriage. In the immediate post-war decades the gendered division of work, paid and unpaid, was sufficiently in line with the male breadwinner model to give rise to a set of normative expectations about the roles of men and women within the family, that underpinned social policies, for example in respect of the lesser contributions and benefits paid by married women under the social insurance system, and in turn reinforced the model.

The erosion of the model in respect of the changing labour market behaviour of women might be expected at some point to have been accompanied by a shift in normative expectations on the part of people and legislators, although the shift need not necessarily be entirely congruent with changes in behaviour. While married women's labour market participation rates have increased hugely in the post-war period, the rate and timing of the increase has been very uneven between different countries. For the UK, Catherine Hakim (1996) has pointed out, there were almost as many women employed full-time in 1951 as in 1981 (30.3 per cent of women aged 20 to 64, as opposed to 31.6 per cent). However, as Lessig (1996: 285) has observed, when norm violation increases (as in the case of the shift away from a single male breadwinner towards a dual earner family) then the meaning of obeying the norm also changes and at some point obeying the norm becomes pointless. Indeed, Stacey (1990) has commented that young working class men in late twentieth-century America were not sure whether to regard one of their number who became a breadwinner as 'a hero or a chump'. This is in large measure because normative meanings and expectations are far from clear. The norm is now that women will engage in paid work, and attitudinal surveys have shown consistent increases in the acceptance by men and women of female employment at all stages of the lifecourse (Dex, 1988). But to what *extent*—full-time or some form of part-time—varies considerably according to social class, ethnicity and sometimes

---

[1] The process by which this occurs is complicated, see for example, Suchman (1997).

region. Nor are the accompanying assumptions in respect of unpaid work predictable.

The increase in women's labour market participation has effected a change in the male breadwinner model: the increase in female employment and in the incidence of the dual earner family cannot be denied, even if women's participation is often part-time, making it less of a 'revolution' than is often supposed. This in turn has shaken the whole fabric of gender roles, which have been widely assumed—by government and by people—to flow from the model. At some point, the gap between changing behaviour and the normative expectations flowing from the male breadwinner model becomes too great, and the rupture gives rise to a new set of normative expectations. Female employment is expected, although to what degree is unclear. Indeed, expectations may actually run ahead of behavioural change, on the part of people and policymakers. This in turn has profound implications for the gendered division of carework and for the extent to which care is located in the public or private, formal or informal spheres.

DIMENSIONS OF BEHAVIOURAL CHANGE SIGNALLING THE EROSION OF THE MALE BREADWINNER FAMILY MODEL

Many have argued that on the work and family front it seems that we are seeing more individualisation. Elizabeth Beck-Gernsheim (1999: 54) has described the effects of individualisation on the family in terms of 'a community of need' becoming 'an elective relationship'. In this interpretation, the family used to be a community of need held together by the obligations of solidarity. But women's increased labour market participation, together with family change and instability, has resulted in new divisions between biography and family responsibilities. Burns and Scott (1994) have made a similar point in their discussion of the way in which male and female roles in the family have become 'decomplementary'.

However, while the male breadwinner model has eroded, the social reality is still far from a family comprised of self-sufficient, autonomous individuals. While women's behaviour has changed substantially in respect of paid work, they still perform the bulk of unpaid care work. Men have changed much less in respect of the amount of either paid or unpaid work they do (eg Gershuny, 2000). The pattern of paid work between men and women in households is now much more difficult to predict, but patterns of unpaid work have not changed so much.

In the case of the UK, the British General Household Survey shows that while in 1975, 81 per cent of men and 62 per cent of women aged 16–64 were economically active, by 1996 this figure was 70 per cent for both men and women (ONS, 1998, Tables 5.8 and 5.9). Married women are as likely to be employed as non-married women. Increases have been similar in other strong male breadwinner countries. For example, in The Netherlands, the rate of increase in the net labour market participation of women has been more dramatic, from 29 per cent of all adult women in 1975 to 51 per cent in 1999. The comparable figures for men were 79 per cent and 76 per cent.[2] But in both countries short part-time working is very common for women. Almost a quarter of British women with children under ten worked 15 or fewer hours per week in the late 1990s (Thair and Risdon, 1999), and 24 per cent of all female employees worked under 20 hours a week (Rubery *et al*, 1998). The vast majority of Dutch women work part-time, 80 per cent in 1994; 33 per cent work less than 20 hours a week. The percentage of dual earner families with two full-time workers actually decreased in The Netherlands from 43 to 33 per cent between 1990 and 1994 (Hooghiemstra, 1997).[3]

In respect of family structure, the pace of change in the recent past for the UK has been greater than in regard to the labour market. The divorce rate increased threefold and the rate of unmarried motherhood fourfold in one generation. Cohabitation is the driver of much of the change; it is now sequel and alternative to marriage and has contributed to the increasing separation of marriage and parenthood, which constitutes a more profound shift than the 1960s separation of sex and marriage (Lewis and Kiernan, 1996). British Household Panel data show that cohabiting relationships in the UK are four times more unstable than marriage (Ermisch and Francesconi, 1998). In The Netherlands the changes have been less dramatic; lone mother families represented only 10 per cent of all families with dependant children in 1993, whereas the equivalent figure for the UK was 22 per cent (Van Drenth *et al*, 2000).

Figure 4.1 shows the range of possible contributions of men and women to paid work at the household level, and speculates on the nature of care provision that accompanies different gendered patterns of paid and unpaid work.

The *precise nature* of the erosion of the male breadwinner model is complicated. There has been no simple move from a male breadwinner to a dual career model. Rather, in most Western countries some kind of dual breadwinner model has become the norm. Whether this is a transitional model is entirely unclear. Often, given women's lower earnings, the dual breadwinner model family amounts to a more-or-less one-and-a-half earner model (that is, the dual earner models 2 and 3 in Fig 4.1). Model 3 in Figure 4.1, is a more gender equal model and has not been achieved in any country, although it is the official policy of the Dutch Government, with its 'combination scenario', and The Netherlands has somewhat more part-time work for men (17 per cent of Dutch men work part-time, but a majority of these are either young or over 55).

Policymakers have recognised the existence of greater individualisation in regard to labour market and family behaviour, without taking on board

Figure 4.1 Patterns of Male and Female Paid Work and Arrangements for Care

Male Breadwinner Model
Male FT* earner   Female FT carer

Dual Breadwinner Model (i)
Male FT earner, Female short PT earner   Care supplied mainly by female earn-
                                                   er and kin

Dual Breadwinner Model (ii)
Male FT earner, Female long PT earner   Care supplied mainly by kin, and
                                                   state/voluntary/market

Dual Breadwinner Model (iii)
Male PT earner, Female PT earner   Care supplied by male and female
                                                   earners

Dual Career
Male FT earner, Female FT earner   Care supplied mainly by the market,
                                                   and kin/state/voluntary sector

Single Earner
Lone parent earner, PT or FT   Care supplied mainly by kin, market
                                                   (childminder), and state sector

* FT full-time; PT part-time

the complexities of the way in which the male breadwinner model has been eroded. Changes in behaviour in respect of the labour market and the family have shaken the whole fabric of gender roles that were assumed by policymakers to flow from the male breadwinner model.

TOWARDS AN ADULT WORKER MODEL FAMILY

Female employment is now the norm, although to what extent and for which groups of women remains unclear. This is not surprising given that the new assumptions may actually be running ahead of behavioural change. Governments in the UK and The Netherlands have moved dramatically towards assuming that women will be in the labour market. This in turn is in large measure because of the broader shifts in ideas about how the modern welfare state should function, and in particular because of the change in emphasis from 'passive' to 'active' welfare, and from an emphasis on the rights of claimants to their responsibilities. These changes in thinking about social provision used the behavioural changes in family formation and in labour market participation as both a stimulus and a justification for shifting towards a set of assumptions based on an adult worker model family.

The strength of the idea that there is an obligation to engage in paid work has been clearly expressed in the English-speaking literature since the 1980s. This view stresses the obligation of all citizens who are able to undertake paid work. In the mid 1980s, Lawrence Mead made the case in the US for the state to assert its moral authority in order to insist that welfare recipients fulfil their obligations as citizens to engage in paid labour. He presented this solution in terms of a model of equal citizenship and something that would bring about greater social integration. Welfare-to-work, implemented first in the USA, embodied these ideas and was applied to all able-bodied adults, lone mothers included. Yet there is also a huge amount of concern on both sides of the Atlantic about 'family's' capacity and willingness to care and about the quality of care that is given to young and old dependants within it. In the debate over the family, care is lauded and there continue to be mixed feelings about the employment of mothers, especially if they have young children. Care is recognised as important, but the implications of the welfare-to-work agenda for the anxiety about the family have not been confronted. In the USA, prior to the passing of the 1996 Work Responsibility and Personal Opportunities Act, it was openly argued that not only was there a fundamental obligation on the part of able bodied people to enter the labour market (Mead, 1986), but it would be better in the case of lone mother families for the children in those families to experience one breadwinner as opposed to none (Novak and Cogan, 1987). In respect of lone mother families, the American Enterprise Institute arrived at a position roughly similar to that taken by many late Victorians: lone mothers should work but should also be brought into social settings where they might be taught mothercraft (*ibid*).

Social democrats have, like Mead but unlike more radical critics of welfare (such as Charles Murray), also stressed the overriding importance of employment as a means to social integration or inclusion. In this country, the effort to get more lone mothers into the labour market has been justified as much by reference to the welfare of the mothers themselves as by condemnation of welfare dependency. But there has been little acknowledgement of the complicated relationship between independence and dependence. After all, the middle aged woman who gives up her job in order to care for an elderly person and becomes dependent on benefits does so in order to allow the elderly person to retain a greater degree of independence. The European Commission has focused in the main on the need for active labour market participation, stressing the importance of adult labour market participation in order to increase competitiveness (CEC 1993, 1995, 2000a, 2000b). Both the EC (CEC 2000a) and the OECD (2000) have emphasised the importance of policies to 'make work pay', and in the words of the EC, of strengthening 'the role of social policy as a productive factor' (CEC 2000b: 2).

A striking example of the paradigm shift in the assumptions underpinning policies took place in the UK and The Netherlands in the mid 1990s in respect of lone mothers. This group of women have always been a particularly problematic group for a male breadwinner regime because it must be decided whether and on what terms the state will step in to replace the father (Lewis, 1998). Both national governments swung from treating lone mothers as mothers, with no requirement to register for employment until their youngest child was 16, to treating them as workers, regardless of the fact that a majority of married mothers actually work part-time (Lewis, 1998). The rationale in both countries had much to do with reducing dependence on state benefits, but was supported by arguments regarding the greater labour market participation of married mothers, without it being acknowledged that the vast majority of these women work short part-time hours.

However, these assumptions come into conflict with the expressed desire of a large proportion of women in these countries to put care work first. If good quality, affordable day care were to be provided overnight, it is not clear that all women would want to work full-time. British Labour Force Survey data report that 90 per cent of women with children who work part-time did not want full-time work (Thair and Risdon, 1999). This is, of course, under the current constraint of poor childcare provision relative to most other European countries. Hakim (1996, see also 2001) has argued strongly that the British female labour force divides into a group of committed career women and another group that is content to choose part-time work (and undertake care). Hakim's model is controversial because it highlights choice and underplays constraints. However, it may be that alternative moral rationalities underpin women's commitment to family work (Tronto, 1993; Ahlander and Bahr, 1995; Duncan and Edwards, 1999) and that given the choice between even a well-paying job and unpaid care work for a child or elderly relatives, some women would prefer the latter. Knijn and van Welss' (2001) evaluation of the new policy that treats lone mothers as workers rather than as mothers in The Netherlands has shown that the policy failed at the local level because neither social workers charged with its implementation nor the mothers themselves believed that they should be pushed into the labour market.

Secondly, the new adult work model often conflicts with the existing mechanisms for delivering social programmes (such as means tested social assistance), which may continue to operate in accordance with older, male breadwinner-based assumptions. The result is a set of policies that is far from consistent. For example, in the Dutch case the signals given by policy-makers regarding the division of paid and unpaid work have been inconsistent (Bruning and Plantenga, 1999; Knijn, 2001). Tax and social security policies continue to privilege the male breadwinner in some respects, while policies on employment and working hours have aimed to increase female participation.

Policy ambiguity and inconsistency in respect of the balance of paid and unpaid work also marks the UK case (Rake, 2000; McLaughlin *et al*, 2001), and indeed other continental European countries (Daly, 2000). In the UK, the working families tax credit designed to 'make work pay' is administered on the basis of joint earnings and may thus actually reduce the incentive for partnered women to enter employment in low-paid jobs. The New Deal for the Partners of the Unemployed (mainly women) treats them both as having an independent relationship to the labour market and as dependants. Their access to the programme is dependent on their being the partner of an unemployed man. Thus while ideas about individualisation have been clearly expressed in the UK and The Netherlands, it is still assumed that married women can depend on their husbands as and when necessary.

When implementing the new set of assumptions regarding an adult worker model family, neither the full implications for the policy logic[4] experienced by women were considered, nor the implications for the gendered division of work experienced by (or desired by) women. In many respects, women's labour market participation has become the new norm and it is increasingly assumed that both men and women will be in employment. However, there is evidence to suggest that the assumptions made by policymakers regarding women's status as 'workers' is rapidly outrunning the social reality, which, in many countries, takes the form of part-time and often 'short' part-time work (Lewis, 2001). This becomes crucially important if it is also assumed to any significant extent that individuals will, in the future, be able to make greater provision for themselves, especially in respect of pension provision (Ginn *et al*, 2001). It is also the case that the persistence of the gendered division of the unpaid work of care has not been anywhere near the forefront of the policy agenda. Thus the coherence of policies with regard to care is markedly less than those delineating the new insistence of labour market participation for all, and the monies allocated to care are considerably less than those designed to get people into work and make work pay. Anything to do with care tends to be poorly valued. Wages in the formal care sector are low and benefits and allowances for carers in the informal sector are also low. This means that in a world in which individualisation and the capacity for self-provisioning is increasingly being assumed by policymakers, carers are profoundly disadvantaged. It also means that care continues to be associated with women rather than with both the sexes.

THE FAMILY'S CONTINUING OBLIGATION TO CARE

There is also a literature that stresses the importance of the continuing obligation of 'the family' to care. Commentators from a wide range of political perspectives have interpreted family and labour market change as evidence that people have become more individualistic, seeking the means to self-expression and self-fulfilment. While there is no agreement as to whether individualism is inherently selfish (Giddens, for example, has argued strongly against such a position), the balance of opinion has tended to be pessimistic. In the USA, David Popenoe (1993: 528) stated bluntly: 'People

---

[4] See Lewis (1998) for a discussion of this term.

have become less willing to invest time, money and energy in family life, turning instead to investment in themselves.' Men's failure to maintain their children after relationship breakdown and women's increasing partic- ipation in the labour market are cited time and again as further confirma- tion of concern for self rather than others within the family.

In this interpretation, any encouragement given to women to enter the labour market is part of the problem, not the solution, and the only solu- tion is to return to some kind of male breadwinner model family. The arguments at the end of the twentieth century are a little different from the older and more familiar ones about the impact of women's work on chil- dren. While these are far from dead, the concerns expressed in the 1990s have revolved around the extent to which women's employment promotes relationship breakdown and the effects it has on men's behaviour. As Valerie Oppenheimer (1994) has pointed out, people with very different politics can buy into the idea that women's employment is a key variable explaining family change. In addition, both American and British commen- tators have expressed fears about the effect of women's employment on male work incentives and willingness to support their families. Geoff Dench (1994: 16–17) has argued that:

> [I]f women go too far in pressing for symmetry, and in trying to change the rules of the game, men will simply decide not to play. ...The family may be a myth, but it is myth that works to make men tolerably useful.

Thus women's employment is blamed for undermining the traditional male role of breadwinner and for creating 'yobbish men' in the next generation (Dennis and Erdos, 1992; Phillips, 1997). Most recently, Fukuyama (1999) has argued that the change in women's employment behaviour has allowed men to behave irresponsibly. Most of these writers do not go so far as to advocate curbs on women's work. Fukuyama's solution relies on a 'sponta- neous re-norming' of society, which he hopes will involve women recognis- ing the importance of staying at home with young children. Galston (1991: 281) has gone further and argued that the liberal state has to take action to protect and promote its distinctive conception of the human good: '[r]easonable public arguments for traditionalism' in respect of the family have been overlooked. These arguments in favour of women doing more care work tend to be tied to a strong desire to resuscitate the male bread- winner model family. As Iris Marion Young (1995) has observed, this is effectively to argue that women be prepared to make themselves dependent on men for the sake of their children and others who may be in need of care.

But there is of course considerable evidence that women want to care, whether out of preference (Hakim, 2001) or, as Gustaffson and Stafford (1994) have noted, because patterns of provision in respect of care in different countries owe much to historical and cultural factors.

Certainly in Britain and The Netherlands there is evidence that lone mothers want to care (Van Drenth *et al*, 2000; see also Duncan and Edwards, 1999), something long acknowledged also in respect of elderly care (Finch and Groves, 1983; Lewis and Meredith, 1988). If good quality, affordable day care were to be provided overnight, it is not clear that all women would want to work full-time in these countries.

MODELS FOR ADDRESSING THE ISSUE OF CARE AS WELL AS EMPLOYMENT

Behavioural change has been rapid and dramatic. The contributions that men and women make to families, especially the financial contribution made by women, have changed and there are many more women solely responsible for bringing up children. But the change in the nature of assumptions that policymakers make about the nature of the family and the way in which it works may well have run ahead of the social reality. The trend in respect of social policies is to assume that there is movement towards, or even that we have already achieved, individualisation. Policies that address the work of care have in general been considerably less well funded than those designed to get people into work and to make work pay. Commentators expressing anxiety about informal care in the family tend for the most part to be rather backward looking, but it would be difficult for government to 'put the clock back' in respect of the family, irrespective of the fact that governments perceive strong economic reasons for encouraging women's labour market participation. However, the terms and conditions under which an adult worker model family is promoted vary considerably between countries and it is possible to suggest a model that pays more attention to care and to gender equality.

The problems of moving towards a full adult worker model in respect of the gender dimension alone are fourfold. Firstly, unpaid care work is unequally shared between men and women, which has substantial implications for women's position in the labour market. Secondly, given the lack of good quality, affordable care in the formal sector, many women have little option but to continue to provide it informally (what Land and Rose, 1985 referred to as 'compulsory altruism') and to depend to some extent on a male wage. Bradshaw's cross-national comparative study of lone mothers' employment rates (1996) showed access to affordable childcare to be the key explanatory variable. Thirdly, a significant number of female carers want to/feel that it is 'right' to prioritise care. Fourthly, women's low pay, especially in care-related jobs, means that full individualisation is hard to achieve, on the basis of long part-time or even full-time work.

These points bring us back to the issue of the context for a policy that is driving towards an adult paid worker model. Without access to affordable, good quality support for care, women may resist the injunction to full individualisation so far as they are able, or substantial dis-welfares may be visited on dependants, young and old. It is highly unlikely that any attempt to put the clock back in respect of promoting the traditional male bread-winner family will be successful. Apart from the fact that policies of Western governments generally are running in a counter-direction, attitudes towards women's paid employment have undergone profound change (Scott, 1997).

The tensions in respect of the place of care in an adult worker model are too grave to be ignored. It is useful to look at the Scandinavian and American models in this regard as well. Both have a fully individualised, adult worker model. However, in the US case, the obligation to enter the labour market is embedded in a residual welfare system that often borders on the punitive, whereas in Sweden and Denmark, it is supported by an extensive range of care entitlements in respect of children and older people. The position of lone mothers—always a border case for the study of social policy—is particularly instructive in this respect because of the problem of combining unpaid care work and employment. The USA has gone much more wholeheartedly than Britain down the road of treating these women as paid workers, imposing time-limited benefits. Employment rates of lone mothers are high in the USA; the push factor is strong. But employment rates are higher still in Sweden and Denmark and lone mothers' poverty rates are much lower than the UK or the USA. Indeed, Sweden comes clos-est to having achieved Mead's ideal in that all adult citizens are obliged to engage in paid work in order to qualify for a wide range of benefits, which then permit them to leave the labour market. However, Swedish lone moth-ers get almost as much income from the state as they do from earnings (Lewis, 1998). The system is based on a commitment to universal citizen-ship entitlements, rather than, as in the USA, grafting equal citizenship obli-gations on to a residual welfare model.

Put simply, the Scandinavian model recognises care. All able-bodied adults are treated as citizen workers, but after that permission to exit the labour market in order to care with wage replacement is granted, and for-mal care services are provided. In effect, Sweden and Denmark operate a similar sex equality model to the USA, but their systems have the capacity to graft on respect for difference that manifests itself in the form of an unequal division of care work (Lewis and Astrom, 1992). However, Sweden does have one of the most sexually segregated labour markets in the Western world.

Care work has to be done. While birth rates are falling in most European countries, the proportion of frail elderly people is increasing; those aged 85 and over are projected to be three times more numerous in 2050 in the UK than now (Cmd 4192, 1999 para 2.19). There remain the questions as to 'who cares and on what terms?'. The major issues involved are the extent to which the care is *shared* unequally between men and women in society, and the fact that care work, whether formal or informal, is poorly *valued* via wages and the benefit system. The recently legislated minimum wage will do something for the lowest paid care workers, but the prospects of self-provisioning for large numbers of mainly female workers will remain poor. The Scandinavian model of providing various forms of recognition by the state of care work is considerably better than its polar opposite in the form of the American system, which admits very little collective responsibility for the support of families. However, given Sweden's sexually segregated labour market, there is an issue as to how far the system reinforces the traditional gendered division of paid work. Many women want to care, but they also want equal opportunities in the labour market.

In this respect, it is additionally important to consider the balance between cash and service provision in the welfare state. It is increasingly common to hear the argument that it does not matter whether provision is made in the form of cash or care services, but in fact this choice has profoundly gendered implications. In Germany, unlike the Scandinavian countries, parental leave policies have been implemented in such a way as to subsidise female labour market exit, while claims under the new social care insurance tend to be for cash rather than services, which also serves to bolster informal care in the home. If we accept that many women want to care, then this may be seen as providing a small amount of financial recognition for work they would have done anyway (Evers, 1998). Nevertheless, it serves to reinforce the gendered division of work. In France the substantial movement towards the provision of cash benefits, designed as a labour market policy to encourage the employment of carers in the home, has created more low-paid female employment, albeit with full access to social protection unlike the position in respect of the social care market in Britain. The issue is thus not just the need to make provision for care work, but to consider carefully the structure of that provision.

The issue of care and the fact that some people must combine unpaid and paid work should prompt urgent thinking about the nature of social protection. If all adults are to be treated as workers, then care must be compensated and collective provision made for it. Diemut Bubeck (1995), from a philosophical perspective, and Julie Nelson (1999), from an economic perspective, have argued strongly that care has to be properly valued if there is to be gender justice. However, this does not address the issue of sharing care work. Quite probably until men do more care work it will not be valued any more highly. Creighton (1999) has concluded that policies to address this aspect of care are vital. At the supra-national level, the OECD (1991) promoted the idea of combining work and care for men and women almost a decade ago, a policy also promoted by some EU countries (for example, The Netherlands with its 'Combination Scenario' produced by the Committee for Future Scenarios set up by the Minister of Social Affairs). Recent research on parental leave has shown that unless the leave is compensated and men are also obliged to take it, in all likelihood it will act to promote female labour market exit. As it is, in Britain men have the longest working hours in Europe. It is very difficult to work full-time and to care properly for dependants. Something has to give. EU member states and EU level policy is concerned above all with paid work and with care chiefly for instrumental reasons, as a means to the achievement of a fully individualised adult work model (Esping Andersen *et al*, 2001). But this is to miss the full complexity of the issues surrounding care, which require a more care-centred perspective. The erosion of the male breadwinner model family and with it the patterns of interdependence based on profound gender inequalities is not to be mourned, but there is a need to promote new forms of family solidarity to meet new patterns of behaviour—and for these to be incorporated in any private as well as public law reform.

REFERENCES

Ahlander, NR and Bahr, KS (1995) 'Beyond Drudgery, Power and Equity: Towards an Expanded Discourse on the Moral Dimensions of Housework in Families' *Journal of Marriage and the Family* 57: 54–68.

Anderson, E (1993) *Values in Ethics and Economics* (Cambridge, Mass, Harvard University Press).

Beck-Gernsheim, E (1999) 'On the Way to a Post-Familial Family. From a Community of Need to Elective Affinities' *Theory, Culture and Society* 15 (3–4): 53–70.

Bradshaw, J (1996) *The Employment of Lone Parents* (London, Family Policy Studies Centre).

Bruning, G and Plantenga, J (1999) 'Parental Leave and Equal Opportunities: Experiences in Eight European Countries' *Journal of European Social Policy* 9 (3): 195–209.

Bubeck, D (1995) *Care, Gender and Justice* (Oxford, Oxford University Press).

Burns, A and Scott, C (1994) *Mother-Headed Families and why they have Increased* (New Jersey, Lawrence Erlbaum).

Council of the European Community (1993) *Growth, Competitiveness and Employment—The Challenges and Ways Forward into the 21st Century* (Luxembourg, CEC).

CEC (1995) *Equal Opportunities for Women and Men—Follow-up to the White Paper on Growth, Competitiveness and Employment* (Brussels, Directorate General for Employment and Social Affairs).

CEC (2000a) *Report on Social Protection in Europe 1999*. Com (2000) 163 final (Brussels, CEC).

CEC (2000b) *Communication from the Commission to the Council, the European Parliament, the Economic and Social Committee and the Committee of the Regions: Social Policy Agenda* (Brussels, CEC).

Cmd 6404 (1942) *Report of the Committee on Social Insurance and Allied Services* (London, HMSO).

Cmd 4192 (1999) *With Respect to Old Age. Report of the Royal Commission on Long-Term Care*, vol 1 (London, The Stationery Office).

Creighton, C (1999) 'The Rise and Decline of the "Male Breadwinner Family" in Britain' *Cambridge Journal of Economics* 23: 519–541.

Crouch, C (1999) *Social Change in Western Europe* (Oxford, Oxford University Press).

Daly, M (2000) 'A Fine Balance: Women's Labour Market Participation in International Comparison' in FW Scharpf and VA Schmidt (eds), *Welfare and Work in the Open Economy,* vol 2, *Diverse Responses to Common Challenges* (Oxford, Oxford University Press).

Dench, G (1994) *The Frog, the Prince and the Problem of Men* (London, Neanderthal Books).

Dennis, N and Erdos, G (1992) *Families without Fatherhood* (London, Institute for Economic Affairs).

Dex, S (1988) *Women's Attitudes Towards Work* (London, Macmillan).

Duncan, S and Edwards, R (1999) *Lone Mothers, Paid Work and Gendered Moral Rationalities* (London, Macmillan).

Elster, J (1991) 'Rationality and Social Norms' *Archives Européennes de Sociologie* 32: 109–129.

Ermisch, J and Francesconi, M (1998) *Cohabitation in Great Britain: Not for Long, But Here to Stay*, Working Paper 98–1 (University of Essex, ESRC Research Centre on Micro-Social Change).

Esping Andersen, G (1999) *Social Foundations of Postindustrial Economies* (Oxford, Oxford University Press).

Esping Andersen, G, Gallie, D, Hermerijck, A and Myles, J (2001) *A New Welfare Architecture for Europe?*, Report to the Belgian Presidency of the EU (Brussels, CEC).

Evers, A (1998) 'The New Long Term Care Insurance Policy in Germany' *Journal of Ageing and Social Policy* 10 (1): 77–97.

Finch, J and Groves, D (eds) (1983) *Labour and Love: Women, Work and Caring* (London, Routledge and Kegan Paul).

Fukuyama, F (1999) *The Great Disruption* (London, Profile Books).

Galston, W (1991) *Liberal Purposes, Good Virtues and Diversity in the Liberal State* (Cambridge, Cambridge University Press).

Gershuny, J (2000) *Changing Times: Work and Leisure in Post-Industrial Society* (Oxford, Oxford University Press).

Giddens, A (1992) *The Transformation of Intimacy: Sexuality, Love and Eroticism in Modern Societies* (Cambridge, Polity Press).

Gillis, J (1997) *A World of their Own Making: A History of Myth and Ritual in Family Life* (Oxford, Oxford University Press).

Ginn, J, Street, D and Arber, S (eds) (2001) *Women, Work and Pensions* (Buckingham, Open University Press).

Gustaffson, S and Stafford, FP (1994) 'Three Regimes of Childcare' in R Blank (ed), *Social Production versus Economic Flexibility: Is There a Trade-off?* (Chicago, Chicago University Press and National Bureau for Economic Research).

Hakim, C (1996) *Key Issues in Women's Work* (London, Athlone).

—— (2001) *Work–Lifestyle Choices in the Twenty-first Century: Preference Theory* (Oxford, Oxford University Press).

Hooghiemstra, E (1997) 'Een-en tweeverdieners?' in M Niphuis-Nell (ed), *Sociale Atlas van de Vrouw, deel 4: Veranderingen in de Primaire Leefsfeer* (Rijswijk, Sociaal en Cultureel Planbureau).

Horrell, S and Humphries, J (1997) 'The Origins and Expansion of the Male Breadwinner Family: The Case of Nineteenth-Century Britain' *International Review of Social History* 42, Supplement: 25–64.

Knijn, T (2001) 'Care Work: Innovations in The Netherlands' in M Daly (ed), *Care Work Security* (Geneva, International Labour Office).

Knijn, T and van Welss, F (2001) 'Does it Work? Employment Policies for Lone Mothers in The Netherlands' in J Millar and K Rowlingson (eds), *Lone Parents, Employment and Social Policy: Cross-National Comparisons* (Bristol, Policy Press).

Land, H and Rose, H (1985) 'Compulsory Altruism for Some or an Altruistic Society for All?' in P Bean, J Ferris and D Whynes (eds), *In Defence of Welfare* (London, Tavistock).

Lessig, L (1996) 'Social Meaning and Social Norms' *University of Pennsylvania Law Review* 144: 2181–9.

Lewis, J (ed) (1986) *Labour and Love: Women's Experience of Home and Family, 1850–1940* (London, Blackwell).

—— (1992) 'Gender and the Development of Welfare Regimes' *Journal of European Social Policy* 2 (3): 159–173.

—— (1998) 'The Problem of Lone-Mother Families in Twentieth-Century Britain' *Journal of Social Welfare and Family Law* 20 (3): 251–284.

—— (2001) 'The Decline of the Male Breadwinner Model: Implications for Work and Care' *Social Politics* 8 (2): 152–170.

—— (2002) 'Gender and Welfare State Change' *European Societies* 4 (4): 331–357.

Lewis, J and Astrom, G (1992) 'Equality, Difference and State Welfare: Labour Market and Family Policies in Sweden' *Feminist Studies* 18 (1): 59–87.

Lewis, J and Kiernan, K (1996) 'The Boundaries between Marriage, Non-Marriage and Parenthood: Changes in Behaviour and Policy in Post-War Britain' *Journal of Family History* 21 (3): 372–387.

Lewis, J and Meredith, B (1988) *Daughters Caring for Mothers* (London, Routledge).

McLaughlin, E, Tewsdale, J and McCay, N (2001) 'The Rise and Fall of the UK's First Tax Credit: The Working Families Tax Credit, 1998–2000' *Social Policy and Administration* 35 (2): 163–180.

Mead, L (1986) *Beyond Entitlement: The Social Obligations of Citizenship* (New York, Free Press).

Nelson, J (1999) 'Of Markets and Martyrs: Is it OK to Pay Well for Care?' *Feminist Economics* 4 (1): 43–59.

Novak, M and Cogan, J (1987) *The New Consensus on Family and Welfare: A Community of Self-Reliance* (Milwaukee, American Enterprise Institute).

OECD (1991) *Shaping Structural Change* (Paris, OECD).

OECD (2000) *Economic Studies* 31, 2000/2 (Paris, OECD).

Office for National Statistics (ONS) (1998) *Living in Britain: Results from the 1996 General Household Survey* (London, HMSO).

Oppenheimer, V (1994) 'Women's Rising Employment and the Future of the Family in Industrialised Societies' *Population and Development Review* 20 (2): 293–342.

Orloff, A (1993) 'Gender and the Social Rights of Citizenship: Sate Policies and Gender Relations in Comparative Research' *American Sociological Review* 58 (3) 303–328.

Parsons, T and Bales, RF (1955) *Family Socialization and Interaction Process* (Glencoe, Ill, Free Press).

Phillips, M (1997) *The Sex Change State* (London, Social Market Foundation).

Popenoe, D (1993) 'American Family Decline, 1960–1990: A Review and Appraisal' *Journal of Marriage and the Family* 55 (August): 527–555.

Rake, K (2000) 'Gender and New Labour's Social Policies' *Journal of Social Policy* 30 (2): 209–232.

Rubery, J, Smith, M and Fagan, C (1998) 'National Working-Time Regimes and Equal Opportunities' *Feminist Economics* 4 (1): 71–101.

Scott, J (1997) 'Changing Households in Britain: Do Families Matter?' *Sociological Review* 45 (4): 591–620.

Seccombe, W (1993) *Weathering the Storm: Working-Class Families from the Industrial Revolution to the Fertility Decline* (London, Verso).

Stacey, J (1990) *Brave New Families: Stories of Domestic Upheaval in Late Twentieth Century America* (New York, Basic Books).

Suchman, MC (1997) 'On Beyond Interest: Rational, Normative and Cognitive Perspectives in the Social Scientific Study of Law' *Wisconsin Law Review* 475–501.

Sugden, R (1998) 'Conventions' in P Newman (ed), *The New Palgrave Dictionary of Economic and the Law*, vol 1 (London, Macmillan).

Sunstein, CR (1997) *Free Markets and Social Justice* (Oxford, Oxford University Press).

Supiot, A (1999) *Au-dela de L'Emploi* (Paris, Flammarion).

Svenhuijsen, S (1998) *Citizenship and the Ethics of Care* (London, Routledge).

Thair, T and Risdon, A (1999) 'Women in the Labour Market: Results from the Spring 1998 LFS' *Labour Market Trends* (March): 103–127.

Tilly, L and Scott, J (1975) *Women, Work and Family* (New York, Holt Rinehart and Winston).

Tronto, JC (1993) *Moral Boundaries: A Political Argument for an Ethic of Care* (London, Routledge).

Van Drenth, A, Knijn, T and Lewis, T (2000) 'Sources of Income for Lone Mother Families: Policy Changes in Britain and The Netherlands and the Experiences of Divorced Women' *Journal of Social Policy* 28 (4): 619–642.

Weitzman, L (1981) *The Marriage Contract. Spouses, Lovers and the Law* (New York, Free Press).

—— (1985) *The Divorce Revolution* (New York, Free Press).

Young, IM (1995) 'Mothers, Citizenship and Independence: A Critique of Pure Family Values' *Ethics* 105: 535–556.

PART II

Regulating New Forms of Relationship Between Adults and Children

5

Changing Ways, New Technologies and the Devaluation of the Genetic Connection to Children

JULIE SHAPIRO

INTRODUCTION

I**N THE UNITED STATES** today, as in most countries, parents have a unique status in the lives of their children. Parents possess rights, including both reasonably well-defined legal rights and more amorphous social rights, that no other individuals can exercise. In law and in society, parents are understood to have a special relationship with their children that is protected from interference by other individuals and from the state. At the same time, parents are also expected to bear special obligations towards their children, obligations which are not shared by the society at large. In this regard, the United States can be distinguished from most European countries, where the obligations of the greater society to children are more developed (Sterrett, 2002).

Sometimes the identification of a child's parents is contested. In some circumstances, claiming the entitlements of parenthood is of paramount importance and hence, parenthood is a status eagerly sought. Individuals compete, either legally or socially, for the status of 'parent'. In other circumstances, the obligations imposed upon a parent may be more salient and so individuals seek to avoid being identified as the parent of a child, denying their parenthood and perhaps promoting the parenthood of another individual.[1] In either case, when the status of 'parent' is contested the question of what defines a person as the parent to a particular child comes to the fore.

What makes a person legally or socially recognisable as a parent to a child is a complex question to which there are and have been many

---

[1] Because courts in the United States consider it highly desirable to have some person identified as a parent and hence, subject to the parental obligations of support, it is often useful to advance the parenthood of another individual if one is denying one's own parenthood.

answers. Even as childhood is socially constructed, so is parenthood. Thus, the definition of 'parent' changes over time and across cultures. Many who might be recognised as parents in the USA today would have passed unnoticed in colonial America or in Renaissance Europe or in ancient Rome. No definition can suffice more than momentarily.

There are distinct yet overlapping spheres within which the definition of parenthood may be contested and resolved. There are social parents—those who act as 'parents' in the real world in which a child lives—and there are legal parents—those the law recognises as 'parents'. It might be ideal (and it would surely be simpler) if being recognised as a parent in one sphere automatically ensured recognition in the other. But this is not the case. Sometimes the law fails to acknowledge the parenthood of a child's social parent and sometimes the legal parent of a child may not function as a social parent in the child's world.

That said, recognition as a child's legal parent is not without great meaning in society at large. Indeed, law plays a significant role in the social construction of parenthood. Exercising rights over, and assuming obligations for, a child are among the primary factors defining a person as a social parent. While a person may be able to do so without legal recognition, legal recognition obviously enhances her or his ability to do so. Indeed, the mere fact of legal recognition itself has social meaning as it provides formal confirmation of a person's status. This is particularly true in the USA, where law is a social institution of primary importance in the lives and ideas of many people.

At the same time, recognition as a social parent is not completely irrelevant in the eyes of the law. In an individual case, the fact of a person's status as a social parent may be influential. Similarly, identification as a psychological parent can form the basis of claims to legal parentage.[2] More generally, the law is responsive to social changes and to shifts in the social definitions of parenthood. Particularly if one considers the evolving meanings of 'parent' over time, the legal and social definitions are inextricably entwined.

In this chapter, I will examine some aspects of these evolving intertwined meanings in the USA today. Changing family structures (or perhaps more accurately, the acknowledgement of changed structures) and emerging technologies are influencing the definition of 'parenthood' in both law and society. And even as these influences undermine an old mainstay of parental definition—the presence of a genetic link between two individuals—they lead to increasing emphasis on other factors. I want to examine the broad implications of the declining importance of the genetic link in defining parenthood.

---

[2] A psychological parent is a person who functions as a parent from a psychological viewpoint. As such it is obviously very closely linked to social parenting. Status as a psychological parent has formed the basis for recognition of legal parentage in several states.

It is important to note at the outset that the ongoing struggle over the definition of parenthood is highly politicised. To be a recognised as a parent is, in some significant regards, to have a privileged status under US law. While parents are not immune from state or third-party intervention in the decisions they make regarding their children, they do possess a high degree of autonomy.[3] The well-entrenched doctrine of 'family privacy' protects most parental decision-making from outside review. Thus, it is hardly surprising that as the US has endured various high-profile 'culture wars' over the definition of family and the promotion of 'family values', part of the struggle has been to define who is (and who can be) a parent.

NEW TECHNOLOGIES

Over the last three decades, advances in reproductive and genetic technologies have wrought far-reaching changes in how we think about defining parents within the social context. These changes are as yet incompletely reflected in the law and in society, though some emerging patterns can be identified.

Two branches of technology are important here. First, reproductive technologies have allowed for the creation of children in ways previously unthinkable—children born from donor sperm, donor eggs and from embryos created outside the uterus and then implanted into the uterus of a genetically unrelated woman. We may well stand on the threshold of even more radical developments—cloning, perhaps, which might allow us to create children without even using genetic material from two different pre-existing people. But even without consideration of the future, the changes we have already seen on a reasonably substantial scale have raised issues aplenty.

The second area in which technology has raised new and disruptive questions is the area of genetic mapping and testing. We are now able to identify those individuals who have in fact provided the genetic materials for the creation of a child with a very high degree of precision. This in turn has allowed us (and sometimes requires us) to assess the reliability of assumptions about genetic relationships we have made for many, many years.

In the following sections I will briefly discuss each of these technologies and identify the challenges they raise for the legal system. In addition, I will consider some of the basic responses of the legal system, although I shall defer more detailed consideration until a subsequent section of this chapter.

1 Reproductive Technologies

The past 30 years have seen both the development of and also the proliferation of assisted reproduction technologies. Of these, alternative insemination

[3] See *Troxel v Granville*, 530 US 57 (2000).

(sometimes called 'artificial insemination') is the least technologically complex. Indeed, alternative insemination has been available for far longer than the other technologies discussed here. However, the enhanced ability to collect and store sperm for significant periods of time, coupled with a development of a lucrative commercial market for such services has dramatically increased the use of this technology.

If the sperm used to inseminate a woman is obtained from her male partner, and most obviously if it is obtained from her husband, who functions as the social father of the child created, then alternative insemination poses little challenge to our thinking about parenthood. However, alternative insemination frequently utilises sperm obtained from a donor (most typically an anonymous donor) who is intended to have no ongoing connection to any child resulting from the insemination. A woman using such a service might be a single woman seeking to have and raise a child by herself; a woman who is a part of a heterosexual partnership, where her male partner intends to serve as a parent to the child but is himself unable to provide sperm; or a woman who is part of a lesbian relationship, whose female partner intends to serve as parent to the child. In any of these circumstances, the law and society must confront the appropriate role to be given to the man who provided the genetic material that made the birth of the child possible. Notably, in all of these instances, the donor is not intended to function as a parent, despite the fact that the donor will have a genetic link to any child produced by the insemination.

The legal response to the use of reproductive technology is epitomised by the Uniform Parentage Act (UPA).[4] The UPA provides that the donor is not the parent of the child. Thus, under the UPA, the legal significance of the genetic link is entirely erased.[5]

Assisted insemination would lose much of its commercial appeal if donors were considered to be legal parents, or if they could later claim that status. In the absence of specific statutory provisions, this would seem to be the likely result, as the man would be seen as akin to one who impregnated a woman following a 'one night stand'.[6] Thus, the passage of a UPA-like statute is a predicate to the emergence of the sperm bank and other related reproductive technologies as commercial enterprises.

More technologically complex and more recent are the technologies typified by in vitro fertilisation (IVF). IVF depends on the ability to 'harvest' eggs from a woman's ovaries. The eggs are then fertilised and the fertilised eggs are then placed in a woman's uterus. The woman gestates and gives birth to the child.

---

[4] The original version of the UPA, published in 1973, has been adopted in some form by virtually every state. A new version was published in 2000. Comments here generally relate to the 2000 version of the UPA unless otherwise noted.

[5] This does not dispose of the question of the social significance of the genetic link.

[6] The UPA distinguishes between children who are conceived as the result of sexual intercourse (where the genetic linkage may be significant) and those who are not conceived as the result of sexual intercourse (where the genetic link is of no significance).

The egg donor and the woman who gives birth may or may not be the same person. Further, the woman intending to raise the child may be the egg donor, the woman who gave birth, or a third person.[7] If one woman occupies all three roles, then as with the case of the sperm donor/social father, the technology poses little challenge to our thinking. It is simply a different path to the same end of unified social parent/genetic parent. If two or more women are involved, however, then the law and society must determine the status of the women involved—the egg donor, the gestator, and the intended parent.

Most obviously, the egg donor could be seen to be in a position analogous to a sperm donor.[8] This might suggest that the legal analysis of the egg donor's status would proceed along similar lines as that for a sperm donor—in particular, that in the absence of specific statutory language like the UPA, she would be deemed to be a parent of the child by virtue of the genetic link.

But in fact, the problem—in both legal and social realms—has proved to be a more complicated one, largely because the determination of the egg donor's status must be considered as against the status of the woman who gave birth to the child.[9] Historically, we have always considered that the woman who gives birth to a child is the mother of that child—at least at the outset of the child's life. Until the advent of these technologies, this assumption has rested firmly on the combined claims of genetic linkage and gestation. No other woman could claim any connection to the child that could rival either of these claims.

Technology has broken the connection between genetics and gestation. IVF with a donor egg presents the problem of competing claims from a woman with a genetic link but without gestation versus a woman with gestation but no genetic link. The first woman is, of course, in a position analogous to a father of a newborn, who similarly has the genetic link but no gestation. As it is widely assumed that the man who provides the sperm, absent the operation of the UPA or a similar statute, is a parent (the father) of the child, it would seem to follow that the similarly situated woman must also be a parent (the mother) of the child. But this conclusion cannot be so

---

[7] A woman who gives birth to a child (whether genetically related to her or not) but is not expected to function as a mother is often referred to as a 'surrogate' mother.

[8] The position is analogous in that in each case the donor has provided his or her genetic material for use by another for the purpose of creating a child. The analogy fails to take into account the difference in the process by which the sperm and the eggs are collected and the impact of the donation on the donor. While these differences are reflected in the market price for sperm as opposed to eggs, they are generally ignored in considering the parental status of sperm and egg donors. The new UPA treats all donors, male and female, the same. Donors are not parents.

[9] It is theoretically possible, of course, that the resulting child might have two mothers. But no court or legislature has reached this result. The generally inflexible (and likely genetically based) requirement that a child has at most two parents and at most one of each sex stands in the way of that result.

easily reached, although it is ultimately the conclusion reached by some influential courts,[10] because it ignores the value of gestation.[11]

In any event, this does not complete the analysis of the problems presented by IVF. As with sperm donation, egg donation has become part of a substantial and lucrative industry in the USA. And thus, a further question is posed: As between the egg donor and the purchaser of an egg (who may or may not be the woman who gives birth), who can claim to be the parent to the child? The answer reached is generally the same as that for purchased sperm. Under the new UPA, the seller (be they egg donor or sperm donor) can claim the genetic linkage to the child, but they do not have the right to claim parental status as a result of that linkage.[12] It may often be that the purchaser of the egg is in fact the woman who gestates the child. If so, her claim to parenthood lies in both her gestation and her status as the purchaser of the genetic material.

Ultimately, the decoupling of the genetic link from the definition of parenthood is a necessary condition for the creation of a market for reproductive materials. It remains widely agreed in the USA that selling children or selling parental rights is unacceptable and therefore, if selling reproductive materials is to be acceptable, it cannot be equated with selling parental rights. At the same time, the extensive and highly publicised markets for reproductive materials[13] reinforces the sense that no parental right inheres in the genetic material itself.

Thus, these new technologies, driven by market forces, have devalued and in some instances erased the significance of the genetic link between an adult and a child. On the horizon, there are even more challenging technologies. Cloning could lead to children who have but one source of genetic material or, viewed another way, whose genetic material can be traced directly to their grandparents. Other experimental techniques might combine the genetic material from three people.

2 Genetic Mapping and Screening

Reproductive technologies are not the only sources of challenge in current society. Advanced techniques now enable us to establish, with a high degree

[10] The prototypical case in the United States is *Johnson v Calvert*, 851 P2d 776 (CA 1993)(en banc). *Johnson* does not employ the reasoning discussed here, but reached the conclusion that the egg donor had parental rights and that the gestator did not.

[11] Of course, gestation is a uniquely female activity and it may be unsurprising that a male-dominated legal and social tradition would devalue this uniquely female activity.

[12] Where it required adoption of a statute to ensure that the sperm donor was not considered to be the father, the same is not true for egg donors. This is likely because there was an extensive body of existing law that a man who was genetically linked to a child was the child's father and hence, was responsible for the child's support. This body of law developed in an effort to identify appropriate men on whom to place the obligations of parenthood where there was no socially related candidate—in an instance where a woman had a brief sexual liaison with a man, for example. There was no parallel pre-existing body of law for women, and hence no need for a statute to distinguish the egg donor from the more ordinary case of socially unrelated genetic parenthood.

[13] Major newspapers and magazines frequently contain ads soliciting either buyers or sellers.

of probability if not certainty, which individuals provided the genetic material that created a child. Not only is this technologically feasible, it has become increasingly common and visible. Several popular television talk shows have recently entertained viewers with the spectacle of men being confronted with the results of DNA testing of those they believe to be 'their' children.

These developments have undermined the significance of the genetic link in a distinct way. We are now confronted with the reality of the disjunction between social and/or legal parenting and the genetic tie. Where once we would have had no reason to confront this discontinuity, happy in the belief that the social and legal parent also possessed the genetic link to the child, now we must come to terms with it.[14] This then poses a question of whether our incorrect assumption about the genetic tie means that our assumptions, be they legal or social, about who are the child's parents are also incorrect.

Of course, the idea that people might parent a child to whom they have no genetic link is hardly a new one. Adoption and fostering are ancient practices. But in the USA today, adoptive parents and foster parents must follow specific steps in order to gain legal recognition of their parenthood. They stand in contrast to 'natural' parents who presumably derive their status not from the operation of the law but from nature itself. The defining characteristic for natural parents is their genetic connection to their children. And thus, to discover that perceived 'natural parents' have in fact no genetic tie to their children is disruptive. Do they cease to be parents in the eyes of the law and/or in the eyes of society? This is the question thrust upon us by developing capacities of genetic testing. At a minimum, it forces us to re-evaluate exactly how important the genetic link really is.[15]

The same capacity to read our genes may also change the significance of the genetic link in another way. Once, knowing one's genetic origins was important for, among other reasons, the ability it gave one to construct a medical history. We could make certain inferences about the potential health risks a child faced from information about the health of their genetic ancestors. Thus, if three closely related relatives had breast cancer at an early age, the likelihood that a child might be at a greater risk of early onset of breast cancer increased.

But soon, technology will allow us directly to read our own genetic codes. Instead of constructing probabilities about our own genetic proclivities

---

[14] This is most typically a problem with regard to fatherhood. But it is not exclusively so. There are instances in which babies have been switched, whether inadvertently or otherwise, in the hospital and each has gone home with a set of parents not genetically related to them. When genetic testing reveals to us the genetic reality we must confront the same disjunction.

[15] There are in fact a small number of legal cases involving switched infants. In general, the legal definition of parenthood has followed the genetic link. But courts have not reached this conclusion without some difficulty. And in at least one case, the newly ordained legal parents agreed to leave the child with her social parents, suggesting the limited importance of the genetic tie. See Justin Blum and Michael Shaw, 'Of One Mind on Two Children' *Washington Post*, 5 August 1993, B1.

from the histories of our ancestors, we will be able directly to examine our genes for risk factors. Thus, at least one fairly modern and pragmatic reason for valuing the genetic link (or at least information about the genetic link) may dissolve.

CHANGING WAYS

At the same time as technologies have emerged and evolved, social struggles over the meaning of family have continued. The myth of the nuclear family may indeed have always been a myth, but its status as such has become increasingly clear over the last 30 years. Rising divorce and subsequent remarriage rates have vastly increased the number of 'blended families'. The incidence of children born outside of marriage is also high. In the last 20 years there has been a significant surge in the number of lesbian and gay families, which may be one-parent or two-parent families. While lesbian and gay people have undoubtedly always raised children (typically children born into an earlier heterosexual relationship) there are now growing numbers of planned lesbian and gay families—often made possible through some of the new technology discussed above. These families have also gained heightened visibility, in part as a result of the culture wars over their existence and legal recognition. Adoption, too, has become more visible than it was as the stigma of adoption has diminished.

For all of these reasons, there are increasingly large and visible numbers of people who act as though they were parents, who are socially recognised as parents, and who have sought and perhaps even won legal recognition as parents, but who do not have a genetic link to their children. They may be step-parents or non-biological mothers or adoptive parents. With increasing frequency they are appearing on soccer fields and at PTA meetings and at doctor's offices as well as on television sitcoms, magazine covers and best seller lists.

Legal recognition has lagged significantly behind social recognition. While there is no shortage of instances where the law has refused to recognise these parents, it is increasingly the case that the failure of the law to recognise them has brought the law under criticism. Several years ago, for example, two state courts were confronted with remarkably similar cases.[16] In each case a child had been placed with a planned adoptive family shortly after its birth. In both cases the woman who had given birth to the child relinquished her rights to parenthood. And then in both cases, several years after placement, the man who was the source of the genetic material (in each case the original mother's then-boyfriend) stepped forward to claim parental rights, in conjunction with the original mother's reassertion of her

---

[16] *In re Baby Girl Clausen*, 502 NW2d 649 (Mich 1993); *In re Kirchner*, 649 NE2d 324 (Ill 1996).

own claim. In neither case had the man's genetically based parental rights been properly terminated.

In both cases, the courts observed that the intended adoptive parents had functioned in every way as the parents of the child for the majority of each child's life. They were clearly the social parents of the child. But in neither case could the court find a way to deny the overwhelming significance of the new male claimants' genetic link to the child. And so in both, the courts declared the men to be legal fathers, entitled to assert rights to custody as against the prospective adoptive parents (the social parents) of the child. And in both instances, custody of the child was indeed transferred.

These cases were closely followed in the local and national media and, as the time for the change in custody drew near and as avenues for legal appeal were exhausted, the press coverage mounted. The coverage vastly favoured leaving the children with the families they had known and minimised the significance of the genetic tie that was the basis for the legal result. Though in neither case was there public outcry alter the result, both states enacted altered statutes in their aftermath, and the new statutes reflected increased recognition of social parents and decreased status for those with genetic connections to children who have not functioned as social parents.

Similarly, a series of cases have focused on instances in which two lesbians raising a child fall into conflict. One invokes legal status as a parent— whether because she is genetically related to and gave birth to the child or because she initially adopted the child. The other invokes her social status as a parent, producing all the social markers of parenthood.

The results here have been mixed. Some courts have recognised the non-biologically related woman as a legal mother, based on a variety of legal theories including de facto parenthood and estoppel. In these instances, the importance of the genetic link is diminished as the non-genetically linked woman is placed on an equal footing by virtue of her performance of the social role. Other courts have denied the social mother recognition, relying on the absence of the genetic link. While these results themselves bolster the importance of the genetic link, they have generally been met by criticism, demonstrating the social willingness to depart from the necessity of a genetic component to parenthood. Recent model legislation provides recognition and protection for people who have performed this role.[17]

THE DIMINISHING VALUE OF THE GENETIC LINK

1 Note on Terminology

All children born throughout history could, at least in theory, trace their genetic material to two people—one male and one female. In general,

---

[17] See *Principles of the Law of Family Dissolution: Analysis and Recommendations*, ch 2 (American Law Institute, 2002).

through most of our history, we might assume these people are the parents—father and mother, respectively—of the child. It has always been clear that there is not a perfect overlap between the people who might be identified as the sources of the genetic material and the people who actually functioned as the child's parents. Adoption and fostering of children are well known throughout the ancient myths and legends of many people. Similarly, the husband who raises a child born to his wife but not genetically related to him is a stock figure of fiction and drama.

As theorists have refined their understanding of the construction of parenthood, the term 'parent' has been paired with modifiers to explicate which sort of parenthood was referred to—so, for example 'legal parents' versus 'social parents', and 'natural parents' versus 'adoptive parents'. In a similar vein, as recent scholarship has struggled with the issues discussed above, it has become common to refer to 'genetic parents'. Genetic parents are individuals in the category who contribute genetic material necessary for the creation of a child.

The term 'genetic parent' is not without utility. It is difficult to discuss the meaning of the genetic tie between those who create children and the children they create without a simple term to refer to the people involved. Indeed, my unwillingness to employ the term thus far in the chapter has made me particularly aware of the term's utility in that regard. But 'genetic parent' can also be obscuring. It prematurely concludes that the person concerned is in fact a parent of some sort.

This inherent presumption confuses analysis when the very question posed is whether the person in question is indeed a parent (in either the social or the legal sense of the word); for it seems impossible to respond that a genetic parent is not a parent. The discourse in recent US case law and scholarship is needlessly complicated by this confusion.

While a term to designate those who provide the genetic material is necessary, 'genetic parent' is not the most useful one. As the technological and cultural changes described here have multiplied, it is important to settle on a new formulation. The very need for such a new formulation reveals the diminished status of the genetic link. The presence of such a link is simply no longer sufficient in all contexts to ensure that one is a parent.

For the moment, I shall use 'progenitors'. The idea that the progenitors of a child may in fact not be those who we would recognise as a child's parents (or conversely, that the parents of a child might not be her or his progenitors) is hardly a new one. But the use of the term (or a similarly nonconclusive one) may assist in clarifying the questions presented.

2 The Diminishing Value of the Genetic Link

I have already discussed a number of contexts in which it is clear that status as progenitor does not ensure status as a parent. Two more recent examples warrant brief discussion.

In *In re Nicholas H*,[18] the Supreme Court of California—a court viewed as generally liberal—conferred parenthood on a man who was not (and had always known he was not) the progenitor of his child. Despite the lack of relationship and his knowledge of it, he had served as the child's social parent for most of the child's six years. In the opinion, which was widely publicised, the court awarded the man custody of the child over the objections of the child's mother. It found that the man's admission that he was not the child's biological father did not rebut the presumption of fatherhood that arose from his social relationship with the child.[19] In seeking custody, the child's mother advanced the progenitor of the child (who had never served as the social parent of the child) as an alternative candidate for parenthood. After an extensive review of case law that had developed over a number of years, the court concluded that status as a legal parent did not depend on genetic linkage.

A second recent case creates an interesting comparison. *In the Interest of TSS*[20] was decided by the Texas Supreme Court. (This court might be viewed as the polar opposite of the California Supreme Court.) A man who had served as the social father of a child for 10 years learned that he was not the progenitor of the child. He sought an order terminating his parental relationship with the child. Consistent with the result in California, the Texas court found him to be the father of the child despite the absence of any genetic linkage. The court, quoting with approval, noted that '[a]lthough DNA testing may provide a bright line for determining the biological relationship between a man and a child, it does not and cannot define the human relationship between a father and child'.[21]

This is not to say that the genetic link retains no force in the law or in our lives. Obviously it does.[22] In many instances, courts continue to recognise parenthood based in whole or in part on genetic connection to the child. On a social level, adoptive children frequently search out their progenitors. And a significant part of the demand for the technology described above is fuelled by people who want to have children with whom they will share a genetic connection.[23] But the overpowering importance of the genetic link has begun to diminish significantly and will likely continue to do so.

---

[18] 120 Cal Rep 2d 146 (2002).

[19] This is an instance in which the use of the term 'biological father' can hardly advance the clarity of the analysis.

[20] 61 SW3d 481 (2002).

[21] The California and Texas cases do arise in distinctly different contexts. In the California case a man wished to be father to a child who would otherwise, in the view of the court, have no suitable home. Thus the court was undoubtedly predisposed to find him the father. In the Texas case a man sought to terminate his obligation to support a child where there was no other available candidate, giving the court reason to deny his request.

[22] The father in the Texas case above declared that he would be entirely unable to visit with or care for his child, having learned that he did not share a genetic link with the child.

[23] See eg *In re Baby M* 537 A 2d 1227 (NJ 1988).

LINGERING QUESTIONS, LIMITLESS POSSIBILITIES

As the importance of the genetic link to defining parenthood diminishes and as the definition of parenthood continues to evolve, new factors must come to the fore. If genetic linkage is not conclusive in defining parenthood, then some other criteria must fill that role. One might approach this as a theoretical question, asking what qualifications we should seek in defining parenthood. To date, courts have generally employed one of two approaches: one focused on the functions performed by the parties and the other focused on the intention of the parties.

Functional analyses, turning on who actually played the social role of a parent, were critical in the cases from Texas and California discussed above as well as in those involving intra-lesbian disputes in which the non-progenitor attained legal recognition. Focusing on function ensures a high degree of correspondence between those who are social parents and those who will gain legal recognition.

The appeal of a functional definition of parenthood is apparent. Although it may be far more painstaking for a court to determine whether a person functioned as a parent than it would be to determine whether they are genetically related to a child, it is also more obviously allied to an apparent concern for the well-being of the child. Its appeal lies in large part in the promise it offers that those recognised by law will in fact be those who have substantial relationships to the children concerned. In other words, those who the law will recognise as parents are those who really are the parents anyway.

These very strengths make a functional analysis intrusive, time-consuming and expensive. In addition, there is little consensus about what it means to act like a parent or to play a parental role. Thus, even when all the facts can be determined, the legal meaning of the facts remains in doubt. Litigants confronted with a functional test will be subject to discretionary decision making by judges, who can never be free of their own bias. Thus, the results of a function test will be uncertain and skewed by bias. By contrast, focusing on genetics gave judges much less discretion.

Though not for these reasons, a functional analysis of who are a child's parents has not been commonly employed in cases arising out of new reproductive technologies. In these cases, the more common alternative to a genetic approach has been to rely on the intention of the parties. Several factors contribute to this result. Some of the new technology cases (notably the disputes over frozen pre-embryos) arise before anyone has had an opportunity to function as a parent.[24] Many of the other cases concern disputes that arise during the pregnancy or soon after the birth of the child.

---

[24] Indeed, these cases arise before there is a child to parent. Pre-embryos are generally frozen when there are approximately eight cells.

Courts are generally reluctant to view gestation as a parental function. This seems curious as it could well be argued that gestation is a quintessential parental function. But the consequences of recognising gestation as a parental function might be more drastic than it would first appear. It might, for example, consistently advantage women over men in determining parental rights, at least in the early stages of a child's life.

It would also call into question the legitimacy of what is known as gestational surrogacy. If gestation is a source of parental status, then it cannot, consistent with our prescriptions on selling children, be bought or sold. And yet this is precisely what is bought and sold in gestational surrogacy (a practice permitted for profit in a number of states). The application of the function test to these cases is therefore both difficult and problematic. Instead, courts have tended to examine the intent of the parties.

In general, parenthood based on intention fits more closely with the marketised version of parenthood on which the market in reproductive technology is based. Intent is a concept that lends itself to the contractarian model that forms the basis of the commercialisation and marketisation of reproductive technologies.

The decline in importance of genetic linkage has potential implications for gender equality. Analyses based on the presence of a genetic link placed men and women on an equal footing. Mother and father made the same genetic contribution to the creation of the child. With the diminishing reliance on the genetic link, this parity might be threatened. In this light, the unwillingness of the courts to consider gestation as a factor in parenthood seems striking. Further, the attraction to intention seems potentially suspect. Focusing on intention again equalizes the position of men and women. While the division of the actual labour of caring for children is sharply gendered, the intentions of the parents to be parents may well be equivalent.

Several other implications are worth noting. The diminishing importance of the genetic link could well lead to a loosening of the attachment to the 'only two parents/one of each sex' model. This model has been under pressure from the social developments discussed above. And adherence to it has been based in part on the formulation that each child has two and only two natural parents, one of each sex. But if instead we understand that the child has two progenitors, but that the progenitors are not necessarily parents, this might loosen the hold and allow the law to accommodate itself more closely to the social reality.

Moving away from reliance on the genetic link to define parenthood also raises the possibility of increasing numbers of fatherless (and possibly parentless) children.[25] As long as parenthood is conferred by genetic relationship, all children have parents, though it may be difficult to identify them

---

[25] In the USA there is considerable anxiety about fatherless children already. Generally, fatherless children are those who have no male playing the role of social father and a significant part of the concern arises from the fact that those children often live in poverty and may well end up requiring public support.

and they may not able to perform their roles. But if parenthood depends on function or intention, the prospect of parentless children is manifest.

The definition of parenthood will undoubtedly continue to evolve as new technologies are introduced and the law responds to them. The declining importance of genetic linkage has created a need for redefinition. The increasing emphasis on the diversity of family forms and the privatisation of family may mean that no single factor rises to take the place of the genetic linkage.

REFERENCES

Sterrett, SM (2002) introductory essay. *Law and Society Review* 36, 2: 209–26 (Special Issue on *Non Biological Parenting*).

6

Can Co-Parenting be Enforced? Family Law Reform and Family Life in France

LAURA CARDIA VONÈCHE and BENOIT BASTARD

P ARENTAL AUTHORITY WAS the subject of one of the last acts of Lionel Jospin's socialist government. The reform process started 15 years ago and finally resulted in the law voted through by Parliament in 2002.[1] This reform process is characterised by a 'modern' vision of parents' obligations regarding their children, and centres around 'co-parenting', that is around the idea that every child must be able to benefit from the support of both his or her parents.

In this chapter, we will describe the provisions of this new law and identify the main underlying values, particularly those relating to the question of how the lives of children whose parents have separated should be organised. We will explain how these values developed to the stage where they have not only become law but also social norms. We will also look at the legal perspective and social and family practices alongside each other, in order to explore the possibility that the two views diverge. The chapter will close with more general discussion of the kind of legal provisions that could fit more closely with social aspirations.

CO-PARENTING: ONE VIEW OF THE FAMILY AND A DOGMA

1 The New Law on Parental Authority

The legal text contains measures that reflect the weight that the legislator attaches to a certain kind of family structure, in which parents find themselves linked together with regard to the care they give to their children. We will present the main elements that constitute this model.

The first article of the new law includes the regulations contained in the International Convention for the protection of Children's Rights in French

[1] Loi n° 2002–305 du 4 mars 2002 sur l'autorité parentale.

law: 'A child has the right to be in contact with his forebears' (new article 371–4 of the Civil Code). Regarding the parents' joint role, the new legislation extends and specifies the idea of 'joint exercise of parental authority', which is the normal mode of childcare whether the parents are together or separated. The new text adds that 'the parents' separation has no effect on rules regarding the exercise of parental authority'. This idea of joint parental authority has gained increasing importance since 1987. In this respect, one of the major innovations of this law is to state that the parents have a *duty* to keep in touch with their children. Even though we do not yet know how this new obligation will be enforced, it is possible that this is a sign that the legislator is interested in promoting lasting relationships between each parent and each child.

Equal treatment of the parents seems to be one of the major themes of the text. Indeed, alternating residence is presented as one, and even the preferred, possibility for the children in the event of a divorce. 'The child's home can be fixed alternatively at each parent's home or at the home of one of his/her parents' (article 373–2–9).

In many ways, the law reveals the growing concern that parents and their children should maintain their relationship, particularly if the parents are going through a separation. Another provision explicitly, yet discreetly, takes into account the fact that each parent should respect the role of the other parent. In order to reach a ruling in a parental authority case, the judge refers, amongst other elements, to 'each parent's aptitude to take on his duties and to respect the other parent's rights' (article 373–2–11).

Following the same approach, article 373–2–6 states that the judge 'can come up with any measure that guarantees the continuity and effectiveness of parent–child relations'. It should be mentioned that this text was included in order to limit some of the parents' choices. The second part of this article reaffirms this idea in that an entry in the parents' passport forbidding a child to leave the country can be ordered by a judge. However, this article can be interpreted in a more positive way. Indeed it can be understood as trying to facilitate the maintenance of ties between a parent and a child if they have been separated after a divorce (Bastard and Gréchez, 2002).

In the same spirit, the new law includes provisions on family mediation.[2] The judge can propose mediation to the parties in order to 'facilitate the parents in obtaining an agreement regarding joint parental authority'. The judge can even require them to meet a family mediator who will inform them of the object and effect of the decision (article 373–2–10). This clearly shows the legislator's intention to make negotiation and understanding between the parents the model.

---

[2] Family mediation was possible if decided by the judge since 1996 according to the Code de procédure civile. The innovation now is to include family mediation in the Civil Code.

2 The Growing Importance of Co-Parenting

The law recently voted through by Parliament has evolved over a 15-year period. We will briefly trace the steps in this evolution in order to analyse the different forces that led to the new importance given to co-parenting. The starting point is the reform of 4 June 1970, which replaced the *father's authority* with the term *parental authority*. Parental authority is composed of rights and obligations belonging to the father and the mother to protect the child and ensure his education.

The increase in the number of divorces led to a clearer definition of principles. The modernisation of the rules on divorce began in 1975, at the same time as the modification of the rules on parental authority. The right to obtain a divorce is granted as soon as both parties agree in principle, and there are different legal paths to divorce. This reform is viewed as the beginning of legal and judicial 'plurality'. The provision stating that child custody is to be given to the 'innocent' spouse was suppressed, but this did not automatically lead to giving custody to one of the two parents.

In 1987, as a result of the change in family practices and in the modifications in the relevant case law, joint parental authority was introduced and extended to unmarried parents.[3] In addition, a provision stating that the judge can decide that divorced parents continue to have joint parental authority was introduced. The idea of custody disappeared. In the event of joint parental authority, the judge sets the child's usual residence at the home of either of the two parents.

The 1987 reform aims at reinforcing the chances of continued parenting, notwithstanding the breakdown of the couple relationship by instigating joint exercise of parental authority after the parents' separation:

(Neyrand, 1994: 89)

In 1993, the idea of joint parental responsibility regarding their children's education, which is present in the UN's 1989 International Convention for Children's Rights, was introduced into French law. Indeed, the law, dated 8 January 1993, established the principle of joint parental authority in the legitimate family, even if a divorce occurs. The law does not force the judge to prescribe where the child will live. The judge does so only if the parents disagree on the subject. The terms 'visiting rights' and 'residence rights' are now only used when only one parent has parental rights.

As the more consensual and egalitarian idea of shared care was developing, opposition to the idea of alternating residence also developed in France and the idea was only barely accepted by the time of the 2002 legislation. One of the reasons behind this opposition was Françoise Dolto's (a respected

[3] Loi du 22 juillet 1987.

psychoanalyst who studied children and teenagers) statements together with those of French magistrates regarding alternating residence:

> When he is young, a child cannot handle alternating residence without feeling confused. ... Up to the age of twelve or thirteen, the concept of alternating residence is disastrous for children. It is a good thing that the child is able to go to either parent's home when he wants to, but only if this does not lead to changing schools as a result of alternating residence. The social context has a major impact on a child's development. This is why rotating homes is not good when the child has to attend two schools. ... It is harmful because there is neither emotional unity, nor spatial unity nor social unity.   (Dolto, 1988)

This hostile position regarding alternating residence was set aside only when the reform of family law was relaunched in 1997.

Irène Théry's report for the government (Théry, 1998) also marks an important stage in this development. The report contains an analysis of the evolution of the family and puts forward the distinction between marriage and parenthood. The dilemma that exists today is underlined. The process of promotion of the individual in modern society appears in two ways: gender equality and personalisation of ties with children. Gender equality has an impact on the increased contracting of conjugal ties, whereas personalisation of ties with the children tends to make child–parent relations unconditional. This unconditionality has been transferred from conjugal ties to inter-generational ties. How can these two types of ties be articulated? (Théry, 1998: 38). The Théry report reasserts the relevance of co-parenting:

> Society believes that there is a strong counterpart to increased freedom for the couple: the accompanying obligation for both parents to maintain their responsibility towards their child and to respect and encourage the other parent's responsibility.   (Théry, 1998: 194)

The report also states that it is necessary in law to continue to suppress the elements creating uncertainty that prevent parents from being able to apply it if they wish to do so.

> The idea is not to change morals by law, nor to transform all ex-couples into co-operative parents, however it appears that legal and judicial obstacles prevent parents who wish to exercise their double responsibility from doing so.
>   (Théry, 1998: 196)

The term 'usual residence' of a child is criticised because it keeps the distinction between principal and secondary parent alive. The persistent use of the terms 'visiting rights' and 'residence rights' is also criticised. The various propositions put forward include to

> specify that joint parental authority involves a right to custody for each parent, but not a 'visiting right'. Therefore, when the terms visiting rights and

residence rights are used in a case of joint parental authority, it is simply a misuse of language. These terms, which have now disappeared from the French Civil Code, should now be banished from case law as well. As a result of the content of parental authority, joint parental authority leads to the existence of a custody right. A parent can fail to exercise this right only in exceptional circumstances. Any unauthorized limitation to this duty by the other parent will probably be punished.   (Théry, 1998: 197)

The following report, written by Françoise Dekeuwer-Défossez, takes the systemisation of co-parenting even further. Indeed, through a large number of recommendations, the report proposes to reinforce filiation ties and parental authority. This is done by way of continuous reference to the term 'parental couple'.

Each parent's individual responsibility is not exercised independently from the other parent's responsibility. A child does not originate in individuals but in a couple, that is two people of different gender tied together by a story. ... Even though there is a great increase in the number of recomposed and single-parent families, this evolution does not seem to have to lead to the questioning of a child's founding reference: his parents as a couple.

(Dekeuwer-Défossez, 1999: 18)

The authors of this report believe that this idea of a 'parental couple' should be maintained in all cases when the parents are separated, whether they were married or not. The Dekeuwer-Défossez commission proposes to 'make contracts between the two parents the reference model in order to deal with the consequences of separations regarding the children'. Once again the aim is to separate, as far as possible, the couple issue and the upbringing of the children issue and to encourage agreements between the parents (Dekeuwer-Défossez, 1999: 81).[4]

These propositions were more or less supported by the legal and family specialists. The reform launched by Elisabeth Guigou, Secretary of State for Justice, continued with the help of Ségolène Royal, as soon as she was appointed Secretary of State for the Family, Childhood and the Handicapped.[5] The extensive reform that was considered at the time included a project to modify the legal rules relating to divorce by suppressing the idea of fault. Unfortunately, the reform failed: Madame Guigou left the Ministry of Justice for another Ministry and only part of the provisions were voted through, including the above-mentioned law on parental

---

[4] It should be noted that the terms used in the Dekeuwer-Défossez report contain a contradiction that will be underlined further in our paper. The report states that 'more freedom should be given to the father and mother' and that agreements between the parents should be encouraged and at the same time constantly mentions the need for agreements that are directed towards maintaining the parental couple. As a result, what is proposed is a very limited freedom. This is the position we put forward at the meeting organised by the Ministry of Justice in May 2000 (Ministère de la Justice, 2001: 154ff).

[5] See the above mentioned conference (Ministère de la Justice, 2001).

authority, which constitutes an important step in the affirmation of new family values.

3 A New Absolute Goal?

Following this evolution, co-parenting has become the solution of choice for the legislator and family law specialists. It is enforced and is now the new 'absolute goal'.[6] This choice is easily understandable. In order to be coherent, a policy that seeks to take the evolution of the family into account must accept that the traditional institution is weakened whereas the birth of an 'individualistic and relational' family is confirmed (de Singly, 1998; Commaille and Martin, 1998).

The provisions voted through during the recent reform tend to give spouses the possibility and encouragement needed to put into effect these new views of the family. Co-parenting and the constant desire to reach agreements by parents regarding their children's education should facilitate a true distinction between parenting and marriage along with solutions regarding the upbringing of the children whatever the situation of their parents may be. Amongst the possibilities available to the parents, family mediation appears in the provisions adopted in 2002. The reform affirms the political will to maintain ties between parents whatever their situation may be. The legislator is convinced that parents are 'parents forever' and has made the extension of family ties a requirement in the event of a divorce.

Even though these decisions are coherent and to the point, a number of surprising aspects remain. Is it possible to impose co-parenting as the only legitimate way to care for one's children, when at the same time it is said that more liberty should be available to couples and that they should be more trusted to define the modalities of divorce on their own? In other words, what remains of the 'pluralism' of French law if a unique model for the care of children exists in the law?

If these questions are taken a little further, we might wonder whether the legislator's choice is not in fact a 'conservative' solution: imposing the continued existence of parental ties, of the 'parental couple'. Is it not the wish to maintain the permanence of family ties? Can it not be, as certain people have noted, an underlying, strong, conservative and 'Catholic' model that seeks to make ties between parents never-ending, in contrast to ideas about the right of parents to choose their own solutions and in favour of pluralism in the field of family life? This is Jean Gréchez's theory:

> Referring to a parental couple which would outlive the married couple, this is reminiscent of the catholic conception of the eternal couple, or even the transfer of religion into the current social version.   (Bastard and Gréchez, 2002)

---

[6] Danièle Hervieu Léger, 'Le mariage, les deux seuils de la désacralisationn' in Ministère de la Justice, 2001: 21ff.

It is now necessary to look at the situation in context: how is co-parenting perceived and enacted by parents, and what alternative solutions could be found?

The study of family practices reveals that the legislator's goals have not quite been reached. All kinds of elements, both family practices and professionals' habits, lead to this conclusion.

1 Difficulties with the Concept of Co-Parenting ...

Modern day parents, even though they have accepted that they are subject to the new law of parental authority and have responded positively to the messages encouraging joint care of their children, have trouble understanding the new family values. It is a fact that certain surveys, particularly those which favour modernising the law and changing practices in the field of parent–child ties, refer to well-informed parents capable of ensuring alternating residence for their children. This is the case in the works by Gérard Neyrand (on alternating residence) and those of Didier le Gall and Claude Martin (on recomposed families). Such parents are depicted as innovating and courageous, yet rare. In some studies, a militant view appears reflecting the approval by these researchers of the new family models which makes their observations less objective.

> In our surveys, we have encountered numerous cases for which alternating residence has proved to be a satisfactory solution both for the parents and for the children, probably less upsetting than any other solution which could have led to conflicts and difficulties, probably the best possible alternative in these cases.   (Neyrand, 1994: 287)

However, the available data suggest that many parents who do not live together still have difficulty in sticking to the values attached to co-parenting. This is clear when one realises that in most divorce cases, the child's main residence is with his mother. In 1994, two million children under the age of 18 did not live with both their parents (17 per cent of all minors and 3 per cent more than in 1986). Yet, 85 per cent of those children lived with their mother, 9 per cent with their father (and 6 per cent with neither of their parents). In other words, in practice, with regard to children's residence, the traditional gender inequality still exists (Théry, 1998: 49). These statistics remain unchanged and there seems to be no progress in the attitudes and practice as regards co-parenting.[7]

[7] These statistics on separated families are echoed in recent studies on the distribution of parental tasks, which also remain affected by strong discrepancies and do not seem to change.

One might think that a child's home is simply a factual element that does not reflect the full picture concerning parenting. However, studies on contact between children and their father show very little change in recent years. A demographic survey carried out in 1994 indicates that children tend to see their father after a separation more often than in the past: between 1986 and 1994, the proportion of children who see their father at least every other weekend has increased by one third and reached 40 per cent in 1994 (Villeneuve-Gokalp, 1999). But one child out of three never sees his or her father and this proportion has not changed since 1986. Children tend to see their father more when he remains single and does not have other children, and when the child's mother has met a new partner but does not live with him. Teenagers tend to live with their father, more than is the case for young children, but those who live with their mother tend to see their father less than their younger siblings. These statistics suggest that for a great number of children, the ties with the parent they do not live with tend to disappear, as is generally the case when their parents are not in contact at all.

Whether it is the disappearance of such ties or more generally the continuation of strong conflicts after the divorce or even non-payment of living allowances—one third are never paid and another third are paid irregularly—it appears that a great number of French couples are not inclined to apply the shared parenting that is expected from them.

Another important discrepancy between the values described and those referred to by couples is the fact that mediation has had little success as very few couples have used it. Mediation is linked to co-parenting. Mediation appears to be a technique capable of leading to agreements between parents and in favour of more egalitarian solutions regarding the care of children, which is why it has been encouraged in recent years, and both praised by the State and institutionalised by the legislator.[8] But mediation appears to be an institution with very few 'clients'. There were a few hundred in 1991 according to the only existing survey (Martin, 1994). There are probably more today because the number of mediators has increased,[9] but mediation services do not want statistics to be released on this matter because they could show how difficult it is to convince divorcing couples to abide by the proposed process. What are the reasons for this hesitation regarding mediation? The practice is not well known and is not appreciated by lawyers. Also, couples' attitudes regarding mediation could be the

---

[8] Before mediation was introduced into the Civil Code, a national consultation group on family mediation was set up by decree in October 2001. It was composed of representatives of institutions and mediators and must formulate propositions to the relevant ministries on the questions of mediators' training, deontology and accreditation for mediation services.

[9] There are around 200 mediation associations organised in two federations. The number of divorces per year in France is more than 110,000 and half of the 600,000 civil proceedings started each year are related to the reorganisation of family relations, whether the parents are married or not.

sign of their difficulty in adopting the parental values proposed by the legislative process.

2 Professional Difficulties with the Concept of Co-Parenting

Couples are not the only ones having trouble adopting the values of co-parenting; professionals have the same problem. Without carrying out a systematic study of this phenomenon, it is possible to illustrate that the previous values—custody and childcare functions carried by one parent only—are still present.

Irène Théry and her criticism of the persisting use of the term 'access right' were mentioned above. This criticism is still relevant today: our recent study of children contact centres in France show that almost 10 years after the introduction of the reform which suppressed the reason for the existence of access rights, judges still set out 'access rights' according to the 'usual' methods—for instance every other weekend and half the school holidays (Bastard and Gréchez, 2002). Knowing that judges want the decisions to come from the spouses themselves (Cardia-Vonèche *et al*, 1996), it is likely that this conformism in setting up meetings between parents and children is the result of lawyers and couples' social values. It is quite surprising that judges who are constantly working towards de-dramatising conflicts have not tried to stimulate change. What we see is the survival of strongly rooted custom and the reflection of continued inequalities between men and women.

All other signs in recent times also show the difficulty for professionals and institutional actors in changing childcare management by modifying the way decisions are reached in the event of a divorce. Without detailing the analysis, we can only mention the impossibility of adopting the proposal for new administrative access to divorce, and the failure of the reform whose aim was to get rid of divorce for fault.

The failure of the project for 'divorce without a judge' was due to the lack of support from lawyers who did not want to lose their part of the 'divorce market' (Bastard, 2000). Lawyers constantly put forward the argument that the reason for their opposition to this project was that couples were not ready to organise their own separations and it was necessary to maintain the role of professionals (lawyers and judges) to accompany them through the formalisation of their breakup. The pertinence of this argument is of no importance, but what can be noted is that the argument goes against the idea that couples are competent and should be trusted as having the capacity of parents that is the heart of the logic behind the family law reform.

Fault based divorce is still the path that people use the most (more than 40 per cent). Many of these cases are disputes only in appearance, and many of them include partial agreements, especially on the question of childcare (Belmokhtar, 1999). The proposal to suppress this type of divorce and replace it with divorce for irreparable breakdown of conjugal ties did not satisfy everyone. Amongst the arguments put forward is the idea that there is a fault or a responsibility in the breakdown of the marriage and this continues to be supported by a large number of divorcing couples. Therefore it seems right to maintain this type of divorce procedure, particularly when one of the spouses believes the other one has committed faults that should be stated and repaired.[10]

In any case, the slowness of movement in this field of reform is a sign that professionals and specialists are suspicious of the actual trend towards giving couples control over their separation. It shows the attachment of the actors involved to a conception of the couple and the family that does not fit in with the legislator's new reforms.

CONCLUSION

Does the solution chosen by the legislator carry a risk: that the values referred to by the law are totally different from those of social and family practices? Legislators were confronted with an unprecedented change in family practices, causing them to initiate a new path that appeared a solution to this new situation: co-parenting seems to solve the difficulty relating to the need, at the same time, to maintain ties between children and their parents and enable the parents to find a new partner. The revolution in ideas that has taken place comes down in favour of negotiations between parents and a joint undertaking of the children's education. But this reform has not yet been put into practice.

From the couple and family point of view, it seems that we are not dealing with a 'traditional' scheme in which an 'advanced' minority manages to apply these new rules but a scheme which is opposed by a majority of people who need help to understand the changes. Couples tend to hold a set of values that are difficult to reconcile into a coherent whole. A new regime has developed over the last 25 years for couples and the family in which all the usual ways of acting and the rules are examined and reinvented. Couples are attached to the success of their union and at the same time put forward the idea that they need to be honest with themselves, which means that they can break up if their relationship is unsatisfactory. They regard gender equality as essential and are prepared to enhance the father's position, however they repeat the traditional distribution of tasks according to gender.

Everything seems to lead to the conclusion that most modern day couples are not ready to apply the new solutions that are offered to them. It

---

[10] In practice, obtaining the admission of such faults and their reparation is extremely difficult, almost impossible because judges tend to prefer to treat both parties in the same manner and not to make a decision regarding the principle of the divorce.

seems that keeping in touch with the other spouse, even if it is for the benefit of their children, is a goal that cannot be achieved. They prefer to stay away from the other party, and operate a 'clean-break' rather than maintain contact with each other as proposed by judges and mediators.

Faced with this opposition, as shown for instance through the large number of divorces based on fault and the relatively low success of mediation, we could see nothing but resistance to new solutions, and difficulty in entering a more modern era represented by negotiation on all issues and the 'parents forever' idea that underlies parental authority. However, such an analysis must not be the end of the story, as it stigmatises couples who are unable to get along. Perhaps it would be more helpful to question the accuracy of the model offered as the only way forward to being modern!

Negotiation, which appears to be all that is expected from the parents, may not be possible. Why should these couples be required to discuss, to maintain ties and reach agreements if this seems impossible to them and causes suffering? Is not maintaining contact in every situation attempting to continue a relationship that has ceased to exist? Is such a project truly 'modern'? Some couples can adopt it, but should it be imposed on all couples, without regard to their specific culture or history, in a period where individuals are particularly attached to their independence and willing to produce their own rules?

Before promoting the unique idea of co-parenting, would it not be advisable to consider other possibilities, which include solutions that correspond to the practices of certain couples who do not seem to fit the proposed model? Should there not be solutions in which the 'death of the couple' is accepted along with the end of any form of contact between the parents, without prohibiting the set up and continuation of ties between the different children and with each parent (Cardia-Vonèche and Bastard, 2001)? By taking these different modalities regarding the family into account, it will be possible to respond to the diversity in expectations that exists amongst parents and respect the plurality that characterises the modern family.

REFERENCES

Bastard, B (2000) 'Administrative Divorce in France: a Controversy Over a Reform That Never Reached the Statute Book' in M Maclean (ed), *Making Law for Families* (Oxford, Hart Publishing).

Bastard, B and Gréchez, J (2002) *Des Lieux d'Accueil pour le Maintien des Relations Enfants–Parents. Propositions pour la Reconnaissance des 'Espaces-Rencontre'*: Rapport remis à Ségolène Royal, Ministre Déléguée à la Famille et à l'Enfance (Paris).

Belmokhtar, Z (1999) *Les Divorces en 1996. Une Analyse Statistique des Jugements Prononcés* Etudes et Statistiques Justice 14 (Paris, Ministère de la Justice).

Cardia-Vonèche, L and Bastard, B (2001) 'Voyage au Cœur de la Question Familiale' in B Bastard (ed), *L'Enfant Séparé. Les Voies de l'Attachement* (Paris, Autrement).

Cardia-Vonèche, L, Liziard, S and Bastard, B (1996) 'Juge Dominant ou Juge Démuni? La Redéfinition du Rôle du Juge en Matière de Divorce' *Droit et Société* 33: 277–98.

Commaille, J and Martin, C (1998) *Les Enjeux Politiques de la Famille* (Paris, Bayard).

Dekeuwer-Défossez, F (1999) *Rénover le Droit de la Famille: Propositions pour un Droit Adapté aux Réalités et aux Aspirations de notre Temps* (Paris, La Documentation Française).

Dolto, F (1988) *Quand les Parents se Séparent* (Paris, Seuil).

Martin, C (1994) 'Les Médiations Familiales: Structures, Modèles d'Intervention, Publics et Rapports au Judiciaire. Justice pour Tous ou Justice Communautariste?' Rapport pour le Service de la Recherche du Ministère de la Justice.

Ministère de la Justice (2001) *Quel Droit pour Quelles Familles?* Actes du Coloque de Paris 2000 (Paris, La Documentation Française).

Neyrand, G (1994) *L'Enfant Face à la Séparation des Parents: Une Solution, la Résidence Alternée* (Paris, Syros).

Singly, F de (1998) *Le Soi, le Couple et la Famille* (Paris, Nathan).

Théry, I (1998) *Couple, Filiation et Parenté Aujourd'hui: Le Droit Face aux Mutations de la Famille et de la Vie Privée* (Paris, Odile Jacob—La Documentation Française).

Villeneuve-Gokalp, C (1999) 'La Double Famille des Enfants de Parents Séparés' *Institut National Etudes Demographique, Population 1.*

7

Supporting Conflicted Post-Divorce Parenting

KATRIN MUELLER-JOHNSON

T HE CHAPTERS IN this book focus on the obligations that arise from family relations and the ways in which these are created or regulated by the law. In the case of divorce, one of these obligations is the duty of the residential parent to allow contact between the child and the non-residential parent. The law, rational as it is, presumes that people will modify their behaviour in accordance with this norm, either because they have internalised the norm, or—where it has not been internalised—because of sanctions that await those who do not comply. In the case of denying contact to a non-residential parent without good reason, UK regulations currently threaten the residential parent with, at worst, imprisonment.

But life is more complex. Humans are not always rational decision-makers. It is a classic finding in social psychology that having a particular attitude, which can mean internalisation of a norm, does not necessarily mean that this attitude is expressed through actual behaviour (LaPiere, 1934; Wicker, 1969). Even if one has accepted a moral value and a legal obligation to do something, one does not necessarily behave accordingly. Likewise where one has accepted an obligation it does not mean that one is always in a position to act upon it.

While there are many factors that influence the actual behaviour of an individual, there are factors inherent to certain situations which make a particular behaviour more difficult. For most people, divorce brings with it a host of difficult adaptation processes. In some situations, even where residential parents have accepted this obligation they might not be in a position to act upon it. This is the case for instance when there is so much conflict among the parents, even physical violence, that it is not safe for the parents to meet face to face.

This chapter argues that rather than merely prescribing a certain type of normative behaviour after divorce, such as the obligation to allow contact to the other parent, society needs to support individuals in a way that allows them to comply with the obligations imposed upon them in a safe manner. It then proceeds to describe a variety of short-term programmes and interventions that have this aim and to delineate the need for a long-term perspective of such interventions.

THE IMPACT OF DIVORCE ON CHILDREN

After separation or divorce all members of a family need to find new roles and ways to engage with each other in order to adapt to the changed situation. This adaptation process is difficult, takes time and effort, and is not mastered by everyone. Separation and divorce is especially difficult for children. Divorce brings a number of stressors into a child's life, relational as well as structural. Structural stressors may include a reduction of available material resources, a move to a different neighbourhood, changing schools, which can also mean a loss of friends. More central to divorce are the relational stressors. The child has to cope with a change in the relationship to the non-residential parent, often an attenuation or loss of contact. This might also lead to a decrease in contact with other members of the non-residential parent's side of the extended family, removing potential sources of support. Children may experience an increased need for support to adapt to these life changes, yet it is likely that the residential parents' availability to attend to the children is diminished, because they have to come to terms with the situation themselves. This can lead to a generally troubled relationship with the parents, and this has been discussed as a potential stressor (Emery, 1999). A further stressor might arise when the conflict between parents becomes more openly expressed. Prior to this phase children may have been buffered from parental disputes (*ibid*), therefore seeing the parents arguing openly might be difficult to cope with. The conflict may also become more visibly focused on matters involving the child, eg residency and contact, bringing the child into loyalty conflicts. Such inter-parental conflict about child-related matters could increase around the time of divorce, as the children form one of the few remaining ties between the former partners. Thus they may provide a point at which the conflicts and disappointments with the broken relationship crystallise. For some children the post-divorce conflict can be worse than the conflict they were aware of during marriage. Yet for others, coming from highly conflicted families, including families where domestic violence occurs, separation may bring a lessening of conflict.

A number of factors have been cited to explain differences in coping and adjustment of children. Quality of communication in the family can be an important issue: in a study by Walczak and Burns (1994), children who adapted well to the parents' divorce had received clear explanations about what was happening and maintained good relationships with both parents. Those who showed more difficulties said there was a lack of explanation and of sensitivity to their own feelings. Similarly, troubled relationships with the residential parent, who is usually the main communicator to the child after the other parent has moved out, are associated with increased internalising problems among children (Buchanan *et al*, 1996; Emery, 1999). Another mediating factor that is frequently discussed is inter-parental conflict. A meta-analysis of the literature found that inter-parental conflict was the most powerful single predictor of children's well being after divorce (Amato and Keith, 1991). The effects of divorce are compounded if there is an emotionally intense and prolonged conflict that involves the child directly (Davies and Cummings, 1994; Emery, 1999). It seems from the evidence that the relationship between residential parent and child is more influential than inter-parental conflict, although both are important predictors for child adjustment after divorce.

Financial resources have also been suggested as mediating variables. However, some researchers suggest that it is actually not lower economic status but its adverse effect on the residential carer's parenting capacity which is influential (see Emery, 1999 for a review).

1 Contact

One of the primary approaches to helping a child cope with the separation of the parents is attempting to keep the non-resident parent in the child's life. Contact is generally regarded by policymakers and legislators as a valuable measure to help the child adapt to the new situation and to ensure his or her well being in the new setting. In general, the focus has been on increasing contact between the non-residential parent and the parent, since research had shown that contact is difficult to maintain. As early as the mid 1980s, Eekelaar (1984) showed for a UK sample that in about a third of divorces involving children, contact stopped altogether. Furstenburg and Nord (1985) reported around the same time for a US sample that about half of the children in their study had not seen their non-custodial parent in the last year. However, this strong belief in the importance of post-divorce contact held by legislators and policymakers has not been unequivocally supported by research findings. Research into the outcomes of contact for children has produced ambiguous results. Some studies have found positive effects (Kurtz, 1994; Owusu-Bempah, 1995) mitigating the effects of the parental separation and divorce and helping the children adapt to the new situation, some had ambiguous results (Burghes *et al*, 1997; Emery, 1994; Healey *et al*, 1990; Seltzer, 1991) and others could not obtain any evidence for the benefits of contact (Buchanan *et al*, 1991; Furstenberg *et al*, 1987). Buchanan *et al* (1996) and Johnston *et al* (1989) found that more disturbance was seen in children where there was greater access. Increased contact may lead to increased conflict and disagreement between the parents, and the children might suffer as a result (CASC, 1999).

Important factors that mediate the effect of contact on children included the time since the separation occurred, the quality of the relationship between the parents (Maclean and Eekelaar, 1997) and the quality of the relationship between the non-resident parent and the children both before and after the separation (Block *et al*, 1986; Hess and Camara, 1979).

A recent doctoral thesis (Stover, 2000) investigated the effect of contact between violent fathers and their three- to five-year-olds, in a sample where mothers had been referred to a hospital's department of psychiatry to receive mental health services, and children had witnessed at least one episode of severe marital violence. The study correlated contact frequency (around 25 per cent of the sample did not have any contact in the last six months, 60 per cent had contact at least once a month, including 42 per cent who had regular contact once a week or more) with the child's adjustment and found that boys who had little or no contact with their fathers showed more internalising behaviours, such as depressive symptoms, than those that did have contact. Contact seems to have had a beneficial effect on three- to five-year-olds, but there may be limitations to this finding: the study did not report details about the circumstances of the contact visits, eg whether visits were supervised or free, or whether the contact arrangement was conflict-laden or not. Furthermore, and this may be a more serious limitation, the study did not control for maternal depression. Maternal depression has been shown to be related to internalising behaviour in children (Goodman and Gotlib, 1999; Lipman *et al*, 2002). All mothers in the sample had been referred to hospital for mental health concerns. It is possible that those children who had less contact with their fathers also had mothers with more mental health problems. In this case it could have been not the lack of contact to the father, but the mother's mental health problems which caused or exacerbated that internalising behaviours in the boys.

A further finding in the study was that children who had frequent contact with their father described their mothers as being less warm, caring, supportive and affirming than those who did not see their father (Stover, 2000). Children who had fewer visits had more positive representations of their mothers. Since it is known that the relationship between child and residential parent is an important predictor of the child's adjustment to divorce and separation, contact poses a dilemma where it impacts negatively on this relationship. For children in families where there has been spousal violence there might an especially difficult trade-off between the potential benefits of preserving the bonds with the absent parent and maintaining a positive relationship with the residential parent.

In domestic violence settings there is frequently a risk of continuation of conflict and abuse (Sheeran and Hampton, 1999). Shepard (1992) found that in settings of post-separation contact in families with a background of domestic violence, children evidenced more behavioural problems when the inter-parental violence (physical and psychological) continued.

In summary, it is clear from the reported research that interventions to support parenting after divorce should attempt to improve communication between parents and children and among parents, should enhance parents' ability to recognise and respond to children's needs and concerns in this difficult phase in their lives, and should improve their ability to reduce conflict with their ex-partner or ex-spouse, building an effective co-parenting relationship. The aim should be to improve the relationship with both parents, not to improve the relationship with only one parent (often the non-residential parent) at the expense of placing the relationship with the other parent under additional stress.

PROGRAMMES AND INTERVENTIONS INTENDED TO SUPPORT POST-DIVORCE PARENTING

1 Information

Research shows that:

> most parents are unprepared for the magnitude of the transitions and upheavals, emotional, social and economic, which they experience during separation and divorce.   (Jan Walker, cited in CASC, 2002: 21)

A measure to support parenting after divorce, which is relatively easy to implement, is to provide parents with information on separation and divorce, particularly on how divorce might affect children, and to raise their awareness for the need of effective communication with their child. Being well informed about the effects of divorce and having an idea of what responsible parenting after separation means is a first step towards making parents better equipped to cope with the difficulties and stress that post-divorce parental contact can bring with it. The recent report of CASC (the Children Act Sub-Committee of the Lord Chancellor's Department's Advisory Board on Family Law in the UK) emphasised the importance of more information for parents on divorce, separation and their effects on children and focused on the need for more widespread availability of such materials (CASC, 2002).

Examples of such programmes in the USA are described in Blaisure and Geasler (2000), such as the SMILE (Start Making It Liveable for Everyone) and Children First programmes that are implemented in parts of the USA. In the SMILE programme, group-meeting court personnel stress the importance of minimising the negative effect of divorce on children. This is supplemented by a 50-minute video in which children of different ages talk about their feelings about and experiences of their parents' divorce, and experts provide background information on the needs of children of different age groups when coping with divorce, followed by a group discussion. Children First, another US programme, consists of two sessions, in which parents watch videos of six vignettes of typical divorce related parent–child interactions. Afterwards effective ways of behaving in these situations are discussed in a group setting (Blaisure and Geasler, 2000). In the UK information giving meetings have been evaluated by Jan Walker at the Newcastle Centre for Family Studies, apparently with some success (CASC, 2002).

2 Skill-Based Programmes

While for some families information and thus increased awareness of children's needs and difficulties with divorce might be sufficient to ensure effective parenting, some parents need more than mere information. Here skill-based programmes can be of use, adding training components to the transmission of information. These programmes can have communication modules that show parents how to talk to their children in the new situation. They might also include general effective parenting education, as often the contact parent has not been the primary caregiver while the parents were still living together and has to learn now for the first time how to take care of their children during the visits. A recent evaluation of a programme to increase non-residential fathers' contact frequency by Kissman (2001) showed that half of the sample of non-residential fathers had initial difficulties in communicating with their children or understanding their children's needs. A third important part of the programmes should include conflict management techniques to keep conflict with the other parent as low as possible. Such programmes typically consist of multiple sessions in small groups. After initial information, awareness raising and discussions of potential solutions to difficult parenting situations, parents are encouraged to engage in role-plays on typical co-parenting situations, while attempting to implement the new skills. A third parent observes the role-play and gives feedback.

3 Institutional Approaches

(a) The Family Court System

While the previous interventions aim at improving parents' awareness and parenting ability directly through educational and psychological interventions, another approach aims to reduce external stressors to the parenting situation. Early diversion of families suitable for mediation from the court process may be a good way to support contact for this subset of families, as litigation is very lengthy and tends to exacerbate the conflict between parents (which is not beneficial to contact, as we have seen above). Although this will not be an option for all parents, especially where there has been domestic violence, such mediation institutions need to be expanded and funded, and this has also been suggested by the recent CASC report (2002).

Improvement of the court process might decrease conflict. The CASC report showed that most respondents to their consultation paper on contact were not satisfied with the legal process as it currently is: courts take a very long time to decide cases, often several different judges are involved. Children and Families Court Advice and Support Service (CAFCASS) reports sometimes take an extremely long time (up to 20 weeks) and may be of poor quality. There is also too much pressure on residential parents to agree to contact and the CASC Guidelines on domestic violence are only implemented inconsistently (CASC, 2002), although where they are applied they seem to work well (Department of Health, 2002). All this shows that there is still a lot of room for improvement in the legal process.

In some cases CAFCASS supervises contact in families where there are concerns about unsupervised meetings between non-residential parent and child. This is done either while CAFCASS prepares a court report, where a Family Assistance Order is in place or where conditions according to section 11(7) Children Act 1989 have been ordered. The latest CASC report suggested that the Family Assistance Order could be used more effectively to support contact (CASC, 2002). Currently these orders are restricted to exceptional conditions, a maximal duration of six months, and to cases where both parents agree with this measure. CASC recommended that Family Assistance Orders be available for longer periods and that they should no longer be restricted to exceptional circumstances and to cases where both parents have consented to it, thus making it possible to extend supervision of contact to more families.

(b) Contact Centres

Recognising that much of the conflict and stress of separated parents revolves around contact and the fact that parents have to meet to hand over the child to the other parent, contact centres were created as places where contact visits or handover could take place safely and without the parents having to meet face to face. Increasingly courts and policymakers have been looking at contact centres to provide support for highly conflicted families in their adaptation to post-divorce contact.

In the UK, contact centres tend to be run by charities, churches or independent non-profit organisations. Most contact centres are targeted at conflicted, but low risk, families and only offer supported contact, in which several non-residential parents play with their children in one room and staff are around but do not monitor contact very closely. Such centres usually consist of a large room where families can meet and a separate waiting room for residential parents. Many centres are housed in premises that are part of a different institution, like a church or a kindergarten, and are open only at specific times, for instance every second Saturday. Most contact centres in the UK are staffed by trained volunteers, whose training includes information on the needs of children experiencing the divorce of the parents, issues of child abuse and domestic violence

There are a few highly professional centres with strong safety precautions that offer supervised contact for families with ongoing risks of spousal violence or violence towards the children or abduction, in which parent–child interactions are monitored closely. The problem is that these centres are still rare and families often have to come from afar to attend.

Perhaps as a result of the sparseness of such specialised centres, supported contact centres frequently find themselves in a position of being asked to accept families with a background of family violence. Centres have a practice of screening families before they start for allegations of violence, abuse against the children, domestic violence and risk of abduction. Many supported contact centres work with families with a background of domestic violence and where there is an ongoing concern about reoccurrence of violent incidents. Most centres use staggered arrivals and departures as mechanisms to keep ex-partners from meeting and have separate waiting rooms for contact parents and residential parents. In a recent pilot survey of English and Welsh Centres (Mueller, 2000), 22 out of 25 centres used staggered arrivals and departures and some have separate entrances (32 per cent). A further effective precaution is the existence of constantly monitored, separate car parks for residential and contact parents, although this is only very rarely possible. Slightly more than a quarter of centres in the pilot study monitor the car park (28 per cent), and two fifths escort parents to their car if they fear they are being followed (44 per cent). Centres differ strongly in the safety precautions they have in place, and they should be aware of the standard of safety that they can offer to families, screening families accordingly and not letting themselves be pressured by referrers into accepting families for which they cannot provide a safe setting.

Generally, families using contact centres are satisfied with the experience. In the first large-scale study on child contact centres in the UK, Furniss (2000) reported that parents generally regarded the staff as helpful (88.5 per cent) and neutral (83 per cent); 69 per cent of parents were happy with the toys, games and books that the centres provided, while 24 per cent said this could be improved. 70 per cent of parents said that there is enough space for visits, while 20 per cent said this could be better. A Canadian study by Jenkins *et al* (1997) showed that more than 90 per cent of custodial parents and 70 per cent of non-residential parents reported that they were satisfied with supervised access in general.

Generally centres do not place limits on how long families can stay. Most of the families in the UK and USA move on to have other forms of contact after about 10 visits, although some families, usually those with bigger problems, stay longer. There is only very limited data on the question of what happens to families after leaving. In their study of Canadian contact centres, Jenkins *et al* (1997) described that during the time of the study (about five months) 22 of the 121 participants had discontinued contact at the centre. Of these 22, 10 had unsupervised contact, 3 informally supervised contact, and 9 (45 per cent) had no contact. More follow-up research is needed to elucidate whether this high rate of contact discontinuation is indeed representative.

Investigation is also required into how many of the cases where contact centre attendance ceases are cases where there should not be unsupervised contact or where parents should not meet, for instance in families where there is a background of domestic violence or because there are other concerns, eg about the parenting abilities of the contact-parent, due to substance abuse, mental illness or mental disability. Where safety issues or parenting concerns are not the cause of lack of contact, a factor at least partially responsible for discontinuation may be ongoing parental conflict. Contact centres may attenuate the stress related to contact only while families are at the centre, but do not put them in a position to cope with contact and related difficulties outside. Jenkins *et al* (1997) found that despite high satisfaction ratings with the contact facilitation at contact centres, the attitude towards the other parent did not change, nor was the level of disturbance in family relationships reduced five months after having started at the centre.

(c) Combination of Contact Centres with Skills Training

In response to such concerns there have been attempts to combine the contact centre approach with educational and psychological interventions for parents, thus enabling them to cope more effectively with the difficulties posed by dealing with the other parent in the context of contact. Many contact facilitation programmes in the USA follow this model, such as the approach described by Braver and Griffin (2000). This model targets divorced parents' motivation for contact and their attitude towards it and provides training on conflict managing skills for the interactions with their ex-spouses. In two individual and eight group sessions fathers are trained in parenting skills, such as active listening or proactive discipline, and conflict reduction. In addition to their scheduled contact sessions, fathers were also encouraged to maintain consistent telephone contact with the child. It will be very interesting to see the results of the evaluation of this programme. Flory and colleagues showed that, in an American approach including low level counselling, the degree of conflict did change (Flory *et al*, 2001). The German model also places a strong emphasis on counselling: it is believed that contact should not be facilitated without accompanying educational and counselling talks with the parents (Haid-Loh *et al*, 2000). In the UK, too, contact facilitators have recognised this issue. The CASC report suggests that more counselling and parenting education should be available at contact centres (CASC, 2002).

Training in parenting skills, communication and conflict management will not be necessary for every family. Families should be allowed to make their own decisions as to how much support they would like to accept, rather than being mandated to participate by courts. But more such programmes need to be available and to be more visible to the public. In addition, attempts should be made to lower the psychological threshold for participation to make it easier for parents to attend.

4 The Long-Term Perspective

The educational and psychological interventions, as well as the contact centre approach are conceptualised as short-term interventions. It is envisaged that after successful completion of these programmes or attendance at the contact centres, families should be enabled to engage in meaningful contact and effective parenting in the future. Legislators and policymakers tend to see contact centres as short-term support, while practitioners regard them as being available for as long as the families need them (Bailey, 1999). At most centres there is no time limit. In many cases, however, there are certain factors that impose at least an indirect time limit on contact centre use, eg the artificiality of the setting and the inconvenience of times and location, which may create dissatisfaction in the child or the contact parent. These factors can create a situation in which the resident parent finds it difficult to maintain their position of restricting contact to visits at the centre and feels pressured to agree to unsupervised outside contact.

(a) Artificiality of the Contact Centre Setting

Non-residential parents often feel under strong pressure when first at a contact centre and they may resent being monitored. As much as contact centre staff and volunteers try to make the situation 'natural', it remains an unnatural situation: fathers' actions are indeed monitored to a certain extent, depending on the level of supervision provided by the centre (supported contact or supervised contact). In supported settings several families are in attendance at the same time, quite often all using the same room, so that it is quite noisy and there is no privacy with the child. In addition, there is a lot of pressure to make contact 'a success' and to spend the two or three hours of the visits' duration as 'quality time' with the child. Even for a skilled parent it is quite difficult to keep the child entertained in a single room for such a period. In family life outside contact centres young children rarely spent such a long time continually engaged with a parent. They might play together for a while, after which the child might go off and play by him or herself for some time or the parent might have to take care of some household chore in between. In family life outside contact centres it is much more common to have parallel activity in the same room than actual engagement between parent and child. Thus, in most centres, contact sessions require a higher level of creativity from a parent to make 'quality time' than what we would expect in unsupported families. Even a parent who has a good relationship with his/her child already and who is good at keeping the child entertained might find the contact centre setting a difficult situation. Many of the contact parents that use the centre lack even this: their relationship with the child might not have been very close in the past, they might have undergone a long period of no contact before coming to the centre, or their parenting skills might not be so good.

A British study of contact with fathers has shown that unsupervised contact visits between children and non-resident parents tended to involve watching television or videos together, followed by playing, shopping and outings (Bradshaw *et al*, 1999). A US study showed that both non-resident mothers and non-resident fathers (41 per cent) tended to spend their time on fun leisure activities, such as going for a picnic, doing sports, going to the cinema or visiting family and friends (Stewart, 1999). None of the respondents in her study reported engaging only in school related or organised activities, although 29 per cent reported a mixed pattern of leisure activities and school or organised activities (the other 30 per cent of the sample did not have contact within the last year). None of the sample engaged primarily in talking, working on a project or playing together (Stewart, 1999), which are basically the activities available at contact centres. Thus contact visits in contact centres are more complicated for contact parents and very different from contact outside.

In Jenkins *et al*'s study (1997) the majority of non-residential parents did not like being restricted to the site for their visits: only 44 per cent rated being restricted to the site as satisfactory. In contrast, 91 per cent of resident parents reported that this was satisfactory. Children up to six years old in this study did not have an understanding of why they were at the centre, and only 46 per cent of the children aged seven years and older knew why they came. Some did not like being watched, felt uncomfortable and tried to figure out why they were being watched. Children were on the whole positive about the staff and found them helpful, but more than two thirds (68 per cent) of children expressed at least mild dissatisfaction concerning the toys or the activities at the centre. Children of seven and older were especially dissatisfied, reporting that the toys were designed for younger children and therefore boring to them, and that they felt restricted in what activities they were allowed to engage in, such as having to stay in the room or not being allowed to play with water, etc (Jenkins *et al*, 1997). Given the availability of sufficient funds, contact centres need to be made more attractive for older children, which is a difficult task, as it is usually necessary to restrict the activities to indoors, and mostly to one room. If funds were plentiful, centres specifically targeted at older children might be an option. But as most centres already struggle for adequate funding to cover existing services, most older children will have to make do with what toys are available.

The research cited above suggests that it is more natural to spend two or three hours in a row in the context of an outing, such as going to the playground, or going swimming, than to spend two hours engaged in activities indoors. Some contact centres make accommodation for this and offer individual sessions that make it possible to leave the centre with a supervisor/facilitator. In Germany, for instance, most contact facilitation is provided in the individual setting so that outings are possible and the child is actively involved in planning how such contact sessions should take place and what activities should be done. In this setting some types of supervised contact can even take place outside the centre (obviously where there is risk of abduction, this might not be the case). This model not only makes visits more interesting to the child but also puts the visiting parent under less pressure to come up with enough excitement to fill the duration of the visit. Centres that offer supported contact in the UK setting also appreciate that contact sessions in the centre can become boring after some time. If both parents agree (usually where successful supported contact inside the centre has taken place for some time already) the non-residential parent can take the child outside, to play in the park or to go shopping etc. Usually this is the last step before families move on to free contact outside the centre, or to the stage where they use the centre as a point for handover only. Once a family has moved on to use a contact centre as a handover point, children and parents can engage in whatever activity they fancy during contact visits but parents do not have to meet face to face. Thus child and parent can have quality time, while at the same time minimising conflict between parents. Most centres in the UK and USA offer handover facilities and this seems to be a simple and valuable source of support. Typically they are used by families who had previously taken advantage of the centre's contact facilitation services. Handover services at contact centres should be more strongly advertised to make more parents outside contact centres aware of them. This could spare many unpleasant arguments when exchanging children at, say, a fast-food restaurant or a shopping centre.

(b) The Need for Long-Term Intervention for Some Families

There are other families where this idea of a brief targeted intervention, such as 10 visits to the contact centre, might not solve the problem they face in the context of contact. In families where there are allegations or substantiated findings of child abuse, of domestic violence or a real fear of abduction of the child (long-term high risk families), the risk these issues pose will be unlikely to have abated after 10 visits to the contact centre. Similarly where there is substance abuse or mental illness there is not much prospect of change in the immediate future. If a mental disability affects a contact parent's ability to care for the child, this issue will be a concern for the family until the child is old enough to look after him/herself (long-term/lower risk). In these cases support of contact as a short-term intervention does not suffice. Long-term/lower risk cases can be accommodated by simply allowing families to stay at a contact centre for longer (this is often already practised). However, in the hypothetical case of a child aged three starting contact sessions at a centre, at least 10 more years of contact support would be needed. It is doubtful that contact centres will be able to sustain support for so long.

For long-term/high risk families, finding a long-term solution is more difficult. Here highly professional supervised contact is needed—which can be provided by only a few centres in the UK. The sparseness of centres will make it necessary for families to move on at some point in order to make room for other families who also need this service. Finding a willing third person supervisor who is accepted by both parties and who can provide a safe setting for the child is a huge challenge, if not often impossible. Many women who suffered domestic violence have experienced this and found themselves in positions where they have had to endure new incidents of violence from their ex-partner in the context of arranging contact visits. It is a robust finding that victims of domestic violence continue to be victimised after separation, and that this often occurs in the context of contact visits (Hester and Radford, 1996). In these cases contact frequently stops after another such violent incident and the parents go back to court. The question is how beneficial such highly dangerous and interrupted contact can be for children. What would be a good solution to this problem? If society has no answer to this, and if future research were to show that such high-risk families do not find a way to continue contact in a manner that is safe for all parties involved, is it ethical to re-institute contact for these families in contact centres when contact cannot safely be maintained outside and is thus bound to stop?

If no safe long-term solution is found, contact centres might have unintended detrimental effects for these long-term high risk families. The mere existence of contact centres makes it more difficult for residential parents with safety concerns for contact outside these centres to obtain a no-contact order. After the non-residential parents have successfully shown that they have been able to provide experiences that the children enjoyed at the centre, judges might be reluctant to order contact to stop only because a safe setting outside a centre cannot be found. They might just order contact to remain in place at a centre without considering available resources at supervised contact centres, the limit on available age-appropriate activities for older children or considering the long-term perspective, ie whether this contact supervision will be viable for an extended number of years. More resources are needed to create safe long-term solutions for high risk families. This needs to go hand in hand with research investigating whether long-term visits at a contact facility are in fact beneficial for the child.

CONCLUSION

This chapter began by suggesting that merely prescribing the continuing involvement with both parents after a separation either as a moral or legal obligation will require support for individuals to comply in a manner which secures the safety of those involved. It has provided an overview of different short-term intervention strategies designed to support post-divorce parental contact. These include information-giving meetings, combination training programmes that provide information and practice skills, and structural support, such as contact facilitation, by trained third parties. It has argued that it is necessary to develop a long-term solution for both long-term/lower risk and long-term/high risk families, if it is continued to be assumed that contact is beneficial for these families, even if they might never be able to have contact without third party facilitation until the child is old enough to look after him/herself. This long-term solution needs to go hand in hand with making contact centres more attractive to older children, so that it is possible to provide long-term supervision without the children getting bored with the activities that the centre offers. If centres are not attractive enough, it is possible that the children themselves will put the residential parent under so much pressure that they agree to leave the centre and enter into unsupervised contact, even when such contact is not safe.

REFERENCES

Amato, PR and Keith, B (1991) 'Parental Divorce and the Well-Being of Children: A Meta-Analysis' *Psychological Bulletin* 110: 26–47.

Bailey, M (1999) 'Supervised Access: A Long-Term Solution?' *Family and Conciliation Courts Review* 37: 478–486.

Blaisure, KR and Geasler, MJ (2000) 'The Divorce Education Intervention Model' *Family and Conciliation Courts Review* 38: 501–513.

Block, JH, Block, J and Gjerde, PF (1986) 'The Personality of Children Prior to Divorce: A Prospective Study' *Child Development* 57: 827–840.

Bradshaw, J, Stimson, C, Skinner, C and Williams, J (1999) *Absent Fathers?* (London and New York, Routledge).

Braver, SL and Griffin, WA (2000) 'Engaging Fathers in the Post-Divorce Family' in Elizabeth Peters *et al* (eds), *Fatherhood: Research, Interventions and Policies* (New York, London, Oxford, The Haworth Press, Inc).

Buchanan, CM, Maccoby, EE and Dornbush, SN (1991) 'Caught Between Parents: Adolescents' Experience in Divorced Homes' *Child Development* 62: 1008–29.

—— (1996) *Adolescents After Divorce* (Cambridge, Mass, Harvard University Press).

Burghes, L, Clarke, L and Cronin, N (1997) *Fathers and Fatherhood in Britain* (London, Family Policy Studies Centre).

CASC (1999) *A Consultation Paper on Contact Between Children and Violent Parents: the Question of Parental Contact in Cases where there is Domestic Violence* (London, Lord Chancellor's Advisory Board on Family Law).

CASC (2002) *Making Contact Work: A Report to the Lord Chancellor on the Facilitation of Arrangements for Contact between Children and their Non-Residential Parents and the Enforcement of Court Orders for Contact* (London, The Advisory Board on Family Law: Children Act Sub-Committee).

Davies, PT and Cummings, EM (1994) 'Marital Conflict and Child Adjustment: An Emotional Security Hypothesis' *Psychological Bulletin* 116: 387–411.

Department of Health (2002) *Children Act Report 2001* (London, Department of Health).

Eekelaar, J (1984) *Family Law and Social Policy* (London, Weidenfeld and Nicolson).

Emery, RE (1994) 'Psychological Research on Children, Parents and Divorce' in R Emery (ed), *Renegotiating Family Relationships: Divorce, Child Custody, and Mediation* (New York, Guildford Press).

—— (1999) 'Postdivorce Family Life for Children—An Overview of Research and Some Implications for Policy' in RA Thompson and PR Amato (eds), *The Postdivorce Family* (Thousand Oaks, Sage).

Flory, B, Dunn, J, Berg-Weger, M and Milstead, M (2001) 'An Exploratory Study of Supervised Access and Custody Exchange Services—the Parental Experience' *Family Court Review* 39: 469–482.

Furniss, C (2000) Research Findings in NAOCC Centres (ed), *Conference Report 2000. Child Contact Centres in the New Millennium: What are the Issues Arising from Research Done in the 1990s?* (Nottingham, National Association of Child Contact Centres).

Furstenberg, FF, Morgan, SP and Allison, PD (1987) 'Paternal Participation and Children's Well-Being after Marital Dissolution' *American Sociological Review* 52: 695–701.

Furstenburg, FF and Nord, CW (1985) 'Parenting Apart: Patterns of Child-Rearing after Divorce' *Journal of Marriage and the Family* 47: 893–904.

Goodman, SH and Gotlib, IH (1999) 'Risk for Psychopathology in the Children of Depressed Mothers: A Developmental Model for Understanding Mechanism of Transmission' *Psychological Review* 106: 458–490.

Haid-Loh, A, Normann-Kossakk, K and Walter, E (2000) *Begleiteter Umgang—Konzpete, Probleme und Chancen der Umsetzung des reformierten Par. 18 SGB VIII* (Berlin, EZI-Eigenverlag).

Healey, JM, Malley, JE and Stewart, AJ (1990) 'Children and their Fathers after Parental Separation' *American Journal of Orthopsychiatry* 60: 531–543.

Hess, RD and Camara, KA (1979) 'Post-Divorce Family Relationships as Mediating Factors in the Consequences of Divorce for Children' *Journal of Social Issues* 35: 79–96.

Hester, M and Radford, L (1996) *Domestic Violence and Child Contact Arrangements in England and Denmark* (Bristol, Policy Press).

Jenkins, JM, Park, NW and Peterson-Badali, M (1997) 'An Evaluation of Supervised Access II—Perspectives of Parents and Children' *Family and Conciliation Courts Review* 35: 51–65.

Johnston, JR, Kline, M and Tsann, JM (1989) 'Ongoing Postdivorce Conflict: Effects on Children of Joint Custody and Frequent Access' *American Journal of Orthopsychiatry* 59: 576–592.

Kissman, K (2001) 'Interventions to Strengthen Noncustodial Father Involvement in the Lives of their Children' *Journal of Divorce and Remarriage* 35: 135–146.

Kurtz, L (1994) 'Psychological Coping Resources in Elementary School-Age Children of Divorce' *American Journal of Orthopsychiatry* 64: 554–563.

LaPiere, RT (1934) 'Attitudes vs Actions' *Social Forces* 13: 230–7.

Lipman, EL, Boyle, MH, Dooley, MD and Offord, DR (2002) 'Child Well-Being in Single-Mother Families' *Journal of the American Academy of Child and Adolescent Psychiatry* 41: 75–82.

Maclean, M and Eekelaar, J (1997) *The Parental Obligation: A Study Across Households* (Oxford, Hart Publishing).

Mueller, KU (2000) *The Management of Conflicted Post-Divorce Parenting: An Investigation into the Contribution of Child Contact Centres to the Facilitation of Contact with the Non-Residential Parent with Special Reference to Families having a Background of Domestic Violence* (Masters Thesis, Oxford University).

Owusu-Bempah, J (1995) 'Information About the Absent Parent as a Factor in the Well-Being of Children in Single Families' *International Social Work* 38: 253–275.

Seltzer, JA (1991) 'Relationships Between Fathers and Children who Live Apart: The Father's Role after Separation' *Journal of Marriage and the Family* 53: 79–101.

Sheeran, M and Hampton, S (1999) 'Supervised Visitation in Cases of Domestic Violence' *Juvenile and Family Court Journal* 50: 13–25.

Shepard, M (1992) 'Child-Visiting and Domestic Abuse' *Child Welfare* 71: 357–367.

Stewart, S (1999) 'Disneyland Dads, Disneyland Moms?' *Journal of Family Issues* 20: 539–356.

Stover, CS (2000) *The Effects of Father Visitation on Preschool Aged Witnesses of Domestic Violence* (PhD thesis, Alliant University, San Francisco Bay).

Walczak, Y and Burns, S (1994) *Divorce: The Child's Point of View* (London, Harper and Row).

Wicker, AW (1969) 'Attitudes Versus Actions: The Relationship of Verbal and Overt Behavioral Responses to Attitude Objects' *Journal of Social Issues* 25: 41–78.

8

Litigation in the Shadow of Mediation: Supporting Children in Sweden

JOHANNA SCHIRATZKI

INTRODUCTION

ONE OF THE key values in Swedish society is individualism (Hallberg and Lernstedt, 2002). Individualism is generally understood to mean that the needs and wishes of an individual are prioritised in relation to the best interests of the group to which the person belongs. The extreme view of individualism advocates that each person should be granted an existence independent of his or her context.[1] In a more moderate version the best interests of the group are understood to be promoted by the well being of its members. In the alternative group-oriented way of reasoning, the wel-fare of an individual is considered to be best endorsed by that individual acting as a member of a well-functioning group, whose interests are placed before the interests of its individual members.

A well-functioning public sector is seen as a prerequisite for a society characterised by individualism. The public sector must have the means, and the will, to satisfy at least some of the financial needs of dependent individuals, ie children and the elderly. If the public sector cannot provide basic protection, the individual is bound to build up formal and informal networks to secure his or her needs of survival. An example of such a network is the family in its various forms.

Financial and other protection for vulnerable individuals is conditional on the obligation of 'someone' to make the necessary financial sacrifices. States in which the public sector takes upon itself the administration of such transfers, by expropriating excess income through the taxation system in order to redistribute it, are generally thought of as 'modern', whereas societies in which transfers between individuals depend on personal relationships, typically by next-of-kin,[2] are seen as 'traditional'. Another characteristic of a democratic society based on individualism is the view that its members should

[1] See Eekelaar (ch 1, this volume) on the growth of self-seeking behaviour.
[2] See Smart (ch 9, this volume) on supportive relatives.

have access to justice, and that the rule of law should prevail in conflict-solving as well as in administration. In a simplified way this implies that conflicts between individuals should be solved by court proceedings, typically in a private law procedure. An individual should also have the right to seek justice in the sphere of administration, primarily by means of public law procedures.

There are several examples in *private* Swedish law of laws which have been profoundly inspired by individualism. Two of these include the no-fault or administrative divorce and the virtual absence of maintenance to divorcees.[3] In Sweden matrimony has ceased to imply a long-lasting personal responsibility. The divorce rate is high and Swedish society is characterised by serial personal and parenting relationships. Compared with private law, *public law* provides a more ambiguous mix of individualism and personal responsibility. Although individuals' integrity and right to self-determination should be respected according, for example, to the Social Security Act, there are situations in which the individual's right to, for example, social security benefit may depend on whether or not he or she is part of a family. In families living on social security any earnings children might have, for example from summer jobs, are deducted from the social security benefit of the family. And even though parents have no obligation to maintain their children beyond the age of 18 (21 if the 'child' is still in school) welfare is not granted to young adults in order to enable them to set up an independent home.[4]

In the following sections financial obligations arising from parenthood are discussed. The focus is on the interaction between public and private responsibility regarding maintenance for children. It is argued that there is a legal gap between public responsibility and private obligations, and that this can be explained partly by what could be described as 'litigation in the shadow of mediation', ie the aim of the legal system being to facilitate mediation and not to provide tools for litigation. It is further suggested that the scope of individualism depends on a person's financial situation.

The scope of the article is limited to the support of children living with one parent, including children alternating their residence between their parents' households. Approximately 500,000 or 25 per cent of all children living in Sweden have parents who do not live together. Of these roughly six per cent are estimated to have alternating residence.[5]

GENERAL AIM OF SWEDISH FAMILY POLICY

In Sweden families with children benefit to a significant extent from public transfers. On average 20 per cent of the families' incomes come from the

---

[3] Maintenance orders to former spouses can be made under the law. However, apart from orders for shorter transitional periods, maintenance orders may only be made according to the Supreme Court after long marriages if the causality between the divorcee's need of maintenance and the marriage has been proven (NJA 1998: 238).

[4] Cf the Administrative Supreme Court in RÅ 1997 ref 79 and RÅ 1997 n 243.

[5] The figure refers to 1998; it seems reasonable to assume that this number has increased slightly (*Socialstyrelsen, Växelvis boende*, 2002).

public purse. The most important of these are the parental benefit (Sw *föräldrapenning*) for the newborn for 450 days;[6] the general child benefit (Sw *barnbidrag*), approximately €100 a month; and temporary parental benefit and housing allowance, the amount of which is assessed on the basis of income and the number of children in the household. For single-parent households the public maintenance support system, discussed in this chapter, is frequently an important source of income.

The general aim of the Swedish economic policy for families is to reduce differences between the financial situation of families with children compared to persons without children. Another goal is that financial resources should be evenly distributed throughout the individual's lifetime. Family policy should also promote equality between men and women by making it possible for all parents to combine parenthood and wage earning or studies. In order to promote equality and to encourage mothers to be active in the labour market, paternal involvement in the children's life is encouraged. Financial inducements to encourage fathers actively to participate in their children's life include the 30 days of parental benefit for newborn children which must be drawn by the father if the parents have joint custody. New fathers are further entitled to 10 days' leave on temporary parental benefit at the child's birth or adoption. In separated families deductions in maintenance are made when the child spends time with the non-residential parent.[7] Non-financial inducements include, for example, joint custody, which is seen as a way of promoting parental involvement.

Family economic policy should also promote good living conditions for children in accordance with the United Nations Convention on the Rights of the Child.[8] The fulfilment of this ambition may be questioned since 14 per cent of all children in Sweden, despite the system of public transfer mentioned above, have a standard of living below the social welfare norm. For children living with a single mother this number is 30 per cent.[9]

MAINTENANCE OF CHILDREN: THE LAW

1 Two Systems

Two statutes are applicable to parental maintenance of children not living permanently with both their parents. These are chapter seven of the Parents

---

[6] The parental benefit amounts to 80 per cent of a yearly income of not more than SEK 284,200 for 365 days and 60 SEK a day during the remaining periods. €1 is approximately 9.20 SEK.

[7] If the non-residential parent has the child for six whole days during a month, or for an uninterrupted period of five days, he or she may, according to both the Parents Code and the Maintenance Support Act, deduct one fortieth of the monthly maintenance payment for each 24-hour period of the child's stay: Parents Code ch 7, s 4; Maintenance Support Act s 23(2).

[8] SOU 2001: 24 *Ur fattigdomsfällan, slutbetänkande av familjeutredningen* p 111.

[9] SCB (1999) *Barn och deras familjer.*

Code,[10] in which the private law provisions on parents' maintenance are set out, and the Maintenance Support Act,[11] which regulates the state's responsibility under public law. Chapter seven of the Parents Code lays down the general private law principles of the parental obligation to maintain children. Maintenance under the Parents Code is determined by court in a private law procedure or by agreement.[12] Under certain conditions the state will advance or supplement maintenance support for children living with a single parent. The idea behind this solution is to promote equality between children regardless of whether they live permanently with both their parents or not. Less overtly, the supplement may facilitate parental separation, since it takes part of the burden for the maintenance of the children off the parents' shoulders.

The two statues differ greatly from each other. Different principles apply to fundamental issues, such as the right to maintenance, the duration of maintenance, the amount of maintenance and the principles for calculating it.

Notwithstanding the fact that chapter seven of the Parents Code lays down the general principles for parental maintenance and has a broader scope, it is the system provided for in the Maintenance Support Act which is used most frequently.[13] This is explained by two factors. Firstly, it is advantageous to parents with lower incomes. Secondly, many parents find it practical and conflict-reducing as maintenance support is administered by the public social insurance office (Sw *försäkringskassan*) which pays out maintenance support to entitled children and reclaims it, or part of it, from the liable parent. To obtain maintenance support for a child the residential parent is not obliged to negotiate or litigate with the other parent. However, the application of the Maintenance Support Act may result in the child receiving less maintenance than if chapter seven of the Parents Code had been applied.

2 Right to Maintenance Payments and Maintenance Support

According to the general rule of the Parents Code, parents are responsible for the maintenance of their children until the child has reached majority at the age of 18.[14] The parents shall share in meeting the cost of maintaining the child, each according to his or her ability. Provided that paternity has been established, the duty to maintain a child applies irrespective of legal custody. If the child does not live with both its parents, the parent not living permanently with the child shall discharge his or her duty to maintain the child by making maintenance payments to the child.[15] A step-parent is

---

[10] Sw *Föräldrabalken*. SFS 1949: 381.
[11] Sw *Underhållsstödslagen*. SFS 1996: 1036.
[12] Parents Code ch 7, s 2.
[13] In 2001 over 69 per cent of c 500,000 children living with a single parent, ie 330,000 children, received maintenance support.
[14] Parents Code ch 7, s 1.
[15] *Ibid* s 2.

responsible for maintenance, provided that he or she is married to the residential parent or has a child with the residential parent. The step-parent's duty to maintain does not apply to the extent that the child receives maintenance from the parent the child is not living with.[16]

Under the Maintenance Support Act a child is entitled to maintenance support if his or her parents are not living together. It is required that the child be permanently living and registered with one of the parents and that the residential parent is its custodian.[17] A child does not have a right to receive maintenance support in the following cases:

1 the child's mother is a residential parent and omits, manifestly without valid reason, to take or to assist with measures to establish the child's paternity;
2 there is reason to suppose that, if there is a parent with an obligation to pay maintenance, that parent will duly pay maintenance at a rate not less than the maintenance support;
3 it is manifest that the maintenance debtor is otherwise ensuring that the child receives the corresponding maintenance;
4 the residential parent omits without valid cause to assist with the measures required to obtain maintenance from a parent abroad;
5 one of the parents is dead and the child is entitled to a child pension.[18]

A child has the right to maintenance from birth. An agreement on maintenance payments may be entered into before the child is born. The parents' duty to maintain their children ceases when the child attains the age of 18 years.[19] However, exceptions are made under the Parents Code as well as under the Maintenance Support Act. The Parents Code states that if the child is still attending school at the age of 18 the parents remain responsible for maintenance for as long as the schooling continues.[20] This applies if the schooling in question refers to studies at primary, lower secondary or upper secondary level or other comparable basic education. It does not apply to higher education. A young person's right to maintenance under the Parents Code ceases finally, regardless of schooling, at the age of 21. According to the Maintenance Support Act a young person is entitled to

---

[16] *Ibid* s 5.
[17] Maintenance Support Act, s 3. The child is further entitled to maintenance support in the rare cases when one or two special custodians have been appointed, and the child is living permanently with them.
[18] Maintenance Support Act, s 4. To have the right to maintenance support it is normally required that the child and the residential parent reside in Sweden. If the child is not a Swedish citizen, the right to maintenance support is subject to the residential parent or the child being of at least six months' residential standing in Sweden. A child who temporarily leaves Sweden is considered, for the sake of maintenance support, to be domiciled in Sweden if the stay abroad is intended to last no longer than six months.
[19] Parents Code ch 7, s 1(2); Maintenance Support Act, s 6.
[20] Parents Code ch 7, s 1(2).

extended maintenance support if he or she is attending or resumes school before the age of 19. However, the duration of maintenance support according to the Maintenance Support Act is shorter than the duration of maintenance according to the Parents Code. The entitlement to extended maintenance support ceases in the month of June in the year of the child's 20th birthday.

3 The Amount of Maintenance Payments and Maintenance Support

The major difference between the private and public system of child maintenance for children lies in determining the amount of maintenance, and in the fact that the state supplements maintenance or part of it if the non-residential parent has a low income. When determining the amount of maintenance according to the Parents Code, regard shall be paid to the needs of the child and the combined financial capacity of the parents. Neither the needs of the child, nor the parents' financial capacity, is considered on an individual basis when the amount of maintenance support is determined under the Maintenance Support Act.[21]

The first step when assessing the amount of maintenance according to the Parents Code is to determine the child's needs. The needs of the child are normally assessed according to certain established standards, based on the child's age and the base amount provided for in the National Insurance Act.[22] Thus, the standard amount for a child up to the age of 6 years amounts to SEK 2053, between the ages of 7 and 12 to SEK 2527 and from 13 years of age it is SEK 3000. Costs for childcare are added to the standard amount and the amount of child benefit and certain types of income of the child are deducted. The needs of the child may be determined according to another amount on a discretionary basis and a different amount than the standard may be set in exceptional cases. The next step is to calculate the excess of each parent. The calculation is based on the parents' income, including wages, unemployment benefit, pension and taxable returns. As a rule the assessment should be made on the presumption that the liable parent works full time. When maintenance payments are determined according to the Parents Code, the maintenance debtor may retain a sum for his or her own maintenance and, if there are special reasons, for the maintenance of a spouse or, provided that they have a common child, an unmarried cohabitee.[23] The cost of housing shall be calculated separately. Other living costs are calculated on the basis of a standard amount.[24] A person liable for the

---

[21] The child's own income and assets shall also be taken into account: Parents Code: ch 7, s 1(1). cf NJA 1996: 134; Maintenance Support Act s 10.

[22] SFS 1962: 381: all figures are given for year 2002, on a monthly basis.

[23] Parents Code ch 7, s 3.

[24] The standard amount is 120 per cent of the base amount provided for in the National Insurance Act (SEK 3790 during 2002). The standard amount that may be retained for a spouse or unmarried cohabitee is 60 per cent of the base amount (SEK 1895).

maintenance of several children may retain a sum to cover the maintenance costs of children living with him or her.[25] Once the needs of the child and the financial capacity of the parents have been determined, the amount of the maintenance payment is calculated as the child's needs multiplied by the liable parent's excess and divided by the parents' combined excess.

In contrast to maintenance payments under private law maintenance, support under the provision of the Maintenance Support Act is not index linked. The monthly amount of maintenance support is SEK 1173. No specific needs of the child are taken into account when maintenance support is determined. If, however, the child has an income of its own, the amount of maintenance support may be reduced.[26] In contrast to maintenance payments under the private law system, maintenance support is paid regardless of the financial situation of the residential parent. The non-residential parent is obliged to reimburse part of or the entire amount of the maintenance support. The repayment is determined as a percentage of the taxable income of the parent obliged to pay, after a deduction of SEK 72,000 per year. The percentage is dependent on the number of children that the parent has to maintain, including biological children living permanently with the parent, but excluding stepchildren. A person liable for the maintenance of one child pays 14 per cent; for two children, 11½ per cent (for each child); and for three children, 10 per cent (for each child). The amount of reimbursement may not be higher than the amount of maintenance support received by the child, and it is assessed anew each year. If the income of the parent liable for payment is not sufficient to cover the full amount of maintenance support, the remaining amount will be paid to the child as financial support for which no reimbursement is demanded.

4 Alternating Residence

Alternating residence as a custodial arrangement is approved by Swedish law and by a significant part of society.[27] If the child shares its time between the parents, living alternately with each of them, the child is—for the sake of maintenance—considered to live permanently with both.

Under the Parents Code if the child has alternating residence, neither parent is under a duty to contribute to the maintenance of the child when the child is staying with the other parent. Instead the parents are to share the actual costs of bringing up the child. Though rarely, if ever, applied, the law opens up the possibility of maintenance litigation in case of alternating

---

[25] Normally, this sum, considered together with what is paid for the benefit of these children by the non-residential parent amounts to 40 per cent of the current base amount (SEK 1263).

[26] Maintenance Support Act s 10.

[27] Alternating residence may be ordered by court against the wishes of a parent. A child is presumed to have shared living if it spends approximately 50 per cent of its time with each parent. In the practices of the Courts of Appeal, a child spending 42 per cent of its time with the non-residential parent has been accepted as alternating residence, not contact.

residence if it can be shown that a parent has neglected his or her duty to support the child.[28]

As opposed to child maintenance payments under the Parents Code, maintenance support, according to the Maintenance Support Act, may be rendered with at most half the amount of maintenance support for each child a month (SEK 586). This amount is reduced by half the amount with which the receiving parent should have reimbursed the state had the child lived permanently with the other parent. It should be mentioned that maintenance support for alternating residence is available only to low-income parents with a monthly income of less than SEK 14,350 (parents with higher income are liable to pay back the whole amount).

In contrast to maintenance support in general, maintenance support for alternating residence is dependent on the income of the receiving parent. In accordance with the general rule for maintenance support it is not dependent on the income of the other parent.

DISCUSSION

1 Exceptions from Individualism

The Swedish law relating to the maintenance of children provides at least two departures from the principle of individualism. The first is the principle according to which the needs of the family, ie the child and the residential parent, may take precedence over the wishes of the parent liable for maintenance under the Parents Code. The second exception relates to the reclamation of maintenance support.

(a) Ongoing Collaboration

The assessment of child maintenance according to the Parents Code is, as previously outlined, based on the parents' combined excess and presumes collaboration between the parents. The assessment of the parents' incomes is made on the presumption that each works full time. If this is not the case the reasons for the deduction of working time should be scrutinised. If the court does not consider these reasons acceptable in the light of a parent's duty to provide for the child, the assessment of the parent's excess should be made from a fictive full-time income. Or as it has been expressed in the preparatory materials:[29]

> [m]aintenance ability should be assessed if possible, with regard to the actual ability in cases when the liable parent without acceptable reasons refrains from procuring an income that would put him in a position to contribute to the maintenance of the child. A parent's preferences of the way in which he

[28] Parents Code ch 7, s 9.
[29] Governmental Bill 1978/79: 12 p 402, translated by author.

wants to live his life may thus be restricted by his or her duty to maintain the children.

What could be considered as acceptable reasons for refraining from procuring a full-time income has been tried by the Swedish Supreme Court in a couple of judgments:

> In NJA 1985 p 768, a parent liable to pay maintenance had given up a permanent position as a bus-driver to move to the countryside supporting himself by small jobs, which gave a very low income. He claimed he could only contribute to the child *in natura*. He further claimed that his change of lifestyle was in accordance with the plans cherished by both parents before the break-up. The Supreme Court ruled that his excess should be estimated on the basis of his previous income as a bus-driver.

The Supreme Court came to the same result in NJA 1990 p 201 regarding a parent who had taken up studies.

> In NJA 1990 p 201 the Supreme Court ruled that the excess of a parent who studied should be estimated on the basis of his previous income as a full-time bread-deliverer. The Supreme Court justified its ruling as follows: 'Considering the age of Göran M, his previous trade and present level of income, there is no sufficient reason for assuming that his studies in the theory of business economics, will have any significant impact on his future financial situation.'

Another issued tried by the Supreme Court concerns what efforts ought to be made by an unemployed parent in order to get employment.

> In NJA 1992 p 550 the issue was whether an unemployed parent had done what could reasonably be expected from him to get a job. Given the rate of unemployment at the time, the Supreme Court found this to be the case and rejected the demand for maintenance.

In these cases very little room seems to be left for individual choices when assessing maintenance under the private law system of the Parents Code. On the contrary, solidarity with the family—the children and the former partner—is demanded. It should be noted, however, that these cases concern parents with low incomes, who were not able to provide for their children in accordance with the standard amounts on which the assessment of the needs of the child are based. As will be outlined below, parents who have the means to pay these standard amounts are under little legal pressure to contribute above the average level.

(b) Parenting: Obligatory Personal Guarantee

In spite of Swedish law's ambiguous position on promoting individualism by public contributions, the Maintenance Support Act, according to which maintenance support is not assessed on the basis of the calculated combined excess of the parents, may be considered as promoting the individualism of the parents. This is explained by the fact that although maintenance support may be supplemented by public means, it is the non-residential parent who usually pays the expenses.[30]

The Maintenance Support Act does, however, provide a clear exception to individualism in the provisions according to which a residential parent receiving maintenance support on behalf of his child may be liable to repay it, if the other parent's taxable income is revised by the tax authorities. If the taxable income of the liable parent is assessed to a higher amount than he has reported to the authorities, and he is considered to have had the ability to cover a greater part of the maintenance support, the residential parent will have to repay that part of the maintenance support to the public social insurance office.[31] The provision assumes strict liability and applies irrespective of fraudulent behaviour on the part of either parent (Bejstam, 1999–2000). In sum, the system of maintenance support presumes a relationship between the parents which could be characterised as that of residential parent acting as a 'forced personal guarantee'.

2 Best Interests of the Child

Sweden is a nation in which the principle of the best interests of the child is very much emphasised in public debate. The importance given to the best interests of the child should be seen in the light of the fact that Sweden has a strong tradition of welfarism and 'social engineering'. However, this alone does not explain the strong emphasis on the best interests of the child. Another explanation is that there are few other common values unifying the nation. This in turn could be explained by the country's strong secularisation, implying that religious values are seldom imposed. Add to this the modern history of neutralism and, in short, no common enemies to unify the country, and you find a nation in search of shared values; a search in which the principle of the best interests of the child appears to be a welcome answer.

There are various views on how to understand the best interests of the child as a legal principle. These views range from the view that the best interests of the child means assertion of a general welfare of children, to the view in which the best interests of the child are equivalent to granting the child a right to express his or her wishes and having those wishes respected.[32] Another view stipulates that the best interests of the child as a legal principle should mean a broader scope for individual and discretionary assessments than is the case when other legal rules and principles are applied.

---

[30] The average rate of repayment was SEK 878, that is 75 per cent of the maintenance support; 50 per cent of the maintenance debtors had debts to the state. Figures for year 1998.

[31] Maintenance Support Act s 20; cf also the Supreme Administrative Court in RÅ 2000 n 162.

[32] Cf Governmental Bill 1997/98: 7 p 105.

Although the best interests of the child understood as general welfare is an obvious point of departure for Swedish child law, the principle is only vaguely present in the system of child maintenance. An example is the number of children of single mothers living in poverty, ie below the social welfare norm, whose right to a reasonable standard of living is presumed to be met by social security benefits.[33] The wishes of the child are not taken into consideration when assessing maintenance payments or maintenance support.[34] Neither is the view stipulating that the purpose of the best interests of the child principle is to secure broader scope for individual and discretionary assessments to be upheld. Although the legal mechanisms for doing so exist in the private law system of the Parents Code, actual rulings where the child's needs are assessed at a different amount from the standardised amounts are rare.[35] No scope for individual assessment of the child's needs is available when the Maintenance Support Act is applied.

The position of the children of a single mother living in poverty reflects on another aspect of individualism—divorce on application. The Swedish divorce process is slowed down only by a period of waiting of six months if the spouses have children living with them. The granting of divorce is by no means dependent on the parents having the financial means to meet the higher expenses entailed by the division of the family into two households. Neither is any other aspect of the best interests of the child considered by the court before granting divorce.[36]

[33] *SCB Barn och deras familjer* 1999.

[34] Maintenance Support Act, s 7. In proceedings under the Parents Code, a person with custody represents the child. If the parents have joint legal custody, the custodian with whom the child is living permanently shall represent him/her. A custodian may represent the child, even if the custodian has not attained the age of majority. A guardian is also entitled to represent the child. Young persons who have attained 18 years may represent themselves. The child is likewise represented by the custodian he/she is living with in issues relating to maintenance support.

[35] This should be seen in light of the fact that maintenance litigation is unusual. In 1996 maintenance allowances for 154 children were adjusted by court, as compared to adjustment by agreement, which was made for 9.937 children (*SCB Statistisk årsbok* 2000 p 402). According to unpublished sources at the National Board of Health and Welfare 14 court cases were decided in conjunction with 396 custody cases during the first six months of 2002. In four of these cases the amount of maintenance payment was set at the same amount as, or less than, the maintenance support. In nine cases the maintenance payment were set between 1200 SEK and 2000 SEK and in one case the maintenance payment was set at 3000 SEK.

[36] The parents' joint custody is not influenced by the divorce. A parent may apply for sole custody. The court, however, is not obliged to grant the request, unless both parents are against joint custody or it can be shown that joint custody is manifestly against the best interests of the child. Joint custody is perceived as being the custodial arrangement most in conformity with the best interests of the child. It is the custodial arrangement most highly recommended by the law. The recommendation is followed to a great extent. During 2001, 97 per cent of all unmarried parents living together registered joint custody at the time of acknowledging paternity, and 55 per cent of unmarried parents not living together registered joint custody (unmarried mothers have sole custody under the law). Six months after the termination of the year of separation the joint legal custody remained for 95 per cent of the children of previously married parents and for 84 per cent of children of previously cohabiting parents (*Socialtjänsten 2002:5 Familjerätt 2001, Socialstyrelsen, Upp till 18, Barnombudsmannen* 2001). Approximately 55 per cent of children born in Sweden are born out of wedlock; approximately 10 per cent are born by mothers not living together with the father (or separated during the child's first year).

3   Self-Regulating System

A general characteristic of Swedish child law is the emphasis on law as a self-regulating system (Maclean, 2000), in the sense that it provides basic rules based on the presumption that parents should negotiate for themselves. In case they cannot reach an agreement only a minimum protection is obtainable by litigation. An example is the procedure for assessing the amount of maintenance payments for children. If the parents are in agreement, they are obviously free to agree on a higher maintenance payment than the standardised amounts of the Parental Code. If, however, the non-residential parent does not agree to contribute more than this amount, the possibility of the child—and the residential parent—getting a higher than standard amount of maintenance payments is limited. The law does offer a possibility of getting higher maintenance payments by means of a court order if the non-residential parent is wealthy, since the child should be maintained on the same financial level as this parent.[37] However, the courts are very cautious in ordering maintenance payments at a higher amount than the standardised ones.[38]

Thus what might at first seem like a conflict-producing, and rather complicated, system of assessment of child maintenance payments is seldom litigated. Instead, Swedish subjects depend to a great extent on individual agreements.

CONCLUSION: LITIGATION IN THE SHADOW OF MEDIATION

Mediation is understood to be conducted generally in the shadow of litigation (Mnookin and Kornhauser, 1979). The presumed result of court litigation is perceived as a boundary for the results obtainable by mediation. The theory of mediation in the shadow of litigation implies that the result of mediation depends on the content of the law; in short, a change in the law will have effects outside the courtroom. When Swedish legislative reforms in the area of family law are made, the impact on mediation is very much an issue for consideration. This has resulted in 'pedagogical' legislation, ie legislation that was never intended to be used by courts in litigation but to influence parents in the raising of their children, including patterns for co-parenting (Schiratzki, 1997).

This approach, in combination with cutbacks in legal aid for family law litigation (Regan, 2000), has been successful in keeping such litigation away from the courts. The result could be criticised, however, as a system in which the law in certain areas only upholds a minimum level of protection for its subjects. An example is child maintenance, which is hardly ever litigated. Child maintenance is, furthermore, an example of how the law

---

[37] Governmental Bill 1978/79: 12 p 105.
[38] Cf Supreme Court in NJA 1989: 700, NJA 1996: p 134, NJA 1985: p 781 and NJA 1995: 297; cf also n 35.

assists in securing minimum or standard levels of maintenance for children. This implies limiting the possibilities of personal choice for low-income parents. Parents with a higher income are free, once they have contributed according to the standardised amounts, to make their personal choices, running little risk of having a higher amount of maintenance assessed by court orders.[39]

Litigation overshadowed by mediation implies that fewer public resources are set aside for litigation. This in turn implies that an individual is more dependent on his or her personal resources to negotiate and reach an agreement within the mediation process. One such resource is a network of friends and personal relationships. In the long run this may lead to individualism as a legal value coming under scrutiny, and bring home the importance of group loyalties.

REFERENCES

Barnombudsmannen (2001) Upp till 18.

Bejstam, L (1999–2000) 'Ett Diskutabelt Beslut om Återkrav—och Diskutabla Återkravsregler' *Juridisk Tidskrift* 722–35.

Hallberg, P and Lernstedt, C (eds), (2002) *Svenska Värderingar* (Stockholm, Carlsson).

Maclean, M (ed) (2000) *Making Law for Families* (Oxford, Hart Publishing).

Mnookin, RE and Kornhauser, L (1979) 'Bargaining in the Shadow of the Law: The Case of Divorce' *Yale Law Journal* 88: 950–997.

Regan, F (2000) 'Retreat from Equal Justice? Assessing the Recent Swedish Legal Aid and Family Law Reforms' *Civil Justice Quarterly*: 168–184.

Schiratzki, J (1997) *Vårdnad och Vårdnadstvister* (Stockholm: Norstedts Juridik).

Statistiska Central Baran (1999) *Barn och deras familjer* (Goteborg: SCB).

Statistiska Central Baran (2000) *Statistical Yearbook of Sweden* (Stockholm, SCB).

[39] To some extent it might be argued that Swedish succession law compensates the low maintenance rates by stating that the direct heirs have the right to a so-called forced share of 50 per cent of the estate.

9

Changing Commitments: A Study of Close Kin after Divorce in England

CAROL SMART

INTRODUCTION

I N ENGLAND AND Wales the levels of divorce have grown considerably since the 1950s and although the rate of increase has substantially slowed, divorce (or separation) is now a common experience in families. The familiarity of divorce suggests that fundamental and widespread changes are occurring in the way people conduct their intimate social lives. This has given rise to a growing interest in the ways individuals manage these processes (see eg Finch and Mason, 1990; Simpson, 1998; Smart and Neale, 1999). More broadly, it has necessitated the search for new ways to conceptualise and understand kinship and family under the fluid conditions of late modernity. In this paper I draw on an empirical project which explores how kin relations are 'worked out' (Finch, 1989) in the aftermath of divorce. Before turning to empirical data I present a brief overview of developments in the field of kinship research, which are beginning to revolutionise our thinking about the meaning of family ties, commitments and caring relationships.

THEORISING KINSHIP AND RELATEDNESS

Until recently English kinship was a relatively neglected field of enquiry (Firth, Hubert and Forge, 1969, and Young and Wilmott, 1957 were notable exceptions). Among both anthropologists and sociologists, the implications of contemporary divorce and remarriage for kin relationships were hardly recognised let alone investigated (Simpson, 1998). Divorce was located firmly within a social problems framework; its significance as a cultural process through which the dynamics of kinship were being played out was simply not recognised. This situation began to change in the 1980s as new theoretical understandings of kinship began to emerge. Early preoccupations with static functions and structures (the formal properties of genealogical systems, principles of descent and lineage etc) were giving way to a concern with the way kinship was *practised*, and attention now became focused on the dynamic nature of these practices, their subjective meaning for individuals and groups, and the moral choices that people make in the continual process of negotiating and crafting their intimate social lives (Finch and Mason, 1993; Flowerdew, 1999; Carsten, 2000).

Perhaps most notably, earlier structural preoccupations with the relationship between the 'biological' and the 'social', seen as discrete dimensions of kinship, began to abate. The boundaries between nature and culture were seen to be more permeable than was once supposed, and attention became focused on how they are infused with each other (Strathern, 1992). The concept of 'fictive' kinship (relatedness founded neither on blood nor legal ties) was called into question as researchers came to realise that kinship is more than a biologically or legally defined category and, indeed, may be defined in neither of these ways (Carsten, 2000). Anecdotal evidence suggests, for example, that informal ties are routinely given a legal or biological gloss in order to create an air of legitimacy and moral force. Thus friends are labelled as 'aunties' or 'uncles', grandmothers who bring up their grandchildren as 'mothers', half-sisters or adopted sisters as 'sisters', and partners as 'common law' spouses. In these ways nature is harnessed to social ends and what we construe as 'natural' is itself a cultural construct, a matter of choice (Edwards and Strathern, 2000). There has been a growing interest in the varied and grounded ways in which individuals build a sense of connectedness and belonging to others, including the language used to do so ('my' mother, my 'partner', 'our' Jim, 'our' family, 'our' house/street/group etc). It is not simply a matter of *being related* to someone but of how and under what circumstances individuals *relate to* one another. In other words, kinship, conceived in terms of the useful concept of *relatedness*, can be seen as a cultural construct, a complex of social and personal considerations, which is as much a matter of choice and moral sensibility, as of legal or biological necessity. Indeed, it has been suggested that ties based purely on personal choice rather than legality or accident of birth (such as those which characterise same-sex partnerships) may assume more value precisely because of their voluntary nature (Carsten, 2000).

The recognition of these insights in the context of 'traditional' societies opened the way for renewed interest in the fluid kinship and family practices of Western societies (Allen, 1996; Flowerdew, 1999). Kin relations (seen as extended family relations) in these settings are no less likely to be imbued with a moral character and a sense of permanence or durability, but they have a strong affective component and are inherently flexible (Finch, 1987; Finch and Mason, 1990). Contemporary kinship is continually under construction through a variety of practices, negotiations and changing commitments. This brings to the fore another important feature of kinship: it is necessarily self-limiting. It is not just about what are seen as the positive and harmonious features of interactions with significant others but is also about disconnection and disjunction (Edwards and Strathern, 2000). It can be characterised, then, as a continuous process of becoming connected to some people and disconnected from others.

KINSHIP AND DIVORCE

As we have seen, English kinship is by its very nature fluid and complex, and is further complicated by changing patterns of family life, in particular by cohabitation, divorce, repartnering and step-family life. Conventional understandings of kinship, which are built upon the edifice of the legal tie of marriage, are inevitably confounded in a society with high rates of divorce and extra-marital relationships. Currently, we still know relatively little about how the kinship processes described above actually work or are 'worked out' over time in these circumstances and the purpose of our research was to shed some light on these issues.

It is evident of course that there is no one single kind of divorce with an inevitable outcome. Different people do their divorces differently, and the same people can do their second divorce very differently from their first and so on. There is a growing cultural resource on how to divorce. For example, several of the adults Bren Neale and I interviewed about divorce in the 1990s reflected on the fact that they wanted to do their divorce differently from the way in which their parents had managed theirs some 20 or so years previously. It is not unusual (or new) to hear of 'good' divorces and 'bad' divorces, but this kind of binary categorisation hardly begins to grasp the range of behaviours, commitments and obligations that people now need to negotiate on divorce. A new etiquette is called for. Does one stay in touch with a former mother-in-law or sister-in-law? Should grandchildren spend as much time with maternal and paternal grandparents? Do the children of former brothers-in-law still come round to play with one's children? Do the children speak to the children of their father's 'new' woman when they see them in school? Should stepfathers act like father figures or as family friends?

The ways in which high levels of divorce affect and change everyday life are only just now being fathomed. It was always assumed that family life ended with divorce and only resumed if spouses remarried and constituted proper nuclear families again. Commonplace terminology such as 'breakdown', 'breakup', or 'splitting-up' all suggest fragmentation and a sundering of relationships. Moreover, the sundering is not presumed to be just the married couple, but also the different 'sides' of the family, shared friends and often the children too. While this picture may be true for many people (and we have no idea how many) it may be that in our eagerness to research the 'breakdown' and the harm it might cause, we have overlooked the continuities and the ongoing nature of many relationships beyond divorce.

THE STUDY

The study that is reported here builds upon previous research[1] carried out at the University of Leeds and is one project in a programme of projects[2] looking at the ways in which childhood, parenthood, marriage and partnering are changing in contemporary Britain. This particular study has used in-depth interviews with divorced people in three very different locations. It has also sought to explore certain cultural differences which are reflected in these different locations. Thus we have interviewed people in a rural, farming based district of Yorkshire where the divorce rate is relatively low (our 'rural' sample); a thriving city location where divorce rates are higher and where there is more cultural diversity (our 'urban' sample); and finally a less economically prosperous city where there is a large Pakistani population and where cultural expectations about divorce are likely to differ (our 'minority' ethnic sample).

Where possible we also interviewed a near relative of the divorced person. This was typically a mother or father but in some cases it was a sibling or even an older child. We found that contacting a relative was extremely difficult and we were unsuccessful in recruiting any parents within our minority sample. Obviously the strategy raised potential ethical issues because the relatives could feel that we wanted to question them about the private details of a son or daughter's life. Equally the divorced person could feel that we might relay things to a parent that they wanted to keep secret. There were also potential elements of bias since it seemed likely that we would only be referred on to a parent (or sibling) who was still in contact and still in a good relationship. In fact, this was not always the case, but it was more usual to be passed on to a 'friendly' relative than a hostile one. In order to try to resolve this problem we sought out a separate sample of older people with divorced adult children to fill some of the gaps in our sample and to try to attend to the problem of tapping into only 'good' accounts of ongoing kin relationships.

For the purpose of this chapter I have drawn on data from 14 families where we were able to interview more than one family member. Of these, 7 families (14 individuals) were from our rural sample and 7 families (16 individuals) from our urban sample. All socio-economic classes are represented but with a bias towards the middle class. Only 5 family members were male. Additionally, 6 individuals described themselves as Jewish, 15 as Christian or Church of England, and 9 as of no religious affiliation.

---

[1] See eg Smart and Neale (1999), Smart and Stevens (2000), Smart *et al* (2001), Wade and Smart (2002).

[2] This project is part of the ESRC funded research group on Care, Values and the Future of Welfare (CAVA) (ESRC ref M564281001) which is being carried out at the University of Leeds.

PICTURING POST-DIVORCE FAMILIES

Jill: It's a very impressive family scenario sometimes. My brother and his
wife last year had twin daughters and we went out for a family meal about
six months ago. And there's my ex-husband sat on one side of me, my
current husband on the other, my ex-husband's girlfriend opposite me, the
children sort of bouncing, with merely a batting of an eyelid, they moved as
easily between Jemma, me and Mark and Colin, which—that's actually
down to me.

(aged 41, middle class, rural sample, all names are pseudonyms)

Typically it is assumed that after a divorce kinship networks are diminished.
Although most concern about divorce has focused on children losing contact with non-resident fathers, there has also been concern about children
losing contact with paternal grandparents. Less concern has been addressed
to losing contact with uncles, aunts, cousins and so on. But in all these cases
the common assumption is that divorce ruptures these relationships. Of
course with more distant relations it is sometimes quite hard to know whether important factors in sustaining or breaking contact might be other than
divorce. It might be that geographical mobility is significant, or stage in the
life course might be influential as younger family members grow up, develop friendship networks or even start their own families. Divorce may, of
course, be associated with moving away, particularly if there is a remarriage. This means that there are complex processes at work. We are trying
therefore in this project to look more closely at some of these processes to
try to work out under what conditions it is more likely that extended kin
stay in contact. This is particularly important in a climate in the UK where
there is a growing emphasis on the legal 'rights' of kin to stay in contact
with children. There is a vociferous Grandparents' Movement and there are
a significant number of cases of legal actions by grandparents to secure contact agreements (or court orders) to safeguard their ability to remain in contact with grandchildren. Children may soon find themselves the subject
of contact orders requiring them to visit not only their non-residential parent but also their grandparents on one or both sides of their families. Yet
this is in a context where we know very little about the dynamics of post-
divorce kinship and whether legal regulation is at all suitable in such personal and sensitive inter-personal relationships.

In the discussion that follows I focus on the following issues: (a) kin
keeping, (b) problem relatives, (c) supportive relatives, (d) taking sides and
(e) remaining neutral. I then go on to consider more broadly the effects on
wider family members of there being a divorce in the family.

1 Kin Keeping

One of the key elements in sustaining family relationships across time
and distance (as opposed to under conditions of co-residence) has been

identified as depending on whether one person is willing to assume the role of kin keeper (Chamberlain, 1998). The kin keeper is the person who remembers birthdays and sends cards and presents, who tells family members what is happening to other kin, who preserves and relates family stories, responds to the need for support or contact in varying degrees, and who is quite simply interested in family members. Usually this is the job of mothers (although we have found that in Pakistani families it is often the job of the father). If there is no kin keeper in a family then it is difficult for people to remain in touch and involved with each other.

After divorce it is usually expected that mothers—who are more usually still the residential parent—will continue this job if they assumed it during a marriage. It is expected that she will sustain relationships between children and a non-residential father, no matter how much she might wish to be free of such a role. But it is also often assumed that she will do this in relation to paternal grandparents and other kin. If she ceases to carry out this role she is often seen as not merely becoming neutral but as obstructing 'natural' relationships. Thus, for example, Jill, who is quoted above, says about her children's paternal grandparents:

> **Jill:** I buy Christmas presents for them, which I put from—I don't put Colin [new husband] on it because I know it would just rub it in so I just buy it from the boys. I'm sure Mark [ex-husband] buys them something from the boys but *I know what they like* so I get them a little something that I know they like and then I put 'from Tom and Joe'. And then they see them on Christmas Day and [it is important for the children]—I wouldn't bother otherwise (emphasis added).

What this passage reveals is that Jill is actively sustaining relationships for the sake of her children. It also reveals that she knows what her former parents-in-law like to receive as presents while her former husband probably does not know. She goes to this trouble notwithstanding the fact that she actually loathes the grandfather in question.

For other kin keepers, divorce becomes an opportunity to give up on relationships that were burdensome or unrewarding throughout the marriage.

> **Molly:** When we were together, if his [husband's] mum rang up, he wouldn't speak to her. I used to have the conversation or I would ring her. And when things started going wrong with us, I stopped ringing her and she knew there was something. But I thought, 'Well, why the hell should I bother' because he's, you know, he isn't in my family [anymore] so I'm not gonna ring for him.
> *(aged 47, middle class, rural sample)*

In trying to understand the way in which families work after divorce we feel that it is vital to understand the position of the kin keeper and to recognise that this is often a purely altruistic task, especially where the kin keeper does not care for or like the kin she (sometimes he) is maintaining contact with. Non-residential families do not cohere and sustain themselves without effort but the effect of divorce can be that the effort feels too much and the kin keepers may wish to divest themselves of the ethical duty to continue to nurse relationships.

2 Problem Relatives

In the case of Molly above, she felt that she no longer had the responsibility to sustain contact with her mother-in-law. She did not express the view that the mother-in-law in question was difficult or unpleasant, but she no longer felt a moral responsibility for keeping her in her family circle. Moreover, her children were of an age to sustain contact themselves should they wish to. But some parents found themselves in situations in which grandparents (either their own parents or their ex-spouse's parents) were quite problematic. One of the main problems facing parents was when grandparents would tell the children things that a parent did not want them to know. This was particularly the case when it was something distressing about a non-residential parent or when it went against the parent's own value system. One small, but typical, example was Jill's former father-in-law who did not like Jill and who resented her new husband's relationship with his grandchildren.

> **Jill:** Colin and I got married a year last June and for a while the children were quite concerned at what their relationship was, what it was called and—you know, 'Well if you marry Colin, what is he to us now?' and I said 'He's your stepfather'. I said 'You've got your real father' I said 'and there's only one real dad and there's only one real mum but if your dad gets remarried, Jemma will be your stepmum'—they call her 'nearly stepmum' because they're engaged—'and now Colin is your stepdad'. So they obviously told Mark's parents this. He said 'No he isn't, you only have a stepfather if your real father dies'. So they immediately, or the little one, thought that Dad was gonna die. I could have killed him!

Jill had to get out several dictionaries to prove to her sons that her definition of step-parent was correct and it took her some time to persuade the youngest son (aged eight) that nothing awful was going to happen to his father. These sorts of incidents can happen between the generations in any family of course, but the problem facing divorced parents is when they feel that grandparents are deliberately undermining a situation or good relationships.

In the case of Nina it was her own mother who was the problem. When her daughter was five years old the grandmother Dorian told the child that her father had been cruel to her when she was a baby, threatening to drop her on the floor in order to frighten Nina. The story was true, but Nina did not want the child to know about it because she felt that the father had done it to be cruel to her and not in order to hurt the child. Dorian had told the girl not to tell her mother that she had told her this story but the child had let it slip.

> Nina: I had this mortified child because she'd been told by my mother not to say anything because I'd go up the wall. Yes I would, because it shouldn't have been said in the first place. She knew she'd done wrong. When I asked her she said 'I will tell them anything I want to because I have a right to as their grandparent'. What about my rights as a parent? [I said] 'If somebody had done that to you mother when you'd had me, would you have settled for it?'. 'That's different'. 'Why is it different?'. 'Because it's you'. 'No it isn't, I'm their mother and I've a right to say do not tell my children things like that, it is not your place to.'   (*aged 28, unemployed, urban sample*)

Following this incident the child refused to go to see her grandmother. Relationships which were already volatile and manipulative, deteriorated and Dorian eventually took her daughter to court to get contact with the grandchildren. She was awarded contact and for a period the children were passed back and forth without mother and daughter speaking to each other. Their accounts of this period vary considerably but both agreed that the grandmother had pretended not to be in when Nina brought the children to see her and both agreed that Dorian never sent any cards or presents on birthdays or Christmas. It appears that the daughter now self harms and the son is violent in school. The grandmother asserts that she has been labelled a vexatious litigant and that no solicitor in the city will now take her case because she wants to take her daughter back to court.

The case of Dorian and Nina is an extreme one but it is important in that it reveals the emotional complexity of some intergenerational family relationships. In policy discussions in the UK it often seems that grandparents are portrayed as kindly, benevolent folk who merely have the interests of their grandchildren at heart and who are the victims of malicious mothers who deny their children the right to know their biological kin. Often the reality is much more complex than this.

3 Supportive Relatives

Most of the stories we heard from divorced parents told of how supportive their own parents were. As I explain above, we heard accounts mainly from divorced mothers and there was likely to be a bias towards hearing about 'positive' relationships. Notwithstanding this, it does seem that at times of divorce, the grandparent generation becomes incredibly important as a source of support and comfort. Often daughters would move in order to be closer to their parents. This support would be particularly forthcoming where mothers had been abandoned, where they received no maintenance or child support, or where they may have been left with debts. For some grandparents this was an incredibly hard blow. Not only might they be devastated on behalf of their daughters, but they often had to change their own expectations about their lives and their retirement plans. In some cases grandparents became the main source of childcare to allow mothers to return to work. Grandfathers took on the father's role with grandsons when it came to playing sports and providing role models for boys. Often grandparents supported their adult children financially and helped cope with depression and worry.

> **Mr Platt:** So as I say we did, we did more or less rescue her from all the smaller type debts, which added up to a few thousand pounds didn't it love?
>
> **Mrs Platt:** Yeah.
>
> **Mr Platt:** And then as I say we tried then for her to keep the house. I mean the building society let her pay a smaller mortgage for a while but then they started pursuing her and pursuing her and pursuing her, which we thought was unfair because his name was on the housing thing. But they didn't pursue him they just pursued her all the time.
>
> **Mrs Platt:** She was easy to get hold of.
>
> **Mr Platt:** And eventually obviously the house had to go, that's it.
>
> **Mrs Platt:** It got repossessed.
>
> *(aged 68 and 62, middle class, urban sample, former son-in-law in prison)*

In return adult children often tried to shelter their parents from what was really going on:

> **Ann:** You do try to shelter your parents, but it was quite sordid in a way all this bizarre stuff I'd found out about him [ex-husband]. I'm still not sure, he might have committed bigamy, I've never found that out. It doesn't bother me, who cares? But I suppose I was trying to shield them from it, they'd never really ever seen me in a particularly distraught state before. It was very hard, I wanted to break down but plus I had [my son].
>
> *(aged 38, middle class, urban sample)*

The majority of grandmothers were quite heartbroken especially where former sons-in-law had gone off with another woman, or refused to support their wives and children. They became highly protective and basically reassumed a parenting role. They were worried about their daughters' futures where they had not remarried and wished ardently that they could meet a 'nice man' who would look after them and be a companion to their (adult) child once they had died.

4 Taking Sides

Some kin felt it was simply natural to take sides when their own adult child or grandchildren had been hurt. Some took sides long before there was any hint of trouble, taking against their sons or daughters-in-law before they were even married.

> **Carol:** Right when she married, what were your expectations or hopes?
>
> **May:** Nothing.
>
> **Carol:** Nothing, why?
>
> **May:** Didn't like it at all.
>
> **Carol:** You didn't like it?
>
> **May:** No, no. No I was very much against it.
>
> **Carol:** Why was that?
>
> **May:** Well he was Black. I couldn't understand her.
>
> **Carol:** So you're unhappy about that then?
>
> **May:** Mm very.
>
> **Carol:** What did he do for a living?
>
> **May:** At the time he was a welder. Don't get me wrong the lad was all right. But I couldn't understand how she could, you know she had had some nice boys and then she'd met him dancing. I couldn't understand what she could see in him and I mean both my sons never spoke to her. I mean they do now but they didn't. They blame me for coming to Leeds to live.
>
> (*aged 80, middle class, urban sample*)

May had made it plain to her daughter that she disapproved of the marriage. Other parents kept their disquiet to themselves, only revealing their 'true' feelings after the marriage had ended. In some cases both sets of grandparents joined forces against a husband or wife who was seen to be behaving really badly. In the case of Clare and her parents, the Platts quoted above, her mother-in-law and brother-in-law also rallied round her and tried to help. The entire family rejected her husband because of his gambling addiction and the terrible mess he had made of the marriage. Sometimes one grandparent was particularly antipathetic to the former son- or daughter-in-law while the other was more accommodating:

> **Bren:** What about other people in your family, what did the end of the marriage mean for them?
>
> **Lucy:** Well me mum was really angry, she didn't want anything more to do with him and it was you know 'If any of your children get married and HE comes to the wedding, I won't be there', you know, that sort of thing. Me dad was much more philosophical, I mean he was—he was supportive and I suppose he was mad with him but you know, it's just that's life. So he wasn't too bad about it. And me sisters, I think they were, they were a

little bit angry about it, they were supportive to me but you know.
(aged 54, middle class, urban sample)

But taking sides was a complex business where grandchildren were concerned. Grandparents could be acutely aware that although they thought a father was worthless, he might be loved by the grandchildren that they too cherished. Grandchildren might refuse to see grandparents who criticised their fathers and so often there grew up an uneasy silence between grandchildren and grandparents on this subject. Where grandparents were taking a role in caring for young grandchildren they could often see how much the children might miss their fathers and could also see signs of disturbed behaviour in some cases. In situations where grandparents disliked or disapproved of a former son- or daughter-in-law, and yet where they were still in regular contact with the children, these grandparents had to adjust to having ongoing links with a person they would much prefer to vanish altogether. Interestingly some came to feel quite sorry for their former in-laws because of their inability to sustain good relationships.

> May: Well they had two [children]. And then she told him to get out. And then he got back again you see and that's when she had Rachael and then she shot him out. Then he turned to me for help. Which I gave, I don't know. I felt so sorry for him.
>
> Carol: When you say he turned to you for help you mean emotional or did he need some financial help?
>
> May: He needed financial. So my husband and I gave him it.
>
> Carol: So although you hadn't been terribly keen on the marriage at that point you were willing to help?
>
> May: Oh yes, I've, well I mean when they'd had children, we got [to be] friends, he was, I was never. Even though they got married I was friendly with them. I went over every Monday and did the blooming house through for them. You know washed and ironed and yeah. But it still went against the grain you know. But you can't do it once they have had children because you can't take it out on the bairns. And they were lovely children, you know the two boys when they were young. Well they used to come to us on a Friday night and go back home on a Sunday. And they loved coming.

May's reactions are interesting because the usual story was one where the grandparents were happy when their daughters married and only turned against their sons-in-law when they discovered later that they had failings. May had argued against her daughter's marriage and was clearly prejudiced. But notwithstanding her son-in-law's failings as she saw them (eg his affairs, other children, irresponsibility and dope smoking) she came to like him and still saw him many years later. Her sense of commitment to him arose because she found him likeable, but also because he was the father of her grandchildren. If there had been no grandchildren it is unlikely that May would have helped him, even though she liked him. Thus her sense of changing commitment towards him was a complex web of kin-based obligation and a personal sense of affinity (she loved dancing with him).

5 Remaining Neutral

Some grandparents felt it was their duty to remain neutral at all times, regardless of their feelings about their adult children's marriages and divorces.

> **Amelia:** No [taking sides] was one thing we definitely were never going to do, partly because we thought if anything it was Jill's fault anyway but we sort of couldn't say that's it never darken our door again, you know that was never in the equation. And of course we were concerned that for the boys, the children's point of view, that we were equally accessible for them from whichever parent. Although we were worried about Jill, cross with her, frustrated by her, there was never any question of taking sides because, as she eventually talked more it became clear that Mark's attitude had not always been very helpful, and he hadn't always come up with the goods as you might say. ... But we always felt that it was not that we didn't want to take sides, [rather] it was important that we didn't take sides.
>
> *(aged 65, middle class, rural sample)*

Remaining neutral made it much easier for strained relationships to survive the divorce process and it also made it easier for children. In the case of Amelia, her former son-in-law would often drop her grandchildren off at her house and this made sharing contact much more relaxed and natural. If grandparents were too judgemental it could mean that parents turned to friends or sometimes siblings more than grandparents for support. And where the older generation regarded divorce as shameful (regardless of the quality of the relationships involved) it could lead to estrangement.

> **Jodie:** And the only thing that she [mother] could come up with when Dean and I split up was 'What have I done to have two children divorced!' ... Whereas me dad was, I must admit the only thing that me dad said was 'Are you going to be happy?' 'Yes'. 'Oh, you do what you think is right then.' Whereas me mother was more bothered in what the neighbours think.
>
> *(aged 40, middle class, urban sample)*

SUSTAINING RELATIONSHIPS

What emerges from these interviews is the outline of an ethics and etiquette of post-divorce relationships between kin. The core element would appear to be the extent to which central relationships transcend the formal status of a legal tie (eg mother-in-law to son-in-law) and move onto the terrain more usually associated with friendship. If diverse individuals, who are brought together solely through a legal contract such as marriage, form bonds based on liking, respect, mutuality and shared interests then the breaking of the legal tie does not have to mean the end of the relationship. As life courses change direction after divorce, it is possible that people will drift further apart, but this does not mean that they become antagonistic or uncaring.

We came across some quite exceptional cases where former in-laws became more important than own biological kin. In the case of Jodie quoted above, her former mother-in-law lent her the deposit to buy a house with her new husband. She also gave practical help on a regular basis and was there whenever there was a crisis with her second husband's health.

> **Jodie:** I said 'You don't have to do that' but her husband had been in intensive care and he'd died, he'd had a stroke and a heart attack and whatever and I'd just stuck with her. His sisters couldn't handle it, and I—I just did and—you know, she said 'I'll not forget that, you were there when I needed you and now you need something and I'll do it for you.' But that's the sort of person she is, you know. I just wish me own mother would understand!

But, of course, not all extended kin can or will like each other. In these circumstances a greater effort is required to sustain working relationships and at times individuals may not think the effort is worth it. Moreover the existence of grandchildren complicates matters because it is clear that many parents feel they need to sustain relationships between grandchildren and grandparents even though they would prefer to opt out of the relationship themselves.

In addition we need to recognise the extent to which divorce often heralds new relationships. In several cases we found situations where adult sons remarried (or repartnered) and started a 'new' family. In these cases grandparents had two sets of grandchildren by different mothers. If there was hostility between their son and his former wife the 'new' grandchildren might start to become more significant than the first clutch of grandchildren. In these cases loyalties could become very stretched and people were faced with very difficult emotional and ethical dilemmas.

The other dilemma facing kin was how to be supportive and yet how to avoid taking sides. Very often the behaviour of a son- or daughter-in-law (or sometimes son or daughter) went against core values. The refusal to pay child support or a lack of inclination to sustain contact with children was very hard for some grandparents to take. It could also be very difficult to remain uninvolved with this aspect of a divorce when the grandparents themselves were making up for the financial shortfall out of their limited savings. Sometimes siblings felt honour bound to step in to help or make reparation where a brother or sister had apparently behaved badly. This could create tensions horizontally across the wider family.

Grandparents who were very supportive, both emotionally and financially, often became privately embroiled in disputes over contact. They might be faced with a daughter who was reluctant to facilitate contact between their grandchildren and their father, or they might themselves be strongly antipathetic to their grandchildren seeing their father even if the mother was in favour. Contact disputes between parents are often seen as simply disputes between mothers and fathers, but in the wings there are often both sets of grandparents and sometimes even siblings. This was something that grandparents found hard to discuss. It was as if they 'knew' they should not interfere and so they tended to skirt around the issue. One couple knew that their daughter had not told her sons that their father was in jail and when one son had asked if he could send a letter to try to find his dad, she had destroyed the letter rather than send it on to the father. They were really worried about whether this was the right decision but none of them had ever faced such a dilemma and they simply did not know what to do for the best.

COMMITMENTS AND CHANGING FAMILIES

In their study of family obligations between former in-laws after divorce, Finch and Mason (1990) found that some relationships remained close and supportive, some took on the quality of the cordial yet rather distant relationships found between secondary kin, while yet others could not be maintained at all. The authors suggest that the cultural rules for shaping kin relations in the aftermath of a divorce are still being written, but whatever normative guidelines are put in place are likely to be interpreted flexibly in practice. Whether such relationships are consolidated or undermined will depend upon a range of factors, most notably the history and quality of the relationship and the practicalities and sensibilities of sustaining the links under post-divorce conditions.

Our own findings support these insights and suggest further that they may be applied to kin relationships defined by blood as well as by law. A divorce in the family requires individuals to look afresh at their existing networks of kin and evaluate them in the light of the reconfiguration in family relationships. At a normative level, a continuation of former in-law relationships is clearly permissible, and indeed may be seen as something of an achievement, deserving of congratulations if things work out well. Yet at the same time, there is no expectation that such relationships will continue and they are likely to undergo a testing time in the aftermath of a divorce, when their contingent nature becomes transparent. The continuation of these relationships is thus seen to be voluntary and to rely on good will and generosity of spirit. Relationships that are built solely on the basis of the legal formalities of 'being related' to someone, and that may, therefore, be practised out of a sense of duty or obligation alone, may have less chance of surviving a divorce than in-law relationships that are bolstered by affection, kindness and mutual support.

One significant finding from our study (also reported in Finch and Mason, 1990) concerns the way in which in-laws may seek to find a new and acceptable basis for conducting their relationships in the aftermath of a divorce and in particular their means of expressing this in everyday language. Former sisters-in-law, for example, may still be accorded their original status, or may even be likened to sisters:

> Rachel: Well I said [to my brother], 'You know Jules [former sister-in-law] has been there as long as you. I've spent more time with her than I have with you, got more memories of growing up with Jules than I have with you, and I love her. I love you, my brother, of course I love you, but I love Jules as well, and I've got a stronger relationship with her than I have with my own sister.' *(aged 33, middle class, rural sample)*

If kin by marriage are referred to in terms of or as more important than biological kin, this becomes a way of expressing a particular depth of feeling. As Finch and Mason (1990) suggest, in these ways, individuals create 'as if' relationships with their former in-laws, treating them as something other than what they now are and thereby ensuring that a version (albeit a slightly different version) of the family can still be preserved.

If we consider blood relationships in contrast to affinal ones, however, different normative assumptions appear to apply. There is an expectation that blood relatives (particularly parents and siblings) will be supportive at the time of divorce and there would be cause for concern or censure if support were not provided. However, there is less consensus over whether being supportive means taking sides, and kin may be careful to avoid doing so unless it becomes necessary to the maintenance of relationships with their blood kin. As I have indicated, in most cases in our sample parents did support their children but there were also some notable exceptions. This indicates that these relationships, no less than those based on genealogical ties, have a contingent quality to them and that where underlying tensions exist they may well be uncovered in the turmoil of a divorce, where relationships are put to the test (Smart, Neale and Wade, 2001).

CONCLUSION

To return to the themes introduced at the start of this chapter, our data suggest that while there may be different expectations placed upon kin depending upon whether they are related by blood or simply by law, in practice the way these relationships are worked out over time, and whether they are cherished and sustained will depend on more than an accident of birth or a genealogical tie. These biological and legal frameworks are interwoven and given substance through a range of social practices and moral sensibilities and it is these qualitative dimensions that may be regarded as the substance of kinship. Divorce poses a particular challenge to relationships but the notion that the rift that occurs between two individuals would automatically create a larger rift along the biological divide between the two families of origin, would be far too simplistic. It would not provide us with a very sensitive understanding of the dilemmas people face, nor the complex accommodations they reach.

In popular discourse, kinship is seen as a positive feature of social life, a part of one's social capital that brings harmony and stability and the promise of tangible and permanent support. Divorce, on the other hand, is hardly viewed as an unmitigated good and is undoubtedly a difficult process for all concerned. Since it brings a marriage to an end it might be viewed as the very antithesis of kinship, a severing not only of the formal and publicly recognised ties between the two individuals but also between their respective networks of kin. In the context of ethnic minority families such a view may still have some currency and some real consequences for family members. But among the samples represented here this was not the case. As I have suggested, kinship is perhaps best viewed not in formal structural terms but as a continual process of becoming connected to some people and disconnected from others. Divorce can be seen as an inevitable part of this process, one of the mechanisms through which the ebbs and flows of our intimate relationships are adjusted and regulated. As Bren Neale and I have shown elsewhere in the context of post-divorce parenthood (Smart and Neale, 1999) divorce does not mean an automatic descent into unethical and uncaring behaviour and this insight applies equally to the reworking of wider kin relations. Studies of stepfamily life, such as those of Stacey (1991) and Flowerdew (1999), show that,

> [i]n the way that people draw on a range of relatives, including 'ex'-partners and 'ex' parents-in-law they turn divorce from a kinship rupture into a kinship resource, creating 'divorce extended' families through which these resources can be mobilised.   (Flowerdew, 1999: 23)

It is through such analyses, Flowerdew suggests, that we can capture the dynamic and vibrant possibilities of stepkinship. Divorce is not so much an ending as a turning point, offering creative possibilities for reformulating kin relations in ways that are no less enduring, ethically binding or inherently valued than they were before.

REFERENCES

Allen, G (1996) *Kinship and Friendship in Modern Britain* (Oxford, Oxford University Press).

Carsten, J (2000) 'Cultures of Relatedness' in J Carsten (ed), *Cultures of Relatedness: New Approaches to the Study of Kinship* (Cambridge, Cambridge University Press).

Chamberlain, M (1998) 'Brothers and Sisters, Uncles and Aunts: A Lateral Perspective on Caribbean Families in Britain' in E Silva and C Smart (eds), *The New Family* (London, Sage).

Edwards, J and Strathern, M (2000) 'Including Our Own' in J Carsten (ed), *Cultures of Relatedness: New Approaches to the Study of Kinship* (Cambridge, Cambridge University Press).

Finch, J (1987) 'Family Obligations and the Life Course' in A Bryman, B Bytheway, P Allatt and T Keil (eds), *Rethinking the Life Cycle* (London, Macmillan).

—— (1989) *Family Obligations and Social Change* (Cambridge, Polity).

Finch, J and Mason, J (1990) 'Divorce, Remarriage and Family Obligations' *The Sociological Review* 38: 219–246.

—— (1993) *Negotiating Family Responsibilities* (London, Routledge).

Firth, R, Hubert, J and Forge, A (1969) *Families and their Relatives: Kinship in a Middle Class Sector of London* (London, Routledge).

Flowerdew, J (1999) *Reformulating Familiar Concerns: Parents in Stepfamilies* (unpublished PhD thesis, University of Leeds).

Simpson, B (1998) *Changing Families: An Ethnographic Approach to Divorce and Separation* (Oxford, Berg).

Smart, C and Neale, B (1999) *Family Fragments?* (Cambridge, Polity).

Smart, C, Neale, B and Wade, A (2001) *The Changing Experience of Childhood: Families and Divorce* (Cambridge, Polity).

Smart, C and Stevens, P (2000) *Cohabitation Breakdown* (London, Family Policy Studies Centre for the Joseph Rowntree Foundation).

Stacey, J (1991) *Brave New Families* (New York, Basic Books).

Strathern, M (1992) *After Nature: English Kinship in the Late 20th Century* (Cambridge, Cambridge University Press).

Wade, A and Smart, C (2002) *Facing Family Change: Children's Circumstances, Strategies and Resources* (York, York Publishing Services for the Joseph Rowntree Foundation).

Young, M and Willmott, P (1957) *Family and Kinship in East London* (London, Routledge).

PART III

Regulating New Forms of
Relationships Between Adults

10

Targeting the Exclusionary Impact of Family Law

LISA GLENNON*

INTRODUCTION

T HE BREADTH OF social relationships which are deemed to be within the legal definition of the family is one of the most contentious issues in family law, particularly in the light of the more visible diversity in family formation and the emergence of a 'rights-based' socio-legal culture. Indeed, at the beginning of the twenty-first century, jurisdictions through-out the world are reconceptualising the 'legal family' and developing new legal modes of recognising 'atypical' family forms.[1] Some reform strategies are more transformative than others and there are many points of divergence. Canada, in particular, is regarded as having a 'broad and pluralistic' approach to family definition (Bala and Bromwich, 2002). This has been exemplified by the recent decision of the Ontario Superior Court of Justice in *Halpern v The Attorney-General of Canada*[2] that the exclusion of same-sex couples from 'legal marriage' amounts to unjustifiable discriminatory treatment under the Canadian Charter of Rights and Freedoms.[3] While the three Justices disagreed over the appropriate remedy, a question which raised constitutional arguments concerning the proper division of powers, all concluded that the equality provisions of section 15(1) of the Charter were violated by the common law rule that defines marriage as being the 'lawful and voluntary union of one man and one woman to the exclusion

* I would like to thank Laura Lundy and Roxanne Mykitiuk for commenting on an earlier draft. Any errors or omissions remain the responsibility of the author.

[1] See Mazzotta (ch 12, this volume) who observes that the traditional concept of the family in Italy has 'long since been in the melting pot' due to the growth in alternative family forms. See also Cottier (ch 11, this volume) who examines a preliminary draft law on registered partnerships for same-sex couples in Switzerland and, in particular, focuses on the views of the different participants in the consultation process. Similarly, Picontó Novales (ch 13, this volume) discusses the legal treatment of de facto couples in Spain where distinctions can be made between the legal regulation afforded by state legislation and that afforded by the Autonomous Communities.

[2] 2002 Ont Sup CJ LEXIS 1417.

[3] Hereafter the Charter. Since writing this chapter, the Québec Superior Court has also ruled that the bar on same-sex marriage violates the Charter. The court suspended the ruling for two years to enable the federal Parliament to respond.

of all others'.[4] This chapter will consider the evolutionary development of same-sex relationship rights in Canada. It will be submitted that the recent decision of the Ontario court, although a landmark step, is an inevitable and necessary culmination of the previous jurisprudence of the Supreme Court of Canada which has subjected statutory schemes containing reference to spousal status to the analytical equality framework of the Charter. It will also be considered whether, in policy terms, the legalisation of same-sex marriage offers a progressive strategy for reform or whether it does little more than reinforce existing social and legal norms.

RE-CASTING THE FRAMEWORK THROUGH A RIGHTS-BASED DIALOGUE

The increasing visibility of 'atypical' family forms in society has brought the application of family law into sharp focus. In Canada, the inception of a rights-based framework within which to challenge existing legal norms has, to a certain extent, reframed contextual family law questions, decentralising the substantive content of the law as the primary focus of law reform and concentrating more directly on breadth of application and 'relational equality'.[5] The driving force has been the Canadian Charter of Rights and Freedoms which came into force on 17 April 1982.[6] Some commentators speculated that the Charter would have limited affect on the perceived 'private realm' of family law (Toope, 1991). In addition, it was argued that the development of a rights-based framework within which to articulate legal norms was potentially at variance with the complex interplay of dependencies, needs, social obligations and existing legal norms which contribute to the substance and application of family law (Boyd, 2000: 297). By the 1990s, however, the impact of the Charter on family law was clear. The equality guarantee of the Charter has been the primary vehicle by which to challenge exclusionary laws and to bring gay and lesbian rights within the mainstream political agenda. Section 15(1) of the Charter states that:

> Every individual is equal before and under the law and has the right to the equal protection and equal benefit of the law without discrimination and, in particular, without discrimination based on race, national or ethnic origin, colour, religion, sex, age or mental or physical disability.

The content of the Charter, in particular the construction of the equality guarantee, was influenced by the formalistic approach which had been

---

[4] This common law definition derives from *Hyde v Hyde and Woodmansee* (1866) LR 1 P&D 130.
[5] This can be defined as the legal assimilation between married and unmarried (both opposite-sex and same-sex) relationships. See Law Commission of Canada (2001) and Cossman and Ryder (2001).
[6] The Charter forms p 1 of the Constitution Act 1982, being sch B of the Canada Act 1982 (UK), ch 11. There was a three year moratorium of the enactment of the Charter's equality guarantee which came into force in 1985.

taken by the judiciary to the application of Canada's 1960 Bill of Rights, section 1(b) of which recognised the right of every individual to equality before the law and the protection of the law. The provisions of the Charter were constructed in an attempt to remedy some of the deficiencies of this provision. One aspect of section 15, therefore, is equality *under* the law which was drafted in order to facilitate a purposive approach to its interpretation and application. According to McColgan, section 15 was designed to 'preclude a reversion to the Diceyan approach' to equality where those to whom the law applied had to be treated equally with no consideration of the substantive content of the law (McColgan, 2000: 40).[7] Although several initial decisions of the lower courts delivered a formal approach to equality under section 15, those who had hailed the Charter as an innovative legal vehicle by which to challenge the oppression of historically disadvantaged groups were not disappointed when in 1989 the Supreme Court handed down its first section 15 decision. In *Andrews v Law Society of British Columbia*[8] the court was clear, a substantive approach to equality was to be taken when interpreting section 15. Indeed, McIntyre J stated that in order to achieve the ideal of full equality under the law, the main consideration must be the impact of the law on the individual or group concerned.[9]

The vision of the Charter's guarantee of equality which was spelt out in *Andrews* has found its place in the three-step inquiry now taken when analysing a claim under section 15. The rights claimant must establish that the impugned law subjects him/her to differential treatment; that the differential treatment was based on one or more of the enumerated or analogous grounds set out in section 15(1) and that the differential treatment discriminates in a substantive sense. In other words, that the treatment is discriminatory in a manner which is contrary to the purposes of section 15 in that it perpetuates or promotes the view that the claimant is less worthy as a member of Canadian society, not equally deserving of concern, respect and consideration.[10] The Supreme Court has listed some factors for consideration at this stage of the analysis, such as pre-existing disadvantage, stereotype or vulnerability experienced by the individual or group at issue; the claimant's actual situation; the ameliorative purpose or effects of the impugned law upon a more disadvantaged person or group in society and the nature and scope of the interest affected by the impugned law. Scrutiny under section 15, therefore, facilitates an assessment of the alleged violation which takes account of the social and political setting in which the question arises, with particular emphasis on the remedial purpose of the

---

[7] S 15, therefore, lays down four basic equality rights: the right to equality before the law; the right to equality under the law; the right to equal protection of the law and the right to equal benefit of the law.

[8] [1989] 1 SCR 143.

[9] *Ibid* 165.

[10] *Law v Canada (Minister of Employment and Immigration)* [1999] 1 SCR 497 at 548–9.

Charter.[11] Significantly, the analysis is conducted from the perspective of the rights claimant. Indeed, although dissenting on the facts in *Egan v Canada*,[12] L'Heureux-Dubé J noted that it was preferable to focus on the impact of the law (its discriminatory effect) as opposed to the constituent elements (the grounds of the distinction), the evaluation taking place from the point of view of the victim rather than the state. This view is reinforced by the analytical separation between section 15(1) and section 1 of the Charter. The focus of the section 15 analysis is on whether the rights claimant can show that the impugned law contains a distinction which is discriminatory. Only then does the burden shift to the legislature to prove, under section 1 (which allows a violation to be upheld if it is reasonably justifiable in a free and democratic society)[13] that the infringement of the claimant's right to equality is justified by reference to the objectives of the law in question.

VIEWING THE RIGHTS OF SAME-SEX COUPLES THROUGH THE LENS OF SUBSTANTIVE EQUALITY

The rights of same-sex couples in Canada have been viewed through the lens of section 15 and, with the emphasis on substantive equality and the amelioration of disadvantage, the net result has been the legal assimilation with their functional comparators, unmarried opposite-sex cohabitants. The process has been an incremental one, with earlier Supreme Court decisions spawning a body of caselaw which has directed legislative policy in this area. The genesis of these developments was the Supreme Court decision in *Egan v Canada*[14] where the court held unanimously that sexual orientation is a deeply personal characteristic that is either unchangeable or changeable only at unacceptable personal costs, and so falls within the ambit of section 15 protection as being analogous to the enumerated grounds.[15] A majority of the court also recognised that gays and lesbians

---

[11] In the words of McIntyre J in *Andrews v Law Society of British Columbia* the purpose of section 15(1) is to promote 'a society in which all are secure in the knowledge that they are recognised at law as human beings equally deserving of concern, respect and consideration' [1989] 1 SCR 143 at 171. The provision is, therefore, designed to remedy the imposition of unfair limitations upon opportunities, particularly for those persons or groups who have been subject to historical disadvantage, prejudice, and stereotyping: [1989] 1 SCR 143 at 180–1.

[12] [1995] 2 SCR 513.

[13] See *R v Oakes* [1986] 1 SCR 103. Under s 1, two conditions must be met by the state to justify a Charter violation. Firstly, the objective of the legislation must be pressing and substantial. Secondly, the means chosen to attain this legislative end must be reasonably and demonstrably justifiable in a free and democratic society (as such the rights violation must be rationally connected to the aim of the legislation; the impugned provision must minimally impair the Charter guarantee and there must be proportionality between the effect of the measure and its objective such that the attainment of the legislative objective is not outweighed by the breach of the right).

[14] [1995] 2 SCR 513.

[15] In the *Egan* case, however, the court, by a narrow majority, upheld the impugned legislation which excluded same-sex couples from the provisions of the Old Age Security Act. Lamer CJ, La Forest, Gonthier and Major JJ ruled that same-sex couples are incapable of meeting the fundamental social obligations sought to be protected by Parliament in this instance; that is, unlike heterosexual couples, they do not have the ability to procreate.

'whether as individuals or couples, form an identifiable minority who have suffered and continue to suffer serious social, political and economic disadvantage'.[16] Once the Supreme Court recognised that sexual orientation was an analogous ground of discrimination for the purposes of section 15 and that same-sex couples have suffered historical disadvantage, stereotyping and marginalisation, section 15 proved to be a fertile ground upon which to challenge ideological assumptions and heterosexist discrimination. The invocation of a rights-based dialogue also helped to galvanise a more cohesive and visible body of right claimants who have utilised the momentum generated by Supreme Court decisions to challenge other exclusionary laws. Indeed, unlike the US debate which centred on the right of gays and lesbians to legal marriage, the corollary of which was the polarisation of activists into assimilation versus anti-assimilation positions (Lahey, 1999: 255), the struggle in Canada has focused on more fact-specific individualised questions in the context of non-discrimination protection and the conferral of benefits, such as the right to spousal support on relationship breakdown. Canadian activists have, until now, tended to avoid the same-sex marriage question and, in the alternative, have sought cohabitation rights parallel to those enjoyed by opposite-sex cohabitants (*ibid*, 257–8).[17] The fact that the latter have been gaining legal recognition in Canada since the 1970s meant that there was a substantial body of law which was ripe for challenge in this way.

Indeed, even prior to the enactment of the Charter, both the legislature and the judiciary began to address the issue of unmarried opposite-sex cohabitation and the 1970s saw the enactment of the first legislation which ascribed spousal status to unmarried opposite-sex cohabitants for certain purposes. Paving the way was the province of British Columbia where, in 1972, legislation was passed which gave support rights to opposite-sex partners who had lived together as husband and wife for at least two years.[18] While other provinces followed suit, the more conservative did not. For example, up until 1999 the province of Alberta had not extended the definition of spouse in the spousal support legislation to include opposite-sex cohabitants. The Supreme Court decision in *Miron v Trudel*,[19] however, expedited the process of uniform assimilation. In this case the differential treatment of unmarried opposite-sex cohabitants relative to legally married couples in Ontario's Insurance Act was challenged under section 15. The court held that the exclusion of opposite-sex cohabitants amounted to the

---

[16] *Egan v Canada* [1995] 2 SCR 513 at 602, *per* Cory J.

[17] Similarly, Pícontó Novales (ch 13, this volume) notes that, in Spain, gay rights defence groups are not currently focusing on same-sex marriage as this would do little more than 'divert public attention from important, achievable issues, which would fade into the background if demands for marriage were made … homosexual couples would be left in a legal vacuum'. In the alternative, such groups focus on securing equal treatment for same-sex couples through parallel legal regulation.

[18] British Columbia Family Relations Act, SC 1972, c 20, s 15(e).

[19] [1995] 2 SCR 418.

denial of the equal benefit of the law on the basis of marital status, which was held to be an analogous ground of discrimination for the purposes of section 15. According to the court, while the legislation was designed to protect those who were in financially interdependent relationships with the insured, 'marital status' was not a reasonable marker of these target recipients. Using the fact of 'marital status' to justify reduced legal recognition for unmarried opposite-sex cohabitants was, therefore, held to violate the constitutional prohibition on marital status discrimination enshrined in the Charter, a violation which could not be saved under section 1. The province of Alberta felt the impact of this decision in the 1998 decision of *Taylor v Rossu*[20] where a woman who had cohabited with her male partner for 30 years brought a claim for spousal support. The Alberta Court of Appeal, relying on *Miron v Trudel*, held that the exclusion of opposite-sex cohabitants from the province's spousal support regime violated section 15. This prompted the Alberta legislature to respond and, for a range of purposes, to extend the definition of spouse to include opposite-sex cohabitants who had lived in a 'marriage-like' relationship for three years or who had a child together.[21]

While the law conferred spousal rights and obligations on opposite-sex cohabitants for some purposes prior to the enactment of the Charter, the familial status of same-sex relationships did not, for the most part, receive legal recognition until the advent of Charter-based judicial scrutiny. Up to this point, gay and lesbian rights had been expressed in individualistic terms, specifically the right not to be discriminated against on the grounds of sexual orientation. In the 1970s, Québec was the first province to include sexual orientation in its Human Rights Code, which made it unlawful to discriminate against gays and lesbians in relation to issues such as employment and public accommodation.[22] Most jurisdictions followed suit although the pace of change was not uniform. Alberta's human rights code was only extended to include sexual orientation after the Supreme Court ruled that failure to do so amounted to discrimination under section 15[23] and it was not until 1996 that the federal government passed Bill C-33 to add 'sexual orientation' to the Canadian Human Rights Act.[24] Same-sex relationship recognition did not, however, enter the mainstream political agenda until section 15 was invoked to challenge the differential legal treatment of same-sex cohabitants relative to their opposite-sex counterparts. The fact that by this stage the latter enjoyed similar treatment in law to

---

[20] (1998) 39 RFL (4th) 242 (Alta CA).

[21] SA 1999, c 20, s 2. See Bala and Bromwich (2002) 158.

[22] Québec Charter of Human Rights and Freedoms, RSQ 1977, c C–12, s 10.

[23] *Vriend v Alberta* [1998] 1 SCR 493.

[24] Such an amendment had been introduced as early as 1980 and on several more occasions between 1983 and 1991. In March 1986, the federal government responded to an earlier report issued by the Parliamentary Committee on Equality Rights committing to take whatever measures were necessary to ensure that sexual orientation was a prohibited ground of discrimination in relation to all areas of federal jurisdiction. As indicated, however, the implementation of this measure took a further 10 years.

married couples meant that gays and lesbians were indirectly seeking to acquire the rights and obligations traditionally associated with marriage.[25]

The most extensive and far-reaching functional assimilation between same-sex and opposite-sex unmarried cohabitants came in the 1999 Supreme Court decision of *M v H*.[26] The question before the court was whether the Ontario legislature was justified in excluding same-sex couples from the province's spousal support scheme. The court ruled that the statutory omission subjected same-sex couples to less favourable legal treatment relative to their heterosexual counterparts which amounted to differential treatment on the basis of sexual orientation. This was held to be in violation of section 15 of the Charter and could not be saved under section 1. The province of Ontario was given six months to correct this legislative defect. While technically the decision was limited to the construction of section 29 of the Family Law Act of Ontario, it was a very clear endorsement of the functional assimilation between same-sex and opposite-sex cohabitants and called into question other legislative provisions which made similar distinctions on the basis of sexual orientation. According to the Law Commission of Canada, the net result of the rulings in *Miron v Trudel* and *M v H* has been the establishment of a constitutional requirement that:

> ... governments respect a principle of relational equality, calling into question the validity of all differences in the legal status of married and unmarried (either same-sex or opposite-sex) cohabitants.[27]

The Supreme Court decision in *M v H* has therefore had implications beyond the province of Ontario and, although not all have acted willingly, legislation has been enacted in other Canadian jurisdictions to pre-empt

---

[25] Although it is worth noting that there remained, and still remain, some differences in the legal treatment of married and unmarried cohabitants. Indeed, provincial legislation governing the division of property at the end of the relationship and possessory rights in the family home still do not apply to unmarried couples. Under such legislation, rights in relation to family property arise on the basis of relationship status and not as a result of judicial assessment of the parties' needs and contributions (although on the facts, an unequal distribution can be awarded). In Nova Scotia, for example, the Matrimonial Property Act RSNS 1989, c 275, creates the presumption that the matrimonial assets be divided equally on marriage breakdown, divorce or death of a spouse. Under Ontario's Family Law Act 1986, the value of all property acquired during the marriage by either spouse is divided equally upon the termination of the relationship. Only the Northwest Territories and the Nunavut Territory have family property regimes which equally apply to unmarried opposite-sex cohabitants, Family Law Act SNWT 1997, c 18. See Bala and Bromwich (2002) 177.

[26] [1999] 2 SCR 3. Prior to this there was some indication of a gradual movement towards granting relationship rights to same-sex couples. In *Anderson v Luoma* (1986) 50 RFL (2d) 127 (BCSC) the court held that a same-sex partner could claim a proprietary interest in his/her partner's property by using the constructive trust doctrine in the same manner as an unmarried opposite-sex partner. In *Canada (Attorney General) v Mossop* [1993] 1 SCR 554, while the majority of the Supreme Court held that the denial of bereavement leave to a gay partner was not discrimination on the basis of 'family status' within the meaning of the Canadian Human Rights Act, the dissenting judgments of L'Heureux-Dubé Cory and McLachlin JJ upheld the interpretation of 'family status' within the act to include same-sex couples. In terms of legislative recognition, the province of British Columbia was first to enact legislation extending spousal and parental rights to same-sex couples for certain statutory purposes: Family Relations Amendment Act 1997, SBC 1997, c 20.

[27] Law Commission of Canada (2001) 14. See also Cossman and Ryder (2001) 275.

comparable *Charter* litigation.[28] The typical response has been to extend ascribed spousal status to same-sex couples in which familial rights and obligations are afforded to those who have lived in a conjugal relationship for a prescribed period, typically ranging from one to three years.[29] Other jurisdictions have combined this with the introduction of registration schemes whereby unmarried couples automatically acquire (partial) spousal status once they register their relationship.[30] Significantly, this allows registrants to bypass the requirement of conjugal cohabitation for a prescribed period before acquiring spousal rights and obligations. On 7 June 2002, Québec passed Bill 84 which is the most extensive registration scheme enacted thus far.[31] However, neither affording same-sex couples parallel

[28] For example, in 1999 the province of Ontario enacted the Amendments Because of the Supreme Court of Canada Decision in M v H Act, 1999 (SO 1999, c 6) which created a new legislative category of 'same-sex partner', the definition of spouse remaining limited to married couples or qualifying opposite-sex cohabitants. Both same-sex and opposite-sex partners must have lived together for a continuous period of three years to acquire spousal rights and obligations, although the decision to restrict the concept of spouse to opposite-sex partners demonstrates the legislative reluctance to bestow full spousal status on same-sex couples. By contrast, the government of British Columbia issued a written statement expressing its support for same-sex marriage and subsequently issued legal proceedings against the federal government seeking the right to marry same-sex couples and claiming that the current bar was in violation of the Charter. Although this action was withdrawn by the British Columbia Liberal government when it came to power, the evidence which had previously been filed by the Attorney-General was able to be used in similar proceedings brought by other petitioners. See *EGALE Canada Inc v The Attorney-General of Canada* [2001] BCJ no 1995 (QL).

[29] The federal response to *M v H* was the Modernization of Benefits and Obligations Act, SC 2000, c 12, which amended 68 statutes to bring the legal treatment of same-sex partners into line with that afforded to unmarried opposite-sex couples. The Act created the category of 'common-law partner', defined as 'a person who is cohabiting with [another] individual in a conjugal relationship, having so cohabited for a period of at least one year'. The desire to affirm the common law definition of marriage, however, is made clear by section 1.1 which states that the amendments made by the act 'do not affect the meaning of the word "marriage", that is, the lawful union of one man and one woman to the exclusion of all others'. See Casswell (2001) 818.

[30] Nova Scotia was the first province in Canada to introduce a registered partnership scheme: Law Reform (2000) Act, SSS 2000, c 29, s 53(1), under which registration is open to same-sex and opposite-sex couples who are cohabiting or intend to cohabit in a conjugal relationship.

[31] Registration is open to both same-sex and opposite-sex couples and provides registrants with the same civil rights and obligations as married couples such as survivor benefits, health insurance, parenting rights and access to support on relationship breakdown. The legislation also removes the opposite-sex restriction on marriage from the Québec Civil Code. Art 365 of the code, which previously defined marriage as 'between a man and a woman', has been amended to read 'between two persons'. However, as the federal government has jurisdiction over the capacity to marry, this does not legitimise same-sex marriages in Québec, although it does indicate a willingness on the part of the provincial government of Québec to legislate in favour of same-sex marriage. Acting within its jurisdiction, the government of Québec has gone as far as it can to establish parallel status, rights and obligations for same-sex conjugal relationships. Their intention is clear from the introductory notes to Bill 84—'[t]his bill creates an institution, the civil union, for couples of the opposite or the same sex who wish to make a public commitment to live together as a couple and to uphold the rights and obligations stemming from such status. ... The bill also amends the Civil Code and other legislation to formalize recognition of the new status of civil union spouses, who will have the same rights and obligations as married couples ....' For the text of the bill, see http://www.assnat.qc.ca/eng/Publications/Projets-loi/Publics/02-a084.htm.

spousal rights and obligations by the process of ascription, nor the availability of registration schemes has quelled the demand for same-sex marriage. Indeed, the Law Commission of Canada in its recent report *Beyond Conjugality* stated that:

> the issue of same-sex marriage cannot be avoided ... The status quo or even the creation of a registration system will not prevent the *Charter* challenges. The introduction of a registration scheme should not be seen as a policy alternative to reforming marriage. Registration schemes in lieu of allowing same-sex couples to access marriage are seen, by those in favour of same-sex marriage, as creating a second-class category of relationships.[32]

The issue of same-sex marriage has thus re-emerged as the next significant question to be tackled by the Supreme Court. That it is now raised against the backdrop of the conferral of spousal rights and obligations on same-sex couples either by ascription or registration alters its substance as the focus is clearly on the denial of choice and the symbolism associated with this.

THE LEGALISATION OF SAME-SEX MARRIAGE

In 2001, challenges were launched in Québec,[33] British Columbia and Ontario against the legal impediment to same-sex marriage. This is not unchartered judicial territory. In 1993, an Ontario Appeal Court dismissed a challenge by a same-sex couple who claimed that the bar on same-sex marriage violated their constitutional right to equality. Based on the argument that heterosexual procreation was the defining purpose of marriage, the majority of the court held that the exclusionary marriage laws did not violate the Charter.[34] Accepting procreation as the principal purpose of marriage allowed the court to conclude that the exclusion of same-sex couples was due to their incapacity to meet the core definitional requirements of marriage as opposed to any 'personal characteristics' (ie sexual

---

[32] Law Commission of Canada (2001) 130.

[33] The Québec hearing concluded in November 2001 but the Justice ordered that the case be reopened the following year in order to review the impact of the newly enacted civil unions bill: see n 31. Since this chapter was written, the Québec Superior Court has ruled that the bar on same-sex marriage violates the equality guarantee of the Charter: see n 3.

[34] *Layland v Ontario (Minister of Consumer & Commercial Relations)* (1993) 14 OR (3d) 658 (Div Ct). Greer J dissented in this case ruling that as 'choice' is a benefit of the law, denying the applicants their right to choose whom they wished to marry was an infringement of section 15(1) which was not saved by section 1 of the Charter. *Re North and Matheson* (1975) 52 DLR (3d) 280 is an example of a pre-Charter challenge to the legality of the bar on same-sex marriage. An application was brought under section 35(1) of the Vital Statistics Act of Manitoba for an order requiring the acceptance of an application to register the marriage of the applicants who were in a same-sex relationship. The Manitoba Court held that the common law definition of marriage was exclusively heterosexual in nature. In the absence of the constitutionally enshrined equality guarantee, there were no legal grounds upon which the applicants could challenge this bar.

orientation).[35] This is not a new argument in the jurisprudence of the Supreme Court and it has been used at two different stages of the analytical framework under the Charter. In *Layland*, the argument was employed to negate, in the first instance, the claim that section 15 was breached. In the more recent decision of *EGALE Canada Inc v The Attorney-General of Canada*,[36] the Supreme Court of British Columbia held that while the discriminatory effect of the bar on same-sex marriage violated section 15 of the Charter, it was saved under section 1. Preserving the original constitutional understanding of marriage as a heterosexual institution was held to be a 'pressing and substantial' objective on the basis that marriage is the primary means by which humankind perpetuates itself in society. Relying on the core biological distinction between same-sex and heterosexual relations, the court concluded that it is not possible to equate same-sex relationships with marriage while simultaneously preserving the fundamental importance of marriage to the community.[37] Conceptualising the institution of marriage as the core social framework for biological procreation allowed the court to justify its primacy and declare it to be exclusively heterosexual.[38] In the most recent challenge to the exclusionary marriage laws, however, the Ontario Superior Court of Justice has reached a different conclusion. Indeed, the judgments in this case are in line with commentators' predictions that the analysis and rhetoric of the majority judgments in *M v H* suggest that the court may be sympathetic in future cases to an argument that the exclusion of same-sex couples from legal marriage is an affront to their 'human dignity' (Bala and Bromwich, 2002: 162).

On 12 June 2002, the Ontario Superior Court of Justice held unanimously in *Halpern v The Attorney-General of Canada*[39] that the legal impediment to same-sex marriage, which derives from the common law definition of marriage as 'the voluntary union for life of one man and one

---

[35] See Mazzotta (ch 12, this volume) who observes similar arguments surrounding the inability of same-sex couples to biologically procreate in social and legal thought in Italy.

[36] [2001] BCJ no 1995 (QL).

[37] *Ibid*, para 211. A consideration of the Charter challenges was largely a redundant exercise in this case anyway as the court held that marriage was a constitutionally defined term and, as such, could only be amended by the formal constitutional amendment process (the Charter could not be used to invalidate another constitutional provision). Any attempt by the federal Parliament to change the meaning of marriage, which was understood as a 'monogamous opposite-sex relationship' when the Constitution was drafted, would amount to a unilateral amendment to the Constitution.

[38] In the words of Pitfield J 'the state has a demonstrably genuine justification in affording recognition, preference and precedence to the nature and character of the core social and legal arrangement by which society endures': *ibid*, para 207.

[39] 2002 Ont Sup CJ LEXIS 1417.

woman to the exclusion of all others',[40] violated section 15(1) of the Charter and could not be saved under section 1. The judgment of Blair RSJ made it quite clear at the outset that the correct decision was to uphold the applicant's challenge:

> the constitutional and Charter-inspired values which underlie Canadian society today dictate that the status and incidents inherent in the foundational institution of marriage must be open to same-sex couples who live in long-term, committed, relationships—marriage-like in everything but name—just as it is to heterosexual couples. Each is entitled to full and equal recognition, and the law must therefore be adapted accordingly.[41]

The guiding principles underlying the judgment are clear from this preliminary statement, that is, that same-sex couples can and do form 'marriage-like' relationships and, as such, should be allowed to acquire both the status and incidents of marriage. The fact that same-sex couples have already been afforded spousal rights and obligations by the process of ascription or voluntary registration meant that the real issue was the conferral of the right to choose the status. The target outcome, therefore, was the realisation of full equality under the law although the crux of the case was the court's view of the purpose of marriage, in particular the role of heterosexual procreation.

While marriage has historically been understood as a heterosexual institution for the purposes of procreation, Blair RSJ considered this to be an outdated view. Taking note of scientific advances which mean that it is possible for children to be born to same-sex couples through procedures such as artificial insemination or in vitro fertilisation, he challenged the view that heterosexual intercourse leading to procreation was the factor which gave marriage 'its principal rationale and unique heterosexual nature'.[42] In de-emphasising the centrality of heterosexual procreation, Blair RSJ provided a holistic vision of marriage and the relationship of parties to a marriage:

> marriage is more fully characterized ... by its pivotal child-rearing role, and by a long-term conjugal relationship between two individuals—with its attendant

---

[40] *Hyde v Hyde and Woodmansee* (1866) LR 1 P&D 130 at 133, *per* Lord Penzance. While the federal Parliament has exclusive authority to legislate in relation to the 'capacity' to marry under section 91(26) of the Constitution Act 1982 (provincial jurisdiction is limited to the 'solemnization' or celebration of marriage under section 92(12)), the court found that there was no statutory impediment to the issuance of marriage licences to same-sex couples who otherwise meet the requisite criteria for legal marriage. The only federal pronouncement on the issue of 'capacity' to marry based upon gender is found in the recently enacted Modernization of Benefits and Obligations Act which, as previously noted, provides that 'marriage' for the purposes of the act means the 'lawful union of one man and one woman to the exclusion of all others'. In the present case, the court held that the intention of this Act was not to define marriage and that this particular legislative pronouncement could not be relied upon as such, although it is indicative of what Parliament considers the definition of marriage to be: 2002 Ont Sup CJ LEXIS 1417, para 97.

[41] 2002 Ont Sup CJ LEXIS 1417, para 32, *per* Blair RSJ.

[42] *Ibid*, para 69.

obligations and offerings of mutual care and support, of companionship and shared social activities, of intellectual and moral and faith-based stimulation as a couple, and of shared shelter and economic and psychological interdependence—and by love. These are the indicia of the purpose of marriage in modern Canadian society.[43]

Blair RSJ thus adopted a functional approach to defining marriage which de-emphasised the biological fact of procreation in favour of asexual functions such as child rearing, companionship, love, care and economic and emotional inter-dependency. Defining marriage in such broad functional terms, read in conjunction with previous Supreme Court jurisprudence which accepted that same-sex couples can and do live in long-term, financially and emotionally inter-dependent relationships,[44] Blair RSJ concluded that there were no legal grounds upon which to justify exclusionary marriage laws.

The impact of the Charter in facilitating this decision is clear. Firstly, section 15(1) allowed the claimants to subject exclusionary marriage laws to judicial scrutiny. Secondly, the outcome depended upon the court's understanding of marriage which, in turn, was directed by the underlying values of the Charter. The nature of section 15 means that the courts are mandated to take a purposive and contextual approach to the question under consideration, paying particular attention to the remedial purpose of the provision in promoting equality and preventing discrimination arising from stereotyping, prejudice and historical wrongs. Given the dramatically shifting attitudes towards marriage and procreation, Blair RSJ had difficulty in holding that heterosexual procreation was the 'compelling and central aspect of marriage in 21st century post-Charter Canadian society'.[45] In other words, looking at the question through the 'prism of Charter rights and values' meant that, for Blair RSJ, the court was obliged to adopt a contemporary vision of marriage unfettered by the historical emphasis on heterosexual procreation. That Supreme Court jurisprudence had already deconstructed the stereotypical characterisation of same-sex relationships meant that Blair RSJ was simply applying accepted judicial principles when holding that the functions of same-sex relationships are approximate to his vision of marriage as a long-term, loving, conjugal relationship.

The judgment of LaForme J did not focus on the 'internal functions' of the marital relationship, accepting at the outset that same-sex relationships can be functionally synonymous with the normative husband-wife dyad. Instead, the judgment was premised on the external social legitimacy conferred by marriage. Accepting the 'pre-existing disadvantage, vulnerability, stereotyping and prejudice' experienced by gays and lesbians, LaForme J

---

[43] *Ibid*, para 71.
[44] *M v H* [1999] 2 SCR 3.
[45] 2002 Ont Sup CJ LEXIS 1417, para 61.

concluded that their exclusion from the optimum conjugal status within society 'reflects and reinforces' stereotypical assumptions about gay and lesbian relationships, thus perpetuating their stigmatisation:

> [e]xcluding gays and lesbians from marriage disregards the needs, capacities and circumstances of same-sex spouses and their children. It declares an entire class of persons unworthy of the recognition and support of state sanction for their marriages. In sum, marriage—as it is currently defined—fails to harmonise with or take into account the issues of gays and lesbians.[46]

In reaching this conclusion, LaForme J focused on the symbolic impact of the exclusion and took a wide interpretation of 'benefit' under the law, thus relying upon the analysis of the majority judgments in *M v H*. The majority in *M v H* recognised that 'choice' is a benefit of the law, holding that section 15(1) encompassed not only the actual conferral of an 'economic benefit' but also access to a court-enforced procedure that could result in the conferral of an economic benefit.[47] In terms of the symbolism associated with the statutory exclusion in question, the majority of the court recognised that this had moral and societal implications as well as economic ones.[48] In the words of Cory J:

> [t]he societal significance of the benefit conferred by the statute cannot be overemphasized. The exclusion of same-sex partners ... promotes the view ... [that] individuals in same-sex relationships generally, are less worthy of recognition and protection. It implies that they are judged to be incapable of forming intimate relationships of economic interdependence as compared to opposite-sex couples, without regard to their actual circumstances ... such exclusion perpetuates the disadvantages suffered by individuals in same-sex relationships and contributes to the erasure of their existence.[49]

In *Halpern*, LaForme J borrowed this analytical framework. In terms of 'choice', the applicants were denied their right to choose whom they wished to marry. This denied them the equal opportunity to participate in society and perpetuated their stereotypical characterisation. Indeed, with specific reference to *M v H*, LaForme J took the view that the symbolic impact of exclusion from marriage was, at the very least, commensurate with exclusion from spousal support legislation. It is clear, therefore, that the symbolic impact of the exclusion became the focus of the analysis under section 15 as opposed to any residual economic benefits which would flow from giving same-sex couples the right to marry.[50]

---

[46] *Ibid*, para 202.
[47] [1999] 2 SCR 3, para 66, *per* Cory J.
[48] *Ibid*, paras 71–72 and 124.
[49] *Ibid*, para 73.
[50] As previously noted, certain spousal rights, notably in relation to family property, continue to be withheld from same-sex and unmarried opposite-sex couples. See n 25.

The heterosexual definition of marriage violated section 15 of the Charter on the basis that it drew a substantive distinction on the grounds of sexual orientation that withheld the equal benefit of the law in a manner that offends the human dignity of gays and lesbians. The question of whether this infringement could be justified under section 1 turned on the issue of procreation.[51] On this point, LaForme J found no evidence by which to conclude that procreation is the essential purpose of marriage and went on to suggest that this argument could be viewed as a pretext in order to rationalise the discriminatory exclusion of same-sex couples.[52] Indeed, one could argue that if procreation were held to be the defining characteristic of marriage, it would be both under-inclusive and over-inclusive.[53] The court, therefore, concluded unanimously that the bar on same-sex marriage violated section 15 of the Charter and could not be justified under section 1. While the court disagreed over the appropriate remedy, the majority suspended the ruling for 24 months to enable Parliament to amend the law accordingly. In response, however, the Minister of Justice has indicated that the Government of Canada will appeal the decision. While accepting that 'the existence of a committed relationship is of great importance to our lives, whether for opposite-sex couples or same-sex couples' the Minister continued that

> there are important reasons why we as a society must consider carefully the issues around changing the fundamental nature of marriage and what the implications of such a change might be.[54]

It is likely, therefore, that this issue will reach the Supreme Court.

The Canadian experience is an exemplar of how relational rights can develop in a libertarian rights-focused socio-legal culture (Bala and Bromwich, 2002: 149). The legal assimilation between same-sex and opposite-sex couples has developed from the spate of judicial victories throughout the 1990s as the robust equality framework of the Charter has been used to challenge opposite-sex definitions of spouse. Once sexual orientation was accepted as an analogous ground of discrimination for the purposes of section 15(1) and gays and lesbians were regarded by the Supreme

---

[51] Although, according to LaForme J, a section 1 analysis was not strictly necessary as the impugned law was a judge-made common law and not a legislative provision. 2002 Ont Sup C J LEXIS 1417, paras 222–8.

[52] *Ibid*, para 242.

[53] *M v H* [1999] 2 SCR 3, para 113.

[54] The Honourable Martin Cauchon, Minister of Justice and Attorney-General of Canada, Press Release, 29 July 2002, http://canada.justice.gc.ca/en/news/nr/2002/doc_30624.html. On 12 Nov 2002, the Minister asked the House of Commons Standing Committee on Justice and Human Rights to consider whether, and to what extent, Parliament should take measures to recognise same-sex unions in light of the constitutional framework and the traditional meaning of marriage. It appears that the Committee will present recommendations on possible legislative reform by April 2003. See http://canada.justice.gc.ca/en/news/nr/002/doc_30740.html.

Court as being subject to pre-existing disadvantage, vulnerability, stereotyping and prejudice,[55] the analytical framework of the Charter became a very useful reform strategy. In particular, viewing under-inclusive legislation through the lens of the rights claimant and within the broader context of society's treatment of the claimant and other persons with the same or similar characteristics or circumstances,[56] allowed the symbolic impact of exclusion to found a claim of discriminatory treatment under section 15(1). In such a climate, exclusionary marriage laws have become ripe for judicial challenge and, as some suggest, the principles established by previous decisions make a favourable outcome likely in the Supreme Court (Bala and Bromwich, 2002: 162). On one hand, this could be seen as the ultimate progressive step, certainly when compared to the position in other jurisdictions where same-sex relational rights have yet to receive any significant space in socio-political dialogue.[57] It certainly represents the culmination of the equality discourse as it has evolved in Canada. Considering the issues in the context of family law policy more generally however, one must question the progressiveness of the outcomes reached by pursuing the goal of 'relational equality'. The next section will consider the relative merits of such an approach.

HOW PROGRESSIVE IS THE 'RELATIONAL EQUALITY' AGENDA?

The legalisation of same-sex marriage is a sensitive socio-political issue which attracts strong polarised opinions. Indeed, it has long since been recognised by commentators as a question which typifies the binarism of the well-known assimilationist/anti-assimilationist debate.[58] From a critical perspective, the demand for the legalisation of same-sex marriage is an acutely visible commitment to the principle of relational assimilation, affirming the status of marriage in society and representing a powerful endorsement of existing norms. In broad terms, the principle of 'conjugal relational equality' (Cossman and Ryder, 2001: 277)[59] which has taken hold in Canada is open to critique on the grounds that it takes 'spousal status' as the primary point of reference and thus reinforces the traditional model of

---

[55] *Egan v Canada* [1995] 2 SCR 513.

[56] *Law v Canada (Minister of Employment and Immigration)* [1999] 1 SCR 497, para 59, *per* Iacobucci J.

[57] See Mazzotta (ch 12, this volume) who observes that, in Italy, despite increasing social tolerance towards gays and lesbians, the Catholic tradition 'remains dominant in social, political and cultural life'. This means that same-sex relationships are currently denied legal recognition and, in terms of reform, the legalisation of same-sex marriage is not an immediate prospect.

[58] See eg Stoddard (1992); Ettelbrick (1992); Hunter (1991); Duclos (1991); Cossman (1994).

[59] According to Cossman and Ryder, this principle calls into question 'the validity of all differences in the legal status of married and unmarried (either same-sex or opposite-sex) cohabitants' (at 275). This is echoed by the Law Commission of Canada in report (2001) 14.

legitimate family relationship.[60] Indeed, judicial and legislative developments have reconstituted the archetypal family form, the marital model, to encompass structurally similar unions through extensive ascription and/or registration. Same-sex couples have thus been given legally equivalent spousal status for a range of purposes outside of a policy debate on the distribution of rights and obligations between adult partners. In a similar vein, Cossman and Ryder admit that the ruling in *M v H* was groundbreaking in that the Supreme Court recognised the 'conjugal nature of same-sex relationships', but point out that the court did not actually discuss the substantive nature of spousal relationships:

> [i]n fact, the ruling in *M v H* steered away from an extensive policy discussion of the meaning of spouse.   (Cossman and Ryder, 2001: 293)

Legal policy in Canada has thus been driven by a formal equality approach to the allocation of familial rights and responsibilities. On the one hand, the Charter has been a powerful tool in the amelioration of historical disadvantage and prejudice, but its remedial nature has also worked to contextualise familial rights and responsibilities from the perspective of an excluded claimant. In terms of gay and lesbian rights, the questions have thus been framed around the legal challenge to opposite-sex definitions of spouse, an approach which has silenced any meaningful debate on, inter alia, the incidence on inter-relationship oppression, expectation levels and normative interdependencies in same-sex relationships.[61] Indeed, without critiquing the assumptions made about spousal relations and problematising their application in the context of same-sex relationships, judicial and legislative responses to the demand for 'conjugal relational equality' have extended spousal status to those whose relationships are deemed to be analogically

---

[60] See eg Ettelbrick (1992), Gavigan (1993), Polikoff (1993), Herman (1990). Cottier (ch 11, this volume) similarly draws attention to the limitations of the equality agenda, in particular the fact that gays and lesbians are judged against the marital model of family form which 'means that there is no room for their own definition of how their partnerships should be regulated'. Indeed, Cottier asserts that the 'claim for equality has been an impediment' to a broader discussion of the needs, values and social reality of those who live in domestic relationships. Vaz Tomé (ch 18, this volume) also notes that current challenges to the concept of family reinforce the marital relationship as the model to which other forms of intimate relationship should aspire.

[61] Reflecting similar concerns, the Ontario Law Reform Commission concluded in a 1993 Report that 'we do not have adequate evidence ... about the nature of relationships between same-sex cohabitants and the expectations of members of those relationships to justify imposing [spousal] rights and obligations upon them. ... [I]n the absence of better information ... it would be inappropriate to impose substantial economic rights and obligations on a group of citizens without adequate information about their experience and needs' (Ontario Law Reform Commission, *Report on the Rights and Responsibilities of Cohabitants under the Family Law Act* (1993) 56–8). Cottier (ch 11) points out that the preliminary draft law on registered partnerships in Switzerland assumes that opposite-sex relationships and same-sex relationships adopt different patterns of internal organisation. It is assumed that the latter are comprised of 'two economically independent adults who do not share the project of raising children' and are thus more egalitarian in nature.

expressive of the marital model of family form. Fineman, in challenging the centrality of the sexual family in socio-legal thinking, critiques such an approach on the basis that it simply extends existing norms rather than offering any 'transformative potential' (Diduck, 2001: 291):

> '[l]iberals' seek to expand the traditional nuclear-family model, urging the recognition of informal heterosexual unions within the definition of the family. There are also calls for acceptance and legal legitimation of same-sex relationships. ... But these reforms merely reinforce the idea of the sexual family. By duplicating the privileged form, alternative relationships merely affirm the centrality of sexuality to the fundamental ordering of society and the nature of intimacy.   (Fineman, 1995: 143)

Reflecting such concerns, other commentators are taking a more root and branch approach, looking at the actual nature of familial rights and responsibilities and not just the breadth of their application in current form.[62] For example, the changing patterns of adult relationships as a result of, inter alia, the displacement of the male breadwinner/female homemaker model of family economics means that for some commentators, the dilemma at the beginning of the 21st century is how far adult family members should be treated as independent individuals (Lewis, 2000: 82). In a similar vein, others comment that financial need and entitlement to societal resources should not be predicated on family status but should be measured by taking the individual as the 'unit of administration' (Eichler, 1997: 124–144).[63] For example, Cossman and Ryder state that in the context of income security schemes, 'relationship status is simply a poor proxy for actual financial needs' (Cossman and Ryder, 2001: 312).[64] By contrast, the approach taken in Canada thus far does not disturb existing assumptions about the role of the family in the provision of financial support, nor does it disturb the assumed nature of spousal relations. The rights-focused discourse, by its very nature, reinforces the dominant paradigm, which 'privileges the [sexual] couple as foundational and fundamental' (Fineman, 1995: 145), and leaves unchallenged existing methods for the distribution of societal resources. Even the most recent indication of legal policy which purports to challenge the centrality of conjugality in family law, fails to deliver any real potential for the development of a new family ideology. In its report, *Beyond Conjugality*, the Law Commission of Canada recommends the legal

---

[62] See Vaz Tomé (ch 18) for a discussion of Portuguese family law and, in particular, the interaction between the family, society and the state. Vaz Tomé critiques current perceptions of the family as a social institution with responsibility for dependent members, a view which, according to Vaz Tomé, perpetuates the gendered division of domestic labour and frustrates the development of truly egalitarian relationships.

[63] See also Deech (1980).

[64] The authors go on to state, however, that relationships continue to be relevant to legislative objectives in some contexts, such as the division of family income and property on relationship breakdown.

recognition of a range of non-conjugal relationships. Calling into question existing reliance on relationship status in determining the allocation of familial rights and responsibilities, the report recommends that the law respond to the 'factual attributes' of relationships rather than their formal status.[65] Defining the state's role in the organisation of domestic relationships as providing an orderly framework to facilitate the voluntary assumption of rights and obligations, the report recommends the legalisation of same-sex marriage and the introduction of a registration scheme for those in both conjugal and non-conjugal relationships. The imposition of rights and obligations by the process of ascription, although considered to be a 'blunt policy tool' in the regulation of relationships, has a residual place in the recommendations in order to prevent exploitation in conjugal relationships. It was deemed, however, to be inappropriate for non-conjugal relationships. Although the report claims to rethink the way in which governments regulate adult relationships, by retaining the presumptive privileges accorded to marriage and recommending the introduction of a registration scheme to give legal expression to the voluntary assumption of a package of legal rights and responsibilities, the proposals simply add another layer of 'status-based' relationship to come under the rubric of legal regulation without altering or seriously challenging existing status-based indicators of family.

THE SEQUENTIAL NATURE OF REFORM

It is clear, therefore, that legal reform and even the latest policy thinking in Canada leaves unresolved many live issues in contemporary family law policy, such as, normative interdependencies and expectations in conjugal and non-conjugal adult relationships, the centrality of status-based indicators in the distribution of familial rights and obligations, the role of the family in the provision of economic support (Diduck, 2001; Boyd, 1994, 1996) and the interaction between the family and the state.[66] It is submitted, however, that such issues can be viewed as conceptually distinct from the equality agenda as it relates to the social and legal treatment of gays and lesbians. Contrary to the arguments of some 'anti-assimilationist' protagonists, supporting 'relational equality' does not necessarily represent unqualified acceptance of current norms. Indeed, to support full 'relational equality' is not to suggest that the current understanding of the family and its role within society remains unaltered or that the nuclear sexual family continues to

---

[65] Law Commission of Canada (2001).

[66] It is for such reasons that Diduck critiques the English House of Lords decision in *Fitzpatrick v Sterling Housing Association* [1999] 4 All ER 705 where the court included a same-sex partner within the legal understanding of 'family' for the purposes of the Rent Act 1977. Indeed, in relation to *Fitzpatrick* and the Supreme Court of Canada decision in *M v H*, Diduck concludes that neither challenged normative assumptions of familial 'duties or functions' nor questioned the relationship between the family and the state. Diduck (2001) 305.

occupy a privileged position in family ideology. The legal assimilation between same-sex and opposite-sex couples does not, and should not, preclude a wider debate on the legal and social functions of the family and its interaction with the state. Once 'conjugal relational equality' has been achieved, it must thus take its place within socio-political dialogue concerning the substantive nature of familial rights and obligations which are bestowed on the basis of marriage, ascription or some form of registration. One can, therefore, view the law reform process as sequential with gay and lesbian rights and the substantive nature and allocation of familial rights and responsibilities, such as financial support, ownership and occupation rights in the family home and entitlement to pension, inheritance and other such benefits, as distinct aspects of reform.

Locating 'relational equality' within this broader reform agenda helps to refute the concerns of those who point to the potential costs of this strategy. Boyd, for example, argues that the:

> positive symbolic benefits of legitimating (some) lesbian and gay relationships by calling them 'family' ... must be balanced against the stigmatizing effects [on] those lesbian and gay individuals who are not in 'conjugal' relationships.
> (Boyd, 1994: 555)

Two points can be made in response to this. Firstly, such a concern would warrant greater consideration if 'relational equality' was taken to be the end product with those who fall outside of the paradigm of the conjugal family continuing to suffer social and legal marginalisation. As indicated, however, gay and lesbian relational rights do not have to be located exclusively within the assimilationist/anti-assimilationist debate. In the alternative, 'relational equality' can be viewed as forming part of a continuum leading to a more transformative vision of the family and its relationship with the state. Secondly, the concern for gays and lesbians who do not conform to the paradigm of the conjugal family should not be any greater than for heterosexuals whose relationships similarly do not conform to this model. Certainly such concerns have not prevented the 'marital model' of family form from acting as the reference point for heterosexual relationships. Indeed, in Canada unmarried opposite-sex couples have enjoyed spousal status for quite some time. Such developments mean that, regardless of the debate surrounding the validity of the assimilationist strategy, subjecting gays and lesbians to continued differential treatment violates their equality rights and perpetuates their stereotypical characterisation as deviant (Ryder, 1990: 46–8). For this reason it would be pre-emptive to jettison 'relational equality' as the first step in favour of a more immediate challenge to existing social and legal norms. There is much to lose by failing to challenge relational inequality on the basis of sexual orientation. In the words of Dalton:

the social and moral costs of leaving state-sponsored discrimination unchallenged are quite high.   (Dalton, 1991: 4)

Considering the social backdrop of the historical disadvantage, prejudice and stereotype suffered by gays and lesbians, pursuing equality for same-sex relationships by assimilation with their heterosexual counterparts is a necessary aspect of the reform process in order to legitimise fully such relationships in social consciousness.[67] It is for this reason that the rights of gays and lesbians must be viewed as an issue for equality-discourse and not as the vehicle to pursue a more transformative ideology of the family. In this sense the Canadian approach has much to recommend it. While the 'relational equality' agenda may not provide comprehensive answers to the many issues which must be addressed by family-policymakers, this neither invalidates the strategy nor renders it redundant. Indeed, Boyd notes the suggestion of some commentators that:

> achieving formal equality is a necessary first step after which questions can be raised about the overall scheme through which we distribute wealth and resources.   (Boyd, 1994: 556)[68]

The logical culmination of the equality discourse in Canada is the removal of the bar on same-sex marriage. MacDougall identifies three sites in the field of rights-discourse—compassion, condonation and celebration which respectively correspond to the underlying nature of the rights fought for in Canada, from the enactment of non-discrimination protection and the conferral of benefits to the positive legal integration of the gay and lesbian community into the fabric of society by same-sex marriage (MacDougall, 2000: 253). Real equality in individual and relational terms requires the state's 'acceptance and celebration' of the group (*ibid* 254) which can be expressed through the legalisation of same-sex marriage but which cannot be achieved against the backdrop of the disadvantageous symbolic impact the bar currently has in society. MacDougall concludes:

> for the state to be involved in celebration means that which is celebrated is not just acceptable but in fact is good. In the context of a group like gays and lesbians, celebration means that society not only accepts or condones this group but approves of it ... [While] benefits may flow from the celebration ... the point of the discourse at this site is not merely these benefits but the celebration itself and what that means for the members of the group and the group itself.   (MacDougall, 2000: 256–7)

---

[67] See Cottier (ch 11) for a discussion of the views of gay and lesbian rights organisations in Switzerland who similarly regard the equality agenda and the quest for same-sex marriage as symbolically important in achieving 'public recognition of the homosexual way of life'.

[68] In a similar vein, Herman notes that '[t]he official acknowledgement that lesbians and gay men form important, useful personal relationships may need to precede rights and entitlements being offered on a different basis': Herman (1992) 147.

The legalisation of same-sex marriage is thus a necessary part of the equality agenda, particularly in Canada where the practical legal assimilation between opposite-sex and same-sex couples has so far been extensive. Indeed, the significance of previous assimilationist decisions such as *M v H* could be downplayed on the basis that individual assessments are fact-specific, thus allowing the rejection of claims from those not involved in financially interdependent relationships. Including couples within the statutory spousal support regime simply gives access to a court-enforced procedure to determine the financial obligations which may be held to subsist at the end of a relationship. The net result is that same-sex couples are deemed to be capable of conforming to the normative husband–wife dyad with its attendant financial integration and dependencies, but that the individual assessment of applications will facilitate the rejection of non-conforming relationships. By contrast, the right to marry is not subject to individual assessment and would be open to all same-sex couples who otherwise meet the requisite criteria for legal marriage. In many ways, therefore, the legalisation of same-sex marriage is a more powerful endorsement of the legitimacy of same-sex relationships. In *Halpern*, the most recent instalment in the evolutionary development of same-sex relational rights in Canada, LaForme J takes a similar view of the relevance of same-sex marriage to the social citizenship of members of the gay and lesbian community and, within the debate, correctly locates the legalisation of same-sex marriage as a transition from tolerance to equality.

In short, therefore, there are more positives than negatives with the Canadian approach, particularly when challenging the legitimacy of 'cultural heterosexism'.[69] The removal of the bar on same-sex marriage avoids leaving gays and lesbians subject to the damaging historical legacy of lawful differential treatment on the grounds of sexual orientation. In terms of how gays and lesbians are socially perceived, this is just as significant as, and may in fact contribute to, the development of a new ideology for the allocation of familial rights and responsibilities.

CONCLUSION

A legitimate question to pose at the beginning of the 21st century is whether the law is responding in an appropriate way to meet the expectations of those within domestic relationships. By failing to challenge normative assumptions about spousal relationships and by failing to problematise the application of existing norms to same-sex relationships, the Canadian reforms do not provide a comprehensive answer to this question. For many commentators, the pursuit of same-sex marriage deflects attention from revisioning policy in terms which would not only foster gender equality and

---

[69] *Halpern v The Attorney-General of Canada* 2002 Ont Sup CJ LEXIS 1417, para 181.

contribute to the development of more egalitarian relationships but would call into question the normative legal and social functions of the family. Indeed, the problems associated with the equality discourse are well documented (Hunter, 1991: 27). From a feminist perspective, same-sex marriage, as a strategy, is not transformative, doing little more than perpetuating a patriarchal institution which legitimises the economic and sexual subordination of women.[70] Boyd, for example, states that seeking family status may:

> reinforce the history of heterosexist and patriarchal family law and support its use to privatize economic responsibility for dependent persons.
>
> (Boyd, 1994: 548)

Without denying the limitations inherent in the assimilation strategy, it is too harsh to label the Canadian approach as regressive. It is progressive when located within the equality agenda in terms of breaking down homophobic societal beliefs and practices. Indeed, the protection of the individual rights of gays and lesbians and the legitimation of same-sex relational rights is a fundamental aspect of 'normalising' (Owen, 2001) gays and lesbians in social consciousness. As an aspiration, this can be viewed as conceptually distinct from the resolution of broader family policy issues which require, for example, changes in the infrastructure of the market in order to reconstitute the typical gendered division of domestic labour in marriage and other domestic relationships.[71] To support same-sex marriage, however, is not to deny the importance of a meaningful debate on such issues, but gay and lesbian relational rights should not become the vehicle by which to pursue an alternative understanding of the family, of relationships within the family and of the relationship between the family and the state. That gays and lesbians have historically been subject to pre-existing disadvantage and stereotype reinforces the view that their legal treatment deserves consideration as a distinct aspect of social and legal reform. Once full 'relational equality' has been secured, more fundamental questions can be raised about the nature of relational rights and obligations for both same-sex and opposite-sex couples. In the words of MacDougall:

> [i]t is possible that marriage is one of the social institutions that needs to be reformed, but gays and lesbians can participate in that reform from within rather than being required to wait on the sidelines until others have solved the problems.   (MacDougall, 2000: 266)

---

[70] There is some disagreement over the potential of same-sex marriage to disturb normative gendered power relations within marriage. cf eg Hunter (1991) with Duclos (1991).

[71] Fineman, for example, states that 'far from structurally accommodating or facilitating caretaking ... workplaces operate in modes incompatible with the idea that workers also have obligations for dependency' (Fineman, 2000: 21). See Vaz Tomé (ch 18, this volume).

REFERENCES

Bala, N and Bromwich RJ (2002) 'Context and Inclusivity in Canada's Evolving Definition of the Family' *International Journal of Law, Policy and the Family* 16: 145–180.

Boyd, S (1994) 'Expanding the "Family" in Family Law: Recent Ontario Proposals on Same Sex Relationships' *Canadian Journal of Women and the Law* 7(2): 545–563.

—— (1996) 'Best Friends or Spouses? Privatization and the Recognition of Lesbian Relationships in *M v H*' *Canadian Journal of Family Law* 17: 321.

—— (2000) 'The Impact of the Charter of Rights and Freedoms on Canadian Family Law' *Canadian Journal of Family Law* 17: 293.

Casswell, DG (2001) 'Moving Toward Same-Sex Marriage' *Canadian Bar Review* 80: 810–856.

Cossman, B (1994) 'Family Inside/Out' *University of Toronto Law Journal* 1: 9.

Cossman, B and Ryder B (2001) 'What is Marriage-Like Like?' *Canadian Journal of Family Law* 18(2): 267–326.

Dalton, HL (1991) 'Reflections on the Lesbian and Gay Marriage Debate' *Law and Sexuality* 1(1): 1–8.

Deech, R (1980) 'The Case Against Legal Recognition of Cohabitation' *International and Comparative Law Quarterly* 29: 480.

Diduck, A (2001) 'A Family by Any Other Name … or Starbucksä Comes to England' *Journal of Law and Society* 28(2): 290–310.

Duclos, N (1991) 'Some Complicating Thoughts on Same-Sex Marriage' *Law and Sexuality* 1(1): 31–61.

Eichler, M (1997) *Family Shifts: Families, Policies and Gender Equality* (Toronto, Oxford University Press).

Ettelbrick, P (1992) 'Since When is Marriage a Path to Liberation?' in S Suzanne (ed), *Lesbian and Gay Marriage: Private Commitments, Public Ceremonies* (Philadelphia, Temple University Press).

Fineman, M (1995) *The Neutered Mother, the Sexual Family and other Twentieth-Century Tragedies* (New York, Routledge).

—— (2000) 'Cracking the Foundational Myths: Independence, Autonomy, and Self-Sufficiency' *Journal of Gender, Social Policy and the Law* 8(1) 13–29.

Gavigan, SAM (1993) 'Paradise Lost, Paradox Revisited: The Implications of Familial Ideology for Feminist, Lesbian and Gay Engagement to Law' *Osgoode Hall Law Journal* 31(3): 589–624.

Herman, D (1990) 'Are We Family?: Lesbian Rights and Women's Liberation' *Osgoode Hall Law Journal* 28(4): 789–815.

—— (1992) *Rights of Passage: Struggles for Lesbian and Gay Equality* (Toronto, University of Toronto Press).

Hunter, N (1991) 'Marriage, Law and Gender: A Feminist Inquiry' *Law and Sexuality* 1(1): 9–30.

Lahey, K (1999) *Are We 'Persons' Yet? Law and Sexuality in Canada* (Toronto, University of Toronto Press).

Law Commission of Canada (2001) *Beyond Conjugality: Recognizing and Supporting Close Personal Adult Relationships* (Ottawa, Law Commission of Canada).

Lewis, J (2000) 'Family Policy in the Post-War Period' in S Katz, J Eekelaar and M Maclean (eds), *Cross-currents: Family Law and Policy in the United States and England* (Oxford, Oxford University Press).

MacDougall, B (2000) 'The Celebration of Same-Sex Marriage' *Ottawa Law Review* 32(2): 235.

McColgan, A (2000) *Women under the Law: The False Promise of Human Rights* (Harlow, Longman).

Ontario Law Reform Commission (1993) *Report on the Rights and Responsibilities of Cohabitants under the Family Law Act* (Toronto, OLRC).

Owen, MK (2001) '"Family" as a Site of Contestation: Queering the Normal or Normalizing the Queer?' in T Goldie (ed), *In a Queer Country: Gay and Lesbian Studies in the Canadian Context* (Vancouver, Arsenal Pulp Press).

Polikoff, ND (1993) 'We Will Get What We Ask For: Why Legalizing Gay and Lesbian Marriage Will Not "Dismantle the Legal Structure of Gender in Every Marriage"' *Virginia Law Review* 79: 1535–50.

Ryder, B (1990) 'Equality Rights and Sexual Orientation: Confronting Heterosexual Family Privilege' *Canadian Journal of Family Law* 9: 39–97.

Stoddard, TB (1992) 'Why Gay People Should Seek the Right to Marry' in S Suzanne (ed), *Lesbian and Gay Marriage: Private Commitments, Public Ceremonies* (Philadelphia, Temple University Press).

Toope, SJ (1991) 'Riding the Fences: Courts, Charter Rights and Family Law' *Canadian Journal of Family Law* 9: 55–96.

11

Registered Partnerships for Same-Sex Couples in Switzerland: Constructing a New Model of Family Relationships

MICHELLE COTTIER

INTRODUCTION

S WITZERLAND HAS ENTERED a new stage in the debate on family values in family law. The turning point is a legislative project which will
introduce registered partnerships for same-sex couples. This project
has been set in motion by the Swiss government's Federal Council, under
pressure from gay and lesbian lobby groups. A preliminary draft law was
submitted to a public consultation procedure in November 2001. The aim
was to collect the opinions of interest groups, political parties and authorities and—in good Helvetic tradition—to design on this basis a regulation
which will find a majority of the Swiss population adhering, or rather not
opposing, in order to avoid the need to hold a popular referendum.

In this chapter, I wish to analyse the competing discourses on family values apparent in the statements made by the different actors taking part in
the consultation procedure and the implications for their position concerning the details of the new legislation. In these statements addressed to the
Swiss government, not only do the variety of opinions concerning the homosexual way of life become apparent, but it is also an occasion for a debate
on family values and the future of family law policy in Switzerland. This
debate centres around the question of equality, ideas about heterosexual
and homosexual couples, and the place of sexuality in family law.

DEVELOPMENTS LEADING TO REGISTERED PARTNERSHIPS

Looking at the history of Swiss sexual and family politics, as well as the
demographic structure of the Swiss population, the fact that Switzerland is
envisaging the introduction of registered partnerships for same-sex couples
may appear surprising. The last Swiss canton decriminalised heterosexual

non-marital cohabitation as late as 1995 (Pulver, 2000: 10). Criminalisation of homosexual practices was removed from the Swiss Penal Code in 1942, but the age of consent for homosexuality remained higher than for heterosexuality until 1992 (Article 194 old Swiss Penal Code). Also, Swiss family law is known regularly to fall behind international developments (Schwenzer, 2001: 199). The marriage-based family is still the basis of Swiss family law and many other legal areas such as tax, immigration or social security laws. De facto relationships are not regulated expressly in most areas of the law including provisions concerning the family home, property equalisation and support on dissolution (Büchler, 2001a: 290ff). It has only recently been possible for unmarried parents to apply for joint parental custody (Article 298a Swiss Civil Code). Additionally, marriage has remained a comparatively popular choice for heterosexual couples, especially when children are born. Although the extra-marital birth rate is steadily increasing, it was still at the low level of 11.3 in 2001. Switzerland does not belong to the group of countries where marriage and the birth of children are disconnected, such as France, Norway or Great Britain (Dobritz, 2000: 257).

The choice of marriage in connection with the birth of a child is however made out of instrumental considerations by an increasing number of couples, basically in order to profit from legal advantages (Fux, forthcoming: 31). In addition, surveys are showing the comparatively high tolerance of the Swiss population of new living arrangements and demographic trends, such as divorce or lone parenting (*ibid* 34). Little is known about the attitudes of the Swiss population towards same-sex cohabitation. It is, however, likely that there is tolerance for this living arrangement also. Gays and lesbians report feeling that Swiss society is comparatively tolerant towards their way of life (Baur, 2001: 532).

In view of this tolerance, the time for recognition of same-sex relationships in Swiss law seems to be ripe. As in many countries which have now introduced legislation about same-sex relationships[1] the Swiss legislative project is the result of lobbying by gay and lesbian rights groups (cf Baur, 2001: 542ff). In 1995 a committee called Equal Rights for Same-Sex Couples handed over a petition to the federal authorities signed by over 85,000 persons, asking for rights equal to those available to couples of the opposite sex through marriage. The National Council, ie the chamber of the National Assembly representing the people, converted the petition into the more binding form of a 'postulate' and mandated the federal government to examine the legal forms which would have to be created in order to stop discrimination against same-sex couples and which rights and obligations such an institution should entail.

As a consequence of this parliamentary postulate, a first report was presented by the Federal Office of Justice in 1999, with the first part comprising comparative law on the regulation of same-sex couples in Europe and

---

[1] Cf The contributions in Wintemute and Andenæs (2001).

the second part analysing the current legal situation of same-sex couples in Switzerland. The report put five legislative possibilities forward for the legal recognition of same-sex couples: (1) a minimalist solution consisting of the revision of selected legal provisions; (2) a contract with restricted legal effects; (3) registered partnerships with self-contained effects, not referring to matrimonial law; (4) registered partnerships mostly referring to the regulation of marriage (Scandinavian model); (5) the actual opening of the institution of marriage to same-sex partners. The report was submitted to a consultation procedure among interest groups, political parties and the cantons in order to investigate whether a consensus could be found as to which model should be adopted. As a reaction to the report, three symposiums organised by gay and lesbian rights groups[2] and universities[3] were held in the year 2000, on the legal situation of same-sex couples as well as heterosexual cohabitants.

In a second step, a preliminary draft law was formulated and published together with an explanatory report (Federal Office of Justice, 2001). The next step is that the final draft will be presented to the Federal Parliament by the Swiss government, the Federal Council. It is a preliminary draft law, and the consultation procedure will be dealt with in more detail below.

In anticipation of legislative activities on the federal level, the cantons of Geneva[4] and Zurich[5] have already established their own cantonal registered partnerships regulations which do not offer a new status, but put registered partners on an equal footing with married couples in the area of cantonal tax, procedural and public welfare law.

THE PRELIMINARY DRAFT LAW:
NOT MARRIAGE BUT CLOSE TO IT

According to the official evaluation of the first consultation procedure, it was the model of registered partnerships with self-contained effects which found most support among the different political actors. This choice led the administration to draft a law on registered partnerships for same-sex couples (couples of the opposite sex are excluded) that in structure and on many points resembles the law on marriage in the Swiss Civil Code (SCC).[6]

---

[2] Symposium organised by NETWORK (Association of Gay Managers) on 4 November 2000 in Zurich, publication of the contributions in *Aktuelle Juristische Praxis AJP*, special issue 'Registrierte Partnerschaft', 3/2001, 243ff.

[3] Symposium at the University of Lausanne on 23 February 2000, publication of the contributions in Guillaume and Arn (eds), *Cohabitation non maritale: évolution récente en droit suisse et étranger* (Geneva, 2000). Symposium of the Swiss Society of International Law on 10 November 2000 at the University of Berne, publication of the contributions in *Schweizerische Zeitschrift für internationales und europäisches Recht* Szier 1/2001, 57ff.

[4] Loi sur le partenariat, of 15 February 2001 (entry into force on 5 May 2001).

[5] Gesetz über die Registrierung gleichgeschlechtlicher Paare, of 21 January 2002. A popular vote was held in the canton of Zurich on 22 September 2002 and 62.7 per cent of the voters gave their consent to the new law.

[6] SR 210 (www.admin.ch/ch/d/sr/210).

As with marriage, registered partnership is an institution binding two persons in a monogamous community of mutual support. From an overall perspective, registered partnership in the Swiss version will not be marriage, but comes close to it.

The draft law not only proposes an actual Registered Partnerships Act, regulating the establishment, the effects and the dissolution of the new status, but also amendments to a series of laws, most importantly the laws on acquisition of Swiss nationality, immigration, asylum, succession, international private law, federal taxes, social security and provision for old age.

The biggest differences from marriage concern the questions of reproduction and child rearing. According to the preliminary draft law, neither adoption nor medically assisted procreation will be available for registered same-sex partners. Furthermore, an important distinction will be made concerning the property system. In matrimonial law the system of deferred com-munity is the legal property regime, which means that basically all property accrued during the marriage is distributed equally between the spouses on dissolution by divorce or death. By signing an agreement, the spouses can however opt for the regimes of separate property or of communal property. For registered partnerships the preliminary draft law proposes separate property as the legal property regime, and the partners can enter into an agreement if they prefer a different solution. Finally, according to the draft, the partnership will not have any effects on the names of the partners. In contrast to this, Swiss matrimonial law still obliges spouses to choose a common family name.[7]

In addition to these more important differences, a series of smaller distinctions to marriage will be introduced: for instance, the registration procedure of the partnership by the civil status registrar is slightly different to that of marriage in that no witnesses have to be present and the partners don't have to say the famous 'I do' but can give their agreement to the registration in writing.

Concerning the legal effects in areas other than family law, registered partnerships will basically be put on an equal footing with matrimony. Registered partners will be treated as spouses in the law of succession, immigration, federal tax, social security and the law on old-age provision. Again, small distinctions will be introduced: naturalisation of foreign nationals living in a registered partnership with a Swiss national will not be as simple as it is for married persons in the same situation. And the social security benefits on the death of a partner will be shaped by the model of the widowers' allowance, which means that women losing their registered partner receive a pension under more restricted conditions than women losing their husband.

---

[7] A reform making the choice of a common family name optional failed in the final parliamentary vote in June 2001, cf Büchler (2001a) 290.

THE PARTICIPANTS IN THE CONSULTATION PROCEDURE
AND THEIR POLITICAL WEIGHT

The interest groups who have taken part in the consultation procedure on the preliminary draft law can be divided into the following 'camps': On one side are the gay and lesbian rights groups and their left-wing, feminist and liberal supporters, who are in favour of making marriage available to same-sex couples or to give registered partnerships the effects of marriage. On the other side are the opponents of the legal recognition of same-sex couples. In the middle we can find liberal-traditionalists, who are only ready to end discrimination as long as the traditional model of the heterosexual family based on marriage is not questioned. On the whole, 73 statements by organisations and 26 by cantons have been collected. In addition 75 statements by individual respondents have been sent in. They are however not accessible to the public.

Nine organisations representing or supporting gay and lesbian interests have sent their statements to the federal government. Their opinions are mostly in agreement, but the question of children in same-sex relationships seems to be mainly a preoccupation of lesbian organisations. The position to be taken concerning reproduction and child rearing is also a point of dispute among the ten private and public women's organisations which participated in the procedure. Smaller numbers of statements have come from private or public organisations for the aged (two), for youth (one) and for the family (two). Organisations from the economic sphere have formulated the point of view of employers (two), employees (two), private insurance companies (one), tenants (one) and home owners (one). Three professional associations representing lawyers, attorneys and notaries have presented their point of view. Five out of eight universities have sent in quite elaborate statements.[8]

The 13 religious organisations that have taken part cannot be classified into one single camp but are divided into liberal proponents of equal rights for same-sex couples and traditionalist opponents of any legal recognition of homosexuality. The proponents are composed of the official Protestant church which has special state recognition and privileges (as do the Roman Catholic and Christ Catholic churches), the Swiss Federation of Protestant Women and the Swiss Federation of Catholic Women.[9] The opponents can be found among Catholics, most importantly the Swiss Catholic Bishops' Conference, and among fundamentalist independent churches.

---

[8] The statements by the Universities of Zurich and Geneva exclusively deal with the issues of private international law.

[9] Several publications and papers testify to internal discussions: The title of the 'discussion paper' published by the Swiss Federation of Catholic Women can be translated as 'Immoral acts or a way of life worth recognising? Lesbians, gay men and bisexuals in church and society'. The Federation of Swiss Protestant Churches indicates references to five of its own publications on the topic.

Among the four governmental parties[10] two parties, the Radical Party (a liberal party representing the interests of economy) and the Social Democrats, can be identified as supporting the gay and lesbian rights groups' claims. The Christian Democrats (the Catholics' party) cautiously support the government's proposal of registered partnerships for same-sex couples while underlining the necessity of the clear distinction between registered partnerships and marriage. This support can, in part, be explained by the fact that the head of the Federal Department of Justice and Police, which is in charge of the preparation of the legislation, is a member of the Christian Democrats. The right-wing Swiss People's Party is however completely against the new law and declines giving any privileges now reserved to married heterosexuals to same-sex couples. Seven smaller non-governmental parties have also formulated their point of view.

When the statements made by the political parties are related to their participation in Parliament, it is striking that if all the members of Parliament voted in line with the official position of their party, registered partnerships with much the same effects as marriage or even the opening of marriage for same-sex couples would become possible.[11] However, the Explanatory Report mentions that a clear majority of the participants in the first consultation procedure were in favour of registered partnerships with self-contained effects. This result obviously does not take into account political majorities, but has added weight to the statements by cantons. This arbitrariness in the weighting of different positions collected by the federal administration is described in the political science literature as one of the shortcomings of the consultation procedure (Klöti, 1984: 323–4). This selectivity is undoubtedly part of the federal administration's strong control over the legislative process.

As most cantons do not collect the opinions of their citizens on federal draft laws, the orientation of the cantonal statements often reflects the opinion of the cantonal government in power, or in practice the opinion of the functionary who has written the statement (cf Sciarini, 1999: 605). For instance the cantons of Appenzell, Ausserrhoden and Aargau, whose populations are known for their rather conservative behaviour in federal votes, are the only two cantons that criticise the exclusion of same-sex partners from

---

[10] Switzerland has a highly fragmented multi-party system. The Federal Assembly is currently composed of 14 parties. But only the four largest parties are represented in the federal government, and have had the same distribution of seats since 1959, cf Linder (1998) 11–12.

[11] In the two chambers of the Federal Assembly, the proponents of same-sex marriage or of registered partnerships with effects mostly like marriage are in a majority: the Radical Party, Social Democrats and Green Party together have 103 of 200 seats in the National Council and would probably have some support from the smaller left-wing parties. The Radical Party and Social Democrats have 24 of 46 seats in the Council of States. The Radical Party has changed its opinion: it was in favour of registered partnerships with mostly the same effects as marriage in the first consultation procedure, and in the second it was in favour of the opening of marriage, although under the reservation of political opportunity. The Social Democrats and Green Party are both in favour of same-sex marriage.

adoption. With such surprising outcomes, many cantons and inter-cantonal organisations[12] are quite cautious in criticising the preliminary draft law and concentrate on questions of applicability by cantonal authorities and the financial consequences of the introduction of registered partnerships.

The cantons are the respondents which put the most weight on political feasibility, a factor that has to be understood in the context of the Swiss political system. A classical explanation of the function of the consultation procedure is that it is aimed at helping to formulate a law that will not be subject to a popular referendum (Sciarini, 1999: 598). In the case of the law on registered partnerships, as for any federal law, the opponents will have the opportunity to collect 50,000 signatures from Swiss citizens within 90 days after the passing of the law in Parliament (Article 141 Swiss Federal Constitution). In this case, a popular vote will have to be organised, and a simple majority of the voters will decide whether the law is approved or rejected. This is why acceptability by the population influenced the work of the drafters and is dominating the debate on registered partnerships in Switzerland.

MARRIAGE AND THE CLAIMS TO EQUALITY

The method of drafting used by the Federal Office of Justice was to take matrimonial law as a starting point and to test every detail to see if it fitted same-sex couples, and then to include or exclude it from the preliminary draft. As described above, differences in regulation were introduced, even if they sometimes appear quite artificial. The creation of this new institution in family law takes place 'in the shadow of marriage'. The main fear appears to be that regulation on same-sex partnerships comes too close to marriage, as the right to marry guaranteed in Article 14 of the Swiss Constitution is understood by the drafters (in contrast to legal doctrine[13]) as excluding same-sex marriage (Federal Office of Justice 2001: 11).

The special law approach is not only criticised by supporters of the opening of marriage for same-sex couples, but also from the point of view of the application of the law by the courts. Problematic consequences for the coherence of family law are foreseen. It is not clear to what extent case law concerning marriage would also be applicable to registered partnerships and vice versa.[14]

[12] Inter-cantonal organisations are eg the Conference of Cantonal Directors of Finance and the Conference of Surveillance Authorities in the Matter of Civil Status.

[13] Swiss legal doctrine interprets Art 14 Swiss Constitution as a guarantee of the right to marry and not as the protection of the institution of marriage in its traditional heterosexual structure (Schoder, 2002: 1296). The decision not to open marriage to same-sex couples has therefore to be understood as motivated rather by political than constitutional motives. In contrast to this, an important part of German legal doctrine interprets Art 6 para 1 of the German Basic Law as containing a constitutional fundamental value judgement excluding the introduction of marriage or marriage-like unions for same-sex couples (cf the contribution by Wolfgang Voegeli in ch 2, this volume).

[14] Cf the statements by the canton of Zurich and the University of Lucerne.

Marriage as a reference point can also be found in gays' and lesbians' claim to equal treatment. The impulse for the legislative process aiming at the creation of registered partnerships in Switzerland came from a committee called Equal Rights for Same-Sex Couples and all the statements made by the gay and lesbian groups in the consultation procedure use the argument of equality in most of the points they make.

Discrimination is a concept linked closely to equality. In the sense of the new Article 8 of the Swiss Constitution of 2000,[15] discrimination is understood as unequal treatment on the basis of certain qualities of a person which cannot be justified by substantial reasons. The Swiss Constitution specifies these qualities as 'origin, race, sex, age, language, social position, way of life, religious, philosophical or political convictions, or physical or mental disability'. The prohibition of discrimination on grounds of the way of life was introduced after the successful intervention of gay and lesbian lobby groups in the Federal Assembly, and refers in the first place to homosexuality (cf Baur, 2001: 534).

The principle of equal treatment and the prohibition of discrimination on the grounds of sexual orientation appear to be the most powerful arguments in gaining access to privileges formerly reserved to heterosexual married couples. Especially in the official statements made by cantonal governments, equal treatment is depicted as an imperative that leaves little scope for political choices.

Using the equality argument has its shortcomings, however. One problem is the reference point which is needed in order to be able to judge whether something is treated equally or in a different way. When gays and lesbians claim treatment equal to married heterosexual couples, the married relation-ship becomes the standard against which their relationships are judged. This means that there is no room for their own definition of how their partnerships should be regulated. This problem is well known from the history of the women's movement (cf Maihofer, 1995: 167).

As in most countries where gay and lesbian rights groups have been actively lobbying for the recognition of their relationships, the decision to head for marriage has not been uncontested inside the movement. Sociologist Aebersold (2001: 34; 2002) shows how the positions of Swiss gay and lesbian activists have changed from a fundamental critique of marriage as a patriarchal institution including claims for its abolition in the 1970s, to the political claim of institutionalisation of same-sex relationships in the 1990s. The opening of marriage to same-sex couples appeared appealing because it would resolve many demands for equal treatment in one fell swoop, and also because it was a provocative idea. Lesbian organisations have however always stayed more reticent in supporting the campaign for 'homo-marriage'.

---

[15] Cf the English translation on www.swissemb.org/legal/const.pdf.

In Swiss feminist legal literature, the idea of creating a marriage-like institution for same-sex couples has been criticised. Büchler (2001b) argues that the discourse accompanying the institutionalisation of same-sex relationships through a new status called registered partnership has the effect of consolidating the bipolarity of the gender order: the emphasis lies on the norm of heterosexual marriage, which appears to be the only adequate institution regulating the gender order. Marriage is reaffirmed as the historical structural core of the sexual and reproductive community, a community in which differences and inequalities between the two sexes are inscribed and constantly reproduced. At the same time, the same-sex relationships' deviance from the norm is underlined, instead of recognising their equal value. As a consequence, Büchler proposes the abolition of marriage altogether, instead of creating a new institution in family law.

As has been the case for women, claims for equal treatment also mean that the majority will not tolerate any special treatment of the group claiming equal treatment. A recurring argument in the statements of respondents critical of the consultation procedure is the equal treatment of cohabiting heterosexual couples with same-sex couples. Furthermore, religious groups demand that religious communities are also given some legal instrument similar to registered partnerships, again invoking equal treatment. For example the Swiss Catholic Bishops' Conference requests the finding of solutions for the situations of members of religious communities or of priests' housekeepers, through the creation of an assistance contract.

The claim for equality has been an impediment to a deeper reflection on the needs, family values and family reality among gay and lesbian lobby groups as well as the whole society.[16] The fact that the Federal Office of Justice has chosen to pursue the model of registered partnerships with a regulation independent from matrimonial law could have been an opportunity to design new legislation. But it has not been possible to liberate the new regulation from the structures of matrimonial law.

THE MODEL SAME-SEX COUPLE AND
THE FUNCTIONS OF FAMILY LAW

Family-related legal regulations regularly provide the mechanisms for the distribution of rights and obligations within the relationship, as well as for social security provisions in favour of families which are financed by contributions or taxes paid by all citizens. Both ensure a certain amount of redistribution of economic resources. This redistributive element is mainly justified today by the unequal distribution of paid and unpaid labour between partners and in society as a whole.[17] In the preliminary draft on

---

[16] Lisa Glennon reaches a similar conclusion regarding Canada (cf her contribution in ch 10, this volume).

[17] See Lewis (ch 4, this volume).

registered partnerships for same-sex couples and the reactions to it in the consultation procedure, the question of redistribution is tackled using models of relationships to shape the legal regulation. This discussion about the 'typical same-sex couple' also makes it apparent that the function of family law is defined in various ways.

1 The Government Version

The preliminary draft law is based on the assumption that married heterosexual couples and same-sex registered partners follow a different pattern of organisation of the relationship. The following comparative definition can be given: Both marriage and registered partnership are institutions of family law,[18] adhering to the model of the monogamous, long-term relationship of two adults sharing bed and table and committed to mutual support. In the marriage version, the two adults are of the opposite sex, normally having common children who are reared mainly by the woman, which results in her being in an inferior economic position. In the registered partnership version, the two adults are of the same sex and do not have common children and therefore are also economically on the same footing (Federal Office of Justice, 2001: 12).

When explaining the differences between registered partnership and heterosexual marriage the Federal Office of Justice thus explicitly makes one main predictive assumption: registered same-sex couples will normally act as two economically independent adults who do not share the project of raising children. At the same time a normative assumption is made: the Federal Office of Justice assumes that, because same-sex partners are not able to have biologically common children, there is no social norm obliging the partner to take responsibilities for the child of the other partner.

The assumptions made by the drafters of the law on registered partnerships appear to correspond to the representation most of the respondents have of same-sex couples, especially as most of the cantons agree on the choice. However, these assumptions were not verified by sociological studies concerning the organisation of family life in same-sex couples, an omission that has not been noted by the respondents. This illustrates how unimportant the role of social science has been in Swiss family law reform.[19]

---

[18] However, the preliminary draft law does not suggest the inclusion of registered partnerships in the family law section of the Swiss Civil Code.

[19] In the preparations of the latest divorce law reform from 2000 at least some sociological and psychological studies about the effects of divorce and the possible role of divorce law in family conflicts were taken into account; cf Message of the Federal Council concerning the amendment of the Civil Code, of 15 November 1995, Bundesblatt (Swiss Federal Journal) 1995, 1. Socio-legal analysis of Swiss family law is however practically non-existent; for an exception cf Monika Binkert and Kurt Wyss, (1997) *Die Gleichstellung von Frau und Mann im Ehescheidungsrecht: eine empirische Untersuchung an sechs erstinstanzlichen Gerichten* (Basel, Helbing & Lichtenhahn): a study analysing how the level of maintenance after divorce is influenced by different gender ideologies embraced by courts and solicitors.

If the propositions by the Federal Office of Justice are followed, the new law on registered partnerships will not be part of the Civil Code by which the rest of family law is regulated. This means that it is not willing to recognise registered partnership as an institution of family law. The question of the definition of family is not entirely a terminological one. The Federal Office of Justice underlines in the report that registered partnerships do not aim at the foundation of a family. 'Family' is seen as a community of two persons of the opposite sex, who have common children. Children may live in a registered partnership, a fact that is not denied,[20] but they are not recognised as being the children of both partners. Only for asylum law are the drafters willing to use a 'wider definition of the family' which includes same-sex partners (Federal Office of Justice, 2001: 39). This means that, in most instances, where a legal provision is supposedly based on the protection of 'the family' in its reproductive function, a different rationale has to be found for registered partners. This becomes quite clear especially in the question of support obligations (cf below).

2 The Version of Gender Equality Experts

A unique perspective on the question of the model that should direct regulation on same-sex relationships was given by the Swiss Conference of Gender Equality Delegates, which is the body where the cantonal offices for gender equality[21] co-ordinate their activities. In their statement, the Swiss gender equality experts draw attention to the connection between discrimination on grounds of sex on the one hand, and on grounds of sexual orientation on the other. They emphasise that the regulation of forms of cohabitation should not only take into account the couple but also the gender order surrounding it, where women and men are limited in their free choice, especially in the question of the division of paid and unpaid labour. This is why they ask the legislator to make sure that the law contains recognition and compensation for domestic work in same-sex relationships by means of support obligations, division of property or social security law. On the other hand, they mention the risk of power imbalances and inequalities internal to the same-sex relationship including the possibility of violence, and the need to protect the weaker party.

3 The Gay and Lesbian Position

Gay and lesbian rights organisations have not expressly developed their own model of partnership but criticise the choice of the proposed model of

---

[20] In this question the report also refers to a judgment of the Federal Court, the highest Swiss court, in a divorce case that stated that homosexuality is not in itself a reason to deny parental custody to a parent (cf Federal Office of Justice, 2001: 17).
[21] Besides the Federal Office for the Equality of Women and Men, 16 of the 26 cantons and 5 cities have their own offices for gender equality: see www.equality.ch.

the egalitarian, mutually independent and childless same-sex couple by the drafters of the law. Some oppose the 'legal prescription of a role model' altogether. The arguments used to oppose differences between matrimonial law and the future law on registered partnerships are—depending on the question: the need for treatment to be equal to that of married heterosexual couples, the will for mutual responsibility and commitment, and recognition of the reality of homosexuals, mainly lesbians, raising children together. The areas where gays and lesbians ask for equal treatment or the possibility for same-sex couples to choose the solutions of matrimonial law concern support obligations, property, name, the dissolution of the partnership and child law.

In their statements, gay and lesbian rights organisations take a position based on the autonomy of the same-sex couple to choose the degree of mutual commitment and community that fits them—while at the same time rhetorically underlining the readiness for mutual commitment and responsibility. Gender inequality is made a topic of concern by lesbian organisations which emphasise that the division of labour between men and women in society should also be taken into account. Gays and lesbians, however, do not preoccupy the gender equality experts with problems of inequality and power imbalances in intimate relationships. The main aim of the campaign for access to marriage is not seeking legislation that protects the weaker party in the relationship, but in order to achieve public recognition of the homosexual way of life. The campaign thus emphasises the symbolic function of family law, and as a minority asking the majority for respect, the minority needs to be united. The hierarchical relationship between homosexual couples and heterosexual couples is called into question but not the possible hierarchy within the partnership.

The starting point for women's claims to more equality and protection in family law was and is different: the aim was to challenge the gender order expressed in family law rules establishing a hierarchy within the couple, such as the right of the husband to dispose of the woman's property and the right to forbid her an occupation outside the household, provisions that were not abolished until 1988 (cf Gerber, Kaufmann and Kaufmann, 1993). Women's campaigns and gays' and lesbians' campaigns focus on distinct hierarchies and power relations. The consequence is a differing sensitivity toward protection and equalisation of power imbalances in intimate relationships, and a distinct way of making use of family law.

4 The Traditionalist Point of View

A traditionalist point of view is taken by those who underline the importance of marking clear differences between the new institution of registered partnership and marriage. The internal organisation of the relationship is of minor interest. It appears to be more important to make sure that the regulation of registered partnerships looks as different from that of marriage as possible. The marriage-based family is looked at as the basic unit and the foundation of the state. Because of its reproductive function it has to be privileged. For some, marriage is the only legitimate institution of family law. Others, who are cautiously in favour of registered partnerships, underline the importance of the application of the same moral standards which are valid for marriage to registered partnerships, such as the obligation to fidelity and the commitment to the community. This moralist attitude has not been without effect on the gay and lesbian movement: as mentioned above, the discourse used in statements by homosexuals' rights groups is to claim equal treatment in exchange for equal acceptance of commitment and responsibility.

5 The Implications for the Regulation

We now turn to some of the implications of the different concepts of the model for the same-sex couple; the functions of family law are discussed with the help of the examples of property, support obligations, dissolution and child law.

(a) Property

According to the preliminary draft law, separate property will be the legal property regime, and the partners can conclude an agreement if they desire a different solution (Art 19ff). However, the draft does not provide other regimes to choose from, as in matrimonial property law. As explained above, matrimonial law, by contrast, states that the system of deferred community is the legal regime, a property regime that brings an equalisation of property accrued during marriage on dissolution (Art 196ff, SCC).

Many organisations giving their opinion on the preliminary draft law have taken the question of the property regime as the occasion to discuss the model of same-sex relationships proposed by the government. The gay and lesbian rights organisations criticise the alleged role model, but do not fundamentally oppose the proposed property regime as it corresponds to their autonomy-based view. Two cantons, one university and two organisations are in favour of installing the legal regime of deferred community as in matrimonial law. Most of them use equality arguments. The gender equality experts, however, underline the need for a mechanism of equalisation for an uneven distribution of paid and unpaid labour that is likely to occur between registered partners.

(b) Support Obligations

According to the preliminary draft law, the partners in a registered partnership are entitled to mutual support during the relationship. On dissolution, each partner is basically responsible for his or her own support, that is a 'clean break'. A support obligation however remains in favour of the partner that has partnership-related disadvantages (Schwenzer, 2002: 235), that is the partner who has given up gainful employment because of the partnership (Art 36).

The question is: when has gainful employment been given up *because of the partnership?* The assumptions underlying the preliminary draft law are of importance: if the future regulation is based on the normative assumption that there is no social norm obliging the partner to take responsibility for the child of the other partner and that registered partnerships cannot have the aim of founding a family, the formulation 'has given up gainful employment because of the partnership' can only mean that if gainful employment has been given up for child rearing by the legal parent of the child, there is no post-separation support obligation. The question arises: what is the rationale for support obligations on the dissolution of a registered partnership?

The search for this rationale makes it clear that the inclusion of same-sex couples in the definition of 'the family' is not without legal relevance. So one canton, Fribourg, which can be counted on to embrace the traditionalist point of view, makes the link between support obligations and the reproductive aim of marriage: for this canton, support obligations between spouses have been conceived with the 'traditional family (parents with children)' in mind. Fribourg therefore questions support obligations between registered partners altogether. Parliament is not likely to abolish the post-separation support obligation and introduce a pure 'clean break system'. It will, however, be the task of the courts to define how the same-sex family with children will be treated in post-separation support law.

(c) Dissolution

Dissolution of the partnership following the preliminary draft law is easier than divorce, in that one year of separation is enough for unilateral dissolution (Art 32), whereas it is only possible to divorce against the will of the other spouse after four years (Art 114 SCC), or if the continuation of the marriage is unacceptable on serious grounds such as domestic violence (Art 115 SCC).

This 'easy way out' for registered partnerships is understood by many respondents as a symbol of a weaker engagement in comparison to marriage. Here the equality argument becomes very important: all supporters of the legal recognition of same-sex relationships underline that same-sex partners are willing to offer the same degree of commitment as opposite-sex partners. Quite in contrast to this, one canton,[22] which is sceptical about the entire regulation, deduces from the easier dissolvability that all legal privileges accorded to registered partners should only be granted after a certain period of time.

---

[22] The canton of Vaud.

(d) Children

When we look at the question of children brought up by same-sex couples the importance of biology for parenthood is at the centre of the debate. The Federal Office of Justice emphasises that 'nature' gives a mother and a father to every child, that child law correspondingly has the aim of giving a legal mother and father to every child and that therefore adoption by a same-sex couple should be excluded, as well as access to medically assisted procreation (Federal Office of Justice, 2001: 17).

On this, the Explanatory Report of the Federal Office of Justice comes closer than on any other issue to the positions taken by fundamentalist Christian groups. These groups also use 'nature' to emphasise the reproductive function of marriage, and that children have the right to a 'natural' upbringing. Thus in their view, this is not possible when they live with two parents of the same sex.

The proponents of a right to adopt, often emphasising that adoption should at least be allowed in the form of stepchild adoption, use the argument of the existing reality of children already living with parents of the same sex. Political parties from the left and liberal wing support the postulate of gay and lesbian rights organisations, that there are women who have children from a former relationship who let their female companion take over a social mother role.[23] As in the case of the organisations which clearly reject any form of adoption, the argument of the 'welfare of the child' is used. It becomes once again apparent that the concept of the welfare of the child depends entirely on the values and convictions of those interpreting it. In the version of gays and lesbians as well as most women's organisations and the youth organisation Pro Juventute, the welfare of the child demands the protection of the relationship between the child and his or her social parent. Stepchild adoption is postulated as one way of achieving this protection, especially in the eventuality of the death of the biological parent or in the case of a dissolution of the registered partnership. In the government version, the welfare of the child is seen as being in danger because the child would be in an exceptional situation in society because he or she has two fathers or two mothers. According to this view, parental responsibility cannot be given to the step-parent, and the stepmother or father can only become the guardian of the child on the death or dissolution of the registered partnership. This, however, means that parental responsibility has to be taken away from the biological parent(s).[24]

---

[23] The statements regularly speak of one third of all lesbians that supposedly have children from former relationships. The source of this figure is however indicated nowhere.

[24] Quite in contrast to this Swiss reticence in recognising same-sex parenthood, in the Netherlands a social parent living in a relationship with the legal parent can apply for shared custody with the legal parent. On death he or she becomes automatically solely entitled to custody rights. Cf Schrama, 2002: 282ff.

SEXUALITY AND THE FEARS OF 'OVERFOREIGNISATION'

Sexuality is not directly referred to in the discussion on models of same-sex and matrimonial relationships. In the legal definitions, neither marriage nor registered partnerships apparently have anything to do with sexuality.[25] The requirement to share bed and table is not explicitly stated in the provisions of matrimonial law or in the preliminary draft law on registered partnerships. According to matrimonial law, the spouses are united in the matrimonial community and they owe one another fidelity and mutual assistance (Art 159, SCC). According to the literature, the community of the spouses comprises the spiritual, physical, domestic and, if children are present, the educational element. The duty of fidelity is thought to concern not only sexual exclusiveness, but also spiritual loyalty. This doctrinal definition of the marital community has however lost its legal significance. Since the year 2000 marital infidelity is no longer a ground for divorce under Swiss law. Family law is not concerned about whether married people really are in an intimate relationship. It has become commonly accepted that marriage can have goals other than that of reproduction. This corresponds to the international development where marriage is viewed as a community rather than a unit responsible for the reproduction of society. The recent judgements of the European Court of Human Rights in the cases *Goodwin v UK* and *I v UK*,[26] in which the right to marry a person of the opposite sex (Art 12, ECHR) has been extended to trans-sexuals, mirror this change. In what concerns the new regulation on registered partnerships for same-sex couples, the preliminary draft law does not mention fidelity as a duty of the partners, and Article 2 speaks of a community of responsibility. Homosexual practices are only an issue for the fundamentalist opponents of the law who argue that, for 'natural sexuality', two persons of the opposite sex are needed.

The requirement of sharing bed and table is however of legal importance in another area of law: immigration law. Firstly, family members who have a residence permit derived from their spouse's permit are obliged to live together with this spouse if both are foreign nationals (Art 17 para 2, Law of Abode and Settlement of Foreigners[27]). This regulation has been challenged because of the effect it has on women who are victims of domestic violence: if they leave their violent partner, they risk loosing their residence permit. Therefore the abolition of this requirement has been decided upon in one chamber of the Federal Assembly, the National Council.[28] However, the Federal Council's new draft immigration law goes into the opposite direction and wants to extend the obligation of cohabitation also to spouses of a Swiss national.[29]

---

[25] See Fuszara and Kurczewski (ch 3, this volume).

[26] Case of *Christine Goodwin v The United Kingdom*, 11 July 2002, Appl no 28957/95; case of *I v The United Kingdom*, 11 July 2002, Appl no 25680/94.

[27] SR 142.20 (www.admin.ch/ch/d/sr/142_20).

[28] Parliamentary initiative Christine Goll of 12 Dec 1996, no 96.461.

[29] Cf Message concerning the Federal Law on Foreigners, of 8 March 2002, Bundesblatt (Swiss Federal Journal) 2002 (www.admin.ch/ch/d/ff/2002/3709.pdf).

A second way of imposing a cohabiting way of life on married couples is the regulation on bogus marriages: if the police have evidence that a marriage has been entered into with the sole aim of attaining a residence permit for one of the partners, this permit does not have to be issued (Art 7 para 2, Law of Abode and Settlement of Foreigners). As one element of evidence of a bogus marriage, the absence of matrimonial community is stated by the Federal Court.[30] The police notoriously visit households in the early morning, in order to check where the spouses have been sleeping. They thus fill the idea of community with their concepts of marriage, which includes sexual community.[31] In the above-mentioned draft immigration law, the fight against the allegedly enormous problem of bogus marriages is attacked in an even more drastic way: in the future, marriage will be refused by civil status registrars if they suspect a bogus marriage.

When taking an overall perspective, it becomes clear that since the reform of the divorce law in 2000, Swiss family law no longer cares about the intimate details of relationships; immigration law however nullifies this liberation for immigrants and their spouses.

This fight against bogus marriages and the obligation to cohabit according to the draft immigration law is taken up in the preliminary draft law on registered partnerships. Only a few organisations criticised this tightening of control over relationships. The argument of equality with the current, less restrictive regulation for marriage used by most critical voices was disarmed quite quickly by the federal administration with reference to the ongoing reform of immigration law. Only one organisation, the Swiss Conference of Gender Equality Delegates, refers to the special situation of victims of domestic violence in same-sex relationships, and that they should not be obliged to stay with their violent partners for reasons of immigration law. In the perspective of the cantons, it appears that fears connected to 'overforeignisation'[32] and the prevention of fraud using civil status by foreigners are the main preoccupation.

More innovative perspectives are formulated by the two opposite sides. Supporters of the recognition of same-sex relationships, as well as some sceptical voices who criticise the privileging of registered partners in comparison with heterosexual cohabitants, ask for an immigration law based not on status but on the actual relationship. As a solution to the problem

---

[30] Cf Swiss Federal Court, decision of 31 May 1996, BGE 122 II 289, 294ff (www.bger.ch).

[31] In a recent decision the Swiss Federal Court accepted the following evidence for a bogus marriage: 'The spouses never lived together since the marriage, an intimate relationship has not been taken up. Encounters occurred basically only on daytime and during a limited period of time. Except for greeting and good-bye, the appellant never kissed or hugged his wife' (Swiss Federal Court, decision of 7 Nov 2002, no 2A 533/2002).

[32] The term 'overforeignisation' (Überfremdung) was introduced by the Swiss xenophobic movement and expresses a feeling that there are too many foreigners in Switzerland and that immigration has to be restricted. The term has even been introduced into federal immigration law (Art 16 Law of Abode and Settlement of Foreigners).

of bogus marriages and now bogus registration, the *Centre Patronal,* an organisation of employers whose statement is marked by scepticism concerning registered partnerships, proposes to issue a residence permit to every person living with and supported by a person authorised to live in Switzerland. This solution surprisingly corresponds to the proposition of the Swiss Conference of Gender Equality Delegates to separate the right to family life from civil status. The motivation is however distinct: the *Centre Patronal* wants to keep the institution of marriage 'clean', whereas the Gender Equality Delegates envisage a legal order where civil status and especially marriage lose their importance.

TOWARDS A LAW OF DE FACTO RELATIONSHIPS?

The statements formulated in reaction to the Swiss preliminary draft law on registered partnerships leave an ambivalent impression. On the one hand, a large number of the important interest groups in society appear to support the idea of passing a regulation on same-sex partners and in this way recognise this way of life. Swiss family law could make a big move away from fixation on the institution of marriage and towards legal recognition of a plurality of living arrangements.

On the other hand, the future institution of registered partnership adds another status to family law, at a time when the evolution of family law is said to be leading away from status to contract and relationship (Schwenzer, 2001). As Coester (2002) comments, status is not a criterion that is indicative of families. Protection by the state and the redistributive function of family law, social security law and tax law should be reserved to those who raise or have raised children—independent of sexual orientation or status. I would like to add that in my opinion, the status should also lose its importance for the regulation of the internal legal relationship of couples. The future lies in unified rules that give the real nature of the relationship priority over legal status.[33] The law could distinguish between different situations of cohabitation, independently from the type of relationship, instead of passing the regulation on a model of the 'typical relationship'. It is even imaginable that the regulation should extend to groups of more than two people living together.

As has been mentioned before, several organisations responding to the consultation procedure demand the enlargement of the circle of relationships recognised by the law. Although these claims are mostly made in order to express opposition to registered partnerships for same-sex couples with the argument of discrimination against other living arrangements, they nonetheless introduce new ideas to the debate on the regulation of personal relationships. The demands of the Swiss Catholic Bishops' Conference on

---

[33] This is the idea of the new law on property division in New Zealand, cf Atkin (2001).

behalf of members of religious communities or of priests' housekeepers have already been mentioned above. In spite of the reservations that have to be made about the motivation for these claims, they appear to be more original and innovative than the equality-based claims of homosexuals' lobby groups to 'homo-marriage'.

REFERENCES

Aebersold, D (2002) 'Nun Wollen Sie Die Ehe Doch' *Basler Magazin* 21, 25: 10.

—— (2001) *LOSgelöst. Die Ehepolitik der Lesbenorganisation LOS vor dem Hintergrund der Bewegungsgeschichte und feministischen Theorien* (Fachprogrammarbeit im Bereich Geschlechtersoziologie (unpublished), Berne).

Atkin, B (2001) 'Reforming Property Division in New Zealand: From Marriage to Relationships' *European Journal of Law Reform* 3: 349–364.

Baur, FE (2001) 'At the End of the Fairy Tale, Will Heidi Stay Single? Same-Sex Partnerships in Switzerland' in R Wintemute and M Andenæs (eds), *Legal Recognition of Same-Sex Partnerships* (Oxford, Hart Publishing).

Büchler, A (2001a) 'Family Law in Switzerland: Recent Reforms and Future Issues—an Overview' *European Journal of Law Reform* 3: 275–296.

—— (2001b) 'Ehe und Geschlechterkonstruktion. Ein Beitrag zur Abschaffung der institutionalisierten Zweigeschlechtlichkeit' in Verein Pro FRI (ed), *Recht Richtung Frauen, Beiträge zur feministischen Rechtswissenschaft* (Lachen/St Gallen, Dike Verlag).

Coester, M (2002) 'Same Sex Relationships: A Comparative Assessment of Legal Developments Across Europe' *FamPra.ch (Die Praxis des Familienrechts)* 3: 748–764.

Dobritz, J (2000) 'Europäische Fertilitätsmuster (European Fertility Patterns)' *Zeitschrift für Bevölkerungswissenschaft* 235–266.

Federal Office of Justice (1999) *Die rechtliche Situation gleichgeschlechtlicher Paare im schweizerischen Recht, Probleme und Lösungsansätze* (Berne, cf www.ofj.admin.ch).

—— (2001) *Bundesgesetz über die registrierte Partnerschaft gleichgeschlechtlicher Paare, Erläuternder Bericht und Vorentwurf* (Berne, www.ofj.admin.ch).

—— (2002a) *Bundesgesetz über die registrierte Partnerschaft gleichgeschlechtlicher Paare: Zusammenstellung der Vernehmlassungen (Collection of the statements concerning the law on registered partnership for same-sex couples)* (Berne).

—— (2002b) *Vernehmlassungsergebnisse: Bundesgesetz über die registrierte Partnerschaft gleichgeschlechtlicher Paare (Results of the consultation procedure)* (Berne, www.ofj.admin.ch).

Fux, B (forthcoming) 'Family Change and Family Policy in Switzerland' in P Flora (ed), *Family Change and Family Policies in Consociational Democracies: Belgium, Switzerland, and The Netherlands*, vol 2 (Oxford: Oxford University Press).

Gerber, J, Kaufmann, R and Kaufmann, C (1993) 'Frauenforderungen an das Schweizerische Zivilgesetzbuch' in Rechtshistorisches Seminar (ed), *Eugen Huber (1849–1923), Akten des im Sommersemesters 1992 durchgeführten Seminars* (Berne, University of Berne).

Klöti, U (1984) 'Politikformulierung' in U Klöti (ed), *Handbuch Politisches System der Schweiz*, vol 2, *Strukturen und Prozesse* (Berne and Stuttgart, Verlag Paul Haupt).

Linder, W (1998) *Swiss Democracy: Possible Solutions to Conflict in Multicultural Societies*, 2nd edn (Basingstoke, Macmillan, New York, St Martin's Press).

Maihofer, A (1995) *Geschlecht als Existenzweise* (Frankfurt/Main, Ulrike Helmer Verlag).

Pulver, B (2000) *Unverheiratete Paare* (Basel, Geneva and Munich, Helbing & Lichtenhahn).

Schoder, C (2002) 'Die Bedeutung des Grundrechts auf Ehe für das Ehe- und Familienrecht' *Aktuelle Juristische Praxis* 11: 1287–96.

Schrama, W (2002) 'Reforms in Dutch Family Law during the Course of 2001: Increased Pluriformity and Complexity' in A Bainham (ed), *The International Survey of Family Law, 2002 Edition* (Bristol, Jordan).

Schwenzer, I (2000) 'Vorbemerkungen zu Art 125-132 ZGB' in I Schwenzer (ed), *Praxiskommentar Scheidungsrecht* (Basel, Geneva and Munich, Helbing & Lichtenhahn).

—— (2001) 'Editorial: The Evolution of Family Law—From Status to Contract and Relationship' *European Journal of Law Reform* 3: 199–202.

—— (2002) 'Registrierte Partnerschaft: Der Schweizer Weg' *FamPra.ch (Die Praxis des Familienrechts)* 3: 223–237.

Sciarini, P (1999) 'La formulation de la décision' in U Klöti *et al* (eds), *Manuel de la politique suisse* (Zürich, NZZ Verlag).

Wintemute, R and Andenæs, M (eds) (2001) *Legal Recognition of Same-Sex Partnerships* (Oxford, Hart Publishing).

12

Same-Sex Relationships in Italy

VALERIA MAZZOTTA

THE EVOLUTION OF THE FAMILY IN A SOCIAL
AND NORMATIVE CONTEXT

THE FAMILY IS a complex phenomenon: as a social institution it has varied and changing characteristics, with differing organisational structures, and cannot be reduced to a single all-inclusive model. The family is subject to the effects of continuous social changes, from both the legal and the sociological point of view, and its characteristics must be constantly re-examined (Puleo, 1996; De Luca, 1996: 2).

Despite the impossibility of defining the family independently of its time and socio-cultural context,[1] Italian legislation has accepted and institutionalised a traditional concept of the family, that is, the legitimate family based on marriage. Such a family, the basic cell of society and the locus for individual integration and socialisation, has clear-cut legal, social and cultural features. It accomplishes educational and affective tasks, and it also gives economic support to its members in an atmosphere of mutual solidarity. Continuity and stability are assured for the socio-economic and political system through the transmission of values and the provision of social control (D'Angeli, 2001: 1).

From a sociological perspective, Professor Donati maintains that a family exists only if the three conditions necessary for it to accomplish its role are present. These essential conditions are:

— full reciprocity between people having a stable relationship (Donati, 1990);
— marriage as a solemn legal act from which codified rights and duties flow, ensuring stability (De Luca, 1996: 3);
— daily cohabitation and sharing of material goods and spiritual aspects, with exclusive sexual relations permitting reproduction (Ventura, 1990).

---

[1] Scalisi (1987) 441; Fruggeri, *I concetti di mononuclearita' e plurinuclearita' nella definizione di famiglia*, in http://www.terapiafamiliare.org/pubblicazioni.htm.

If one of these essential conditions is missing, a family cannot really exist. With reference to homosexual relationships, it has been observed that stable cohabitation does not constitute a validating factor for identifying a family, even where adoption or assisted procreation is involved, because 'no valid environment of socialization would be provided for the child' (Donati, 1990).

Thus, as Ventura maintains, assigning legal importance to alternative forms of cohabitation would mean legitimising simple social facts and placing such unions on a par with the legitimate family, so creating relational models that are not analogous to, and present many incompatibilities with, the legitimate family (Ventura, 1990).

Despite the resistance offered by the legal establishment and sociologists from a Catholic culture, the traditional concept of family in Italy has long been in the melting pot (Francescato, 1974), as a result of the proliferation of alternative models which lack the essential characteristics of marriage. A multiplicity of family forms have come into being partly as a result of historical or socio-cultural influences. In any industrialised society, in the same social context, legal system and historical moment, different family models can coexist.

Legal rules and social procedures must go hand in hand, so that realistic legal provisions, sensitive to social change, can evolve to deal with the new phenomena. The law must assume as a reference parameter actual family models. As Cassano argues, law can be compared to a glove: the better it fits, the better it wears (Cassano, 2002: 1408). In elaborating and applying legal rules, the judiciary must have regard to the whole population, both those members with majority values and others.[2]

According to recent sociological analysis,[3] a legal response to the new family forms could be attempted from two opposite starting points, one inspired by a normative perspective and the other by pluralism. A normative perspective takes the traditional family model as the point of comparison, in respect of which the so-called 'new families' turn out to be unsatisfactory, because investigation of their deficiencies and malfunctions proceeds from the theoretical models derived from study of the nuclear family. The pluralistic perspective is based on 'the model of difference' (Rapoport, 1989) and refers to multiple family models, treated as different forms with particular aspects, so that the traditional form is only one of many. The researcher's task is to question views about the new family and to redefine the analysis. I suggest that only by accepting the pluralistic perspective will it be possible to classify different sorts of relationships.

The time is ripe for abandoning reference to the conjugal family as a prototype of family relationships in general in the light of emerging ethical pluralism. The values of the Catholic tradition, though undeniably

---

[2] Bessone, Alpa, Ferrando *et al* (1995) 'Quanti Statuti ha l'Embrione?' note to Manifesto di Bioetica Laica, in http://www.dirittofamiglia.it/Docs/Giuridici/dottrina/artificiale1.htm.
[3] Fruggeri, above n 2.

previling, co-exist today with other common shared values. Different attitudes towards values and moral rules which, in turn, influence one another, co-exist in contemporary society. Certain traditional social values are less appreciated, whereas others, inherent in the individual sphere—such as freedom, happiness, tenderness, health, good appearance and reciprocal tolerance—are sought after more and more. The satisfaction of individual and family needs stands out as a primary aim, to which the demands of the community are subordinated. In the moral field, a relativist attitude prevails: good and evil do not depend on absolute, universally valid principles, but are redefined from time to time according to circumstance.

Until recent times, the law simply used to 'register' the kind of family socially recognised in a specific historical phase as the general form consistent with the dominant socio-political conceptions. Thus the family based on marriage strengthened its image of normality. In practice the role of the lawyer and legislator in such a context becomes that of the arbiter of normality. Then follows the risk of diversity being seen as abnormality, and widely accepted as such. That would be detrimental to non-discrimination and the principle of equality.

Assuming that the conjugal family is the dominant 'normal' model and legislative parameter, putting new families on a par with the legitimate family, and evaluating them by the same criteria inevitably leads to a negative value judgement, and even the illegitimacy of new models.[4]

However, if the social importance of new family structures is recognised, then the currently unassailable notion of the heterosexual monogamous family might best be abandoned. In its place, a wider concept of family could be preferable, whose fundamental characteristic of affectivity is also shared by the traditional legitimate family.

It is relationships and affective ties which define the new family which, as De Luca maintains, is 'bound by affectionate ties and common interests and ruled by freedom and autonomy for its members' (De Luca, 1996: 1). The new family plays a fundamental educational and cultural role and accomplishes, on a social level, its main function of solidarity and affective support.

Affectivity is a common denominator for a number of heterogeneous—not necessarily comparable—family forms, and is sufficient to sanction them within their own terms. Recognition of and a guarantee of the right to express feelings freely within different forms of partnerships, which are stable and characterised by reciprocal solidarity between the partners, including those of the same sex, would acknowledge the free expression of affectivity as a fundamental aspect of the personal identity which characterises human nature. Disputes on the meaning of the 'natural' character

---

[4] However, as Cottier (ch 11, this volume) found in Switzerland, the preliminary draft law on same-sex relationships took marriage as a reference point and tested whether it fitted same-sex couples. This approach led to an interesting outcome, as eventually it did prevent the draft law being made.

of the family (Constitution, Art 29) might finally be settled. To compare the legal recognised conjugal family with other personal forms of 'familiar' interaction is not helpful because each model is defined by its own characteristics.

Thus, affectivity, an irrepressible demand of human beings, is the common parameter, capable of reconciling demands for the privileged status of the institutional family with the need to protect and permit pluralism, the right to self-determination, and the citizen's private sphere. According to these principles, the Italian family, far from dying, will enjoy a renaissance, and the form that best meets the requirements of its members will emerge: the legislator must recognise the impossibility of turning back the clock and must refrain from ethical and moral judgements. To persist in recklessly professing a conservative ideology would mean the relegation of Italy in the European integration process, which is heading unequivocally towards cultural, political, social and legal openness.

THE CONSTITUTIONAL FOUNDATION OF HOMOSEXUAL UNIONS: RELATIONSHIPS BETWEEN LAW AND THE FAMILY

Only recently (as a result of gay rights activists, changes in public opinion and legislative initiatives undertaken in many European countries) has Italian legal science begun to appreciate the legal importance of homosexual relationships.[5] Jemolo has spoken of the family as 'an island around which the sea of law merely laps' (1948). That means that the family, 'societa naturale fondata sul matrimonio', represents a social reality unrelated to the law but not outside it. The regulation of family relationships aims to grant them sanction. As Bianca argues, the legal system, confronted by a relevant individual interest inside the family, 'devises the necessary remedies for those cases in which the spontaneous development of family relationships overwhelms such interests' (Bianca, 2001: 8). So the rule of law guarantees and impinges upon the family when there is a need for legal protection. Consequently, a lack of legal rules leaves individuals without any remedy. These considerations apply to everyone without distinction, regardless of sexual orientation.

Moreover, the fact that the law is oblivious to homosexuality makes those involved absolutely invisible to law and society, thus defeating any potential claim to rights. In practice, in many Western countries the move towards identifying the homosexual as an individual deserving rights originated in the discriminatory criminalisation of homosexuality, which provoked individuals to claim recognition for their rights. In Italy, the legislative silence engendered a kind of tolerance that hides a reality of rights

---

[5] Balletti (1996); Schlesinger (1994); Costanza (1994); Forder (2000); Grillini (2000); Longo (2000); Bonini Baraldi (2001); Ferrando (2000); Rodotà (2001: xIII); Marella (2001); Quadri (1999); Solaini (2000: 510); Sesta (unpublished).

denied, and of wrongs and discrimination. As Rodotà maintains, there is still evidence of 'a very big distance between attempts at civil renewal and the actual condition of the homosexual in Italy' (Rodotà, 2000: 7).

As far as the Italian Constitution is concerned, there are three relevant rules. First of all, the legal relevance of homosexuality can be traced back to Article 2 of the Constitution: 'The Republic recognises and guarantees man's inviolable rights, both as an individual and in the social formations where his personality is developed': that is the *personal* principle, according to which the legal system recognises and assumes the pre-existence of the person, his fundamental rights and defence. The former is recognised as primary, and not awarded by the state: that is, the person is the centre of an undetermined series of social relationships which fulfil his personality: the person is the goal, the state the instrument.

By granting free development of the personality within those human groups in which the need for social interaction is expressed, Article 2 also admits social pluralism. Social formations constitute a wide range of organisations, which stand between the citizen and the state, aiming at the development of human personality, of which the traditional family represents only one model.

Article 3, para 1, according to which 'all citizens have equal social dignity and are equal in the eyes of the law, without distinction of sex, race, language, religion, political opinion, personal and social rank', emphasises the equality principle, which applies also to homosexuals, as it forbids sexual discrimination. Paragraph 2 states that the Republic has to eliminate the social and economic obstacles which prevent the full development of human personality, by limiting freedom and equality.[6]

So, from reading Articles 2 and 3 of the Constitution, it may easily be inferred that the family is one of the social formations within which the individual's personality is realised and finds protection. Within this basic cell of society, formal and substantial inequalities are to be resolved whatever the sexual orientation of the individual concerned (Bessone *et al*, 1995: 16).

Article 29 of the Constitution refers to the conjugal family as a constitutional family model (Puleo, 1996). It states that the Republic recognises the rights of the family as a natural social unit founded on marriage, substantially equating family and natural society (Jemolo, 1966: 52; Bin, 2000). The expression 'natural society' has long since been subject to different interpretations. According to students of natural law (Stella Richter, 1965; De Cupis, 1961), the family is an autonomous entity, constitutionally protected, pre-existing the state (Puleo, 1996). Therefore by 'divine reasoning' it

---

[6] As Glennon (ch 10, this volume) found in Canada the equality guaranteed by s 15(1) of the Canadian Charter of Rights and Freedoms 'has been the primary vehicle by which to challenge exclusionary laws and to bring gay and lesbian rights within the mainstream political agenda'.

would be absolutely impenetrable to any state interference (Bessone *et al*, 1995; Grassetti, 1950), thus making it impossible to legitimise different family forms.

Openness towards the legal admissibility of other family forms is shown by laymen, who offer an interpretation of the phrase 'natural society' in contemporary terms, by changing its meaning according to a concept of family which is constantly evolving.[7] This view represents a step towards the admissibility of other forms of union as social formations wherein the individual develops his personality, according to Article 2.[8] So, Article 29 of the Constitution would add specificity to Articles 2 and 3: the family is a social group where the individual's personality develops and his inviolable rights are protected by the Republic. Establishing a family is the natural aim in any person's life, the spontaneous and unavoidable response to the request for affective and material needs.

The conjugal family's favoured position and its protection does not involve any restriction or violation of the rights and values of the person as such. But a guarantee of protection must also be offered to other different form of cohabitation which share equal values, affectivity and mutual solidarity between partners. This interpretation of 'natural society' therefore corresponds to the idea of a natural family: it meets an innate and fundamental need of individuals, and is connected to the demand for social contact and affectivity. Such a family could be a homosexual one, because the *personae* principle implies full recognition of the human person and protection of its dignity, independent of status and sexual orientation.

Notwithstanding this 'liberal' conception of the family, in Italy the traditional interpretation of the fundamental constitutional values still applies. This view stems from the Catholic tradition, which remains dominant in social, political and cultural life.

Is there an argument for denying legal relevance to the homosexual family? In Italy, as in many other Western countries, the current trend is for homosexual partners to live together like a married heterosexual couple. The partners look for full affective and sexual satisfaction within the relationship, and emotional as well as cognitive support, in addition to autonomy from their original families (Barbagli and Colombo, 2001: 201ff). And yet, no form of legal recognition of the relationship is available, with unavoidably negative effects for the partnership's stability, because, whereas legal rules provide a guarantee of social respectability, the lack of them facilitates social disapproval (Bianca, 2001: 8).

The legal rights and obligations associated with reciprocal solidarity, economic support and inheritance only accrue from marriage. So with regard to homosexual partners the discrimination is double: on the one hand, they are denied marriage as a freely chosen act, on the other, they

---

[7] Mancini (1963); Bessone (1976); Bessone (1979); Ferrando (1998), Ferrando (1997).
[8] Bessone *et al* (1995) 13; Campagna (1966); Prosperi (1980) 53.

receive no protection from the law. On the basis of sexual orientation, the law ignores the innate need for a family in which it is possible to develop the personality according to personal choice.

The foundation of this discrimination originates from negative views of homosexuality, treating it as a free choice or rebellion against rigid rules imposed by the system. Homosexuality is instead an individual characteristic, neither chosen nor modifiable (Grillini, 2000), and in no way worthy of censure by those who hold a different ethical or moral opinion.

RESPECT FOR HUMAN RIGHTS AND THE PRINCIPLE OF NON-DISCRIMINATION BASED ON SEXUAL ORIENTATION: THE EU PROVISIONS

Full implementation of the equality principle should lead to the abolition of any difference in legal treatment on the basis of individual characteristics. Equality is strictly linked to the non-discrimination principle, according to which any inferior treatment of some subjects, with respect to distinctive characteristics, should be forbidden. But equality and non-discrimination are relevant when it comes to the human and civil rights of homosexuals: with regard to same-sex relationships, a general recognition of non-discrimination based on sexual orientation has been reached.[9] Historically homosexual conduct was often strongly repressed, and in many countries today homophobic abuses are still committed. However, the huge energy and determination of the gay rights movement has played a determining role in increasing awareness and sensitivity.[10]

Within the wider intervention in the area of fundamental rights, EU provisions and international treaties have supported the non-discrimination principle based on sexual orientation, initially in Article 13 of the Amsterdam Treaty, which explicitly equates discrimination based on sexual orientation with that based on gender, race, ethnic origin, religion, opinion, physical handicap or age.

Another fundamental step was taken by the resolution of the European Parliament on 8 February 1994. In *The Equality of Rights for Homosexuals in the Community*[11] (confirmed by the resolution of 16 March 2000[12]), it invites Member States to promote homosexual rights and to abolish any form of discrimination, showing an openness to same-sex marriage or at least a legal status equivalent to heterosexual marriage, as well as the possibility of parenthood for homosexuals. Reactions from jurists were not

---

[9] Garneri (1999); Wintemute (1995) 6ff; Bonini Baraldi (2001). Eg Cottier (ch 11) points out that the prohibition of discrimination on grounds of the way of life was introduced in the Swiss Constitution in 2000, thanks to the pressure of gay and lesbian lobbies.

[10] In 1998 the homosexual movement only existed in 36 countries whereas in 1993 an increase of 55 per cent was registered: Heinze (1995) 58.

[11] In *Guce (Gazzetta officiale)*, 28 Feb 1984, n 61, p 40.

[12] Art 56, Res A5–0050/2000.

unanimous: some were positive (Costanza, 1994), but others were very critical (Schlesinger, 1994; Balletti, 1996), principally because of the supposed
exclusion by Article 29 of alternative forms of affective union.

A move towards full legitimation of new models of cohabitation can be
found in the Paper of the Fundamental Rights (Di Majo, 2001; Conetti,
2001), signed in Nice in December 2000 in which Articles 7, 9 and 21 refer
explicitly to homosexual relationships. Article 7 refers to respect for private
and family life, and the right of privacy is also relevant here, in
that it included the right to have affective and intimate sexual relationships
as an expression of individual personality and freedom, secure from hostile
reactions.[13] Article 9, modifying Article 12 CEDU, mentions the right to
marry and establish a family without specifying the gender of the partners
(Rodotà, 2001: XIII). Finally, Article 21 forbids discrimination based on
sexual orientation. The Paper is in itself innovative and arresting,[14] although
its binding power and validity will depend on its integration into subsequent treaties.

As regards the effectiveness and the importance of the Paper for the
Italian legal system, the Commission for Community Policies of the Chamber
defined it as a legally binding document, the lowest common denominator
of 'a Europe which is able to realize its unity in respecting its diversities, by
trying to build such unity on common factors'. However, in the conclusive
resolution, changes to the Paper were desired, above all in relation to the
Italian Constitution.

It is with reference to constitutional principles that major problems will
arise, if and when the Paper becomes binding. Serious difficulties could
emerge with reference to the incompatibility between Article 29 of the
Constitution and Article 9 of the Paper, which potentially grants the right
of marriage to homosexual couples too. Conflict amongst jurists, adverse
reactions from the Catholic Church[15] and questions about relations between
sources of law are to be expected. The crux of the matter will be the recon-
ciliation of non-discrimination based on sexual orientation with the traditional principles of civil law.

THE ITALIAN SITUATION AND POSSIBLE SOLUTIONS

The gay movement in Italy dates back about 30 years. Public opinion has
recently become more tolerant, but this development is not reflected in the
state of the law. Little has changed, and a great deal remains to be done to

---

[13] Bloustein (1964); Richards (1977), (1979); Ceccherini (2001); Torbati (1996–97);
McClain (1995); Reiman (1976); Saunders (1991).

[14] Rodotà (2001), according to which the Charter 'politicamente vincola già tutti i soggetti,
sovranazionali e nazionali, che ad essa hanno dato il loto consenso'; Ruscello (2001).

[15] The Consilium of the Episcopal Conferences of Europe was critical of the paper in relation to both the attempt at legitimising alternative unions and for having omitted any reference to God.

remove discrimination and satisfy the claim for rights. The hope is that the legislature will soon respond to these urgent demands.

Those who favour a normative intervention will pin their hopes on the European integration process (Grillini, 2000) and propose solutions inspired by foreign experience, for many European governments have long since implemented equal rights for homosexuals.

1 Case Law

Until now cases concerning homosexual couples have seldom gone to court. From the few judgments we have, however, the application of the same principle elaborated with reference to heterosexual cohabitation, namely that of a stable and lasting affective relationship, emerges as the ratio decidendi.

In a case some years ago,[16] where a landlord evicted a tenant claiming that his cohabitation with another man concealed a sublease, the court stated that the expression 'living together as husband and wife' means a *way* of living together, which could refer both to heterosexual and homosexual cohabitation. The judgment went further and said that in homosexual relationships, mutual assistance or disbursement of money in case of illness or need is a moral and social duty, ie a natural obligation.

Similarly, in two other cases,[17] the court held that moral support and expenses paid by one partner in favour of the other constituted a natural obligation. The Court of Florence, in a case where a man claimed money spent on looking after his dead partner, stated that, as the partners were linked by a close and stable bond of affection, their relationship was not a simple cohabitation but involved specific duties. Finally in 1993[18] the Turin Assizes recognised the right of a homosexual to abstain from testifying against his partner, in the same way as the rule applies to heterosexual partners.

2 The 'Registry Family' and Civil Union Registers

The 'registry family' is defined by Article 4 dPR n 223/1989 as 'people bound by marriage ties, relationship, affinity, adoption, protection or affective ties, cohabiting and having habitual residence in the jurisdiction of the same council'. So, it could refer to a couple of the same sex,[19] though only for registration and without further legal relevance.

---

[16] Trib Roma, 20 Nov 1982, n 13445, in *Temi Romana* (1983: 379).

[17] Trib Firenze, 11 Aug 1986, in *Dir eccl* (1989) II, p 367; Court of Cassation, 22 Feb 1995, n 1989, in *Arch civ* (1960) I, p 484, n by De Tilla.

[18] Corte d'Assise di Torino, 19 Nov 1993, in *Riv pen* (1994) p 55.

[19] Balletti (1996) believes that a registered family is the only form of homosexual relationship possibly recognised.

Some councils, in order to facilitate their functions, have set up a register of civil unions in which 'the relationship of civil union between two people, even of the same sex', appears.[20] Such initiatives have often been opposed by Regional Control Committees and subsequently rejected by Regional Administrative Courts, in view of the constitutional irrelevance of civil unions and the limitations on council competence in registration and other civil matters.[21] However, in the district of Bologna the practice turned out to be very positive, and council housing was also accorded to same-sex couples.

3 Bills

A few Bills refer to homosexual relationships.[22] Some are very significant, such as the 'Soda' law Bill,[23] which specifically regulates 'affective' homosexual relationships. It imposes anti-discriminatory provisions, and also regulates same-sex marriages, on the basis of the Danish model. The Bill was partly modified and subsequently reintroduced.[24] More recently, another Bill was proposed which referred to 'registered domestic union' for homosexuals and confers on cohabitants the power of regulating their assets as heterosexual couples do (Grillini, 2002). So far as non-discrimination is concerned, a Bill was introduced for the first time in 1999.[25] Its aim was to put the equality principle into full effect by removing any discrimination, including that based on sexual orientation. As a result, those who suffer discrimination might have been able to take out an 'injunction' in order to stop it. If the Bill were to be enacted, it would represent a real advancement towards the recognition of equal rights for homosexual couples, bringing Italy into line with European legislation.

Only if we interpret existing regulations in the light of natural law are we obliged to deny that same-sex unions are 'luoghi degli affetti' (literally 'places of affection') (Bessone, 1976) where the values set out in the Constitution are achieved.[26] With reference to homosexuality, attention must be

[20] Bologna City Council, 3 March 1997; Pisa City Council, 8 July 1997; Firenze City Council, 20 July 1998; Prato City Council, 30 Oct 1997; Vaiano Cremasco City Council, motion 1, April 1997.

[21] Tar Toscana, 9 Feb 1996, n 49, in *Foro it* (1996) III, 524, n by Romboli and Rossi / *Registri Comunali Delle Unioni Civile Ed / Loro Censori*.

[22] Many bills were presented in Parliament: eg 'Vendola' 17 May 1996, n 1020; 'Buffo' 11 December 1996, n 2870; 'Cioni' 30 July 1997, n 2725.

[23] 12 March 1998, n 4657: see FM Colorni, *Matrimonio, Convivenze, Unioni Civili: la 'Soluzione Scandinava' del Progetto Soda*, in http://www.gay.it/view.php.

[24] Bill, 20 Sept 2001.

[25] Bill, n 6582, 'Measures against the Discriminations and for the Promotion of Equal Chance', presented in Parliament for discussion on 11 Jan 2001, examination postponed. Subsequently, another bill was presented in Senate: 'Measures Against Discrimination and Equal Opportunities Promotion', not yet examined.

[26] According to Barile (1984) 358, homosexual unions, as well as heterosexual ones, are based on affection, and the spiritual aspect is even more essential.

drawn to Article 3 para 1 of the Constitution, which explicitly prohibits discrimination on grounds of personal characteristics: in fact, according to scientific data, homosexuality is a personal characteristic intrinsic to the individual, neither chosen nor willed. Homosexual inclination hinges on the nature of the individual: as such, ideology or lifestyle choice should not be considered, and it cannot be ethically or morally judged. Homosexuality pertains to human rights,[27] and should be regarded and legally recognised as belonging to this sphere. Moral hostility in Italy cannot prevent legal recognition of stable same-sex relationships.[28]

A further objection invoked against homosexuality is the lack of procreative purpose, so whilst homosexuality may be respected 'as an interpersonal relation', it could not assume any further relevance.[29] Although the argument is plausible, at least some regulation of economic assets would be appropriate, in order to facilitate an awareness of the responsibility of individual choices, and to avoid unjustified favour or disadvantage.[30]

Denial of protection leads to clear inequities. Rights ascribed to heterosexual couples are not accessible to homosexuals: no benefits exist for carers, there is no right to succession in a lease in the event of the death or incapacity of the partner, nor indeed any other succession rights, not even reversion of pension. Only a few district legislatures recognise the right to council house allocation and no protection is given to the weaker partner in the case of relationship breakdown.

The legal invisibility of the homosexual makes it difficult to identify both the damage and the person responsible: if the right to an affective tie is not recognised, who has violated whose rights? What tools can be employed against verbal aggression which does not carry a penalty?

Daily experience of clear discrimination, in which the subjects involved are powerless, are many and frequent throughout life. Quite often, once personal sexual identity starts to manifest itself, homosexuality is understandably thwarted by well-meaning parents or teachers, who may end by damaging the full and free development of the individual's dignity (Concetti, 1997: 6, 29, 46, 64) and right to privacy (Rodotà, 1995: 105). Further discrimination may take place in the working environment. For

---

[27] Colorni, *L'Italia laica e i diritti degli omosessuali*, in http:/www.gay.it/view.php.

[28] Sacra Romana Rota 28 July 1981, *Foro it*, Rep 1983, voce *Matrimonio*, n 148, n by Gullo, in *Dir eccles* (1982) II, p 48.

[29] D'Agostino (1994); Castello (1994). According to ecclesiastic court trends, homosexuality is a cause for the nullity of marriage, as it is a 'psychic nature cause' that prevents *consortium vitae coniugalis*, due to the psychological impossibility of sharing a sincere sexual donation with a partner of opposite sex and of creating a Christian family with children: Trib eccles reg Umbria, 26 Feb 1993, *Foro it*, Rep (1994), voce *Matrimonio*, n 120; Trib Apostolico Romana Rota, 24 Nov 1987, *Foro it*, Rep (1990), voce *Matrimonio*, n 104; Trib eccles reg A 18 June 1987, *Foro it*, Rep. (1989), voce *Matrimonio*, n 93; Sacra Romana Rota 24 Nov 1983, *Foro it*, Rep (1985), voce *Matrimonio*, n 85, and 31 Jan 1980, *Foro it*, Rep (1981), voce *Matrimonio*, n 88.

[30] Romboli and Rossi, above n 21.

although no disciplinary measures can be adopted against employees by reason of sexual orientation, homosexuality is often a reason for verbal and sexual harassment by colleagues.[31]

Other difficulties occur in social relationships and other areas giving rise to a consciousness that wrongs and discrimination affect the social and existential balance of homosexual individuals. So the possibility of a remedy based on 'existential damage' emerges. This is a new kind of damage originating in the law of tort, but covering a wide range of cases, and is increasingly cited in situations that were unprotected in the past (Menzione and Manna, 2001). Thus, for example, the eviction of a surviving partner causes economic damage, but also has repercussions in the emotional sphere, as he/she may be forced to abandon the house where many years were spent together. In cases of death, the loss of goods of sentimental value causes damage in the intimate and social sphere. Failure to recognise the right to a 'family' business involves double damage, both economic and emotional. To take this line of argument to extremes, the impossibility of procreation or adoption involves the impossibility of psychological projection in children, from which an undeniable diminution in the affective and social sphere results.[32] 'Existential damage' opens the way to protecting the development of the gay personality and the removal of discrimination, even though exhaustive protection is still a long way off.

Finally, legal protection for the homosexual family is inconceivable if resistance to normative regulation of the de facto heterosexual family is not overcome. In fact, only in those legal systems that have recognised heterosexual cohabitation for a long time (Marella, 2001) have specific rules for same-sex relationships subsequently been introduced.

In general, there are undeniable analogies between the two forms of cohabitation, with special reference to the lack of legal protection and the denial of fundamental rights. But homosexuals' needs for legal protection differ from heterosexuals' needs. In terms of equality of treatment, and the prohibition of discrimination, the heterosexual couple can opt for informal cohabitation and, in those legal systems which admit it, registered partnership; or they can freely choose marriage, from which stems an exhaustive regulation of personal and economic relations.

To permit the homosexual family the minimal protection granted to the de facto heterosexual family would not satisfy the requirement for equality under the law.[33] For this reason the gay movement demands some kind

---

[31] Confederazione Generate Italiano del Lauoro, *Una piccola storia ignobile: le molestie sessuali sui luoghi di lavoro: Come far valere i propri diritti*, in http://www.cgil.it/donne.

[32] *Ibid.*

[33] However, some believe that achieving a specific legal system for de facto couples would lead the government in the future to institutionalise same-sex couples. As Picontó Novales (ch 13, this volume) points out, that is what gays and lesbians tend to believe in Spain.

of legal regulation permitting homosexuals to regulate their relationships in the same way as a heterosexual couple can do through marriage.

This brings us to the admissibility of the legalisation of same-sex marriage. Although I agree that denying marriage to homosexuals violates the principle of equality under law, I do also believe that Italian society is not yet ready to extend the old-fashioned definition of marriage to include loving same-sex couples. The legislator, in making laws, must have regard to social practice and moral beliefs, as any regulation of family matters has its origins in the social and cultural tradition. Same-sex marriage is not yet a shared and common practice in Italian society, which still considers marriage accessible only to heterosexual couples.

But reasons for treating marriage as out of the question collapse in the face of various proposals, for example a registered partnership with patrimonial consequences solely for the partners, without reference to the possibility of children. Before homosexual relationships can be legally recognised, they must be fully accepted in society. Some signals that this process is in progress already exist (Forder, 2000), primarily the abrogation of penalty rules[34] and the related prohibition on discrimination based on sexual orientation. Homosexuality cannot be considered a disease[35] or voluntary, but rather as a structural and irremovable part of the person's emotional life. Public declaration of their sexual orientation by institutional figures might also help.

At least three reasons for special regulation are identifiable: respect for private and family life; the practical considerations stemming from concrete events (such as consciousness of the consequences of Aids); and anti-discriminatory rules (Forder, 2000). The latter has strong symbolic meaning and relevant practical effects: the rules prohibiting discrimination by sexual orientation represent the legal justification for rejecting statutes explicitly forbidding same-sex marriage or partnership, and artificial procreation and adoption.

Italy could draw inspiration from solutions adopted elsewhere in Europe,[36] not least as a result of demands for harmonisation of human rights. Legislative models point to the following possibilities:

Unregistered partnership: some countries safeguard same-sex partners when the relationship breaks down, with special regard to patrimonial assets;[37] rights and duties flow from the simple fact of stable cohabitation, with no need for registration. Rights and duties are limited to certain situations and are

[34] In Italy, penalty rules for homosexuals were abolished in 1889.

[35] Colorni in *Uguaglianza formale e movimento gay* in http://comunita.gay.it/arcigay/udine/allgay/docum/mill5.htm.

[36] With reference to the regulation in the rest of the world, see Ceccherini (2001), Forder (2000). For example, this is the approach made in Switzerland by the Federal Office of Justice in 1999 in preparing the preliminary draft law on registered partnerships for same sex (see Cottier ch 11, this volume).

[37] Eg Hungary and Sweden.

usually inferior to those of heterosexual couples. But in some cases, rights flowing from marriage are expressly attributed to homosexuals.[38]

Registered partnership: protection is the same as that derived from marriage. Two cases are identifiable: registered cohabitation and registered partnership. Registered cohabitation usually applies to any couple independent of sexual orientation.[39] Registered partnership confers the same rights as those derived from marriage: mutual assistance, that is, social security and welfare rights. Except for those who reject any regulation at all, Italian jurists accept registered partnership, because it does not interfere with marriage nor with the notion of family as stated by Article 29 of the constitution.

Marriage: although the homosexual lobby has claimed free access to marriage, there is strong political and cultural resistance to the idea, because of the implied threat that such recognition would constitute for the traditional institution of marriage.[40]

Cohabitation agreement: a contractual tie between two adult people, aimed at regulating their economic relationship during cohabitation and even afterwards. A bill on this subject has been presented to the Italian Parliament, which does not reject its admissibility to homosexuals, but understandably this is not the way fully to satisfy demands for protection and equality.

In Italy the only practicable solution may be the regulation of the patrimonial assets without reference to marriage or to children or adoption. That would satisfy legitimate requests for equal treatment and absence of discrimination, because same-sex cohabitants could choose between regulating their patrimonial and legal relations and waiving this right. However, the path to full equality in respect of rights is a long one, and even in those countries where full regulation is in force, the process was gradual and took many years.

In order to deprive same-sex relationships of any protection, some invoke the natural impossibility of procreation. Reproductive capacity would be a specific element characterising both marriage and the de facto heterosexual

---

[38] Usually in the working circle, such as in the USA, or in immigration matters, such as in England.

[39] For example, such a regulation is in force in Belgium, France, Aragona, Navarra, and Valencia, whereas in Catalonia there is a distinction between heterosexual and homosexual couples; a registration system also works in Scotland and it applies mainly to homosexuals in California, Vermont and Hawaii.

[40] In the USA, for example, the debate was centred on the right of homosexuals to marry, whereas, on the contrary, in Canada, as Glennon found (ch 10, this volume), the question of marriage was voluntarily avoided, and the debate centred on non-discrimination and conferral of benefits. In Canada, some commentators within the gay and lesbian community argue that the institution of marriage should be decentralised, both socially and legally. However, according to Glennon, questions of whether the institution of marriage itself continues to bestow certain rights and obligations on spouses (whether heterosexual or same-sex) are separate policy questions. The argument that marriage should not attract the bundle of rights and obligations which it currently does, should not be used as an argument against legalising same-sex relationships.

family, so that its impossibility within same-sex couples would preclude all regulation.[41]

An alternative approach points out that the different sex of the partners is not referred to in any legal disposition as a necessary condition for a family; furthermore, many heterosexual couples cannot or do not want to have children.[42]

Ostracism of same-sex couples may be partly due to the fact that historically homosexuality has been identified with paedophilia or pederasty. But such an idea stems from a faulty conception of homosexuality, as a perversion or illness and not as an individual's personal condition.

The right to children cannot be denied to anyone without contravening the principle of equality and non-discrimination that exists in a democratic society. According to current Italian legislation, the law with regard to children functions within the traditional family model—the only one accepted by Article 29 of the Constitution—the place where the best interests of the child find full realisation. So the legal system is built on and thought of as referring to the conjugal heterosexual family, naturally destined to procreate. In short, the law concerning children is used for preserving the role of the heterosexual conjugal family in contrast to any other family model. No disposition explicitly denies custody to a homosexual parent, so that the opportunity to grant it should be taken into consideration in specific cases. But parental responsibility could not be assigned to the parent's new partner, because Italian law requires marriage and the adoption of the partner's child by the step-parent, according to Article 44(b) l.184/1983 (Adoption Law). These provisions create obstacles for same-sex couples: namely the impossibility of marriage and adoption of children. Assisted fertilisation, according to a new bill, is accessible only to the heterosexual couple whether married or not.

Theoretically, homosexuals could adopt a child only in the special cases mentioned by Article 44(a), (c) and (d) l.184/1983,[43] exceptionally available to single people. But there have been no test cases and such a request would be likely to be rejected. Italian adoption law is inspired by the so-called *imitatio naturae* principle: parents of opposite sex are a natural presupposition

---

[41] The impossibility of procreating is strongly maintained by the Catholic Church in order to deny legal relevance to same-sex relationships. See Giovanni Paolo II, *Discorso al Tribunale della Rota Romana*, 21 Jan 1999; and Pontificio Consiglio per la Famiglia, *Dichiarazione sulla Risoluzione del Parlamento Europeo che equipara la famiglia alle 'unioni di fatto', comprese quelle omosessuali*, 17 March 2000. Children are considered a presupposition of the existence of family also in Switzerland (see Cottier, ch 11, this volume), where the child living in a homosexual registered partnership is not considered as child of both partners.

[42] Wintemute, 'An Overview of Changes Within and Outside Europe', paper presented to the meeting 'Stare Insieme', Pisa, 5–6 Nov 1999.

[43] According to Art 44, cases of special adoption are: (1) the minor is an orphan and the adopter is within the sixth degree of kinship or is bound to the child by stable relationship pre-existing his parent's death; (2) the adopter is the parent's spouse; (3) there is no possibility of applying for fostercare; (4) the minor is both handicapped and orphaned, according to Art 3, 1° para, L. 104/1992.

and parents will 'naturally' be married, as the conjugal family is the exclusive admissible parameter. The legislature is not interested in other family models; their existence in social reality is recorded but not regulated, for fear that reforms involve radical change and a threat to the social order. The same-sex family is seen as a 'monster without any valid justification' (Balletti, 1996), outside what is natural and therefore ignored by law (Costanza, 1994). But homosexuals are individuals, with the same needs as heterosexuals and with the same desires for parenthood.

But does the understandable longing for children conflict with the minor's interest whose right to a conventional family should be protected? In what kind of family has the child the right to be brought up? The same-sex family could be a proper 'place of affection' for the child's development and same-sex partners could be the best of parents. In many instances, parents of different sex prove incapable of bringing up a child and loving him or her, so parents of opposite gender are not a necessary prerequisite for the expression of love and affection. Any negative impact on children deriving from their parents' sexual orientation has never even been scientifically tested: in fact homosexuality usually develops inside the heterosexual family.

However, modern psychological, psychiatric and psychoanalytic science has demonstrated the child's need for a model of parenthood founded on parents of the opposite sex, for balanced personality development, proper character-building and a regular process of socialisation (Finocchiaro and Finocchiaro, 1983: 72). Above all, in spite of rare enlightened points of view, a cultural obstructionism persists, which could in itself harm a child's development if living in an unusual family setting.

The principal impediment to the recognition of the right to parenthood for homosexuals is a cultural one. Apart from the undeniable need to purge Italian society of any discriminatory attitude to sexual orientation, no right to parenthood (whether biological or by adoption) exclusively aimed at satisfying selfish individual desires or desire for self-fulfilment exists. The prime concern is the minor's right to develop in the most suitable environment. There are many legal stumbling blocks in the way of achieving parenthood for homosexuals in Italy. For the moment, acknowledgement that a same-sex couple could be regarded as a suitable parental family would represent a symbolic step in the right direction.

In conclusion, no explicit discriminatory or anti-discriminatory dispositions in relation to sexual orientation are traceable in the Italian legal system, so that the only protection given is that available to individuals in general, and in this sense Italy differs from the approach taken by the European Parliament.

A normative revision is at present quite unlikely. However, Italy remains a Member State of the European Union. As such, it has chosen to participate in a system which enunciates rules and common principles, whose observance, though not compulsory, is generally promoted.

With the utmost respect for Italian cultural traditions, some changes could be made. First, Article 3 of the Constitution could be modified by adding sexual orientation as an element in non-discrimination. Further, an anti-discriminatory law with reference to personal and social homosexual relations is necessary. Judicial decisions would also constitute an important step forward, but only if cases are brought to court. The next step would be legal recognition of homosexual relationships, in keeping with the European trend.

The time is not ripe for legal or social acceptance of same-sex marriage as the hand of tradition continues to rest heavily on the Italian legislature. But regulation of patrimonial assets and their relevance in respect to third parties might be more feasible. Intervention in matters of parenthood is not currently desirable: society is not ready for it nor would it currently be to the advantage of children.

The hope is that the legislature will soon accept the need to regulate same-sex relationships and so keep in line with other Western governments in promoting the principles of equality and non-discrimination.

REFERENCES

Balletti, S (1996) 'Le Coppie Omosessuali, le Istituzioni Comunitarie e la Costituzione Italiana' *Rassegna Di Diritto Civile*: 241.

Barbagali, M and A Colombo (2001) '*Omosessuali Moderni: Gay e Lesbiche in Italia* (Bologna: Il Mulino).

Barile, P (1984) *Diritti dell'Uomo e Libertà Fondamentali* (Bologna: Zanichelli).

Bessone, M (1976) 'Rapporti Etico: Sociali (artt. 29–31)' in V di Branca (ed), *Commentario della Costituzione* (Bologna and Roma: Società Editrice del Foro Italiano).

—— (1979) 'Favor Matrimonii e Regime del Convivere in Assenza di Matrimonio' *Diritto della Famiglia e delle Persone*: 1192.

Bessone, M, G Alpa, G Ferrando, A D'Angelo and MR Spallarossa (eds) (1995) *La Famiglia nel Nuovo Diritto* (Bologna: Zanichelli).

Bianca, CM (2001) *Dititto Civile: La Famiglia, Le Successioni* (Milan: Giuffrè).

Bin, M (2000) 'La Famiglia: alla Radice di un Ossimoro' *Studium Luris*: 1066.

Bloustein, EJ (1964) 'Privacy as an Aspect of Human Dignity: An Answer to Dean Prosser' *New York University Law Review* 39: 962.

Bonini Baraldi, M (2001) 'Società Pluraliste e Modelli Familiari: il Matrimonio tra Persone dello Stesso Sesso in Olanda' *Familia*: 419.

Campagna, L (1966) *Famiglia Legittima e Famiglia Adottiva* (Milan: Giuffrè).

Cassano, G (2002) *Manuale del Nuovo Diritto di Famiglia* (Piacenza: La Tribuna).

Castello, M (1994) 'Sulle Proposte, di Istituzione dei Registri delle Unioni Civili e di Introduzione del Matrimonio tra Persone dello Stesso Sesso' *Giurisprudenza di Merito*: 993.

Ceccherini, G (2001) 'Il Principio di Non Discriminazione in Base all'Orientamento Sessuale in Alcuni Ordinamenti Stranieri: lo Stato del Dibattito' *Diritto Pubblico Comparato ed Europeo* 1: 39–60.

Concetti, G (1997) *Diritti Degli Omosessuali* (Casal Monferrato: Piemme).

—— (2001) 'La Carta dei Diritti Fondamentali dell'Unione Europea' *Studium Juris*: 1163.

Costanza, M (1994) 'Adottare è un Diritto di Tutti?' *Diritto della Famiglia e delle Persone*: 1079–83.

D'Agostino, F (1994) 'Le Coppie Omosessuali, Problema per i Giuristi' *Iustitia*: 80–81.

D'Angeli, F (2001) *La Tutela Delle Convivenze Senza Matrimonio* (Turin: Giappichelli).

De Cupis, A (1961) 'Il Concubinato nel Diritto Privato' *Foro Padano* 3: 75.

De Luca, L (1996) *La Famiglia non Coniugale. Gli Orientamenti della Giurisprudenza* (Padova: Cedam).

Di Majo, A (2001) 'La Carta dei Diritti Fondamentali dell'Unione Europea: Aspetti Giuridici e Politici' *Europa e Diritto Privato*: 50.

Donati, T (1990) 'La Famiglia di Fatto come Realta' Sociale e come Problema Sociale Oggi in Italia' *Iustita*: 239.

Ferrando, G (1997) 'Assegno di Divorzio e Convivenza More Uxorio' *Famiglia e Diritto*: 30.

—— (1998) 'Convivere senza Matrimonio: Rapporti Personali e Patrimoniali nella Famiglia di Fatto' *Famiglia e Diritto*: 185.

—— (2000) 'Gli Accordi di Convivenza: Esperienze a Confronto' *Rivista Critica di Diritto Privato*: 163.

Finocchiaro, A and Finocchiaro, F (1983) *Disciplina dell'Adozione e dell'Affidamento dei Minori* (Milan: Giuffrè).

Forder, C (2000) 'Riconoscimento e Regime Giuridico delle Coppie Omosessuali in Europa' *Rivista Critica di Diritto Privato*: 107.

Francescato, G (1974) *Famiglie Aperte: La Comune* (Milan: Giuffrè).

Garneri, S (1999) 'Le Droit Constitutionel et les Discriminations Fondées sur l'Orientation Sexuelle (Premiere Partie)' *Reviste Franceze Droit Constitutionel* 40: 727.

Grassetti, C (1950) 'I Principi Costituzionali Relativi al Diritto Familiare' in P Calamandrei, A Ievi and A Barbera (eds), *Commentario Sistematico alla Costituzione Italiana* (Florence).

Grillini, F (2000) 'Omosessuali e Diritti: Il Pacs in Francia e il Confronto con la Situazione Italiana' *Rivista Critica di Diritto Privato*: 183.

Heinze, E (1995) *Sexual Orientation: A Human Right Act* (Dordrecht, Boston and London: Nijhoff).

Jemolo, AC (1948) 'La Familiglia e il Diritto' *Annuario Facoltà Giuriursprudenza Universita Catania* 2: 38.

—— (1966) 'La Costituzione: Difetti, Modifiche, Integrazioni' in Ornaghi (ed), *La Costituzione della Repubblica* (Milan: Giuffrè).

Longo, F (2000) 'Le Convivenze "Registrate" Nei Paesi Dell'U.E.' *Notariato*: 186.

Mancini, G (1963) 'Uguaglianza tra Coniugi e Societa' Naturale nell Article 29 della Costituzione' *Rivista di Diritto Civile*: 223.

Marella, MR (2001) 'Il Diritto di Famiglia Fra Status e Contratto: il Caso Delle Convivenze Non Fondate Sul Matrimonio' *Stare Insieme. I Regimi Giuridici della Convivenza Tra Status e Contratto*: 3.

McClain, C (1995) 'Inviolability and Privacy: The Castle, the Sanctuary, and the Body' *Yale Journal of Law and Humanities* 7: 195.

Menzione, D and Manna, E (2001) 'Omosessualità: Torti e Discriminazioni' in P Cendon (ed), *Trattato Breve dei Nuovi Danni*, vol 1 (Padua: Cedam).

Prosperi, F (1980) *La Famiglia non Fondata sul Matrimonio* (Naples: Jovene).

Puleo, S (1996) 'Voce I Famiglia. II) Disciplina privatistica. In Generale' in *Enciclopedia Giuridica Treccani* (Rome: Treccani).

Quadri, E (1999) 'Problemi Giuridici Attuali della Famiglia di Fatto' *Famiglia e Diritto*: 503.

Rapoport, R (1989) 'Ideologies about Family Forms: Towards Diversity' in K Boh *et al* (eds), *Changing Patterns of European Family Life* (London: Routledge).

Reiman, JH (1976) 'Privacy, Intimacy, and Personhood' *Philosophical and Public Affairs* 6: 26.

Richards, J (1977) 'Unnatural Acts and the Constitutional Right to Privacy' *Fordham Law Review* 45: 1281.

—— (1979) 'Sexual Autonomy and the Constitutional Right to Privacy: A Case Study in Human Rights and the Unwritten Constitution' *Hastings Law Journal* 30: 957.

Rodotà, S (1995) *Tecnologie e Diritti* (Bologna: Zanichelli).

—— (2000) Pamphlet in D Menzione (ed), *Diritti dei Gay. Istruzioni per l'Uso: una Guida Pratica per Lesbiche e Gay* (Rome: Enola).

—— (2001) *Presentazione al Volume Stare Insieme: I Regimi Giuridici della Convivenza Tra Status e Contratto, a Cura dDi Grillini-Marella* (Naples: Jovene).

Ruscello, F (2001) 'La Famiglia tra Diritto Interno e Normativa Comunitaria' *Familia*: 710.

Saunders, C (1991) 'Privacy and Social Contract: A Defense of Judicial Activism in Privacy Cases' *Arizona Law Review* 33: 811.

Scalisi, V (1987) 'La Famiglia e le Famiglie (Il Diritto di Famiglia a Dieci Anni dalla Riforma)' in AA.VV. *Scritti Catanzaresi in Onore di Falzea* (Naples: Esi).

Schlesinger, P (1994) 'Una Risoluzione del Parlamento Europeo Sugli Omosessuali' *Corriere Giuridico*: 393.

Sesta, M (Unpublished) *Le Convivenze Omosessuali Nell'esperienza Italiana*.

Solaini, L (2000) 'La Famiglia di Fatto' in P Cendon (ed), *Il Diritto Privato Nella Giurisprudenza: La Famiglia*, vol 1 (Turin: Giappichelli).

Stella Richter, G (1965) 'Aspetti Civilistici del Concubinato' *Rivista. Trimestrale di Diritto e Procedura. Civile*: 1123.

Torbati, M (1996–97) 'The Right of Intimate Sexual Relations: Normative and Social Bases for According It "Fundamental Right" Status' *Southern California Law Review* 2: 1817.

Ventura, S (1990) 'La Famiglia di Fatto, Famiglia Legittima e Giusta Familiarita' *Iustitia*: 420.

Wintemute, R (1995) *Sexual Orientation and Human Rights* (Oxford: Hart Publishing).

13

Cohabitation: The Ideological Debate in Spain

TERESA PICONTÓ NOVALES

MARRIAGE IS NO longer considered to be the only way into conjugal life by an increasingly large part of the Spanish population (Meil Landwerlin, 1999). The idea of cohabitation 'without papers' appears as a legitimate means of entering into a partnership and as a basis for the family.

However, the fact that de facto couples or unions are now a visible part of society, does not necessarily imply that they are seen as a new alternative to marriage. In the developed countries, this model tends to function either as an option in itself, or as a trial marriage. In European countries de facto cohabitation takes either of these forms, depending on the family culture and the legislation of each country, together with the presence or otherwise of children (Hague Academy of International Law, 1999).

What is clear is that Spanish society has opted for a plural, open and liberal family ideology, but, as Assier-Andrieu (1995: 88) has pointed out, 'perhaps much more linked to the idea of freedom (everybody is equal by virtue of their birth, free to practise their sexuality as they wish) than to the idea of equality'. More specifically, the Spanish Constitution contemplates the possibility of different forms of non-marital cohabitation, including any form of stable cohabitation, all of which are guaranteed with the different rights, firstly to freedom and dignity and then to the equality of those involved (Alberdi, 1995: 382; Roca Trías, 1990: 1072).

However, as Meil Landwerlin (1999: 18) has pointed out, we might ask if this freedom 'also extends to relationships between homosexual people: that is, is Spanish society tolerant towards homosexuality?'. The first thing to be underlined is that such tolerance is not uniformly present among the different groups within Spanish society. More specifically, it is determined by factors such as religiousness, age, level of education, marital status and, to a lesser extent, ideology. Two out of three non-believers, young people, university students, single or separated/divorced people with a left-wing or centre ideology do not condemn it. But at the same time, two out of three

Table 13.1 Opinion of Spanish People Regarding the Best Kind of Relationship
for a Stable Couple

Form of Cohabitation	Young People[a]	Population over 18[b]
Church marriages	36	54
Civil marriages	6	9
Living together without being married	18	11
Living together followed by a church marriage	24	9
Living together followed by a civil marriage	11	8
Not living together	1	1
Other answers	2	4
Doesn't know/no reply	3	4

Sources
[a] CIS-Instituto de la Juventud (Central Statistics Board, Youth Institute) Study 2.262.[1]
[b] CIS Study 2.283, March 1998.

or more elderly people, those practising any religion, those with only primary or lower education, widows/widowers or married people and those with right-wing ideology, consider that it is always wrong. On the other hand, the general trend in Spain is that, first, cohabitation ceased to be considered as immoral and then began to be understood as simply another way of living as couple.

The data in Table 13.1 reflect the evolution of the opinion of the Spanish people on the best kind of relationship for a stable couple. If we contrast the data in the CIS Instituto de la Juventud Study 2.262 in this respect with those of the CIS 2.283 (Barometer of March 1998), the trend reflected in the table above indicates the evolution of the opinion of younger people, who are increasingly in favour of cohabitation as the best kind of relationship for a stable couple. As can be seen in Table 13.1, 18 per cent of young people are in favour of living together without marriage as opposed to 11 per cent of the population aged over 18. This fact is even more significant if we bear in mind that for another 35 per cent of young people, cohabitation is a temporary option to be considered before church or civil marriage, as opposed to 17 per cent in the case of the population aged over 18.

Nonetheless, these views do not coincide with actual behaviour with respect to marriage. To be more specific, we are faced with a considerable difference between the preferences expressed and what actually happens in practice (Hernández Rodríguez, 1999: 18–19). In Spain, the changes in attitude outlined above do not alter the fact that real family behaviour and, more particularly, entry into family life and the formation of a stable couple continue, nonetheless, to be subject to institutional norms; that is, they occur through marriage. The arguments put forward in favour of marriage

[1] Cf CIS (1999).

are more patent in Spain than in other countries. As the CIS data reveal, the decision to marry continues to involve more public than private factors in Spain. More specifically, it may be said that family, social and even religious pressure are still important reasons for couples deciding to marry (CIS Instituto de la Juventud, 1997).[2] Some have pointed out that if the religious factor, which is decisive when it comes to opting for marriage, is combined with the level of education, it transpires that, no matter what the level of education is, the number of couples wishing to live together without marrying increases as we move away from religious practice (Flaquer, 1991: 62).

Furthermore, the Spanish defend marriage as opposed to living together, not so much for reasons of emotional security but more because of the support given by the partners' families in establishing the home, and the acquisition of greater security to support the stability of the couple. In summary, marriage is widely preferred as a form of stable cohabitation for the couple, even if this is only for reasons of social or family pressure or because the couple is going to have children (Hernández Rodríguez, 1999: 25–6).

There are other factors associated with the prevalence of cohabitation in Spain. De facto couples are found more often in the big cities and in the region of Catalonia and the Balearic Islands, together with Ceuta and Melilla, and are rarely found in small towns and in Navarre and Extremadura. It has also been pointed out that this cohabitation is more characteristic of the younger population, from the higher income bracket (Alberdi, 1995: 89, 108, 167; Flaquer, 1991: 61–67; Meil Landwerlin, 1999: 15, 19). Similarly, the average age for couples starting to live together is generally higher the higher the educational level, the social position and the socio-economic family status.

There are a number of reasons given for not formalising cohabitation, for example, the fact that the couple find it 'impossible' to marry (late termination of studies, difficulty in finding work, difficulty in finding a house), they may reject marriage for ideological reasons, and when it comes to negotiating becoming a couple may wish to minimise the risk of failure by means of trial cohabitation (FOESSA, 1995: 163; Camarero Suárez, 1998: 152–3). But overall the traditional ideological or financial reasons for not marrying seem to be giving way to reasons linked to the dynamics of the couple or the transition of its members to adult life.

In fact, it has been said that a process of 'pluralisation' of the models for and stages in entry into a living-together situation is taking place (Kaufmann, 1993: 46). This 'pluralisation' is reflected in the ideological and political debate that stable de facto couples are stimulating with their claims for legal recognition, which questions the exclusivity of the traditional family law model of marriage. It is expected that we will move towards consideration of equality, and away from what has up to now been

[2] Cf CIS (1999).

a constant trend in the legal reforms and social policies pertaining since the Spanish Constitution came into force in 1978. All of these have so far been more concerned with protecting people's freedom to organise their cohabitation than with equality in the treatment of diversity in existing cohabitation situations in our society (Picontó Novales, 1998).

INSTITUTIONAL RECOGNITION OF UNMARRIED COUPLES

In the case of Spain, first the courts and then the legislator, without formulating a generic treatment of de facto couples, started to correct some of the injustices that the current legislation was giving rise to for this new, growing family form. More specifically, Spanish jurisprudence has played an important political, social and legal part in bringing the rights of de facto couples into line with those of married couples (Mesa Marrero, 1999: 74).

Given the absence of any specific regulation governing the situation of de facto couples in Spain, as with other developments and situations pertaining to the family (Picontó Novales, 2001), there has been a succession, not only of social demands, but also of jurisprudential work which, although it has been hesitant, has gradually created a legal body of opinion able to respond to at least some of the problems and some of the questions posed by de facto couples.

The Constitutional Court (TC) considers that permanent affective relationships are worthy of legal and constitutional protection, but it does not believe that these and married couples are equivalent realities. For this reason, it is not logical to propose an equivalence of effects between the two types of couple, married and unmarried. But this does not prevent the de facto couple being given some of the rights pertaining to marriage, given that cohabitation *more uxorio* deserves legal and constitutional protection (Talavera, 1999a: 37).

More particularly, the Constitutional Court tends to attribute different consequences to unmarried people when it comes to Social Security pensions and urban leases (O'Callagan, 1998: 35; Pérez Canóvas, 1996: 173; de Verda y Beamonte, 1998: 480; Saura, 1995: 91). As far as pensions are concerned[3] there is an underlying idea that people who decide not to marry cannot automatically benefit from all the legal consequences that the law attributes to people who decide to marry, because there is an objective reason that justifies unequal treatment (ATC 156/1987, 11 Feb; Rulings of the TC: 29, 30, 35, 38, 14 Feb 1991; STC 77/ 1991, 11 April; STC 66/1994, 28 Feb; ATC 222/1994, 11 July). Regarding leases, the TC holds that the

---

[3] However, there are some rulings by the TC that do concede the widow's/widower's pension. Thus, for example, TC ruling 260/1998 of 22 December, in the Legal Basis of which the TC states: 'All the forms of extramarital cohabitation are not included in the sphere of the precept, but only those whose cause lies in the impossibility referred to, that is, those stable unions that were unable to be transformed into a conjugal bond.'

application of constitutional law to marriage is not in itself sufficient reason to justify not applying the benefits contemplated for the tenant's spouse to the unmarried 'cohabitating' person (STC 222/1992, 11 Dec; STC 6/1993, 18 Jan; STC 47/1993, 18 Feb).

Perhaps what lies behind the TC's approach is a desire to avoid being faced with the possibility of having to establish two different kinds of legal instrument, a marital and a non-marital one. This approach has been widely rejected both in Spanish jurisprudence and doctrine. In this sense, it should be said that, while it is a solid argument in the case of heterosexual couples who have the possibility of opting for marriage and do not do so; it would not appear to be so solid in the case of homosexual couples (Herrero Brasas, 1997: 49), many of whom have long been demanding the right to marry.

For its part, the jurisprudence of the Supreme Court has had to deal in cassation with several kinds of situations affecting de facto couples; including those in which the woman presents a claim as a result of the couple breaking up, or a claim is made upon the death of one of the 'cohabitants' (O'Callagan, 1998: 40; Pérez Canóvas, 1996: 259). While the Supreme Court (TS) jurisprudence has been categorical in denying similarity between marriage and the de facto couple, in some specific cases it has modified this attitude, allowing the analogous application of some personal or property-related effect of marriage to the de facto couple (eg in the TS Rulings of 18 May 1992 and 21 October 1992) (Talavera Fernández, 1999a: 40).

Furthermore, TS jurisprudence, by requiring heterosexuality in almost all its rulings for the acknowledgement of certain legal effects for de facto couples, has excluded homosexual couples. But the fact that in some of its rulings the TS does not apply this requisite when *more uxorio* cohabitation is established (for example, TS Ruling of 18 May 1992) could be interpreted as the TS being open in some cases to the possibility of homosexual couples being included in this kind of cohabitation (Talavera Fernández, 1999a; 45).

The Spanish legal system regulates only some of the legal effects of de facto couples and does so in a fragmentary and dispersed manner. More specifically, the acknowledgement of the rights and duties of stable, unmarried couples derives from specific legal practices, which bring this form of cohabitation into line with marital cohabitation or, where relevant, with the jurisprudence of the courts. Thus, for example, the Spanish state legislator allows de facto couples to adopt children jointly (but only heterosexual couples, 3rd Additional Clause of Law 21/1987 of 11 Nov); it also acknowledges their subrogation rights in the event of one of the tenants dying for both heterosexual and homosexual de facto couples (Art 16.1, Urban Lease Act of 24 Nov 1994); to use methods of assisted reproduction (only heterosexual de facto couples: Art 6 and 8.2, Assisted Reproduction Techniques Law of 22 Nov 1988); the right to obtain certain Social Security

Health Benefits and the relevant widow's pension[4] only exceptionally, in some legally determined cases (10th Additional Clause of Law 30/1981, 7 July, which regulates separation and divorce). Lastly, not only the spouse of a prisoner, but also the person united to him or her by a relationship of analogous affectivity, can use the 'Habeas Corpus' procedure, with no distinction for reasons of 'sexual orientation' (Art 3, Organic Law 6/1984, 24 May).[5]

At this point, we should note that it is the Autonomous Communities that have taken legislative initiatives to provide de facto couples with their own regulation in Spain. Thus, the Autonomous Communities of Catalonia, Aragon, Navarre, Valencia, Madrid, the Balearic Islands and Asturias have all decided to provide a regulatory framework for de facto couples. We have, firstly, the Catalan law for stable couple unions (L 10/1998, 15 July) and, secondly, the Aragonese Law relating to stable, unmarried couples (L 6/1999, 26 March). The Navarre parliament has also approved the legal equality law for stable couples (Law 6/2000, 3 July). This law, together with that of the Principality of Asturias on stable couples (L 4/2002, 23 May), stands out as a consequence of the social, political and institutional reaction to the recognition these give of the right of homosexual couples to adopt (Art 8, Navarre Law 6/2000) and foster (Art 8, Asturian Law 4/2002) children. More recently, the courts of Valencia have approved the law by which de facto unions are regulated (L 1/2001, 9 April 2001), followed by the Autonomous Communities of Madrid and the Balearic Islands who have respectively approved the De Facto Unions Law (L 11/2001) and the Stable Couples Law (L 18/2001). Finally, other autonomous communities are preparing their parliamentary proposals for de facto couples. Among these are, for example, those of Andalusia, the Basque Country, Castilla–La Mancha and the Canary Islands.

The Catalan and Aragonese Laws were the first to recognise the 'maritality' or marriage-like nature of a homosexual relationship in terms of equality with heterosexual couples. Furthermore, the Aragonese, Navarre and Asturias legislation grants stable de facto couples their own legal statute, which aims to resolve the main questions posed by these non-marital forms of cohabitation. These Aragonese, Navarre and Asturias laws

---

[4] The exceptional conditions in which there is a right to a widow's pension in de facto couples are reflected in the 10th Additional Clause of Law 30/1981, of 7 July. More specifically, the clause referred to acknowledges the right to this benefit to the survivor of a de facto union or unmarried couple when such a couple was unable to contract marriage due to an insoluble conjugal bond with another person.

[5] In this section I have only referred to some of the legal effects that the different laws grant to de facto couples, without aiming to be exhaustive and leaving out the negative effects reflected in the Criminal Code or in other laws. In any event, a more detailed analysis of both the negative and positive effects for de facto couples within the Spanish legal system can be found in Reina and Martinell, 1996: 64–79 and Mesa Marrero, 1999: 64–68.

Table 13.2 Legal Regulation of De Facto Couples in the Autonomous
Communities of the Spanish State

Autonomous Community	Legislative Situation	Distinction Between Hetrosexual And Homo-sexual Couples	Possible Recognition Adoption For Homo-sexual Couples in the Law[a]	Possible Recognition Fostering for Homo-sexual Couples in the Law[b]
Andalusia	Under way			
Aragon	Law 6/1999	1 single system	No	No
Asturias	Law 4/2002	1 single system	No	Yes
Balearic Islands	Law 18/2001	1 single system	No	No
Canary Islands	Under way			
Cantabria				
Castilla–La Mancha	Under way			
Castilla–Leon				
Catalonia	Law 10/1998	2 different systems	No	No
Extremadura				
Galicia				
La Rioja				
Madrid	Law 11/2001	1 single system	No	No
Murcia				
Navarre	Law 6/2000	1 single system	Yes	Yes
Basque Country	Under way			
Valencia	Law 1/2001	1 single system	No	No

[a] According to state legislation, only heterosexual de facto couples may adopt children. However, since it is legally possible for single people, widows or widowers, separated or divorced people to adopt individually, in practice there have been cases of minors being adopted by homosexual people, regardless of whether or not they were in a relationship at the time.

[b] Some of the autonomic legislations on the protection of minors allow fostering or even the adoption of minors by homosexual de facto couples, eg Valencian Law 7/1994, 5 December, on Protection of Children.

contemplate a single model, that of the stable couple, regardless of its sexual orientation: while the Catalan law contemplates two different systems depending on whether the couple is homosexual or heterosexual and distinguishes between them concerning inheritance (favouring heterosexuals) and the possibility of adoption (limited to heterosexual couples). With regard to the latter, we should note that the Aragonese law breaks with the overall approach of unitary treatment for both kinds of stable couple by introducing an article in which only heterosexual couples can adopt (Art 10).[6]

From another viewpoint, it should be pointed out how the Catalan, Aragonese, Navarre and Asturias laws, when defining the de facto couple, understand it explicitly as 'an effective relationship analogous to the married relationship' and add the appendix: 'regardless of its sexual orientation'. While the other Autonomous Laws, in which the Partido Popular has had the parliamentary initiative or has finally approved the law (in the case of Valencia or Madrid) do not include either of these two terms, they both avoid equating the relationship established between this kind of couple with that which is established between married couples and, of course, exclude any reference to sexual orientation.

To conclude this section, it should be underlined that there is still no state legislation on de facto couples in Spain, despite the fact that at different times there have been legislative initiatives in this regard. Among the more recent ones, reference should be made to the initiatives of 1996 and to their renewal in 2000. The bills presented to the general courts were as follows: Bill by which Legal Effects are Recognised for De Facto Couples, presented by the Socialist Group of the Congress (General Courts Official Bulletin, 8 Nov 1996); Bill on Legal Equality for de Facto Couples, presented by the Grupo Federal de Izquierda Unida – Iniciativa per Catalunya (General Courts Official Bulletin, 15 Nov 1996); Bill on the Recognition of Legal Effects for De Facto Couples, presented by the Coalición Canaria Parliamentary Group (General Courts Official Bulletin, 14 April 1997); Organic Bill on Civil Union Contract, presented by the Grupo Popular (General Courts Official Bulletin, 29 Sept 1997). The first three bills are characterised by the fact that they reflect a concept of the de facto couple based mainly on the existence of 'a relationship of affectivity similar to that of the married couple ... regardless of the sexual orientation' (Art 1, Socialist Group's Bill; Art 1.2, Izquierda Unida – Iniciativa per Catalunya Bill; Art 1, Canaries Coalition Bill). All of them apply some of the legal effects of marriage to de facto couples (tax, labour, administrative, health care, and widow's pension benefits). On the other hand, the Partido Popular's bill is not in itself a law for de facto couples, but rather claims to recognise certain legal effects for any relationship that exists between adults who, by means of a contract which is incompatible with the marriage contract, agree to live together and mutually help each other. The only bills eventually approved in the Chamber of Deputies for subsequent

---

[6] All these autonomous laws are only applicable to those who belong to the Autonomous Community in question. The communities can only legislate in matters in which they are competent, which means, among other things, that the Autonomous Communities cannot legislate in some of the most important practical questions for de facto couples, because these questions fall within the competence of the state. Among these are issues relating to Social Security, pensions, taxes, etc. In parallel fashion, neither can they establish a civil register system for de facto couples similar to that which is available to married couples.

parliamentary processing were those proposed by the Coalition Group of the Canaries and the Popular Group.

Since none of the bills presented during the previous legislative term had been approved, these were renewed during the year 2000 on a state level and new ones appeared. These include Bill by which some Legal Effects are Recognised for De Facto Couples, presented by the Socialist Parliamentary Group (12 April 2000); Bill on Measures for the Legal Equality of De Facto Couples, presented by the Izquierda Unida Parliamentary Group (14 April 2000); Bill on Stable Couple Unions, presented by the Catalan Parliamentary Group (3 May 2000); and Bill presented by the mixed group, at the proposal of Iniciativa per Catalunya–Els Verds. The most outstanding feature of these bills is that they all extend their legal effects to both heterosexual and homosexual de facto couples. The proposals of Izquierda Unida and Iniciativa per Catalunya–Els Verds also clearly contemplate the possibility of homosexual couples adopting. These four bills were rejected once more at the end of 2000. Lastly, reference should be made to the Bill of Legal Equality for Stable Couples of the Navarre Parliament, presented for consideration by the General Courts, which was rejected with 133 votes in favour, 154 against and 11 abstentions[7] on 3 April 2001.

De facto couples have been ignored for a long time by the Spanish state legislator. This is why, in the absence of a specific legal system to regulate the situation of de facto couples in Spain, jurisprudence has had to respond to the problems and questions that are posed by de facto couples. To be more specific, court decisions have been based on constitutional jurisprudence. Legal pronouncements on the requisites and effects of 'de facto cohabitation' have always appeared a posteriori; that is, once a specific question has been brought up and solved by the court, which decided whether or not certain effects pertaining to marriage could be applied to the case in question.

THE CONTROVERSY ON THE NAVARRE AUTONOMOUS LAW ON DE FACTO COUPLES: A CASE STUDY

In this section a more in-depth study will be made of the Navarre Law of Legal Equality for Stable Couples (Navarre Law 6/2000, 3 July), as it is the first law on de facto couples which grants homosexual couples the possibility of adopting (Art 8, Law 6/2000) and because of the controversy it gave rise to, both during the period of parliamentary debate and when it came into force. The first paragraph of Article 8 establishes: 'The members of a stable couple may jointly adopt, with the same rights and obligations as couples who are united by marriage.'

---

[7] *Diario de Sesiones del Congreso de los Diputados, Pleno y Diputación Permanente*, VII Legislature, no 73, 3 April 2001, ss 3600.

This Article, originally Article 6 in the Autonomous Bill for the Legal Equality of Stable Couples, presented by the Parliamentary Group of Izquierda Unida, had been rejected at the Plenary Session of the Commission with the UPN (Unión del Pueblo Navarro) voting against, and CDN (Convergencia de Demócratas de Navarra) abstaining. However, other political parliamentary groups (Izquierda Unida, Euskal Herritarrok and the Mixed Group) maintained their support for Article 6, and succeeded in having a new vote held in the Full Commission. As a result of having maintained their support and with the votes in favour of PSN and CDN, who changed their position, the text of Article 6 was eventually approved by the plenary session of the commission.[8]

No sooner had the law been passed, on 6 October 2000, than 83 deputies of the Popular Parliamentary Group presented an appeal against it on the grounds of unconstitutionality. This was an appeal that contested the whole Navarre Autonomous Law. The alleged reasons included various lines of argument related to the central intention of the contested law to establish complete equivalence between marriage and stable couples in the name of equality. Moreover, they argued that due to this intended equality, the possibility of homosexual couples adopting would go against 'the natural biological order, according to which children need a father and a mother, or a father or a mother, but not two fathers or two mothers'; together with placing the minor in a 'living environment that would be clearly damaging to the harmonious development of his or her personality'. Lastly, according to the appellants this autonomous law violates the exclusivity of the state's competence to regulate the legal system of civil relationships on forms of marriage.[9]

Probably one of the most important reasons for the social and political upheaval caused by this Navarre Law was the legal and institutional recognition of homosexual de facto couples as affective family cohabitation and, in particular, the explicit legal recognition of the right of these couples to joint adoption (Art 8 of L 6/2000). More recently, the Asturias Law of Stable Couples (Law of the Principality of Asturias 4/2002, 23 May) has led to the same political and social upheaval for having set stable de facto couples on an equal footing with married couples, regardless of their sexual orientation (Art 8, Law 4/2002).[10]

With respect to this issue, both the Navarre Autonomous Law 6/2000 and the Asturias Law 4/2002, because they contemplate the possibility of homosexual couples adopting or fostering, would be in line with the

---

[8] *Diario de Sesiones del Parlamento de Navarra*, V Legislature, no 22, 22 June 2000, ss 16.

[9] Appeal of unconstitutionality presented on 6 Oct 2000 by 8 deputies of the Partido Popular against Autonomous Law 6/2000, 3 July, for the legal equality of stable couples of the Navarre Parliament (Legal–Material Grounds 1, 2, 3).

[10] In relation to Asturias Law 4/2002, 3 July, the Partido Popular of this Autonomous Community is studying the possibility of presenting an appeal of unconstitutionality as it considers that the law constitutes an invasion of the competencies of the state administration.

European Parliament Resolution of 8 February 1994, on equal rights for homosexuals and lesbians, which, with the aim of avoiding any discrimination that might exist in homosexual couples for reasons of sex, suggests the possibility of 'being parents', 'adopting', or 'bringing up children'.

The proposals approved in this Resolution are advanced and innovative in bringing homosexual couples into line with the marriage of heterosexuals or an equivalent legal situation, enabling the registration of the cohabitation situation, and fully guaranteeing the same rights and benefits as those enjoyed by married couples. Among these, it considers that 'the recommendation should, at least, attempt to put an end ... to any restriction of the rights of lesbians and homosexuals to be parents, to adopt or bring up children' (proposal 14). What is clear is that this resolution of the European Parliament, by taking on the form of a 'recommendation', is not obligatory for the member states, as it would have been if it had taken the form of a directive, as was intended in the initial proposal for the Resolution.

In any event, the possibility of joint adopting already existed for stable heterosexual couples since the coming into force of State Law 21/1987 of 11 November, regulating fostering and adoption. In particular, as has been mentioned above, the third Additional Clause of this Law explicitly permitted joint adoption 'for the man and woman who are part of a couple and are permanently united by a relationship of affectivity analogous to the marriage relationship', although homosexual couples were excluded from this possibility. Nonetheless, since it is possible for single people, widows or widowers and separated or divorced people to adopt individually according to the state law referred to above, a homosexual person can adopt individually, whether or not he or she is involved in a stable homosexual relationship at that time. For its part, the Valencia Law 7/1994 of 5 December, on the Protection of Children had already included the possibility for couples of the same sex to adopt jointly, in Article 28. However, there has been constant controversy around the interpretation of this regulation.

POLITICAL AND SOCIAL REASONS FOR THE INSTITUTIONALISATION OF DE FACTO COUPLES IN SPAIN

In this section, I shall attempt to present some of the most significant arguments put forward in favour of the institutionalisation of de facto couples. I shall begin by presenting the reasons that have either explicitly or implicitly appeared in the political sphere. I shall then proceed to deal with the arguments that the jurists use. Finally, I will reflect upon some other important opinions present in Spanish society.

From among the different political groups with parliamentary representation, two general ideological approaches can be distinguished, together with some important differences of opinion expressed by several groups within them. Thus, on one side we have the Partido Popular for whose political representatives the family model means marriage, and this is why its state legislative proposal provides for the regulation of a 'civil contract' in which de facto couples might be included. This is a contract that has nothing to do with either marriage or the legal family model that they see as being protected by the Spanish Constitution of 1978. This civil contract goes beyond the strict problems involved in the reality of de facto couples, as any two people of age who commit themselves before a notary public to living together and helping each other can sign (Díaz Moreno, 1999: 127).

On the other side are the other parliamentary groups, who hold both heterosexual and homosexual de facto couples to be real families, and to be protected by the Spanish Constitution of 1978 and, therefore, deserving of specific legal regulation. Among others, this view is held by the Socialist Parliamentary Group, in Izquierda Unida, in Convergència i Unió, in the Coalición Canaria, Iniciativa per Catalunya–Els Verds, Izquierda Unida de Navarra, Grupo Mixto del Parlamento de Navarra, etc. However, within this large group, it is necessary to distinguish between the political groups which propose total and absolute equalisation in all spheres between married and unmarried people, with no distinction in terms of the 'sexual orientation' of the couple, such as Izquierda Unida and Iniciativa per Catalunya–Els Verds, and another group of those who propose a unitary legal system which would attribute various legal effects, without considering the sexuality of those involved, except for restricting adoption for homosexual couples. Among those belonging to this group would be the Socialist Party, the Canary Islands Coalition and Convergència i Unió in Catalonia.

Factors such as the protection, the recognition and the guarantee of certain rights, together with the need for legal security concerning property, have led many jurists to defend the model of marriage as the only way to generate the legal rights and effects pertaining to marital cohabitation. More specifically, many of the civil law experts working in the sphere of family law consider that the constitutional protection for marriage has an element of exclusivity.[11] For this reason, to consider de facto couples as existing on the same level as married couples would involve going against what is recognised and protected in the Spanish Constitution of 1978. Besides representing an attack on the constitutional protection of marriage, it would also involve a kind of interference into the right of free decision for those who wish to live together outside marriage. Any other kind of cohabiting relationship, either because it is not stable or not formalised, or because it is not heterosexual, does not fulfil the conditions for being protected institutionally by family law.

For another substantial group of Spanish jurists, there are reasons to think that the Spanish Constitution *does* protect and recognise a plurality

---

[11] Among this group of civil law experts are the following: Navarro Valls (1994); Lledó Yagüe (1997) 339ff; Martínez de Aguirre (1996).

of models for couples living together.[12] Despite this, the current regulation of civil marriage is a rigid model that excludes other alternative models of cohabitation for the stable couple. This is why these jurists defend the need to regulate these other non-marital models, thus providing an institutional response on the part of the law to the social reality of unmarried couples. Nonetheless, the majority of this group of jurists remain inflexible regarding homosexual couples. What these couples are fighting for is not the legitimacy of their relationship but recognition within family law that they are part of a union that can be equated to marriage or heterosexual de facto couples. More specifically, the jurists consider heterosexuality as an essential requisite for any cohabitation to be recognised by the law, due to the symmetry that this sort of unmarried couple has with the married couple.[13]

Lastly there is a group of Spanish jurists who defend a particular legal system for de facto couples as an alternative to that which exists for married couples, regardless of the sexual orientation of the members of the couple. For these, the fact that they may (in the case of heterosexuals) or may not (homosexuals) marry would not affect the *more uxorio* nature of the relationship.[14] However, some, voicing the social demands of gay rights groups, consider that homosexuals have the right to marry. In the face of the difficulties involved in their social acceptance, they end up concluding that the problems related to gay couples will have to be solved in some other way. The preferred way would be to apply to them whatever legal system is designed for heterosexual de facto couples (Ferreres Comella, 1994: 195–6).

Almost all the gay rights groups claim equality in one form or another. For pragmatic reasons these claims are being channelled through the claim for the same rights as heterosexuals (Ortega, 2000). They do not think this is the most suitable time to make the question of marriage a central demand because the only thing they would achieve by doing so would be to divert public attention from important, easily achievable issues, which would fade into the background if demands for marriage were made, and homosexual couples would be left in a legal vacuum. For this reason, achieving a specific legal system for de facto couples is much better than nothing for the majority of Spanish homosexual couples, who trust that the social and legal normalisation that this would give rise to could, after a certain time had elapsed, lead the Government to institutionalise the reality of homosexual couples (Herrero Brasas, 1997: 49–51, 54; Ugarte Pérez, 2000: 38–40).

---

[12] In this sense, among others, the following may be consulted: Estrada Alonso (1991); Ferreres Comella (1994); Calvo Soler and Pérez Triviño (1998); Llebaría Samper (1997); Mesa Marrero (1999); Pérez Vallego (2000); Reina and Martinell (1996); Roca Trías (1990); Zorrilla Ruiz (1997).

[13] See, among others: Estrada Alonso (1991) 52; Llebaría Samper (1997) 87–88; Pérez Vallejo (2000) 25–27; Reina and Martinell (1996): 34–35.

[14] Namely, Talavera Fernández (1999a) 66–68; (1999b) 156–7; Pérez Cánovas (1996) 118–123, 142–150; (1997) 25–27; Bayo Delgado (1999) 38; Borrillo (1997) 17–19.

The Catholic Church has also been concerned about the existence of de facto couples. For this reason the Pontifical Council for the Family (2000) drafted a document expressing its position in which it insists on the institutional value of marriage with respect to which the situation of unmarried couples must not be in the same position. More specifically, the subjective dimension of the unmarried couple, which is not a matter of public interest, is underlined. De facto unions are the consequence of private behaviour and should remain limited to this sphere. This document also takes a stand on the demand for homosexual couples to be considered on the same level as married couples. In this regard, 'the recognition or even bringing up homosexual relationships to the same level as marriage' is considered 'more serious, which, furthermore, does not involve discrimination, in any way, against these people' (Pontifical Council for the Family, 2000). In the end, the Catholic Church continues to hold a negative view of de facto couples in general, although this did not prevent it from approaching these family realities with discretion and respect from a more personal standpoint. In doing so, it has left behind any penalties for de facto couples, which were reflected in the Canon Law of 1917 and did not disappear until the Canon Law of 1983, as a result of the influence of the Vatican Council II. Thus, for example, the offences of cohabitation and adultery were listed in the 1917 Code, and the members of these de facto couples (people with neither fame nor honour) were considered despicable (Canon 2357.2, Canon Law 1917).

Beyond the legal problems that may arise, the distinction between these two kinds of cohabitation and their different regulation is due more to ideological factors than anything else. Thus, the appeal of unconstitutionality presented by 83 deputies of the Grupo Parlamentario Popular against the Autonomous Law 6/2000, among others, uses the following arguments in order to reject it. In the first place, this law somehow identifies the marriage relationship of married couples with the relationship that exists between unmarried couples. In this regard, this autonomous law attributes the legal effects pertaining to the institution of marriage to unmarried couples. In the second place, with regard to homosexual de facto couples, this Law has not regulated a new form of marriage because it could not do so, as this is a matter of state and not autonomous competency. This led the Navarre legislator to approve a text that, legally speaking, is a new form of marriage, disguising it in the euphemistic expression 'the legal equality of stable couples' united in a relationship of affectivity analogous to the marital relationship.[15]

One member of the Parliamentary Group of the Partido Popular in the Chamber of Deputies, in the debate that ensued when the bill for the legal equality of stable couples presented by the Navarre Parliament[16] was discussed, pointed out that

---

[15] Above n 9.

[16] *Diario de Sesiones del Congreso de los Diputados*, VII Legislature, 3 April 2001, no 73, 3614–15.

this Bill, in the end, gives shape to an institution in which all the benefits and no obligations are granted to de facto couples as opposed to married ones. Practically no requisites are made or formalities required to constitute it ... .

Therefore, the Partido Popular could not justify establishing a legal system for de facto couples as an alternative to the legal system for married couples because, among several other reasons, de facto couples would be left in a situation of clear advantage over married couples, not to speak of the complete rejection by this political group of homosexual couples being legally comparable to heterosexual couples.

SOME CONCLUSIONS AND A NUMBER OF LOOSE ENDS

The de facto couple phenomenon has attempted to make its mark, first as a social fact, encouraging an increasingly plural, open and democratic Spanish society, and then as an institution recognised and protected by the law. As indicated in the first section of this chapter, de facto couples are already an unquestionable reality in many of the countries of the European Union and in countries such as ours, everything indicates that there should be institutional recognition in the future. Without entering into the controversy regarding whether the number of people involved is 200,000 or 600,000 couples,[17] it is clear that we are witnessing an increase. This, together with the generational differences outlined in the first section, means that at present de facto or stable couples are now present in rather more than a marginal way in our society.

Furthermore, partial recognition of certain legal benefits is being granted to de facto couples by the Spanish legal system, though this is not synonymous with recognition of true 'institutional status'. More specifically, without entering into whether this is a consequence of questions of competence, the autonomous parliaments have hastened to regulate the situation of de facto couples, allowing themselves to be influenced, at least in part, more by the social pressure of certain associations and political groups than by a deep, well-founded reflection on what conditions should exist to enable this legitimate plurality of forms of alternative family cohabitation to be regulated. It should not be so much a question of granting certain financial, administrative and criminal law benefits to these alternative forms of cohabitation, as of granting them effective legal equivalence, especially in cases where *more uxorio* cohabitation is taking place between two people, as in marriage. In the end, what is lacking is a legislative intervention more geared towards configuring a 'cohabitational' model as an alternative to marriage, given that in these cases there is true cohabitation that is fully comparable to marital cohabitation in legal terms. For this we

---

[17] Figures presented respectively by the Partido Popular and the PSOE (socialist party) in the debate on the latest legislative initiatives referred to above.

would need a precise definition of this institutionalisation of an alternative cohabitational model, which is being rejected by many jurists, politicians and important social sectors of Spanish society.

In general, the autonomous regulation of de facto couples, together with the State bills which were not accepted, have developed a regulatory framework for this social reality, which lies in the cohabitation contract. But at the same time as they establish it, they place it outside the institutional sphere of family law, thus conserving the exclusiveness of marriage. This should not prevent us from making a positive judgement of the progress represented by the fact that these laws recognise more rights and legal effects for extra marital unions than those previously contemplated in the Spanish legal system.

In another respect, homosexual de facto couples as affective and family cohabitation, have also been fighting for full legal recognition. The legislative changes that affect morality involve conceptions of life that can and should be analysed and discussed rationally but which, in general, conceal deeply rooted feelings of acceptance or rejection, which prevent people from engaging in rational discussion. Thus, the political groups are very reluctant to grant rights that would normalise the life of a large number of people because electoral considerations oblige them to be cautious. From a sociological viewpoint, the homosexual relationship is still not generally perceived in our cultural environment as a form of family cohabitation comparable to that of the heterosexual couple, and this has been reflected in the different laws. It is not so much a question of granting specific partial legal regulation, as of establishing clearly whether or not people of the same sex can be involved, legally speaking, in real *more uxorio* cohabitation and finally whether or not heterosexuality defines family cohabitation in an absolute and definite way.

The treatment of homosexual de facto couples requires not only a legal approach but also a sociological and psychological approach that avoids the use of stereotypes as well as dealing, among other things, with their social recognition, and with whether or not both kinds of unions are comparable. The constitutional recognition of basic rights such as those of freedom, equality and non-discrimination, the free development of the human personality and dignity and the right to privacy is important, but are they socially accepted?

The option chosen in large part by the autonomous laws has been to establish a different kind of legal regulation for stable heterosexual and homosexual couples. This has very probably occurred in order to avoid the creation of a single legal status for both types of family cohabitation. This solution is intended, above all, to avoid heterosexual and homosexual de facto unions having the same effects.

All in all, I believe it is insufficient to offer a legal solution to homosexual couples that is only geared towards finding a legal status for them, with the least possible degree of interference in the current civil regulation of the family, because this would involve leaving the real nucleus of the problem unsolved. The issue is expressed by Talavera Fernández (1999a: 5), by means of three basic questions: (a) can true *affectio maritalis* exist between people of the same sex?; (b) can two people of the same sex constitute a family unit, even with children in the home?; and (c) is heterosexuality an essential requisite of any cohabitation as a couple for it to be recognised by the law?

Without going into any other kind of legal or competence problems that might arise, the distinction between these two kinds of cohabitation and their different regulation raises ideological rather than any other kind of issues, as was shown by the demonstrations that followed the approval of *Ley foral navarra 6/2000* in dealing with the possibility of the freedom of homosexual couples to adopt. This regulation, as indicated above, is in line with the Resolution of the European Parliament of 8 February 1994, *on equality of rights for homosexuals and lesbians*, which, reflecting the demands of homosexual groups and based on the principle of equality and non-discrimination, establishes full equality of rights between homosexuals and heterosexuals, and even recommends putting an end to any kind of marital prohibition affecting them or any regulations forbidding them to 'be parents', 'adopt' or 'bring children up'. In any event, and despite its non-binding nature for Member States, the significance of this resolution is that it is a pronouncement by an institution of the stature of the European Parliament, in which all the Member States are represented. It reflects demands that are becoming louder and increasingly widespread in European countries.

There is no doubt that the issue of the adoption of minors by homosexual couples is, and will continue to be, the subject of controversy. I believe[18] that in the case of homosexual couples there should be an open debate of the kind that has not yet been held in Spain, both in the social and legislative spheres, with discussion by expert psychologists, educationalists, specialised educators, etc, without losing sight of the fact that there is no right to adoption for adults in any of the cases (married couples, unmarried heterosexual or homosexual couples, etc). The argument is precisely the opposite: it is the children who have the right to grow up in a suitable family environment, whether this is their own or an alternative one. It should therefore be the interest of the child and not any other criterion that indicates, case by case, that a particular child with his or her rights and needs should be fostered or adopted, regardless of whether the child is to be adopted by a married couple, a heterosexual de facto couple, a homosexual couple or an individual. Child welfare regulations are being applied in

[18] The issues relating to fostering and adoption are very complicated and go beyond the scope of any simplification of the arguments brought up in this debate, the majority of which are ideological. See Picontó Novales (1996).

cases in which a child, or several brothers and sisters, are requested for fostering or adoption by heterosexual, married or unmarried couples, and the legislative possibility of homosexual couples adopting or fostering should exist. The decision should be left to the social experts, as is done in the other cases, who can evaluate and decide in each case whether or not the supreme interest of the child, together with his or her need for affection, right to education, development or personal maturity, the right not to be separated from brothers and sisters if at all possible, and the continued, non-intermittent reference of the same adults (which may not be the case in child welfare centres) are going to be guaranteed.

REFERENCES

Alberdi, I (1995) *Informe Sobre la Situación de la Familia en España* (Madrid, M° de Asuntos Sociales).

Assier-Andrieu, L (1995) 'Politique, Science et Droit naturel' in L Assier-Andrieu *et al* (eds), *Politique des Lois en Europe* (Paris, Librairie Generale de Droit et de Jurisprudence).

Bayo Delgado, J (1999) 'Problemas Subsistentes en el Derecho de Familia' *Jueces para la Democracia* 35: 36–9.

Borrillo, D (1997) 'Uniones del Mismo Sexo y Libertad Matrimonial' *Jueces para la Democracia* 35: 15–19.

Calvo Soler, R and Pérez Triviño, JL (1998) 'Igualdad, Discriminación y Parejas de Hecho' *Sistema* 142: 47–61.

Camarero Suárez, MV (1998) 'Uniones de Hecho y Conflictividad Matrimonial' in JM Martinell and MT Areces Piñol (eds), *XI Jornades Jurídiques: Uniones de Hecho* (Lleida, University of Lleida).

Campo, S (1991) *La Nueva Familia Españo* (Madrid, Eudema).

Centre de Investigasiones Sociologicas (1999) 'Los Jóvenes de Hoy' *Boletín* 19.

CIS, Instituto de la Juventud (1997) 'Estudios 2257, 2262 y 2265' (Madrid, CIS).

Díaz Moreno, JM *et al* (1999) *Las Uniones de Hecho: Una Aproximación Plural* (Madrid, Universidad Pontificia de Comillas).

Estrada Alonso, A (1991) *Las Uuniones Extramatrimoniales en el Derecho Civil Español* (Madrid, Civitas).

Ferreres Comella, V (1994) 'El Principio de Igualdad y el 'Derecho a no Casarse' (A Próposito de la STC 222/92) (1)' *Revista Española de Derecho Constitucional* 42: 163–196.

Flaquer, L (1991) 'Hogares sin Familia o Familias sin Hogar? Un Análisis Sociológico de las Familias de Hecho en España' *Revista de Sociología* 36: 57–78.

La Fondacion FOESSA (1995) 'Informe Sociológico Sobre la Situación Social en España (Síntesis)' *Documentación Social* 101: 163.

Hague Academy of International Law (1999) *Fifth European Conference of Family Law: Legal Regulated Forms of Non-Marital Cohabitation and Registered Partnerships* (Strasbourg, 12 Feb 1999).

Hernández Rodríguez, R (1999) 'Análisis y Perspectivas Sociodemográficas de las Uniones de Hecho' in JM Díaz Moreno *et al* (eds), *Las Uniones de Hecho: Una Aproximación Plural* (Madrid, Universidad Pontificia de Comillas).

Herrero Brasas, JA (1997) 'El Matrimonio Gay, un Reto al Estado Heterosexual' *Claves de la Razón Práctica* 73: 41–54.

Ibañez Pascual, M (2001) 'Construcción de Pareja, Individualización y Cambio Familiar' *Abaco* 29/30: 61–70.

Iglesias de Ussel, J (1990) 'La Familia y el Cambio Político en España' *Revista de Estudios Políticos* 67: 247–256.

Kaufmann, JC (1993) *Sociologie du Couple* (Paris, Presses Universitaires de France).

Llebaría Samper, S (1997) *Hacia la Familia no Matrimonial* (Barcelona, Cedecs).

Lledó Yagüe, F (1997) 'Los Matrimonios de Hecho Contra el Derecho y el Sentido Común del Legislador' *Revista del Poder Judicial* 45: 339–87.

Martínez de Aguirre, C (1996) *Diagnóstico Sobre el Derecho de Familia* (Madrid, Rialp).

Meil Landwerlin, G (1999) *La Postmodernización de la Familia Española* (Madrid, CESMA Escuela de Negocios).

Merino Hernández, JL (1999) *Manual de Parejas Estables no Casadas* (Zaragoza, Librería General).

Mesa Marrero, C (1999) *Las Uniones de Hecho: Análisis de las Relaciones Económicas y sus Efectos* (Madrid, Aranzadi).

Navarro Valls, R (1994) *Matrimonio y Derecho* (Madrid, Tecnos).

O'Callagan, X (1998) 'Consecuencias Jurídicas de las Uniones de Hecho' *Cuadernos del Derecho Judicial* 20: 15–57.

Ortega, RM (2000) 'Rechazo del Partido Popular a las Leyes de Parejas de Hecho' http://www.Colegaweb.net/COMUNICADO%20hecho%202000-2.htm/.

Pérez Cánovas, N (1996) *Homosexualidad, Homosexuales y Uniones Homosexuales en el Derecho Español* (Granada, Comares).

—— (1997) 'El Derecho de Gays y Lesbianas a la Vida Familiar' *Jueces para la Democracia* 30: 25–27.

Pérez Vallejo, AM (2000) *Autorregulación en la Convivencia de Hecho (a Próposito de las Recientes Disposiciones Prelegislativas y Legislativas Tendencialmente más Dispositivas)* (Almería, Universidad de Almería).

Picontó Novales, T (1996) *La Protección de la Infancia: Aspectos Sociales y Jurídicos* (Zaragoza, Egido Editorial).

—— (1997) 'Family Law and Family Policy in Spain' in M Maclean and J Kurcewzeski (eds), *Family Law and Family Policy in the New Europe* (Aldershot, Dartmouth).

—— (1998) 'Sociología Jurídica de la Familia: Cambio Legislativo y Políticas Sociales' in MJ Añón *et al* (eds), *Derecho y Sociedad* (Valencia, Tirant lo Blanch).

—— (2001) 'La Regulación Jurídica de las Parejas de Hecho en España: Un Análisis Socio-Jurídico' *Revista Educación* 325: 57–77.

Plaza Penedés, J and Tamayo Carmona, JA (1998) 'Artículo 28 de la Ley Autonómica Valenciana 7/1994, de la Infancia, y sus Repercusiones en Materia de Adopción por los Posibles Integrantes de una Unión de Hecho' in JM Martinell and MT Areces Piñol (eds), *XI Jornades Jurídiques. Uniones de Hecho* (Lleida, University of Lleida).

Pontificio Consejo para la Familia (2000) 'Familia, Matrimonio y'Uniones de Hecho' http://www.vatican.va/.

Reina, V and Martinell, JM (1996) *Las Uniones Matrimoniales de Hecho* (Madrid, Marcial Pons).

Roca Trías, E (1990) 'Familia, Familias y Derecho de la Familia' *Anuario de Derecho Civil* 1057–91.

Saura, LF (1995) *Uniones Libres y la Configuración del Nuevo Derecho de Familia* (Valencia, Tirant lo Blanch).

Silva, JM (1999) 'Futura Regulación de las Uniones de Hecho en España' in JM Díaz Moreno *et al* (eds), *Las Uniones de Hecho. Una Aproximación Plural* (Madrid, Universidad Pontificia de Comillas).

Talavera Fernández, PA (1999a) *Fundamentos para el Reconocimiento Jurídico de las Uniones Homosexuales: Propuestas de Regulación en España* (Madrid, Universidad Carlos III-Dykinson).

—— (1999b) 'Presupuestos para un Reconocimiento Jurídico Coherente de las Uniones Homosexuales en España' *Anuario de Filosofía del Derecho* 20: 145–159.

Ugarte Pérez, J (2000) 'Parejas de Hecho y Matrimonio Homosexual' *Claves de la Razón Práctica:* 103.

Verda y Beamonte, JR de (1998) 'Principio de Libre Desarrollo de la Personalidad y 'Jus Connubi' (a Próposito de la ATC 222/1994)' in JM Martinell and MT Areces Piñol (eds), *XI Jornades Jurídiques: Uniones de Hecho* (Lleida, University of Lleida).

Zarraluqui Sánchez-Eznarriaga, L (1999) 'Las Uniones de Hecho en el Derecho Español' in JM Díaz Moreno (ed), *Las Uniones de Hecho: Una Aproximación Plura*l (Madrid, Universidad Pontificia de Comillas).

Zorrilla Ruiz, MM (1997) 'Consideraciones de Principio en Torno a la Unión Libre' *Revista del Poder Judicial* 45: 389–414.

Part IV. A

Regulating the Relationships Between Adult Children and Elderly Parents

14

Maintenance of the Aged by their Adult Children: an Adequate Legal Institution?

JEAN VAN HOUTTE and JEF BREDA

INTRODUCTION

S OME YEARS AGO, the Centre for the Sociology of Law (UFSIA, University of Antwerp) conducted research into 'the maintenance of the aged by their adult children' (Van Houtte and Breda, 1976; Van Houtte, 1977; Van Houtte and Breda, 1978). At that time, legal measures were being taken to confirm the right of recourse of the Public Centre for Social Welfare (OCMW) against the adult children of elderly persons on the basis of this maintenance obligation.[1] In recent years, a new confrontation has arisen between proponents and opponents of maintenance obligations or, to be more precise, the right of recourse of Public Centres for Social Welfare.

A BRIEF HISTORY OF CHANGES IN THE MEANS OF SUBSISTENCE, FAMILY SOLIDARITY AND MAINTENANCE OBLIGATION

A study of the present implementation of the maintenance obligation cannot ignore the origins and transformations of this institution over time. Because the sociology of the family has not focused upon the role of family solidarity in guaranteeing subsistence, we need to re-examine and reinterpret that literature, and also the contribution of legal history.

1 Family Solidarity and the Maintenance Obligation in Ancient Rome

Because of the parallels between the evolution of society, law, and especially the family in Rome and the West, we will pay special attention to family

[1] The Law of 7 Aug 1974 concerning the introduction of the right to subsistence welfare; the Organic Law of 8 July 1976 concerning the Public Centre for Social Welfare.

solidarity and the maintenance obligation on the former. Comparison should permit generalisations about how family law interacts with socio-cultural reality. Furthermore, it must be remembered that Roman law significantly influenced the shape of the family law provisions of the Civil Code.

Roman society experienced a dramatic shift from an agricultural to a mercantile economy, a development with far-reaching cultural and structural changes. The extended family is particularly fitted to, and tends to predominate in, an agricultural economy. Roman kinship was structured in terms of the *gens*,[2] the *consortium*,[3] and the *familia*,[4] a series of concentric circles of which the innermost and smallest—the *familia*—was to survive the longest. These kinship structures supported, and were supported by, a system of rigid stratification, inflexible property relations, and a sense of sacredness pervading all social life.[5]

The *gens* and the *consortium* declined fairly early as important means of support but the *familia* continued to guarantee subsistence to its members. The *paterfamilias* felt obliged to provide a livelihood for the members of his *familia*, whose activities simultaneously contributed to the preservation and growth of the patrimony. Similarly, it was customary for the wife to bring a *dos* from her father, thus increasing her husband's property and the latter's ability to provide for his wife and children (Lebras, 1959: 420–1).

Although maintenance was guaranteed only by the mores, this was nevertheless a solid basis. Legal claims were not common at first because Romans preferred to keep family matters out of the courtroom.

---

[2] The *gens* was the largest kinship unit, a political and economic entity consisting of a large number of persons who considered themselves descendants of a common male ancestor. The structural and functional characteristics of the *gens* are uncertain. See Kaser (1955) 44; Gaudemet (1963) 53–63; Johnston (1969) 73–81.

[3] Gaius defines the *consortium* as a *societas naturalis* (a natural community) which was automatically created among the heirs when the *paterfamilias* died. It is more than joint ownership, which arises from inheritance and may not be permanent (Gaudemet, 1963: 63–83). Kaser argues that it is not only a community of goods ('Vermögensgemeinschaft') but also an association of persons on a family basis ('Familienrechtliches Verband') (1955: 44).

[4] The *familia* can be considered a household consisting of a number of persons and goods under the authority of the *paterfamilias*. Its members include his legitimate children, and his wife if he has acquired authority over her by a *conventio in manu* (in which case she left her natal family completely, and even her gens, and was accepted *filiae loco* in the wider kinship structures of her husband, in which she even acquired certain hereditary rights). Adopted persons were also full members. Finally, there were the slaves. The basis of the familia was thus quite clearly the *patria potestas*. Its members were those under that authority, not those related by blood or marriage. See Kaser (1955) 44.

[5] In the absence of other data, anyone wishing to understand traditional Roman family structures is compelled to use Roman law as his starting point. But such reliance can be justified on other grounds as well. Roman law was pre-eminently a common law, reflecting contemporary mores. It is therefore legitimate, following Durkheim (1947) to take law as the crystallisation of social relations, and thus a proper basis for social analysis. At a later period a discrepancy developed between the 'mores', fixed in the rules of law, and changing familial and social reality; this discrepancy is related to the adaptation and extension of the legal structures. Because Roman law was the law of and for the patricians, the *beati possidentes* (just as the *Code Civil* is the law of and for the bourgeoisie), the structures and developments described are mainly those of the patrician family.

> The Roman's strongly marked sense of dignity and decency keeps him from taking the privacy of marital and familial life into court: a modern divorce suit would seem disgraceful to him. He does not, therefore, like having 'the privacy of family life' made transparent in law: as little law as possible is his watchword in this field.
>
> (Schulz, 1934: 15)

But social developments soon changed all this. In the course of extraordinary military and mercantile expansion the Roman autarchy was destroyed, the rigid class structure dominated by patricians dissolved, and the power of the sacred to legitimate social institutions gravely weakened. The *familia* as an extended family structure was endangered—eroded from within and crumbling from without (Lebras, 1959: 421–9; Kirkpatrick, 1963; Piganiol, 1954; Zimmerman, 1947).

The erosion of the *familia* tended to undermine family solidarity, with the result that the *paterfamilias* felt less obliged to provide assistance to all his members, some of whom had ceased to participate effectively in the household. Mores alone no longer possessed sufficient authority to secure the performance of family obligations and thus counteract the economic insecurity of family members. Eventually the emperor tried to restore family solidarity by permitting legal claims for maintenance. Customary law was thus transformed into state law.

The oldest rescripts,[6] from approximately AD 100, relate to a son's legal claim against his father. Because a young man could acquire independence and be granted his own *peculium*,[7] through his activities as a soldier, tradesman or manufacturer, some fathers may have thought that they were no longer obliged to pay maintenance for a son in need. The first rescript in favour of a daughter is found in the time of Antoninus Pius (AD 138–161). That this appeared later than maintenance claims by sons may be explained by the daughter's greater integration in the *familia*: if she was not married, she remained active in her father's household and received what she needed; when she did marry, she received a dowry intended to ensure her subsistence. In the second half of the second century AD all legitimate children (*liberi*) of either sex were recognised as having claims for maintenance against their father, though this was restricted to those *sub potestate*, who belonged to the *familia* proper.

At the same time the *familia* was crumbling and had fewer members *sub potestate*. More women married *sine manu*[8] and thus did not come under

---

[6] A rescript is a reply by a Roman emperor to a magistrate's query about a point of law. There is little systematic information on the maintenance obligation in handbooks and articles on Roman law. The first author to treat the matter thoroughly was Albertario (1925). Sachers (1951) has written the most recent study, critically synthesising the others.

[7] *Peculium* is the capital that the *paterfamilias* provides to the *filii*; it remains the property of the *paterfamilias*, but the *filii* administer it and collect the proceeds.

[8] The earlier form was the marriage *cum manu*, in which the woman leaves her own family and enters that of her husband. A woman married *sine manu* still belongs to her natal family and does not live under the authority of her husband; this form became dominant at the beginning of the Christian era.

the authority of their husbands, the *paterfamilias*, or belong to the *familia*. And more adult sons were emancipated. This had two possible consequences. Firstly, persons who were emancipated could subsequently become needy. And secondly, if they prospered on their own, this did not augment the patrimony of their original *familia*, with the result that the *paterfamilias* and other members of the *familia* might become needy. The question thus arose whether family solidarity persisted between members and former members of a *familia*.

Rescripts were an attempt to counteract the crumbling of the *familia* and its adverse effects on subsistence. Thus by the time of Ulpianus (third century AD) the father was responsible for emancipated children, the mother became legally obligated to support her children, and at the same time both parents were granted legal claims against their children. In this way the mutual obligations of maintenance, originating in the sacred mores regulating all Roman society, were translated into a statute that helped to preserve the *familia* not only during the Roman empire, but even after its fall.

2 Means of Subsistence, Family and Relatives in Western Society

(a) From the Middle Ages to Modern Times

In the Middle Ages, there were also extended families composed of two or more related families, their servants and apprentices, integrated by their economic functions in agriculture or handicrafts. The strongest guarantee of subsistence for an individual was to be a member of such a household. But membership was voluntary, and persons were free to leave (Gaudemet, 1963: 89). Obligations to relatives outside the household varied regionally. Roman law applied in southern Europe. In the north, ethical values expressed in *costuymen* (usage, custom) encouraged family solidarity, but their partial failure is apparent in the role of other institutions—the church, religious orders, and public authorities—in caring for the poor.

Starting in the 15th century the number of households containing more than one adult couple began to decrease and by the 18th century the nuclear family had come to predominate. This progressive nuclearisation probably occurred more smoothly in northern Europe (northern France, the Netherlands and the Germanic empire), where the legal superstructure was more compatible because paternal authority in the Germanic *mundium* was less extensive and less absolute than the *patria potestas* (Gaudemet, 1963: 120). As a result, both individuals and families were thrown back upon their own resources and could not, as in southern Europe, look to the Roman law regarding the *familia* as a basis for obligation.

Initially, the maintenance obligation between members of a family who lived in different households was probably ethical and supported by severe informal sanctions. But it soon came to be regulated by custom and usage, extending beyond parent and child to include the obligation of a natural grandson to support his grandfather, and sometimes even subsisting between siblings. The particular rule varied from one *costuym* to another. Thus the usages of Santhover and Gelderland gave children *de plano*[9] a right to subsistence, whereas other relatives could only ask for it ('soo d'alders dat versuecken') (Defacqz, 1873: 370–5).

But even in 'le pays coutumier' Roman law constituted a 'raison écrite' for custom (Domat, 1695: 4) and, when confirmed by usage and adopted by legislation, became the basis for substantive law. Thus Pothier, a 'national' jurist, discusses the institution of maintenance in ancient French law almost entirely by reference to Roman law (1830: 83). In proportion to their means, parents were obligated to support their adult children in need, even if the latter had reached an age when they would normally be able to provide for themselves; if parental support was not forthcoming, grandparents were similarly obligated. This obligation could be nullified if the law permitted the parent to disinherit the child for gross disrespect. The obligation was also mutual: adult children were required to maintain needy parents and, where children failed to do so, adult grandchildren were so obligated. (Apparently, it was not possible for a child to reject this duty because of disrespect by a parent.) As will be seen below, these rules have significantly influenced the civil law.

Pothier also offers some evidence of family nucleation. He notes that judges preferred to order children to make a financial contribution to parental maintenance and only if this was difficult would they order that the parent be admitted to the child's household. That adult children were leaving the parental household and were less willing to assume obligations of support voluntarily can be seen in Pothier's observation:

> The corruption of morals, which has constantly been growing, and which today has reached its peak, makes these claims, unheard of in the past, very frequent in the courtroom, to mankind's shame.   (1830: 83)

(b) The 19th and 20th Centuries

The laws governing maintenance, which were incorporated in the *Code Napoléon*, are still in force in Belgium. These give shape to family solidarity, and seek to ensure a minimum subsistence for the whole family. Adult children and their parents, other ascendants, and parents-in-law, are bound

---

[9] The judge is required to order the maintenance of needy children; the claims of other needy relatives are judged individually, guided by principles of equity.

by mutual obligations of maintenance, in proportion to the needs of the claimant and the means of the obligor.[10]

The reciprocity of the maintenance obligation gave rise to controversy (Locré de Roissy, 1836: 342). Some argued that the justifications for maintenance of an aged person could hardly apply to a son or son-in-law old enough to support himself. Others favoured mutuality. Napoleon cut the knot:

> The first consul says that it would be outrageous to give a rich father the right to expel his children from his house after having reared them, and to have them provide for themselves, even if they are physically handicapped. Such is, however, the idea presented in the draft. If it were to be adopted, one should also forbid fathers to give an education to their children, because nothing would be more unfortunate for the latter than to have to break away from the habit of opulence and the tastes their education would have given them, in order to devote themselves to difficult or mechanical labour they would not be accustomed to. If the father does not owe them anything as soon as he has reared them, why not deprive them of the right of succession as well? The maintenance money is not only measured by physical needs, but also by habits, it must be proportionate to the wealth of the father liable for it, and to the education of the child needing it ... The son has, indeed, a legal right to his father's property, and though this right is suspended as long as the father lives, even then it is effected in the provision for the son's needs. However, if the law stipulates that maintenance is no longer due to a son who is of age, it makes it impossible for the courts to grant any.
>
> (Locré de Roissy, 1836: 342)

It appears from this debate that issues of status played a part in shaping the maintenance obligation in the *Code Civil*. Such considerations would not have carried as much weight with Pothier, even though he belonged to the *ancien régime*; for him, children were only entitled to maintenance if they were incapable of working. Thus the concrete features of the maintenance obligation could not be deduced from the nature of man alone.

The question arises whether this bourgeois interest in 'status preservation' was also reflected in the actual administration of the maintenance obligation. We sought to answer this by analysing published judgements (Jamar *et al*, 1814–1965; Van Reepinghen, 1949–70). Our study revealed

---

[10] Children are liable for the maintenance of their parents and other ascendants in need.

Art 206: Sons-in-law and daughters-in-law are likewise and in the same circumstances liable for the maintenance of their parents-in-law, but this obligation comes to an end: (1) when the mother-in-law enters into a second marriage; (2) when the one spouse who caused the relationship and the children by his marriage with the other spouse are deceased.

Art 207: The obligations resulting from these provisions are mutual.

Art 208: Subsistence is only granted in proportion to the needs of the one who claims it and the wealth of the one who owes it.

Art 209: When the one who provides subsistence or the one who receives it, finds himself in such a position that the former can no longer provide it or the latter no longer needs it, either in whole or in part, exemption or reduction of it can be claimed.

that until 1880 courts did not award simply the minimum necessary for survival, but an amount influenced by 'status-related need'. Sometimes the judge even stated explicitly that he had taken 'status' into account. After 1880 the awards were closer to subsistence level, though some were so far below it that they probably had only symbolic value. Awards proportionate to the status of the claimant appear sporadically. Finally, after the Second World War, in addition to subsistence awards, a new type of legal proceeding appears in which the Public Assistance Agency (Commissie van Openbare Onderstand), having provided maintenance to the elderly, seeks redress from those liable for support. Although the published cases are not necessarily representative of the universe of proceedings, they do suggest that the initial interest in status preservation has largely disappeared, either because the claimants have changed or because of a change in public opinion concerning what is just maintenance.

3 The Maintenance Obligation and the Present Socio-Cultural System

The nucleation of the family, which began in the 15th century and greatly accelerated in the 19th and 20th centuries, is often said to have led to the isolation of families and the devaluing of family solidarity, especially the sense of financial obligation. As a result, it is said, the community assumed this role, rendering obsolete the maintenance obligation in the *Code Civil*. Both sociologists of the family and gerontologists studying the plight of older couples in urban environments have contributed to the view that the extended family and wider kinship groups have been totally extinguished, leaving the nuclear family entirely isolated.

In fact, however, such isolation does not occur. Recent empirical studies have shown that although the family has been nucleated as a result of industrialisation, it is not isolated from relatives but embedded in a modified extended family. Demographic factors have altered the structure of the kinship group. Its vertical span has increased (there are more three and four generation families) and age differences between generations are diminishing (Shanas *et al*, 1968: 171).

In the contemporary 'verticalised' family there is typically frequent contact between parents, whether or not they are elderly, and their adult children. There is more than mere contact, however. The elderly declared that they gave financial support to their children or grandchildren, and almost twice as many acknowledged receiving aid from them. Such assistance includes household help, medical care, gifts in money or kind, and lodging. But regular financial support of the elderly by their children or relatives is rare. When demands for financial assistance from their children interfere with emotional ties, the elderly feel that those ties are more important. Thus many are reluctant to ask for assistance for fear that this would harm relations with their children and also damage their own independence.

There appears to be no fundamental inconsistency between the family relationships just described and the maintenance obligation. Indeed, mutual solidarity between parents and children is still both a behavioural and an attitudinal reality. The legal institution seems simply to give it shape. On closer investigation, however, the integration of legal institution and social reality is not without problems. Because it expresses a basic value and thus performs the symbolic function, the maintenance obligation is phrased in general terms. When it is applied concretely it may not always be customary, or socially acceptable. We have observed above, for instance, that regular financial assistance is rare, and that most people believe that the state should share the obligation. Furthermore, the children who are liable to fulfil the obligation may themselves be needy. Because the maintenance obligation may thus be inadequate to guarantee subsistence to elderly persons in need, the next section will focus upon problems that arise when it is coercively applied.

THE COERCIVELY APPLIED MAINTENANCE OBLIGATION

1 Justice of Peace versus Public Centre for Social Welfare

So far we have described the general relationship between the maintenance obligation and social structure. What are the specific repercussions of subsistence difficulties on family solidarity? Under what circumstances does need produce conflicts between parent and adult child, in which the coercion of legal obligation is invoked? At the beginning of our research Justices of the Peace (JPs) suggested to us that it is rare for ascendants to seek to enforce the obligation in court. But our exploratory research also revealed that liability is imposed within the framework of the Public Centre for Social Welfare (OCMW). These two institutions adhere to different principles, and consequently reach different client populations. We have sought to ascertain these differences by analysing records and judgments.

The meaning of a rule of law can only be understood in the context of the institutional framework in which it is applied. The judicial institution in which the maintenance obligation of the *Code Civil* is applied is the JP court, in which the person seeking maintenance claims it from the one who is liable to pay it. The number of such claims heard by judges does in fact appear to be small.

The PCSW is a municipal agency that provides support to those in need. It has the legal right to ask descendants to support needy ascendants at a level fixed by the agency, and can sue those descendants in the JP court to enforce that obligation if they do not pay, although the court will make its own judgement on both need and ability. Nevertheless, in 1969 the PCSWs in the Antwerp district supported more than 3000 people, 1200 of whom had descendants who were asked to contribute; in only 25 cases were those descendants sued in court. Current figures are more or less the same. Thus the PCSW dominates this area. But the PCSW itself should be seen as simply one of many agencies intercepting persons slipping through the net of the overall social security system.

There are other differences between the two institutions. The PCSW provides immediate support to the needy elderly applicant, out of its own funds, and the descendants are involved only at a later stage. The court has no funds from which it can furnish support; all it can do is relate the claim of the ascendant to the liability of the descendant. Thus it is only able to reallocate money among the parties involved, and even this it can only do at the end of the proceedings. The PCSW employs qualified personnel who obtain objective data by standardised methods. They apply fixed financial norms concerning both the ascendant's needs and the financial means of the descendants. The court's only informants are the parties themselves. It is completely adverse to fixed norms, using flexible substantive standards and following individualised procedures.[11]

The two institutions operate autonomously and in isolation from each other. Where a descendant is unwilling to support an ascendant who has applied to the PCSW for assistance, the PCSW refers the matter to court. Judges and lawyers mention the PCSW as the most important referrer for cases. But that is where relations between the two institutions end: judges are quite ignorant of the method the PCSW uses in handling the cases. Clients, on the other hand, appear to be aware of the different functions of the two institutions, and use them accordingly. Interviews with social workers revealed that it is mainly the ascendants who go to the PCSW, where they seek assistance with the entire range of their problems, not just their financial needs.

As a consequence of these differences concrete decision-making also varies between the institutions. The PCSW distinguishes between those clients who only need financial assistance and those who require institutional care. The latter group is further divided into those who do and those who do not need medical help. Each of these three categories is deemed to require a particular level of support. If the elderly person cannot afford this support, the PCSW assumes the burden of paying the difference and then seeks to recoup it from relatives.

2 Is the 'Coercively' Applied Maintenance Obligation Still a Social Problem?

One might expect that the ongoing expansion of the social insurance and social security systems would provide an adequate safety net for an increasing

---

[11] These procedures and methods of data collection are similar to the differences between courts and administrative agencies.

number of individuals. While this is true to a certain extent, it would however appear that some people are still confronted with social insecurity. Moreover, the ageing of the population has given rise to a new problem. Over the past 10 years, the daily cost of rest homes has increased by 30 per cent, which is considerably higher than the rate of inflation (Ministry of Economic Affairs). The Association of Flemish Cities and Municipalities estimates that one in three residents in rest homes run by an OCMW (Public Centres for Social Welfare) call on the OCMW to help foot the bill. For the oldest pensioners in particular, the gap between the amount of their pension and the cost of living in the rest home is becoming very substantial, yet these people are most likely to require residential care.

The ageing of the population also means that the need for medical care is increasing, especially in the oldest age groups. While an elderly person in residential care is, in principle at least, required to pay accommodation costs, the costs of nursing and care are borne by the federal authorities. The rest home population not only requires more care, but also more intensive care: some estimate that 65 per cent are now very care-dependent. Moreover, the government is allegedly failing to meet the additional costs, so that the elderly are being made to pay.

Against this backdrop, it is not surprising that a social debate has emerged regarding the partial recuperation of the cost of residential care on the basis of the maintenance obligation for elderly parents. Moreover, the debate is becoming increasingly acute, as the legal regulation regarding right of recourse is not applied equally strictly by all OCMWs. Some municipalities (such as Herentals, Menen, Ostend and Mechelen) are said to reclaim costs rarely. In other words, depending on where one lives, one might or might not be required to contribute towards the costs of residential care for one's elderly parents.

3 The Debate on Maintenance Obligation

It is therefore worth analysing and assessing the arguments that are put forward in the debate on maintenance obligation. Firstly, however, we would like to draw attention to a persistent misunderstanding in this debate. Those who argue against maintenance obligation would appear to be opposed to the right of recourse of the OCMWs on the basis of the maintenance obligation under the Civil Code. We shall, therefore, deal separately with the issues of maintenance obligation under the Civil Code and the right of recourse of OCMWs on the basis of the Civil Code.

(a) The Civil Law Institution of Maintenance Liability

The relationship between the moral and legal duties of next of kin, on the one hand, and those of the community, on the other, is of central importance to the legal institution of maintenance liability. Clearly, though, this issue cannot be resolved on the basis of empirical data alone. We shall therefore take as our starting point existing value orientations in society, which obviously implies a normative choice. Factual arguments will, however, also come into play.

The civil law institution of maintenance should not be reduced to its coercive aspect, however important this may be. It also has a symbolic purpose in the sense that it refers to living ethical principles and allows everyone to participate in an existing normative awareness. It is a law that holds up an ideal to the people and encourages them to translate this ideal into concrete action, thereby fulfilling a socio-pedagogical purpose. The fact that solidarity, especially between parents and children, is still considered an important value and indeed is put into practice, is also quite apparent from sociological data. It is therefore not surprising that the legal institution of maintenance liability was not abolished from French and Dutch family law when this legislation was reformed. Yet, we submit, that its concrete legal form in the Civil Code is no longer adapted to the needs of society and the mechanical application of the law would appear to be outmoded.

Therefore, the question arises as to whether the legal interpretation of the notion of solidarity within the family needs to be reassessed. We would argue that its ethical dimension should be emphasised more clearly. The notion of gratefulness rather than that of lineage ought to occupy a central position. Those who never cared for their children can hardly demand, by legal process, that their children support them. It should also be noted in this context that receiving such support is no longer vitally important, as the person entitled to maintenance can now count on special social provisions that guarantee subsistence income. On this basis, we submit that judges should be granted power of appraisal, so that they would no longer be forced to order maintenance payment automatically.

(b) The Right of Recourse of OCMWs on the Basis of Maintenance Liability under the Civil Code

There are empirical indications for and against right of recourse on the part of OCMWs. Let us first consider arguments for its abolition. The requirement to call on relatives for financial help or knowledge of the fact that right of recourse is being exercised can be humiliating for the person in need, especially for parents vis-à-vis their adult children. The adult children, for their part, may be reluctant to pay out of concern for their own household rather than out of self-interest in the narrow sense. If right of recourse is exercised, this may well undermine the relationship between the aged and their adult child(ren). Clearly, though, this relationship is crucially important to the psychological balance and well being of the former.

Moreover, maintenance obligation tends to affect the most vulnerable individuals and enhances differences in welfare. After all, needy parents are often encountered in families where some members, or even one member, have succeeded in attaining a modest level of welfare. This welfare may be undermined by the amount of care that children in these households receive. After all, the first generation is likely to require financial assistance at a time when the second generation faces the choice of whether the third generation should be given an opportunity to carry on studying or should be told to find a job.

Furthermore, by exercising its right of recourse, the care-providing institution might undermine its own purpose, as such action will be perceived as repressive by the elderly person in question. Moreover, the question arises whether the effort and cost associated with exercising one's right of recourse do not seriously compromise the assumed benefits.

There are also a number of arguments against abolishing right of recourse. Abolition of OCMWs' right of recourse would undermine the moral obligations of kinship. Those who decide to make sacrifices, nevertheless, will put their own household at an economic disadvantage compared to less morally sensitive persons who fail to provide assistance in similar circumstances. It would be particularly objectionable if persons who are 'rolling in wealth' were to neglect their needy parents.

Abolition of the maintenance obligation would entail an additional burden for the community. At present, the maximum recourse amount is relatively small, but if the maintenance obligation were to be abolished, the community may well be required to make a larger contribution. Abolition of the maintenance obligation would result in a number of abuses. Elderly parents could be tempted to have themselves declared indigent, knowing that no recourse can be taken against their children.

While we concede that empirical arguments may play a role in this debate, we also feel that people's diverging views on the respective role of the family and society ultimately determine where they stand on this issue. Those who feel that society is responsible for guaranteeing subsistence income under all conditions, including the case of admission to a rest home, will find the arguments against maintenance obligation compelling. Conversely, those who attribute a subsidiary role to society and the state will find it hard to accept that the relatives of an elderly person in a rest home refuse to contribute towards the costs of residential care in accordance with their own financial situation.

REFERENCES

Albertario, E (1925) *Sul Diritto Agli Alimenti* (Milan, Societa Editrice 'Vita e Pensiero').

Centrum voor Bevolkins en Gezinsstudien (1969) *De Bejaarden in België, III, Familiale en Sociale Relaties* (Brussels, Centrum).

Defacqz, EH (1873) *Ancien Droit Belge ou Précis Analytique des Lois et Coutumes Observées en Belgique avant le Code Civil* (Brussels, Centrum).

Domat, J (1695) *Les Lois Civiles dans leur Ordre Naturel,* vol 1, 2nd edn (Paris, Coignard).

Durkheim, É (1947) *The Division of Labor in Society,* trans G Simpson (Glencoe, IU, Free Press).

Gaudemet, J (1963) *Les Communautés Familiales* (Paris, M Rivière).

Jamar, L, Waleffe, F and Delahaye, P (eds) (1814–1965) *Répertoire Général de la Jurisprudence Belge* (Brussels, Bruyland).

Johnston, HW (1969) 'The Roman Family' in JK Hadden and ML Borgatta (eds), *Marriage and the Family* (Itasca, IU, FE Peacock).

Kaser, M (1955) *Das Römische Privatrecht,* vol 1 (Munich, Beck).

Kirkpatrick, C (1963) *The Family as Process and Institution* (New York, Ronald Press).

Lebras, G (1959) 'Capacité Personelle et Structures Sociales dans le Très Ancien Droit de Rome' *Droits de l'Antiquité et Sociologie Juridique, Mélanges Henry Lévy-Brühl* (Paris, Sirey).

Locré de Roissy, JG, Baron de (1836) *La Législation Civile, Commerciale et Criminelle de la France ou Commentaire et Complément des Codes Français,* vol 2 (Brussels, Librarie de Jurisprudence de H Tarlier).

Piganiol, A (1954) *Histoire de Rome,* 4th edn (Paris, Presses Universitaires de France).

Pothier, RJ (1830) 'Traité de Contrat de Mariage' *Oeuvres Complètes de Pothier,* vol 7 (Paris, E Crochard).

Sachers, E (1951) 'Das Recht auf Unterhalt in der Römishen Familie der Klassischen Zeit' *Festschrift Fritz Schulz,* vol 1 (Weimar, N Böhlaus Nachfolger).

Schulz, F (1934) *Principien des Römischen Rechts* (Berlin, Duncker and Humblat).

Shanas, E *et al* (1968) *Old People in Three Industrial Societies* (New York, Atherton Press).

Van Houtte, J (1977) 'Familiesolidariteit versus Gemeenschapssolidariteit (Family Solidarity Versus Social Solidarity)' *Tijdschrift voor Sociaal Welzijn en Maatschappelijk Werk* 4: 194–9.

Van Houtte, J and Breda, J (1976) *Behoeftige Bejaarden en Onderhoudsplichtige Kinderen: Een Rechtssociologisch Onderzoek in Commissie van Openbare Onderstand en Vredegerecht (Elderly Persons in Need and Children Liable for Their Maintenance: A Sociological Survey of Law Practices in Public Assistance Agencies and Justice of the Peace Courts)* (Deventer, Van Loghum–Slaterus).

—— (1978) 'Maintenance of the Aged by their Adult Children: the Family as a Residual Agency in the Solution of Poverty in Belgium' *Law and Society Review* 12: 645–664.

Van Reepingen, C (1949–70) *Recueil Annuel de Jurisprudence Belge* (Brussels, Bruylant).

Zimmerman, CC (1947) *Family and Civilization* (New York, Harper).

15

Obligations of Grown-Up Children to their Elderly Parents: Bulgarian Legislation and Practice

VELINA TODOROVA

INTRODUCTION

T HE PRIMARY OBLIGATION for maintenance of the elderly according to Bulgarian family and welfare law is based on family relationships and kinship. There is a public obligation only when the elderly person is unable to support him or herself and has no relatives under a legal duty to provide maintenance.[1] Current amendments to the Social Assistance Act confirmed and even strengthened the maintenance liabilities of family members. This gave rise to a public debate on the moral price of requiring elderly parents to sue their adult children for maintenance.[2]

Legal norms are only one of a number of sources of mutual obligations between the generations. These obligations derive mainly from the traditions and culture of Bulgarian society, where the family has been and still is the structure which provides security and maintenance for its vulnerable members. The state still relies very much on the family and kinship solidarity to substitute for or to complement the safety nets provided by society.

There are both demographic and economic reasons for the increasing importance of family solidarity nowadays. The economic crisis which accompanied transition made the obligations of the family towards the elderly

---

[1] See the last amendments to the Social Assistance Act 2002—which made the old provision even stronger.

[2] See *Sega*, daily (11 Dec 2002). On the arguments in such a debate see Van Houtte and Breda (ch 14, this volume).

more important and more burdensome.[3] This was due to the drastic reduction in the resources available to the elderly at the beginning of the transition period in 1989. This was caused by the deterioration in public financing for pensions[4] and they fell to low levels as a result of budgetary limitations.[5]

The demographic trends also affected intergenerational relations. Comparative data show that Bulgaria has a rapidly ageing population. The proportion of elderly people is already very high, and is expected to grow over the next 20 years.[6] As a result of this the middle generation, that is the economically active, who are decreasing as a proportion of the population will have to provide maintenance for two generations—the children and the elderly.

This chapter explores family relations as a source of personal obligations over time in Bulgarian society. By looking to the interpretation of effective legislation in its historical and cultural contexts I will analyse what drives

[3]

Table 15.1 Bulgaria: Major Economic Indicators

Indicator	1995	1996	1997	1998	1999	2000
GDP growth %	2.9	–10.1	–7.0	3.5	2.4	4
Inflation %	34	310	579	1	6.2	3.5
Nominal exchange rate BGL (BGN)/USD	71	487	1776	1675	1974	2100
Unemployment rate %	11	12.5	14	12	16	19
Average salary in USD	130	56	108	128	122	122
Total budget income (% of GDB)	36	32	33	39.5	42.5	37
Total budget costs (% of GDB)	41	42	36	38	43.5	38
Retirement pay costs (% of GDP)	8.2	6.9	6.3	–	8.5	9.4
Child benefits costs (% of GDP)	0.8	0.6	0.6			

Sources: World Bank (1999) *Bulgaria: Poverty in the Transition Process* (Washington) 2–5; World Bank (2000) *Balance Between Protection and Opportunities: Social Protection Strategy in Transition Economies* (Washington) 59.

[4] The reasons are familiar: the reduction in pension funds income due to high unemployment, migration abroad, and the non-payment of security contributions.

[5] In 1999 the average monthly pension was about $35, which means that for 10 years it marked a decrease by approximately 60 per cent. See Bulgaria Country General Assessment, UNDP, (2000) 26. Currently, the minimum pension for paid service, old age and full employment duration is about US$25, whereas the highest pension is about US$90 (per month).

[6] According to the data from the last census (2001) the population of the country is decreasing continuously. In 2001 it amounts to a total of 7,977,646 people. As compared to the previous census of 31 Dec 1992, there is a drop of almost half a million people, whereas the decrease in comparison to 1986 is almost one million people. The reasons for this are both the drops in the birth rate, and the increased death rates, which results is a negative growth of minus 5.6 per cent. According to demographers, Bulgaria's problems are related more to the comparatively high death rates rather than to the low birth rates. During the last 10 years, the total death rate factor fluctuates around the figure of 14 per cent. Male super-high death rates are very explicit. For instance, in 1997, 118 men died per 100 women. The total death rate factor for men is 16.3 per cent as compared to 13.2 per cent for women. Also, one further reason for the absolute decrease in Bulgaria's population during the last twelve years is the migration of young people to Western European countries and the USA. The Bulgarian population is ageing. For the last 37 years (1960–97) the population had aged by about 7 years, and for the last 7 years only by 1.4 years. Decreased birth rates and the higher life expectancy, although it is still low as compared to that in the European countries, are the major reasons for this effect.

intergenerational support and assistance—is it primarily legal or ethical norms? The answer to this question could suggest how influential law is in the area of family relations and personal obligations (see Eekelaar, ch 1, this volume). It is also interesting to examine the views of today's young people about their obligations to elderly parents (or relations) and whether these obligations should be shared with society as a whole. It is yet another question to ask how the state takes into account family resources in drawing up its social policy. I will also draw on results of empirical research carried out specifically for the purposes of this chapter.[7]

THE ELDERLY IN THE FAMILY LAW CONTEXT

Bulgarian law supports solidarity within the family. As soon as the first family laws were adopted, legal relations were established within the extended family in two directions—the responsibilities of the elderly to the children and vice versa, the responsibilities of grown-ups (and minor) children to their elderly relatives. These interrelations could be characterised as both personal and economic.

The primary question in considering the regulation of personal relations is: which are the significant relations and what is the degree to which kinship

Table 15.2 Average Life Expectancy

Year(s)	1980	1992–94	1998–2000
Average life expectancy	71.35	70.91	71.70

Women have a higher average life expectancy of 75.34, whereas for men it is only 68.15. Ageing is also accelerated by other processes, such as migration abroad of the young generation (mainly)—176,000 for the period 1992–2001.

Table 15.3 Population Average Age by Years

Year	1960	1990	1997	2001
Population average age	32.4	37.4	39.2	40.1

The rural population is ageing faster than the urban population, irrespective of the higher birth rates in the villages. Migration to towns is the major reason. As a result, the total number of retired people is growing. In 1999 they constituted 29.1 per cent of the country's total population. The same applies for their relative share against the population total.

Table 15.4 Age Structure, 2000

Age groups	Below 18	18-65	Over 65
Number	1,550,000	5,055,595	1,366,250
Relative share	19.5%	63.4%	17.1%

[7] The research was carried by the Alpha Research Sociological Agency in April 2002. It covers 1220 respondents. The registration method is a standardised interview.

has a legal meaning? The Family Code (FC) legitimises relations between two groups of relatives. One group comprises the close relatives, such as parents and grandparents. The grandparents, for example, have a special status. They are entitled to have contact with a child[8] as well as to adopt a child.[9] The child may be placed with them if parental rights and duties are restricted or terminated, or in the case of divorce.[10] There are also opportunities for placement with relatives or friends. But on the other hand, the child owes maintenance and respect to his/her parents or grandparents.

The more distant relatives, defined as 'relatives and friends', form the second group of relevant relations. The goal here is to provide for a legal opportunity for the inclusion of a broader circle of persons in the upbringing of the child. The Child Protection Act (2000) also uses the term 'relatives and friends' to identify the circle of persons with whom the child can be placed as a measure of protection.[11] According to the interpretation of the Supreme Court, the concept of 'relatives and friends' covers 'the persons, who maintain immediate contact and relations with the family and know well both the parents, the children and their relations'.[12] The degree of kinship is not identified, as the actual relations of proximity and the will of the relative to take care of the child are significant.

Family law settles also some economic relationships between relatives, that is the obligations for assistance and maintenance. Parents and children, brothers and sisters as well as grandchildren and grandparents are mutually obliged to provide maintenance to each other.[13] The absence of close relatives who might provide maintenance provides the ground for access to public assistance.

FAMILY LAW AND PERSONAL OBLIGATIONS
BETWEEN GENERATIONS

All the family laws adopted in Bulgaria in the period 1907–85 contain the rule that children owe respect and assistance to their parents. The obligations

---

[8] Art 70 FC reads: '(2) The grandfather and grandmother are entitled to personal relations with their grandchildren who are minor. Where there are obstacles in the way of maintaining personal relations, the regional court at the place of residence of the grandchildren, at the request of the grandfather or the grandmother, decrees measures for personal relations with them, except where this is not in the interest of the children.'

[9] Art 52 FC reads: '(2) The grandfather and the grandmother or any one of them may adopt their grandchild only where the child has been born out of wedlock or where both or one of its parents are deceased. The court also takes into account the opinion of the other grandfather and grandmother of the adopted. (3) Where petitions for adoption of a grandchild have been filed by the grandfather and the grandmother by the parental and by the maternal lines the court decides the case in view of the interests of the child.'

[10] Art 75 and 106 FC.

[11] Art 26 Child Protection Act.

[12] See Supreme Court Decision 1/1974, para 1. Mladenov and Bratanova (1996) 290. From here onwards, case law references are cited from this collection.

[13] See Arts 80 and 81 FC.

of children towards parents have developed gradually from the duty of respect towards the duty of maintenance (in 1937). Since 1968, in response to the developing forms of family life, this obligation has been expanded towards step-parents. In 1985, the new Family Code expanded the circle of relations to whom children owe respect and assistance: their parents, their step-parents and their grandparents. The norm cannot be enforced through a civil action. Its aim is to transfer an ethical message to the younger generations. Violation has no direct consequences at all, but can indirectly damage the situation of children. In fact, where the lack of esteem and disrespect for parents assumes an extreme form, serious consequences may result for the child such as deprivation of status (by terminating an adoption, for instance[14]), or loss of rights (by depriving the child of an inheritance[15]).

Besides its 'quasi legal' effect the legislature has persisted in keeping this provision irrespective of the social and political context. This indicates the intention to use the power of law in creating personal obligations. As has already been pointed out, it is not only the law which creates and maintains mutual obligations between family members. More important, in my view, is to ask what creates the necessity for such legal interventions. In the context of Bulgaria it is for the family to guarantee the maintenance of its members during times when no other structure is able to do this (van Houtte and Breda, ch 14, this volume).

HISTORY OF THE RULE

As early as the very first law which regulated the relations between parents and children, the Persons Act (1907), an obligation was constituted for children towards their parents: 'The child, irrespective of his/her age is obliged to esteem and respect his/her parents.'[16] This provision originates in Roman private law. The reason for its introduction into French law was the cancellation of 'paternal power' over children on becoming of age. Therefore, according to French commentators, the important words in the text are: 'irrespective of his/her age'.[17] According to the French authors, as at the time of its adoption, the rule constituted a *moral obligation*, and a reminder that 'reaching the age of majority did not exempt children from their obligation towards their parents'. However, the will of the legislators can be perceived as to preserve, even as an ethical rule without any legal consequences, the old norm, which set up a life-long dependency between generations. Moreover, emphatic reference is made to children's duty to respect

[14] Art 64, paras 1–3 FC.
[15] Art 3 Inheritance Act.
[16] Art 63 Act on the Persons. It reproduced a regulation contained in the Italian Civil Code (CC) (which in itself borrowed it from the French Civil Code). Same text in Art 371 of the French CC, Planiolle (1928) 17. All comments on French law herein have been quoted from this work, translated into Bulgarian.
[17] See Planiolle (1928) 17.

their ascendants in general, regardless of the fact that Article 371 of the French CC mentions only the mother and the father. Since that time, French judicial practice has firmly supported the rights of grandparents to maintain contact with their grandchildren.

The reasons for the creation in Roman law of legal obligations between members of the family can be found in two different areas. The first is in the area of economic solidarity between the members of the family and the weakening of the ethical rules to support this (van Houtte and Breda, ch 14, this volume). The status of the child in Roman family and law provides a second explanation.[18] It was actually intended to preserve the power, although modified, of the father after the children became of age, that is after the child leaves the family of his/her father. Thus, the law serves as a tool to introduce interdependency between generations as an element of social order. It serves as a means to protect the family in times of insecurity and weak public institutions.

THE LEGITIMACY OF THE NORM TODAY

Following this reasoning the question arises, what could be the justification for the existence of this norm today? The obvious answer is that personal obligations towards the elderly create a resource for the maintenance of an ageing population thus relieving the public purse. It can also be said that in this way the law establishes the connection between inter-personal relationships and the obligations of the community to vulnerable social groups.

The Persons and the Family Act, which in 1949 superseded the Persons Act, however, abandoned this rule. The reason probably lies in the radical change in the ideological environment and the influence of Soviet law. Historically, at that time, children were regarded as a special resource for the regeneration of society and the building of socialism/communism. Therefore norms were adopted through which parents served their children rather than the other way round. The emphasis was placed on parental obligations towards children and the interests of the latter. Another reason is that the state took on the general obligation to guarantee social justice through state social security nets rather than the family structure. This situation changed during the 1960s.[19]

---

[18] See Andreev (1975) 196–7. It is known that *paterfamilias* had the absolute power (*patria potestas*) in respect of descendants within the family. *Patria potestas* was not only a power of a very broad scope over the members of the family, including children, but in its content, it limited the capacity of inferiors in terms of their personal and property rights. Therefore, within the relationship between parents and children, the father or *paterfamilias* is almost entirely constituted as the subject of rights, whereas the child is the subject of obligations. This power had lasted until the death of *paterfamilias*, which meant that children were subjected to it irrespective of their age. Even full age did not terminate their obedience to *paterfamilias*.

[19] For more on this issue see Todorova, 'Rights or Duties: the Parents' Views and the Arguments of the Court in Parental Rights Litigation', paper presented to the 11th ISFL World Conference, 2–7 Aug 2002, Copenhagen/Oslo.

In 1953, the obligation of children towards their parents was reintroduced and expanded. Children were legally obliged not only to respect their parents, but also to help them. Obviously, economic maintenance is being referred to:

> children are obliged to respect their parents and help them according to the latter's needs and the former's capabilities.[20]

The subsequent family law, the 1968 Family Code, adopted this norm and even elaborated on the obligations of children towards their parents:

> Children are obliged to respect their parents and help them according to their capabilities. Children shall have the same obligation for their stepfather and stepmother.

The obligation for assistance has remained, but the criteria for the conduct have become milder. The obligation is narrowed to 'children's capabilities' whereas 'parents' needs' are left out. However, the addressees of the obligation have increased—step-parents are also included. The 1985 Family Code developed the rule even further, by placing it in a separate provision. According to Article 69:

> children shall respect their parents and help them. They shall have the same obligation to their stepfather or stepmother (para 1). Children who are of age are obliged to take care of their parents where the latter are old-aged, unable to work or sick (para 2).

The new text already makes a distinction between the obligations of minor children in para 1 and those of full-age children.[21] Minors owe only respect and help, which does not mean financial maintenance. Children who are of age, however, have special obligations. They owe care to a category of parents in need, who find themselves in a difficult position: 'old, unable to work or sick'. A similar obligation for assistance and respect is also assigned to grandchildren towards their grandparents.[22] Article 70(1) reads: 'The grandchildren are obliged to respect their grandparents and to help them.'

Thus, in the period of late socialism, probably as part of the search for additional resources, the obligations of grown-up children towards their parents were increased. This is probably an expression of the intent of the state of finding a way of sharing its obligations towards the elderly. And, probably, the reasons are not only economic. The resource of law is being used again for the creation and the establishment of new moral imperatives.

---

[20] Art 84, para 3.
[21] See more in Nenova (1994) 447–9.
[22] See Art 70, para 1 FC.

In this case, however, the law expressed a norm which is supported very widely within Bulgarian society.

SOCIAL NORMS REGARDING THE ELDERLY: JUSTIFICATION OF THE LEGAL NORM

How does the legal obligation of children 'to respect their parents and assist them' relate to customary law? Unlike other imports, in this case, irrespective of the fact that the legal norm was literally transferred from Western legislation, it was not new in the context of the customary norms of Bulgarians. This fact was appreciated at its very adoption, at the beginning of the 20th century. The legislator stated that it corresponded fully to Bulgarian tradition and morals.[23]

It is a part of the tradition of Bulgarian society that the mere existence of family ties creates personal obligations, which are of particular significance for the individual irrespective of how burdensome they are. A proof not only of the existence, but also of the effect of this customary norm,[24] can be found in the survival of mutual assistance between generations, which runs in both directions: towards the young and towards the elderly, taking several established forms, which have been preserved irrespective of changes in the historical context. These include the obligation of the oldest child to take care of elderly parents, the duty of a successful family member to share his/her success within the family, and personal sacrifices of parents to children. The role of the law is to demonstrate the value of these obligations to a society where the state institutions meant to ensure assistance to the vulnerable have been weak. That is why the norm has never been questioned. The only period when it was not so frequently discussed was the time of the socialist welfare state.

Traditional family behaviour requires the younger (or the youngest) child to stay with his/her parents and take care of them in their old age (Benovska-Sabkova 2002: 95, 140). This continues to be a moral obligation today, and deviation from it is rare, although its fulfilment involves conflicts. Living with elderly parents in a common household today, in addition to being a form of fulfilment of the filial duty of 'taking care',[25] is also a

---

[23] According to the commentators 'the provisions of these civil legislation acts constitute a consistent legal form suitable for the social and economic relations of our life, which, during the last two decades of the nineteenth century did not diverge very much from the economic and social life of France from the beginning of the age and that of Italy from the mid-century period' (see Fadenchecht, 1923). Another commentator stated that it is exactly in the area of family relations that Bulgarian and French customs parted. That was why the French CC was used as the source of Bulgarian family law (see Kojuharov, 1923).

[24] See Eekelaar (ch 1, this volume). He refers to Finch and Mason (1993) in explaining the nature of 'social rules' of the responsibilities of the members of the family.

[25] Finch and Mason (1993) 115. According to one of the old women interviewed in a village, 'I never thought I would be alone here, now that I have three children.' The separation of the three children in nuclear families is considered to be a deviation from the norm whereby one of them had to stay together with their parents and take care of them in their old age.

form of maintenance for the economically dependent young. This traditional norm has been used by the state as a resource to support its social
housing policy. This happened particularly under socialism at the time of
urbanisation, and could be seen as a compromise with the regulated modernisation of society during that time.[26]

In contrast with that firmly rooted social norm, another has developed
during recent years, namely, direct financial assistance to the elderly from
the young. This applies to successful young people, who set up a 'private
social policy' or 'safety nets', supporting not only their parents, but a
broader circle of relatives: grandparents, aunts, etc.[27] Our research into this
comparatively new phenomenon in the discourse of individuals and groups
values leads to the conclusion that family solidarity could be a burden on
the individual and an obstacle to success and development. As the
researcher states:

> the successful entrepreneurs today in Bulgaria live in two parallel worlds—the
> world of success and wealth that promises freedom of choice and the one of
> the traditional community that demands a kinship solidarity from them:
> (Alexandrov, 2001: 179)

Other analysts offer a different interpretation of the same phenomenon,
studying it from another perspective. 'For the first time', they state, 'the
older generations are not in a privileged position as regards access to resources. Just the opposite, they would not make it without the maintenance
of descending generations.'[28] According to them, this has resulted in the loss
of power resource for the older generations, which was the basis of the
patriarchal family. They regarded this as a ground for announcing the modernisation of the Bulgarian family.

However, very recent research provided an ambiguous answer to the
question: 'Do grown-ups provide assistance to their elderly parents?' Respondents hesitated to answer affirmatively: 41.7 per cent are sure that they
do 'in most cases', whereas 39.7 per cent think that this happens only 'from
time to time'.[29] Hesitation can be observed in both age groups, that of the

---

[26] Eg the Ordinance on the Sale of Housing Facilities (1978) recognised the individual housing needs of 'young newly married couples when they share the house of their parents at an
area of 10 sq.m. or less per person' (Art 11). The same act, however, continues to encourage
the common sharing of housing between parents and adult children. Thus, according to Art
11, para 5, 'The children who have reached majority shall be taken into account (as members
of the family) if they live with their parents and if they sign a declaration that they accept not
to be included in the list of the citizens in need for 5 years after the acquisition by their parents of their home.' See more in Todorova (2000) 164–5.
[27] Interview with H Alexandrov for *The 24 Hours* daily (29 March 2002).
[28] Outcomes, coming from a study on the qualitative aspects of poverty, conducted by the
Association for Balkan Anthropology in 1998, published in Ivanov (1998) 62.
[29] Research done by Alpha Research, dated April 2002.

young (from 18 to 30) and the elderly (over 61). The groups, which could be defined as more conservative, eg farmers and families from the Turkish ethnic group, show higher confidence in the effect of the norm: over 50 per cent. With both groups, however, there is a steady share of 19 per cent who state that the young do not help their elderly parents today. Can this be regarded as an indication of the decrease in family solidarity in contemporary society? If this is not a change in values, the reasons should be traced in the deprivation that affected the majority of families during the crisis of transition, and the channelling of the resources to the young children.

Denial of maintenance is negatively regarded by the majority of respondents (60 per cent). Mostly, it is attributed to 'bad manners and egoism' (36 per cent) and 'lack of responsibility' (24 per cent). However, quite a few of the respondents try to justify this behaviour with the 'lack of financial capacity with the adults' (24 per cent) or 'other problems' (12 per cent), thus identifying the conflict between generations over access to the limited resources. The latter group covers mainly people from multiple households or those having three or more children.

THE DEPENDENCY OF ADULT CHILDREN ON THEIR PARENTS

The traditional and sustainable practice of adult help for the elderly does not exhaust the inter-generational relations and dependencies. Dependency also exists in the opposite direction: from elderly parents to their grown-up children. Researchers, irrespective of their approach, are unanimous that dependency on the parents is preserved after children grow out of childhood, irrespective of the facts, which, especially during socialism and transition, point to the emerging emancipation of the younger generations.[30] Dependency is related to several factors: sharing a common household, raising children, economic reliance on 'products from domestic farming'. Therefore, we cannot disagree with the view that the economic independence of the young is both real and relative.[31]

The reasons for this dependency are contained in both the family behaviour of the young and in some deficits in social policy. For instance, until quite recently, the age for the first marriage remained traditionally low, which, for years on end, made the young dependent on their parents. Assistance from the parents used to take the form of both the provision of housing and direct material maintenance for children. Parents used to take an active part in the upbringing of grandchildren. This custom demonstrated sustainability even

---

[30] See Benovska-Sabkova (2002) 115, 155, 157. See also Case Study 'Young People—Needs, Risks and Perspective' in *Bulgaria—Early Warning Report* (United States Agency for International Development (USAID), United Nations Development Programme (UNDP), Open Society Foundation (OSF), 2001) 51–55. See also Stoyanova *et al* (1997) 181.
[31] See Benovska-Sabkova (2002) 140.

during the well-developed day care system under socialism. Moreover, this practice is supported by the legislation.[32] Recent years saw a change towards a later marriage and the birth of the first child, which shows an attempt to achieve economic independence before marriage.[33]

Conclusions can be drawn following a number of different directions. On the one hand, economic difficulties restrict the formation of nuclear families and make the ones already formed unstable. Therefore, the organisation of family life in Bulgarian society is still marked by both complexity (meaning the extended family) and nuclear structures. This is seen as one of the family strategies for both coping with economic difficulties and the survival of both the family and the individual.[34] In a situation where social safety networks are undeveloped, the family remains the only supportive environment that can provide for the young. Recent research proves the existence of these family mores: the family exerts enormous material effort to push up the social scale its younger members and the children.[35] This was observed not only in the area of education (where the families invest one third of their annual income) but also in the personal care for the child and his/her leisure time.

On the other hand, however, according to anthropologists and ethnographers, this feature of inter-generational relations in Bulgaria has its negative aspects, too. They assess the preservation of the economic reliance of the young on the older generations as a factor leading to dependent and passive social behaviour, which reproduces old models and practices. There is also concern that the strong kinship relations result. These carry a big price— such as high levels of corruption.[36]

Finally, inter-generational relations in the Bulgarian context are one of the features of the poverty and deprivation in the broader society. There are positive sides, such as the fact that the emancipated young are independent, they demonstrate autonomous behaviour and are led by values such as mutual assistance, solidarity, etc. The reverse practice, however, in the ongoing maintenance from the elderly to the young, creates dependencies and maintains power relations that do not favour the development of modern relationships both within the family and in society.

---

[32] The Labour Code (Art 164, para 3) provides for the right of the grandparents to a leave instead of the mother, for the upbringing of the child until he/she reaches two years of age. The FC provides for the settling of the child with the grandparents as the first opportunity available in litigation alienating or restricting the parental rights of the parents or for the cases of divorce (Art 74, para 1; Art 106, para 4). The grandparents enjoy an individual and executable right to personal relations with their grandchildren. Art 52, paras 2–3 FC provide for the opportunity for the child to be adopted by his/her grandparents.

[33] In 2000–02, the age for contracting the first marriage changed as follows: from 21.5 years in 1989 to 23.5–23.8 years and the age of the woman at the birth of the first child increased from 22.0 years in 1989 to 25.1 years.

[34] Benovska-Sabkova (2002) 122, 140, 155 and Ivanov (1998) 62.

[35] See A Raichev 'Why the Young Live Better than the Elderly?' *Sega*, daily (28 Sept 2002).

[36] *Ibid.*

ARE CHILDREN LEGALLY OBLIGED TO RESPECT THEIR PARENTS?

Bulgarian family law has traditionally perceived children as subjects of obligations rather than as rights holders. The duties of children towards the older generation have been expanding. As discussed above, legal regulation reproduces a moral norm. The goal, as explained by theory, is to use the law as a means for the socialisation of younger generations.

To analyse the legal obligation of children I will use the list suggested by J Herring of ways whereby one could establish an obligation on grown-up children to maintain parents (Herring, 2001: 558–9). It includes the following grounds: reciprocated duty, relational maintenance, implied contract or dependency. My goal is to establish the degree to which these ways of justifying reasons for the obligation have been discussed in Bulgarian legal theory and case law. I will start by noting that the theory of family law has always emphasised the moral grounds of children's obligation towards their parents, irrespective of whether the children have attained full age or not.

The reciprocated duty is the most frequent explanation of the norm: children owe respect and help because they themselves received care and maintenance when they were young. According to Nenova, the obligation of the child 'is based on parental care and authority, whereas the respect of children is the major moral satisfaction of parents for their efforts and sacrifice' (Nenova, 1994: 447; 1977: 496). The interpretations of other authors are in the same spirit, whereby a grown-up child 'is bound to repay his/her parents by his/her labour and resources for the fact that they have prepared him/her to pursue an activity of public benefit' (Georgiev *et al*, 1975: 311). Therefore, the norm has the function of reminding and helping the assumption of a moral obligation, which, in any case, is being transferred and assumed through both custom and tradition and in the specific economic conditions in society.

The second explanation, which exhausts the attempts of the theory to explain the norm, is the feeling of love and affiliation between parents and children. Here, the question arises of the correspondence between the motivation of the legislators and that of the persons observing the norm and how that law relates to the conflict between those offering and seeking assistance, be it children or parents.

To the question: 'What is the motivation governing those, who provide help?' opinions split into two equal groups. The first group were occupied by the 'feeling of responsibility' and 'love and affiliation' (two groups of 35 per cent of the respondents). The elderly attribute more importance to the 'feeling of responsibility', whereas the young regard 'affiliation' as more important. Those who help their parents are not guided by utilitarian reasons. They do not expect any material or other benefits for what they do, although, according to effective legislation, taking care of elderly parents is related to some material benefits. The Inheritance Act provides for such heirs to receive additional property, over and above their legitimate share.[37]

As regards the just distribution of assistance and maintenance between generations, the respondents prefer children to elderly parents: 68.4 per cent against 23.3 per cent. Residents of the capital and people with academic education (30 per cent) were most likely to grant maintenance to parents (42 per cent, almost equal to children, who received 53 per cent). Maintenance is granted to children by groups with more traditional behaviour: rural population (74 per cent), multiple households' representatives (79 per cent) and the followers of Islam (80 per cent).

The research shows that society is aware of the existence of conflict over the use of resources by the two groups in need: the children and the elderly. As regards the distribution of resources, society gives preference to the younger generation. Subsequently, competition between the two groups has to be resolved through the social policy of the state. In the case where public expenditure on pensions is available, we may expect that the resources of the family will be directed mostly to the rearing of the young generation.

There could be another possible interpretation of this issue. Where it is stated, for instance, that children owe respect and care as a correlation to what they received from their parents, is it a reference to the actual care they received from parents? Here we come to another explanation offered by Herring, which is 'implied contract'.

Bulgarian law obviously tackles the presumption that parents are always good providers of care and they always do this in compliance with legal and moral norms. Therefore, children are assigned the obligation of respect and maintenance. However, there are numerous examples of inadequate, unsatisfactory or poor parental care. What then of the children of such parents? The only hypothesis where the law expressly states that children do not owe maintenance for their parents is that of the termination of parental rights due to the behaviour of parents.[38]

Outside these comparatively rare cases, the obligation of children towards their parents remains, even where parents have never assumed personal custody. An established practice exists, which is legally regulated, for parents to place their children in residential care.[39] This practice has been approved not only by society, but according to the case law as constituting a legitimate form of parental care.[40] Therefore, children owe assistance and maintenance

---

[37] According to Art 12, para 1 of the act, 'the heirs, who had lived with the bequeathor and taken care of the latter shall receive as inheritance the household furniture and utensils and, if they deal with land farming and receive no other remuneration thereto, they receive the farming machinery and stock of the bequeathor'.

[38] Art 91, para 3 FC.

[39] In 2001, 25,000 children were placed in residential care, where only 2 per cent of them were orphans.

[40] According to Decision 2904 1975, Supreme Court—'the placement of a child in a residential establishment by the parent ... constitutes a legal, legitimate parental action in fulfilment of parental obligations under the law'.

even to such parents. Irrespective of whether children received care and maintenance, they always owe to their parents. This is unacceptable. Of course, we can exclude the extreme cases of placement, which are the last resort for bringing up the child.

In this context, it would be more convincing to explain the grounds for the constitution of the obligation by the mere fact of biological origin rather than the actual care received. This thesis is confirmed by the case law, as the law assigns to children the same obligation with respect to step-parents. As regards the obligations of the latter, the court states that 'the obligations, which stem for the stepparent, do not cover the obligation of providing maintenance to step children. The grounds for the obligation of mainte-nance are kinship, adoption, ownership'.[41]

In conclusion, I believe that no such behaviour can be required from chil-dren if it is not placed as a requirement on parents themselves in the first place.[42] If we adopt the reciprocity thesis, what grounds do we have to demand respect and care from children who have been deprived of this by their parents? In these cases reciprocity is out of the question since no repayment can be made of what has been invested in the children. Here, even the 'implied contract' theory will not be effective if we exclude the 'cons' arguments of Herring.

FAMILY LAW AND ECONOMIC RELATIONS
BETWEEN GENERATIONS

The deep meaning of the norm being discussed here articulates the value of personal obligations to society. However, the provision creating a duty for children to respect and assist their elderly parents has no specific econom-ic meaning. It is not enforceable and contains only an ethical message. Definitely, greater significance in this respect is attributed to the provisions that establish maintenance liability of grown-up children to their elderly parents.

Maintenance and assistance for older generations are provided for in the Constitution. According to Article 50, 'The old people, who have no rel-atives and are unable to provide for themselves from their own property ... are placed under the special protection of the state and society.' The persons expected to fulfil the obligation of maintenance are within the circle of rela-tions,[43] which includes parents, spouses, full-age children, grandchildren, brothers and sisters. Where no such persons exist and the old person is unable to support him or herself, a right to social assistance arises. A simi-lar provision is also contained in the Family Code. As Article 93 reads:

[41] See Ð 109 1977 SC.
[42] The same observation in van Houtte and Breda (ch 14, this volume).
[43] See the interpretation of the term 'relations' in the Social Services Ordinance (1999)—para 2 of the Supplementary Provisions.

'Under the social assistance system the State takes over the care for the persons in need where there are no persons under the rules set out in Article 80 who are obliged to provide the maintenance or where these are unable to provide it.'

Relatives, in a sequence set out by the Family Code, have an obligation to provide maintenance to their elderly relatives in need (who cannot provide for themselves from their property). Elderly parents are placed by the Family Code (1985) in the second position, after the spouse and children, among the persons, to whom a grown-up child owes maintenance.[44] Respectively, an elderly parent is entitled to seek maintenance from his or her children, except where such a parent has a spouse who can provide him/her with such maintenance.[45] This provision was introduced as early as 1937, by the first Act on the Obligation of Maintenance. The Social Assistance Act, adopted in 1998, in force in 2000, was the first piece of legislation to regulate social assistance. Until recently, these relations were regulated by secondary legislation. The 1951 Decree on Public Assistance, which was in effect by 1998, does not contain any similar provisions. Irrespective however of the lack of explicitness in social legislation about the primary importance of the family obligation for maintenance, and the subsidiary nature of its public counterpart, it has always been present in family law acts.[46]

The right to maintenance has consequences in terms of both family law and social assistance law. In addition to establishing a legal family obligation for maintenance, it also affects the right of the elderly person to social assistance. For a maintenance claim to be upheld, two facts need to be proved. Firstly, the need of the elderly parent: such a parent should not have property generating means of maintenance. Secondly, the person under the family obligation has to be able to provide such maintenance. Maintenance affixed by a court decision is collectible with priority over that of any creditor.

The right of the elderly to social assistance arises where the persons obliged to provide maintenance under of the Family Code are found incapable of performance (or if incapacity is temporary, while it lasts[47]). According to Article 11, para 3 of the Social Assistance Act:

---

[44] According to Art 81 FC, sequence of the persons entitled to maintenance: The person who is liable to provide maintenance to several persons entitled to maintenance is obliged to do it in the following sequence: to children, to spouse or a former spouse; to parents; to grandchildren and great-grandchildren; to brothers and sisters; to grandparents, and to ancestors of a higher degree.

[45] According to Art 80, the persons entitled to maintenance may claim it in the following order: from a spouse or a former spouse; from children; from parents; from grandchildren and great-grandchildren; from brothers and sisters; from grandparents and ancestors of a higher degree.

[46] See the Ordinance Act on the Obligation of Maintenance 1937, the Act on the Persons and the Family of 1949 and the Family Codes of 1968 and 1985.

[47] See Art 2, para 6 of the Act on Social Assistance (1998).

> The right to social assistance arises for persons, who, due to age, health, social or other reasons outside their control are unable to provide for their basic living needs by themselves or with the help of the persons obliged thereto by the law.

In fact, access to social assistance may be denied only to an elderly person who brought a suit against his/her child for maintenance and received the adjudicated maintenance on a regular basis. The claim of maintenance depends entirely on the elderly person and no obligation exists for the right to be exercised, and, thereafter, an application to be filed before social funds.

However, cases where claims for maintenance against grown-up children are brought to the court by the elderly parents are very rare. There is a stronger ethical norm that it is not right for children to support their parents, which prevents parents from acting that way. This demonstrates that there are limits to the law in creating personal obligations in the family sphere. Instead, parents value good personal relations with their children more than their legal rights.

The maintenance of the elderly by the young, or at least the direct form of financial maintenance, is not regarded unequivocally by older generations. Parents do not expect their children to provide them with financial means and take care of them when they grow old.[48] To the question: 'What do children owe to their parents?' the most frequent answer is 'Respect' (75 per cent of the respondents). Only 15 per cent of the respondents expect that their children will take care of them when they grow old, 6–7 per cent expect to be morally helped and 1 per cent expect economic maintenance. A confirmation of this widely shared belief appears in a letter from a retired person, placed in a newspaper:

> I lie to my children that my pension can provide for me. If I told them I could not afford proper food, they will do their best to help me. I will never take money from them, as cows are never seen suckling from their calves. Both of their wives are unemployed and they have schoolchildren to maintenance.[49]

Parents believe that their obligations are much greater than those of their children towards them. The forms of help approved by parents are the assumption of care and access to grandchildren, or communication of their experience and practices. The latter fact is the subject of study by some researchers. According to them, 'the behaviour of the young', both under socialism and today, is compromising; they consider their elderly, consult them and take their opinion into account. This is 'esteem' and 'respect'.[50]

---

[48] According to the research of the National Statistical Institute and the Institute of Demography of 1997, published in *Women and Men in Bulgaria* (Sofia NSI and Institute of Demography 35).

[49] *24 Hours*, daily (26 March 2002).

[50] See Benovska-Sabkova (2002) 139.

CONCLUSION

Two provisions of the Family Code are aimed at legally binding adults to provide respect, assistance and maintenance to their elderly parents. The norms could be valued also as a means for the redistribution of resources of families to all family members where the state is too weak to ensure social assistance to the vulnerable groups.

It is not only the law but also ethical norms and customs in Bulgarian society, which support family solidarity, especially where family strategies are concerned in economic and other crises. The analyses clearly show that it is not the law but family ethics and personal relationships that give rise to personal obligations within the family. It is obvious if we compare two legal provisions—the non-enforceable and the enforceable ones. Elderly parents readily accept any assistance in the form of esteem and respect or involvement in a common household with their grown-up children. They do not wish to sue their children, which they consider as undermining the personal relationships within the family. Moreover, parents in Bulgaria still believe that they are morally obliged to make sacrifices for children no matter how old they are. The elderly believe it unacceptable that they should rely on direct financial maintenance. They rely on the voluntary and not the forcible granting of maintenance. This is mainly because the elderly do not consider it fair to compete with minor children. The law also promotes this ethic. Minors are awarded priority in receiving maintenance from their parents and the public also firmly backs up this norm.

These family values are used well by the state in sharing responsibilities for the elderly between the private and public sectors. The current public debate, however, clearly seeks more involvement by state funds instead of overburdening the families. And one more concern—allowing families to create their own social safety nets—provides a breeding ground for negative effects such as dependency and corruption. This is the price that the society and the state would pay for failing to develop appropriate social policy. To close the circle I would suggest that it is not so difficult to implement this public provision, if and when public wealth allows.

REFERENCES

Alexandrov, H (2001) *Brain Hunters (Lovci na Ymove)* (Sofia: New Bulgarian University).

Andreev, M (1975) *Roman Private Law* (Sofia, Nayka I Izkystvo).

Benovska-Sabkova, M (2002) *Political Transition and Everyday Culture* (Sofia, M Drinov).

Fadenchecht, J (1923) 'Codification of Civil and Commercial Law' *Juridicheska Missal* 1:1.

Finch, J and Mason, J (1993) *Negotiating Family Responsibilities* (London, Routledge).

Georgiev, H, Palazov, I, Beshkov, P and Damyanov, T (1975) *Family Code—Commentary* (Sofia, Nayka I Izkystvo).

Herring, J (2001) *Family Law* (London, Longman).

Ivanov, A (1998) *National Human Development Report: Bulgaria 1998* (Sofia: United Nations Development Programme).

Kojuharov, I (1923) 'The Pursuit of the Father' *Juridicheska Missal* 2–3.

Mladenov, VN and Bratanova, P (1996) *Family Code: Text, Judicial Practice, Bibliography* (Sofia: Sibi).

Nenova, L (1977) *Family Law* (Sofia, Nayka I Izkystvo).

—— (1994) *Family Law of the Republic of Bulgaria* (Sofia, Nayka I Izkystvo).

Planiolle, M (1928) *A Course on French Civil Law*, vol 1 (Sofia, Herman).

Stoyanova, K *et al* (1997) *Family Social Policy* (Sofia, Gorex Press).

Todorova, V (2000) 'Family Law in Bulgaria: Legal Norms and Social Norms' *International Journal of Law, Policy and the Family* 14:2.

Part IV. B

Harmonisation of Law and Diversity: the Fit Between Family Law and Family Values

16

Ethnicity and Expectations Concerning Family Law and Family Values in Bulgaria

STEFKA NAOUMOVA

INTRODUCTION

T HE ETHNIC SITUATION in Bulgaria is one of the most important features of social and political life and has a permanent influence on national legislation. The question of diversity in expectation between minority ethnic groups has become very important in the context of the European harmonisation of private law in general and family law in particular. The process of harmonisation in family law has given rise to a large number of problems that have to be resolved. One of these is the problem of diversity in expectations between different European countries, as family law is deeply rooted in cultural and ideological values. It is not surprising that these values are not homogeneous even within each European country.

The contemporary Bulgarian family in general, and family law in particular, cannot be reviewed separately from the more general question of the impact of ethnic differences on the cultural and ideological values of society. These differences give rise to a range of expectations about the future development of family law not only at the national, but also at the European level. The attempt to impose these differences on pan-European family values and some culturally alien European family law has not yet been subject to empirical analysis, so it is not yet clear how European family law will respond to a context of diverse expectations.

Bulgarian society is traditionally oriented as regards family and family law and each ethnocultural community has its own family culture. There is also an institutional framework incorporating the general principles of contemporary family law, the family values in different ethnic communities and protection of their rights. The Bulgarian Constitution, adopted in 1991, proclaims the principle of equality and non-discrimination for all

Bulgarian citizens. The Constitution guarantees the right to freedom of mind, conscience and religion; the right of representatives of minority groups to dispose and develop their culture freely, and to use and study their native language. At the same time, Article 11, paragraph 4 of the Constitution prohibits the formation of political parties on an ethnic, racial or religious basis. They are given the same status as parties whose aim is the violent seizure of state power. Representatives of ethnic and religious groups in Bulgaria have the right to establish their own cultural, social, educational and other organisations and associations, but not political parties.

The constitutional framework for regulating equality between the sexes can be found in Article 6, section 2. According to this provision 'all citizens are equal before the law. Any restrictions of rights or privileges based on race, nationality, ethnicity, sex, origin, education, beliefs, political affiliation or property status are inadmissible.'

The constitutional principles provide the legal basis for any new developments in family law, however, but need to be reviewed separately in the context of the more general question of the impact of economic transformation on the social status of ethnic minorities and their family situation in a post-totalitarian system. Two main questions are addressed in this chapter: the first deals with diversity in expectation among minority ethnic groups concerning the family from a traditional perspective. The second question considers the problems arising from new European provisions based on a new vision of family life.

THE IMPACT OF ECONOMIC TRANSFORMATION IN BULGARIA ON THE SOCIAL STATUS OF THE MINORITIES AND THEIR FAMILY SITUATION: A BRIEF OVERVIEW

It is over 10 years since the beginning of change in Central and Eastern Europe (including Bulgaria). This makes it possible to review all that has been achieved up until now, as well as to make predictions about the future. After the euphoria which followed the change in the political system, we entered a period of sober economic analysis and concrete decision-making to control the pace of transition towards a market economy.

In general terms, countries from Central and Eastern Europe had to choose between two existing models of economic transition—the American model and the European model. The American model was grounded in a number of economic and sociological analyses dating from the turn of the century. The general message is that government should attempt to correct, through democratic policy, the dehumanising influence of severe market competition, the depersonalising industrial organisation of labour, and the city ghettos in the industrial centres. In the American social and cultural context this theory, as implemented in practice, appeared to be really effective, since it stimulated the economy, stabilised politics, and ensured a good life for millions of people. The European model, which was dominant in the Old Continent until the Second World War, and reshaped after the war, finds that the optimum variation for Europe is the institutional implementation of liberal democracy. On the other hand, this model, according to Ralf Dahrendorf, may fail to ensure the best of all possible worlds.

In the present dynamic world situation where neither of the two main economic models can be directly implemented in the countries of Central and Eastern Europe, we note the words of Francis Fukuyama:

> We can imagine future worlds which are much worse than the one we know, worlds in which racial and religious hate have returned, or worlds in which we are facing a number of wars or environmental catastrophes. But we cannot imagine a world that is *essentially* different from the present world and at the same time is a better one.

This discreetly suggests that a new vision of the best possible world is probably not a match for the reality. Even in the most developed liberal democracies conflicts and change continue, and new models for social rationality are looked for. Today, in a period of change, the East Europeans together with Americans and Europeans, have their chance to move forward if they manage to avoid some of the imperfections of the existing models and if they manage to create some new ones.

In spite of the differences between the American and European models, they share a relatively successful approach to the question of private enterprise and private initiative. It is beyond doubt that the over-centralised political and economic system which was dominant in Central and Eastern Europe for decades, has been proved ineffective in economic, political, and moral terms. The main reason for this is that it limited individual initiative and as a consequence limited individual responsibility. As a result technological development was slow and there was a permanent deficit in the economy. This led to a long period of recession in the countries in Central and Eastern Europe, including Bulgaria. Over-centralisation and the merging of economics and politics in Eastern Europe led to the impossibility of differentiating between structures and activities—which are differentiated in countries with a highly developed technological base and a high level of labour separation.[1] After the beginning of transition in almost all the countries of Central and Eastern Europe efforts were made to integrate society through practical administrative measures—as economic life became free from political tutelage. At the same time, though, transition toward economic and political pluralism caused new problems. Some of these concerned all transition countries (for example,

---

[1] Still Durkheim foresaw such dependence—the more developed is one society in technological aspect, the stronger is the differentiation not only in the frame of the economic cycle, but in the other spheres of social life as well. In this way, according to him, a transition is executed from solidarity based on common kinship and culture, to solidarity integrated through functional dependencies.

the short-lived naive expectations that an organic market evolution would be reached, slowing down privatisation, and the growth of unemployment, crime, etc), and some were specific to separate countries.

Change to the political system in Bulgaria, as in other countries of Central and Eastern Europe, did not automatically lead to change in the economic system. Political transition freed up an enormous amount of energy which, with correct channelling, should have led to a rapid move to rational forms of social and economic organisation. This process gave priority to problems of political freedom, minority rights protection, ethnic tolerance, political pluralism, etc. As for economic prosperity, though, the situation sometimes looks rather uncertain, which is not surprising as it is not possible to wave a magic wand and leap from yesterday's centralised model to a free market initiative and entrepreneurial activity.

The actual problems facing economic reform in Bulgaria in general may be outlined in the following points:

1 the accelerated process of privatisation;
2 joining restitution with privatisation;
3 harmonising legislation and making it conform to EU directives for the purpose of speeding up the process of full Bulgarian membership in the European Community;
4 the ethnocultural situation and protection of the rights of minorities in the context of the Balkan situation.

Each of these points could be analysed in depth and guidelines drafted for the future development of the country.

It should be noted, however, that these key pointers for economic reform are organically integrated. It is not possible for privatisation to be put into effect without the legislation. On the other hand, the dynamics of economic and social life require changes to legislation to be timely, so that economic policy becomes grounded on a solid legal base.

The first basic question was which of the following three main approaches to transformation should be chosen: (1) shock therapy; (2) step-by-step transition; or (3) a combined approach. Bulgaria at first used the shock therapy method but within a few years gave it up. This caused the following problem— the shock therapy approach is based on the presumption of building market institutions over a short period of time. Now it is known that such an assumption is incorrect because the development of market institutions requires a long period of time. At the same time, though, legislation went through different metamorphoses until a relatively clear way was found for a long-term economic strategy aimed at step-by-step privatisation of the industrial giants, stimulating private enterprise, and avoiding social problems such as unemployment, negative GNP, and social conflicts (including ethnic conflicts).

It is a marked feature of transition in Bulgaria that the restitution process overtook privatisation. Restitution of land and forests was executed in a

very short period of time, and this provided the conditions for private agriculture. As for privatisation, it should be stated that in Bulgaria the process
was too prolonged and drastically delayed. There are a number of reasons
for that, but the most serious ones are the following:

— Lack of clarity about choosing the best acceptable privatisation model.[2]
  In Bulgaria, different variants were implemented for combining privatisation with liquidation of the state enterprise. This provoked unemployment and mass poverty.
— Lack of clear strategy regarding combining economic with financial
  reform. It is impossible to achieve an efficient labour market policy
  without implementing strict budget limitations.
— Lack of clear policy regarding income. Which policy could ensure market stimulation of the workforce in the direction of the conditions of
  market economy?
— Lack of legal guarantees to support private enterprise and private initiative, moreover, this legal gap exists in a situation characterised by an
  enormous freeing up of the workforce and a lack of alternative ways to
  use this workforce in the private sector.

Today the main question is how transformation could avoid social conflicts,
and through what mechanisms that problem could be resolved.

It has been observed that minorities are deeply concerned by the transformation. This is because, in the framework of the centralised economy
when the main slogan was to ensure jobs for everyone, even at a minimal
wage rate, representatives of different ethnic groups had relatively good
conditions. It was due to state policy and to the fact that in different regions
in the country inhabited mainly by minorities, specific economic activity
was developed—stock breeding, tobacco growing, and state sponsored
small industry. Bearing in mind that the ethnocultural situation in Bulgaria
is a permanent factor in determining the level of stability or destabilisation,
this problem deserves special attention.

ETHNIC PROBLEMS AND WAYS TO RESOLVE THE
ECONOMIC AND SOCIAL STATUS OF THE MINORITIES
AND THEIR FAMILY SITUATION

Some of the elements of transition are common to all Eastern and Central
European countries, in particular their desire to be integrated into the

---

[2] There are six basic models known in practice: (1) spontaneous privatisation—when management of the enterprise takes initiative for changing the state ownership towards a new owner; (2)
preliminary privatisation—part of the enterprise material property (actives) is sold; (3) liquidation of enterprise—new owner receives the actives together with his/her counteragents; (4) hidden privatisation—new owner does not pay anything to the state; (5) state initiated privatisation;
(6) privatisation initiated by the municipality which sells its own land or facilities.

European Community and on that basis to build a stable pan-European partnership. The issue of minority rights in the context of European integration has a prominent place in the public debate process in all of these countries. This theme should be considered as one of the points of contact between Western societies and post-Communist societies.

While in the past the importance of the minorities was often doubted in various political contexts, today it seems as if everybody is seeking to solve their problems. It looks as if, in the face of disconnected social reality, it may be possible, through attitudes towards minorities and their families, to find a way to restore social solidarity and give substance to claims that society does still exist. As for questions about Bulgarian family life and family law, this topic cannot be viewed separately from the more general question of the social status of the minorities and their family life and family customs. The ethnic situation in Bulgaria is still one of the most important factors affecting national legislation. In contemporary Bulgaria, four main ethnocultural groups can be identified: Bulgarians (Bulgarian-speaking Christians), Turks (Turkish-speaking Muslims), Pomaks (Bulgarian-speaking Muslims) and Romas. These four ethnocultural groups differ from each other not only in their culture, style of life, and attitudes toward democratic institutions, but also in their opinions about new family legislation against the background of the relationship between European standards and the national legal system. It is one of the most important issues from the point of view of European integration to construct a model of new family values which could be implemented for all existing ethnic groups.

The former institutional view of minorities is far from simple and took a different shape at different times and in different places. During transition some of the traditional problems concerning minorities continued to exist, but there are also new ones (unemployment, increasing poverty, changes in social welfare provision, violence against minorities under the pressures of economic transformation and so on). There is little reason to believe that post-Communist transformation will improve the conditions of minorities as citizens, as human beings, and as workers.

There are several basic connected factors affecting the development of views about minority rights in Bulgaria. Firstly, there are the constitutional aspects of the problem. Secondly, we need conformity with European standards in the context of European integration. Thirdly, there are the non-legal aspects, more specifically, legal–sociological aspects.

The new Bulgarian Constitution adopted in 1991 included several basic principles which placed Bulgaria in line with the rest of the European countries. In the first place, for the first time for over 50 years, the principle of the division of power was restored. In the second place, the principle of political pluralism was restored. In the third place, there is already conformity for the constitutional provisions with the main international acts, more specifically the UN International Civil and Political Rights Pact, the

UN International Economic, Social and Cultural Rights Pact, the Universal Human Rights Declaration, the European Convention for the Protection of Human Rights, as well as the Convention Attached Protocol. Here we should point out Article 5(4) of the Constitution which states:

> international treaties, ratified constitutionally, promulgated, and made effective by the Republic of Bulgaria, are part of the country's internal laws. They take precedence over conflicting domestic legislation.

This means that international treaties are beginning to play a greater role in the process of drafting internal legislation including minority rights legislation.

The second basic point concerns relations between Bulgaria and European institutions. Bulgaria is now represented in Strasbourg as a member of the Council of Europe, and being within the sphere of European Human Rights (including minorities rights), we may now observe directly how the European dimension slowly begins to take precedence over regional and national differences. In this context it is very important to provide reference material for policymaking in the further Europeanisation of local laws and policies. Bulgaria, like other Central Eastern European countries, is in the process of becoming associated with the European Union. Bulgaria is expected to harmonise their laws with those of the EU, which is not an easy task if one takes into account the difficulties encountered when harmonising within the EU itself.

In principle, it should be pointed out that there is a difference between implementing Article 5(4), on the one hand, and the requirements coming from the European Accession Treaty, on the other. In the first case, the question is about a permanent process, in the second case it is about harmonising legislation with the directives of EU. As for implementing the first principle grounded in the constitutional text cited above, we should point out that since adopting the Constitution the Bulgarian Parliament has ratified more than 150 international treaties, but only a few concern minority rights *sensu stricto*. This is because in many of the international treaties minority rights are dealt with indirectly and not in a direct way.

As for harmonising legislation within the EU, it should pointed out that after signing the Accession Treaty, effective for Bulgaria from 1 February 1995, many directives were adopted, but few of them concerned minority rights and their family situation. This has two implications. Firstly, minority rights problems are a priority of the EU. Secondly, there is a classical legal scheme working here, according to which ethnic factors can or cannot be viewed as a separate factor impacting on the creation of independent legal standards. Therefore, the topic of minority rights is more or less connected to either the classical problem of the place of the minorities in the new democratic states or there is a priority for internal legislation which can conform to the traditional peculiarities of each country when solving this complicated problem.

In this context a socio-legal approach is much more fruitful than the traditional legal one. It means that we should examine whether or not ethnic differences are central to the processes of democratisation and marketisation (for example, the growing demand for protection for ethnic minorities raises questions as to whether violence against minorities has increased under the pressures of economic transformation) or have simply become public for the first time, since these problems were excluded by the parameters of past official theory on minorities.

There is also a demographic issue here. Bulgaria is one of the countries in Central and Eastern Europe with the most clearly noticeable demographic decline. This trend is longstanding. But during the past few years its negative features have become obvious. The result of this demographic development and of the wave of emigration has been a substantial decrease in the county's population. The population density has dropped from 81 per square kilometre in 1989 to 75.9 people in 1997. The rate of depopulation is far higher in the villages. In 1994 it amounted to 10.4 per 1000. In the towns and cities the depopulation became manifest in 1994, amounting to 0.7 per mile. These differences can be explained by the predominance of old people in the villages. The birth rate is lower, while the death rate is twice as high as in the urban centres. Infant mortality is rising too.

BULGARIAN FAMILY LAW, EUROPEAN STANDARDS AND NEW FAMILY VALUES

According to data from the census of the Bulgarian population in December 2000, 85.7 per cent of the 7.9 million population describe themselves as ethnic Bulgarians, 9.4 per cent as Bulgarian Turks, 3.7 per cent as Gypsies (Romas), and 1.3 per cent as representatives of other smaller ethnic groups. What is the connection between the European policy of protecting the rights of ethnic minorities and the new role of the family? Bulgaria strictly fulfils EU directives regarding legislative reform in the areas of: health protection, medical care, health insurance, and so on. In addition, the requirements of the IMF (arising from the fact that the country is a Currency Board) are that free health care has to be removed step by step. All hospitals are already business organisations, legally speaking. All hospital services (childbirth, children's services, etc) are paid for. But with high unemployment among minorities, low wages (barely enough for most basic needs), and lowering the number of hospital services in the villages and small towns, a great number of those from ethnic minority communities cannot afford the luxury of planning and having children. According to recent data, approximately 40,000 children each year do not start school. The IMF requires that the number of schools, kindergartens, and even universities be reduced. If that is European integration, then this model obviously is hard to implement in Bulgaria. In other words, integration can be only at the legislative level while the social cost of implementation is so high.

Another typical element of transition and economic crisis is the increased social instability of minorities within the labour force. The low incomes and high cost of health care, education and social protection undermines or entirely eliminates a series of social benefits for minorities, which were acquired during the previous period. After living for almost half a century in a centrally planned economy, Romas have enjoyed relative equality in social life. Since transition their social position and roles are changing substantially. These changes in the socio-economic position of minorities are determined predominantly by their position in the new labour market. Roma unemployment varied from 48.2 per cent in September 1993, to 46.8 per cent in June 1996 and 89.3 per cent in June 2001. There is a clear change in Roma participation in social and economic life, and they have become more discriminated against and restricted than in the conditions of compulsory employment. The change in the work status of the Roma occurs in the context of drastically declining living standards. The decreased demand for labour is forcing Roma out of the labour market. This is the reason why Roma are prone to take up any job suggestions. This new type of economic activity was imposed on the Roma, it is not a result of their free choice. Outside the labour market, a part of the Roma workforce has gone to the informal sector. The years of transition became a period of increasing prostitution, and of the export of 'Gipsy bond-slaves'.

Serious problems, connected with social status, economic welfare and employment in different ethnic groups are due to substantial differences in their educational and qualification level. According to data from the Central Statistical Department, in 1946 82 per cent of Bulgarian Turks were illiterate, and more than half of them did not speak Bulgarian at all. Illiteracy among Roma was even higher. During the following decades great success was achieved in the widespread reduction of illiteracy among these two ethnic groups, but their educational and qualification level kept lagging behind in comparison with the vast majority of the population. The lower level of education of Bulgarian Turks and Roma places them in an inferior situation compared to the Bulgarians and other ethnic communities in the country. Bulgarian Turkish and Bulgarian Muslim families represent the rural population. Unemployment among the Roma population in some villages has reached 90 per cent. Hundreds of schools in the regions with a mixed population will have to be closed down. The additional worsening of the low educational level of representatives of the Roma community leads to its progressive marginalisation. A large number of Roma women are prostitutes. Crime committed by Roma increases as a consequence of their miserable life.

In 1997, the Bulgarian parliament ratified the Convention on Minority Rights Protection. According to the Constitution, Bulgaria is a unit-national state. From the point of view of European integration this act is very significant. The ratification has a mainly political effect. But still the rights of minorities are not respected. At the same time, there are some very contradictory points. The convention that is European in spirit contradicts some traditions of the Roma community in Bulgaria (such as paying for the bride).

It could be said that the way towards a sustainable democracy in Bulgaria must lie through social and ethnic stability. Minority rights in the context of social system solutions, as well as in the context of political approaches leading to the integration of marginalised groups, has to be viewed through the prism of the European model of social stability. Moreover, the position of minorities is inevitably the basis for evaluating any social situation—therefore, their rights in political and social terms would only by disregarded if avoidance of real state and institutional responsibilities were to be introduced through secret discrimination.

In correspondence with the constitutional arrangement and CMRP, the Ministry of Education is obliged to organise and steer education for four hours weekly, from first to eighth grade, for those students whose native language is not Bulgarian. Such an education is organised in Turkish, Hebrew, Armenian, Romany and Greek. Teaching in the mother tongue, as well as the school books and appliances needed for it, is financed by the state. Four Muslim secondary religious schools and a Muslim religious college where Muslim priests are educated have been opened. The restrictions on cultural performances by different ethnic communities and on the publishing of newspapers and magazines in their languages have been abolished. Nevertheless, the state does not engage in financial support of them.

According to the current legislation in Bulgaria, if a person in a court trial does not speak the official Bulgarian language well enough, the court is obliged to provide him/her with an interpreter free of charge. All political prisoners until 1989, including the ones convicted for their opposition to the relation of the assimilation policy, have been rehabilitated.

In 1990 Bulgarian Turks, together with a group of the Bulgarian Muslims and the Muslim Gypsies, established their own party—The Movement for Rights and Freedoms (MFR). It actively joined in the political life of the country. Members of the movement have been elected Members of Parliament at all five parliamentary elections since the beginning of the democratic changes (1990, 1991, 1994, 1997, 2001). The new Bulgarian Parliament was elected on 17 June 2001. The political party which has a majority in the Parliament is a very new one called The National Movement of Simeon the Second, led by the former Bulgarian king Simeon Sachs-Coburg-Gotski. Simeon declared that immediately after forming a government he would propose to Parliament a special Ministry for Minorities. One of the Gypsy parties in Bulgaria, Evro-Roma, is also represented in the new Parliament.

In this way, in the future it will be possible for society as a whole as well as the state to be involved in the process of integration of the Roma population. That is why the brotherly participation of Gypsy intellectuals in the discussion and development of social programmes for the improvement of the social and economic status of their groups is very desirable. The fast implementation of such programmes in practice should be among the priorities of the new Bulgarian government in the forthcoming years.

THE MOVE OF THE FAMILY TO BEYOND THE TRADITIONAL FRAMEWORK: EMPIRICAL CHARACTERISTICS OF THE DIVERSITY OF EXPECTATION IN BULGARIA

The first part of this chapter looked at the range of experience for the ethnic groups within Bulgaria during and after transition with respect to family life and family law. In this final section we turn to the available empirical evidence which looks at the range of opinion in Bulgaria on two issues which are key points differentiating between Bulgarian and EU norms and legislation. The survey, conducted by the National Centre for Public Opinion of the Bulgarian National Assembly in June 2002, focuses on the two main topics that generally express the new policy of the EU as regards the family and its new role in dynamic contemporary society. The first topic deals with the need for a special law establishing equality of the sexes. The second one focuses on the question of homosexual relationships in the context of EU requirements.

The constitutional framework for regulating equality between the sexes can be found in Article 6, section 2 saying that

> All citizens are equal before law. Any restrictions of rights or privileges based on race, nationality, ethnicity, sex, origin, education, beliefs, political affiliation or property status are inadmissible.

This provision corresponds directly to Articles 46 and 47 of the Constitution, which provides that marriage is a 'voluntary union between a man and a woman' and that 'spouses have equal rights and obligations in marriage'. The Bulgarian Constitution does not allow marriage between partners of the same sex, which means that if such a law were passed it would be against the Constitution. At the same time the Constitution is the basic framework for additional regulation of equality between the sexes.

It should be mentioned that the question of equality between the sexes is still not a central focus for public debates in Bulgaria. Some NGOs are very active in this direction, but they lack influence on the legislative decisions. At the same time, in the absence of systematic empirical research on this topic, it is difficult to quantify the ratio of proponents and opponents to the idea of regulating equality between men and woman in Bulgaria by law as part of the process of legal European integration.

Data from the above mentioned research can serve as an illustration of public opinion about a law to regulate equality between men and woman. What do the empirical data concerning this topic show? Table 16.1 shows the distribution of answers to the question 'Should equality between men and woman in Bulgaria be regulated by a law in the process of legal European integration?'.

Table 16.1 Necessity of a Law Regulating Equality between Men and Women

Answers	%
Quite agree	39.9
Rather disagree	58.0
No opinion	2.1

Table 16.2 General Classification of the Arguments

Arguments 'For'	Arguments 'Against'
It is obvious that the new legal system of Bulgaria needs a special law to regulate this topic and in this way to give guarantees against any kind of discrimination.	There is no real need for introducing such a law because equality between sexes is deeply rooted in our country and national tradition of Bulgarians.
There is a real need for introducing such a law because it is a requirement of the EU.	There is no real need independently for introducing such a law.
There is real discrimination in practice. If one looks at the existing laws dealing with equality between men and women in Bulgaria it could be seen that the woman in comparison to the man is in the same position to make decisions on certain questions connected with determining the future of children, but in practice it is not the same.	There is no discrimination either in regulations or in practice. On the contrary, if one looks at the existing laws dealing with artificial human reproduction, it could be seen that the woman in comparison to the man is in a better position to make decision on certain questions connected with determining the future of children.
Agree that if is not a matter of opinion, but represents an international obligation of the country. Technically, it does not have to be a separate Act.	The question whether Bulgaria is legally obligated to adopt certain regulations in the process of integration to the EU has one solution, which is in compliance with the concrete requirements of the relevant chapter of the Agreement Assessment.
If the specific problems are identified we could say that there is a need for more detailed regulation.	Basically, the equality of sexes before the law is provided in Article 6 of the Constitution, so one could not say that generally the quoted text is insufficient and we need a special act against discrimination.

The lawyers interviewed did not agree on the necessity to regulate sex equality in Bulgaria by a special act. The opinions of the experts are divided. On one hand, harmonising Bulgarian and European legislation is deemed sufficient grounds for adopting such a law. Those arguing against, who formed the majority of experts interviewed, hold the view that inequality of the sexes is not a problem for Bulgaria and that there is no need for a special law. These lawyers quoted Article 6 of the Constitution of the Republic of Bulgaria, which provides for the equality of sexes before the law. The arguments in favour of a law for equality are connected mainly to the obligation of Bulgaria to harmonise its legislation with European law and in addition with the need to provide guarantees against discrimination.

The second topic of the research is more complicated since it touches upon a question, which remains difficult to discuss in Bulgarian society. This is the topic of homosexual relations, which are anyway a fact in Bulgaria, and more and more non-governmental organisations are appealing to the legislators for a more tolerant attitude to them. The aim of the survey was to research attitudes to homosexuality, focusing on differences in each ethnic group.

As a whole, the research shows an extremely rigorous attitude to homosexual relations. At the same time, European legislation is becoming more tolerant which argues for change to the Penal Code, which provides punishment for active homosexual practice.[3] To be more specific, changes would be required to the provisions according to which persons performing homosexual or heterosexual acts with persons below the age of 18 (regardless of whether the act is performed with or without the consent of the under-age person) are liable to criminal proceedings. Some of the data in that respect are set out in Table 16.3.

For 84.5 per cent of the respondents the performance of a heterosexual act with a person under the age of 14 with their consent is a crime; 88.8 per cent are of the opinion that the performance of a homosexual act with a person under the age of 14 with their consent is a crime. The percentage of respondents classifying the performance of a heterosexual act with a person aged between 14 and 16 with their consent as a crime is comparatively lower (68.6 per cent). However, with regard to the performance of a homosexual act with a person of the same age, the percentage of people seeing it as a crime is high again (77.0 per cent).

The negative attitude toward performance of heterosexual or homosexual acts with a person under 18 years of age provokes a logical conclusion that such acts should be punished by the law. The difference in the percentage ratio between the people classifying such acts as crimes and those explicitly supporting the opinion that they should be punished is due to the

---

[3] It could be seen in the 2002 Memorandum of European Commission: 'Bulgarian Parliament should change all the articles in the Criminal Code according to which homosexuals are treated as criminals.'

Table 16.3 Assessment of Attitudes to the Heterosexual or Homosexual Act

Questions	It is a crime	It is not a crime	Cannot decide	No answer	Total (N)
Is the performance of a **heterosexual** act with a person under the age of 14 with their consent a crime?	84.5%	8.4%	3.6%	3.5%	850 (100%)
Is the performance of a **homosexual** act with a person under the age of 14 with their consent a crime?	88.8%	5.1%	3.0%	3.1%	850 (100%)
Is the performance of a **heterosexual** act with a person aged between 14 and 16 with their consent a crime?	68.6%	19.1%	7.1%	5.2%	850 (100%)
Is the performance of a **homosexual** act with a person aged between 14 and 16 with their consent a crime?	77.0%	10.2%	7.2%	5.6%	850 (100%)

selection of the possible answer, 'Don't agree with the performance of a heterosexual or a homosexual act with a person under 18 years of age'.

The survey is on a topic which is difficult to discuss. At the same time we registered great interest in the question. The percentage of the respondents feeling too uncomfortable to discuss the topic is insignificant (less than 5 per cent of all respondents). If the draft for legislative changes on these questions were to be made public, it would lead to a wide public response. What main conclusion could we reach from the data collected?

(1)   The respondents classified as a crime the performance of heterosexual or homosexual acts with a person under the age of 14 with their consent. This attitude is shared by almost all parts of Bulgarian society and it

Table 16.4 Assessment of the Necessity of Punishment for the Performance of a Heterosexual or Homosexual Act*

Do you agree with the following statement?	Yes	No
The performance of a heterosexual act with a person under the age of 14 with their consent should be punished.	26.1%	69.2%
The performance of a homosexual act with a person under the age of 14 with their consent should be punished.	26.1%	69.2%
The performance of a heterosexual act with a person aged between 14 and 16 with their consent should be punished.	28.5%	63.5%
The performance of a homosexual act with a person aged between 14 and 16 with their consent should be punished.	28.5%	63.5%
Don't agree with the performance of a heterosexual or a homosexual act with a person under 18 years of age.	35.1%	61.1%

* The total percentage is below 100 because those who did not answer are not included in the Table.

Table 16.5 Assessment of the Age of Understanding of the Meaning of the Sexual Act with Young Persons

Under the age of 12	3.3%
Between 12 and 14	9.6%
Between 14 and 16	14.1%
Above the age of 16	64.7%
Cannot decide	5.2%
No answer	3.1%
Total (N)	**850**

is serious evidence of the high level of conservatism in Bulgarian public opinion. People under 40 are more likely to classify as a crime the performance of heterosexual or homosexual acts with a person under the age of 14 with their consent. The opposite opinion (performance of heterosexual or homosexual acts with a person under the age of 14 is not a crime) prevails among young people below the age of 30 and respondents from Sofia and from the big cities.

(2) Public opinion differentiates between persons below the age of 14 and those between 14 and 16. The respondents are more tolerant of heterosexual or homosexual acts with a person between the age of 14 and

16. 41 per cent of young people below the age of 29 do not regard this as a crime.

(3)   Public opinion strongly differentiates the heterosexual act from the homosexual act. The data clearly show a more tolerant attitude towards heterosexual contact. On the contrary, homosexual contact, regardless of age, is more often seen as a crime. A possible explanation of this is that homosexuality is seen as a more serious threat to under-age persons. Bulgarian society still regards homosexuality as a kind of deviation, having a negative influence on the family.

(4)   If they could influence legislation, 35 per cent of the respondents would not accept as something normal and usual the performance of sexual acts with a person below the age of 18. It is striking that even young people are very cautious and do not support a lower age for sexual contact.

(5)   Two-thirds of adult Bulgarians are of the opinion that the sexual act can be understood by persons above the age of 16. Those questions proved to be very difficult for the representatives of ethnic communities (especially Bulgarian Turks and Pomaks), as well as for respondents with a low level of education. Public opinion is even more strong and categorical when we speak of the transition from awareness to action: 74 per cent of all respondents are of the opinion that the decision to engage in a sexual act should be made by persons above the age of 16. The percentage of Gypsies sharing such an opinion is not as high as for the other ethnic communities (25 per cent). The view that young people between the ages of 14 and 16 can assess the meaning of the sexual act and make a decision as to performance is held more often by people with college education, more by men than by the women, as well as by citizens of large towns. Relatively highly educated people from big cities oppose the conservatism and tradition found in smaller towns and villages. The survey registers a discrepancy between public judgement as to the age at which people understand the meaning of the sexual act, and the age at which the sexual act should be performed. In the public opinion, the maturity connected with understanding the meaning of the sexual act after the age of 16 is a prerequisite for its performance.

(6)   The question of liability to criminal proceedings when performing sexual acts with persons under the age of 16 turned out to be difficult to judge. 35 per cent of the respondents stated their disagreement in principle with the performance of heterosexual or homosexual acts with a person under 18. Respondents could not decide whether the performance of heterosexual or homosexual acts with a person between the ages of 14 and 16 should be regarded as a crime. Reduction of the age limit is supported mainly by people between 18 and 30. The same opinion is shared by people living in small towns and by the Roma population. The assumption that anyone performing a sexual act with a person below the age of 16 is liable to criminal proceedings is shared mainly by older people, the people with college education and the ones living in Sofia and the regional centres.

(7)   The attitude and orientation of the respondents are influenced by the following demographic factors: age, education, place of residence, ethnicity. As to this last factor we can say that the highest percentage of rigour as regards to heterosexual and homosexual acts (irrespective of age) is found among Bulgarian Muslims, where values reach 100 per cent. The same ethnic group demonstrates tolerance to heterosexual acts with persons between 14 and 16 years of age.

(8)   People realise the necessity of establishing legally significant criteria on the basis of the following factors:

—   age limit from the point of view of the principles involved in the Penal Code for liability to criminal proceedings of under-age persons: young (14 years), under-age (18 years), transitional age (16 to 18 years);

—   agreement of the person (in all three categories);

—   understanding of the substance and meaning of sexual act (heterosexual or homosexual);

—   additional criteria in the context of the emerging European tendency for legislative tolerance in that respect.

a   The judgements and opinions of the respondents have been placed on a scale from rigour to tolerance. In that respect the data obtained are a sufficiently reliable landmark for the legislator as to how far the legal consciousness of the people corresponds to the legislative changes offered or to the preservation of the status quo.

b   As a whole the survey shows that Bulgarians have a rigorous attitude to the performance of a sexual act (heterosexual or homosexual) with young or under-age children (under the age limit of 18).

c   There is a certain variance in the percentage distribution concerning the attitude toward heterosexual acts with people between 14 and 16 years of age, where the factor 'person's agreement' is of great importance.

Bearing in mind the complications in defining the legal criteria for criminalisation of the above acts, we have to draw the general conclusion that there is a high level of solidarity with the current provisions of the Penal Code and that any variation towards a more tolerant attitude has to be interpreted in the context of the traditional values of Bulgarian society—protection of children, family honour, and preservation of health, moral and human dignity.

REFERENCES

Genov, N (1999) *Managing Transformations in Eastern Europe* (Paris, Unesko-Most).

17

Family Values and the Harmonisation of Family Law

MASHA ANTOKOLSKAIA*

INTRODUCTION

I T WOULD NOT be an exaggeration to say that the last two years have been quite decisive for the course of European harmonisation of private law in general and in particular. It started in the summer of 2001 when the European Commission issued its Communication *From the Commission to the Council and the European Parliament On European Contract Law*,[1] where it asked the academic community to contemplate four possible options for the further development of harmonised private law in Europe.[2]

Although family law was explicitly excluded from the scope of the Communication's operations, the challenges with respect to the drafting of harmonised family law are generally the same as those formulated in the Commission's Communication. The Commission's neglect of family law was partly reversed by the European Council, which devoted significant attention to the need to include family law in its response to the Communication.[3] Also the broad academic discussion instigated by the Communication did not leave family law without attention.

The establishment of the international *Commission on European Family Law* (CEFL)[4] in September 2001, which decided to start drafting a set of non-binding *Principles of European Family Law*, has transferred the harmonisation of family law from a purely academic to a more practical issue.

---

* This chapter expresses the personal opinion of the author. This research has been made possible by a fellowship from the Royal Netherlands Academy of Arts and Sciences.

[1] Further referred to as the Communication. Brussels (11 July 2001), COM(2001)398 final—C-0471/2001, OJ C255 (13 Sept 2001).

[2] Option one was not to embark upon any activity and to leave the problem of harmonisation to the market. Option two was to promote the drafting of non-binding *Principles*. Option three was to improve existing European legislation. Option four was to elaborate binding European law. *Communication, Executive Summary* p 2: see above n 1.

[3] See above n 1, pp 9–12.

[4] Established on 1 Sept 2001 in Utrecht, the Netherlands. For more information see the website of the Commission: http://www.law.uu.nl/priv/cefl. For more on the Commission see: Boele-Woelki (2002).

It is not surprising that simultaneously with the progress of the harmonisation of family law, the number of problems that have to be resolved has
grown. One of these problems is the compatibility of the harmonisation
endeavour with the cultural and ideological dimension of family law and
with the expectations of the European population. Family law is deeply rooted in cultural and ideological values, and these values are not homogeneous
even within each particular European country. Therefore the expectations
regarding the further development of family law differ from country to country and even within one country from stratum to stratum. Which values then
shall form the basis of the *Principles of European Family Law*? Whose
expectations should be met by the *Principles*? Is it possible to extract some
shared pan-European family values and to build upon them? Or are the
Principles doomed to reflect nothing more than the compromise between
the positions of the different drafters? And in this last case, would the whole
harmonisation project not end up in an attempt to impose upon the Europeans some culturally and ideologically alien family law? In the absence of
any empirical research on this matter, both the opponents and the proponents of the harmonisation of family law can only speculate upon the actual position of the European population regarding such harmonisation.

Addressing these questions I will give a brief survey of the cultural constraints argumentation in the first section. Thereby I will try to show that
cultural and value discords exist not only between various European countries, but also inside each particular country, and provide for very different
expectations for further developments in family law on the part of various
groups of the population. I will suggest that these discords reflect the general progressive–conservative divide in Europe, manifesting itself in the difference in the timing and extent of the modernisation of family laws. In the
next section I will elaborate on the possibilities to bridge the above-mentioned discord by way of extracting some shared pan-European family values. Therefore I will search for such shared values, using the right to obtain
a full divorce as an example, first in the common core of European domestic laws, then in the practices of the European Court of Human Rights
(ECtHR) and the European Court of Justice (ECJ), and finally in the
European Charter. Finally I will try to argue that even in the absence of
shared pan-European values and expectations in respect of family law, it is
possible to draft a harmonised family law with a high level of modernity,
provided that such a law would not be deemed to be binding.

CULTURAL CONSTRAINTS

1 Introducing the Problem

Due to the commonly acknowledged cultural and ideological connotation,
family law has been subject to a persistent and continuing time lag regarding

deliberate harmonisation efforts.[5] For a long time it not only remained almost completely outside the harmonisation activities, but was also perceived as a paradigmatic example of a subject which was unsuitable for such harmonisation. The reluctance to accept the fact that the ongoing harmonisation of family law is a reality and to act accordingly can be attributed to the steadfast perception of the differences between the family laws in the various European countries as part of their cherished cultural heritage. This attitude forms the nucleus of a powerful cultural constraints argument, and is widely shared by family law experts.[6] Culture and tradition are therefore perceived as self-evident values that do not need any external justification.[7] In this vision culture is perceived as something static and given, and the dynamic nature of culture is largely underestimated (Hastrup, 2001: 175–186). The cultural identity argument is then often evoked in order to justify the stagnation and rejection of any reforms (Brems, 2001: 333).

Cultural constraints were so often used as a standard argument against the harmonisation of family law that it seemed as if no one was interested any longer in what this cliché really entails. It is common knowledge that, in spite of far-reaching convergence (Pintens and Vanwinckelen, 2001: 14–16; de Oliveira, 2002: 127–9) the differences between European countries in respect of family law are still very significant. Unfortunately most analyses do not extend any further than to affirm this difference and its cultural dimensions, without insightful investigation of the roots and the essence of the culturally embedded divergence in family laws. Even those who try to put the cultural constraints reservation into perspective do not often investigate this argument in any depth. The most common counter-argument is that certain peculiarities of the family law of the country in question cannot be explained by cultural factors,[8] or that certain changes in long-standing family law concepts have not brought about any cultural shocks.[9] The most convincing criticism so far presented against the cultural constraints argument is that some culturally embedded rules do not coincide with the modern notion of human rights (De Groot, 1995: 29); that tradition is not 'holy' and should not at any rate be protected; and that even culturally laden family rules are

---

[5] For example the first projects dealing with the harmonisation of the law of contracts: *The UNIDROIT Commission for the Principles for International Commercial Contracts* and *The Commission on European Contract Law*, also known as the *Lando Commission*, started their work in 1980 and in 1982 respectively.

[6] Müller-Freienfels wrote in the 1960s: 'Family law concepts are especially open to influence by moral, religions, political and psychological factors; family law tends to become introverted because historical, racial, social and religious considerations differ according to country and produce different family law systems' (Müller-Freienfels, 1968–69: 175).

[7] An opposite view is that the traditions must be judged using universal pluralistic moral values. See An-Na'im *et al* (1995).

[8] For instance, Hondius (1993) 180 has doubts concerning the fact that the Netherlands is the only European country that has a total community of assets as a legal regime for matrimonial property and that this may be explained by the peculiarities of the national culture.

[9] Pintens and Vanwinckelen (2001) 15 therefore use as an example the introduction of the notion of *mater semper certa est* in Belgian family law.

not an end in themselves but rather a means by which to promote a desired regulation of human relations.[10]

The reluctance to investigate the roots and essence of the cultural constraints argument seems to have much to do with the post-modern inclination to avoid value-laden analysis and with the post-modern association of diversity with democracy and open-mindedness. A genuine comprehension of the cultural constraints argument is, however, impossible without a value-based assessment of various national legal solutions constituting this diversity. The cultural constraints argument gives rise to at least two questions: what are the origins of the diversity of family law in Europe, and does each European country really have a homogenous family culture?

2 The Origins of Diversity: The *ius commune* of Family Law

If one looks at the current multicolour palette of family laws in Europe, one could hardly imagine that this diversity did not always exist. However, around a millennium ago the whole of the West had one and the same law on marriage and divorce and some related issues.[11] The *ius commune* of family law, in contrast to other fields of private law, was not Roman law as rediscovered in the Middle Ages and developed in the European universities after the 12th century (Zimmerman, 1998), but the uniform medieval canon family law. Again, unlike the economically related areas of private law, this *ius commune* was equally shared until the Reformation by the Western European civil and common law countries as well as by the Scandinavian region and the Eastern European countries with a Catholic tradition. The Orthodox Eastern European countries were, strictly speaking, never part of this *ius commune*.

This *ius commune* took shape within the framework of the first attempt at the unification of family law which occurred in Europe.[12] This unification represented the final point in the gradual replacement of the wide spectrum of pre-Christian marriage and divorce law, characterised by its informal rules as to the formation of a marriage, easy divorce, tolerance towards concubinage and the acceptance of illegitimate children, by an entirely new set of uniform canon law rules. That was quite a radical and even, according to Berman (1983: 85–115), a revolutionary change. Many legal concepts and

[10] See for instance, Pintens and Vanwinckelen (2001) 15: 'law, even if embedded in our culture, is primarily an instrument to regularize human relationships and is not a purpose in itself'.

[11] The uniform canon law mainly concerned the rules on marriage and divorce, but because of the crucial importance of those institutions for the determination of the legal position of offspring, for inheritance and for the rights to family property, the whole area of family law was influenced. Therefore it is possible to speak, with some reservations, of medieval canon family law in general.

[12] The unification process evolved slowly through the centuries, before accelerating at the time of the reforms of Pope Gregory VII and it was almost complete by the beginning of the 12th century. However, the final point was only reached in the 16th century at the Council of Trent.

family values (marriage as a sacrament, the indissolubility of marriage, strict monogamy and the exclusion of illegitimate children from the family) which were influential in some parts of Europe until deep into the 20th century, were vested or developed during that time.

3 The Conservative–Progressive Divide in Europe

The uniformity of canon marriage and divorce law only lasted until the Reformation. The roots of the current diversity therefore lie in the regulations of the different Protestant Churches and the secular laws of the advancing nation states. But the end of uniformity did not mean the end of the dominance of the ecclesiastical concepts and values of the Middle Ages. Although the Protestant countries rejected the sacral character of marriage and the principle of its indissolubility, most of the canon heritage survived. As Glendon (1989: 31) puts it: 'secular government simply took over much of the ready-made set of the canon law'. After the decline of the authority of the Catholic Church there was no binding ideology that could unify the whole of Europe (Holleman, 1987: 212), ideological pluralism increased, and it became increasingly difficult for the state to justify the canon law values which it had inherited. Nonetheless, they were upheld for a considerable period of time, much longer than other medieval political and religious concepts. Subject to serious discussion for the first time during the Enlightenment[13] and the French Revolution, they again ruled almost uncontested for a long time thereafter. They remained an integral part of the status quo. They only came under serious fire towards the end of the 19th century. The 20th century witnessed a wave of revolutionary changes in the field of family law, especially in the Scandinavian countries (Bradley, 1996), and the Soviet Union's family law was rapidly and radically reformed during those first decades. The southern European countries needed almost the entire century in order to achieve the same level of modernity.[14] The remainder of Europe fell somewhere in between.[15]

The essence of this transformation of family law was to leave behind the surviving concepts and values introduced into family law at the time of the medieval canon unification and to replace them by modern ones. The liberation from medieval heritage occurred throughout Europe, although in some countries it is not entirely complete even today.[16] The value discourses

---

[13] The most remarkable example of the modernisation of family law before the French Revolution was the Prussian *Allgemeines Landrecht* of 1794.

[14] Divorce in Italy was only introduced in 1970, in Ireland in 1996 and Malta remains the last European country not to allow a full divorce.

[15] This of course is a rather simplistic sketch of a more complicated situation. Eastern European law was not modern in all respects. Portugal was the first country where radical reform, albeit not long-lasting, took place. In some other countries the modernity of family law differed significantly from one particular institution to another.

[16] For instance Malta still adheres to the notion of the indissolubility of marriage.

(personal freedom–moralistic duty; autonomy–family solidarity; equality of men and women–patriarchal role division), and the direction of this process (towards a liberal, person-orientated[17] family law) were the same everywhere, but the process was far from synchronised in the different countries (see also Willekens, 1997: 48). From the beginning of the 20th century onwards, a rather clear distinction can be made between countries in the vanguard and those in the rearguard. The differences that colour the map of current European family laws are directly linked to the difference in the timing of this modernisation of family law. This, to my mind, constitutes the very core of the conservative–progressive discord that has constituted the main tension in the development of family law during the last centuries. The point I am trying to make is that the diversity of family laws within Europe is mainly a difference in the level of the modernity of family laws in the various countries in Europe.

4 Does Each European Country have Homogenous Family Values?

Regardless of one's appreciation of the nature of the connection between the diversity of family laws within Europe and cultural diversity, one can ask oneself to what extent the European countries are internally culturally homogenous. Pierre Legrand, one of the best known proponents of law as an emanation of culture, perceives the 'cultureness' of law only from a national perspective (1999: 5),[18] or from the perspective of the common law/civil law dichotomy (*ibid* 64). I would suggest that in family law cultural differences do not usually lie along state borders but are present in every particular European country. I am not even referring to the growing multiculturalism resulting from immigration from non-European countries. What I mean is that even the innate population in each particular European country is split into various different 'cultures', based on different values.[19]

---

[17] My own view is that the change from a transpersonal to a personalistic approach was the most important transformation that occurred in family law in the last two centuries. The essence of the old transpersonalistic attitude is the sacrificing of individual interests to abstract values (eg the stability of the family). Since the family gradually came to be regarded as a union based on love, with the primary purpose being to serve the happiness of its members, the transpersonalistic attitude started to be replaced by the personalistic one. The essence of the personalistic attitude is that the interests of the individual receive priority over abstract moralistic values. It is as simple and old as: 'The Sabbath was made for man, and not man for the Sabbath.' In family law this means that the interest of the person requesting, for instance, a divorce shall not be overruled by such abstract values as the 'stability of the family' or the 'indissolubility of the marriage'.

[18] He speaks in this sense of the 'Frenchness' of French law.

[19] According to recent research, in 2000, 27 per cent of the Dutch population still associated themselves with 'traditional marriage and family ideals', namely lifelong marriage, parentage coupled with marriage and the woman as the housekeeper and child rearer. At the same time 60 per cent of the Dutch population adhere to a 'modern family ideal', defined as not necessarily being lifelong marriage or cohabitation, and women working outside the home. See Liefbroer (2002).

The 'culture' and 'values' of an urban family of highly educated young professionals differs significantly from the 'culture' and 'values' of a rural family of middle-aged traditional farmers in any European country, be it
Ireland, Sweden, Malta or the Netherlands. The modernity of family patterns and family culture and values differs greatly from one social environment to another.[20] Rothenbacher concisely labelled this phenomenon 'the
contemporaneity of the noncontemporaneous' (1998: 21). Each country
has of course a predominant culture and values, which are generally those
of the majority of the population or the *élites dirigeante*.[21] Thus the perti-
nent family law is either a reflection of the predominant values,[22] or a
compromise between the values of the various groups. Following this reasoning one can suggest the existence of a progressive–conservative divide in
Europe, based on the existence of a conservative and a progressive pan-
European ideology of family values. Each of those values has its own rank
and file in each European country. Sometimes this is a majority, sometimes
a tiny stratum. The countries with modern family laws also have a population group with conservative family values and the countries with conservative family laws always have population groups that represent the most
modern views on family life. The expectations regarding the further development of family law that the members of these opponent groups may
have, could vary very significantly. On the other hand, the members of the
affiliated cultural groups will share the same expectations about the desirable changes in family law. They understand each other across the borders,
often looking abroad to support their ideas, and they repeatedly call on the
European courts to adjudicate their confrontations with their compatriot
opponents (Freeman, 2001).

ARE THERE ANY PAN-EUROPEAN FAMILY VALUES?

Does the existence of this conservative–progressive discord preclude any
attempt to embark upon the harmonisation of family law? Value divisions
mean that harmonised law could never provide an answer to the expectations of the whole of the population of any European country. But this is
also so for any domestic law. The difference is that the domestic law reflects

---

[20] An interesting example is a recent comparison between certain aspects of family values
associated with students form the Moscow State University and those of an 'average' British
young person. 51.6 per cent of Russian students as against 62 per cent of British young
persons find homosexual relationships between adult men to be wrong. Regarding lesbian
relationships of adult women this correlation is 38.0 per cent as against 58.6 per cent respectively (*source*: Denissenko *et al*, 1999). Although I do not have any empirical data about the
attitude of the general Russian public on this issue, I am quite convinced that a survey conducted among a less elite and educated group would show a completely different outcome,
considering the notoriously negative view of homosexuality that is still prevalent in Russian
society at large.

[21] I am indebted to Örücü (1999) 86 for this term.

[22] As Kymlicka (1995) 108 has noted, 'the state unavoidably promotes certain cultural identities, and thereby disadvantages others'.

the value compromise reached in each particular country. It is of course a great temptation to suggest that the harmonised law could reflect some pan-European values, common to every European country. In a search for pan-European values one can generally do two things. Firstly, compare the existing family laws; try to trace the underlying values, and extract a common core shared by every stratum in every country. Secondly, one can check whether any set of pan-European values has been developed by the ECtHR and ECJ. Illustrating the difficulties in finding shared European family values, I will deliberately focus on only one rather extreme example, where the level of shared values seems to be as low as the lowest common denominator: the existence of a pan-European consensus regarding the possibility of the legal dissolution of marriage (full divorce).

1   Shared Values and Common Core: No Right to Divorce

A search for the common core of European values regarding full divorce in the various European jurisdictions shows that even the appreciation of the fact that a person must have a right to have his or her long-time broken marriage legally dissolved and to enter into another one, is not shared throughout Europe. The right to obtain a full divorce is not common for all European counties: this right does not exist in Malta. This can of course to a great extent be attributed to the strong Catholic convictions of the majority of the Maltese population. However, the history of the introduction of divorce in Ireland can show that denying divorce is not always solely a question of strict adherence to the Catholic notion of the indissolubility of marriage. The discussion preceding the first unsuccessful Irish divorce referendum in 1986 was conducted from both conservative and progressive sides not merely with recourse to spiritual or secular moral arguments, but with a prevailing reliance on empirical and sociological ones.[23] This means that the rejection of divorce in the first referendum was not only a result of devotion to religious values, which is beyond rational appreciation, but also the product of a rational choice made by the Irish population. The persistent rejection of divorce in Malta illustrates the absence of a total European consensus on the level of very basic values regarding personal autonomy and the functions of marriage.[24]

2   Shared Values and the European Charter: A Search for Legitimation

The case law of the ECtHR and the ECJ shows that both courts often seek legitimation for their value judgements in the European consensus or the European common ground. Because the texts of all three articles of the

---

[23] Dillon 1993: 62 (progressive side); 104–7 (conservative).

[24] If an important function of the marriage is seen in the individual happiness of the persons involved, the acceptance of divorce and remarriage is inevitable.

European Convention on Human Rights (ECHR)relating to family rights (Art 8 (protection of family life), Art 12 (right to marry and to found a family) and Art 14 (prohibition of discrimination)) do not always provide relief, the ECtHR, in deciding cases, has to contemplate factors which are external to the Convention, and has considered that 'the Convention must be interpreted in the light of present-day conditions'.[25] The same applies to the practices of the ECJ. The long road towards the recognition of EU capacity in respect of human rights (see eg Alston, 1999: 9–11; Von Bogdandy, 2000) and especially those relating to family law, and the subjection of the protection of the family to the economic goals of the union, casts its shadow on the development of EU policy regarding family rights (Neuwahl and Rosas, 1995; McGlynn, 2000). The ECJ is also restrained by the subsidiarity principle and often seeks additional authorisation in the consensus argument (McGlynn, 2000). Since the political mandates of the ECtHR and the ECJ are indubitable only within the margins of the European Convention, and the EU legislation respectively, they need additional sources of authorisation every time they employ an extensive or even contra legal interpretation. In seeking such authorisation both courts generally refer to the consensus or the 'common European standard' among the Contracting States (Carozza, 1998). An overall consensus or common core almost never exists. One should not forget that the court has to decide its cases in a Europe divided into conservative–progressive family ideologies, and that the composition of the judges, representing the Contracting States, also reflects this divide. One thing and another oblige the courts to be cautious in using their power.

3 *Johnston v Ireland*: No Right to Divorce

A good illustration of the scale of the political tension under which the European courts have to pursue their goals is provided by one of the classic family law ECtHR cases: *Johnston and others v Ireland*,[26] where the ECtHR took one of its most conservative family law decisions ever.

As is well known, in the *Johnston* case Mr Johnston, an Irishman who many years previously had obtained a judicial separation from his first wife, and his second partner challenged the Irish law that did not permit full divorce and remarriage. In this case the court refused to provide a dynamic interpretation of Article 12, in contrast to *Marcks* where it stated that the whole Convention and not only Article 8 'must be interpreted in the light of present-day circumstances'.[27] Instead of this, the court referred to the *travaux préparatoires* of the Convention, in order to argue that the omission of the right to dissolve marriage was deliberate.[28] The court stated

---

[25] *Marckx v Belgium*. Judgement of 13 June 1979, Series A, no 31, para 41.
[26] *Johnston and others v Ireland*. Decision of 18 Dec 1986, Series A, no 112.
[27] See above n 25.
[28] See above n 26, paras 52–53.

without any reference to the relevant laws of the Member States that 'having regard to the diversity of the practices followed and the situations obtaining in the Contracting States, the nation's requirements will vary considerably from case to case'. This is remarkable considering that at that time only two Member States, the defendant Ireland and Malta, had not introduced full divorce, thus the 'great majority' of the states did share a consensus upon this matter. Accordingly, the ECtHR proclaimed divorce law to be 'the area in which the Contracting Parties enjoy a wide margin of appreciation in determining the steps to be taken to ensure compliance with the Convention'.[29] Finally, the Court refused to recognise the right to dissolve marriage as a right protected under the ECHR.

One could wonder how the ECtHR, which had ensured the progressive development of European family law in *Marckx*, could reach such a decision in *Johnston*. I am, of course, not the first to pose this question.[30] I am inclined to look for an explanation in the political legitimisation of the innovations brought about by the court. One should bear in mind that on 26 June 1986, some four days before the final deliberation in the *Johnston* case, the overwhelming majority of the Irish population rejected divorce in a referendum. The absence of divorce had just acquired the highest political legitimation.[31] An opposite decision by the court would therefore have been clearly contrary to the expectations of the majority of the Irish population. There was also almost no possibility that the Irish government would acquiesce in an opposite decision on the part of the court. It is quite plausible that 'the Court carefully backed down in the Johnston case in order to preserve its own authority' (Johnson, 1995: 513). In *Marckx*, in contrast, there was clear evidence of the intention of the Belgian government to change the contested filiation law, discriminating against extramarital children, and therefore the judgment of the court was in line with the expected changes of the relevant legislation. The court was probably quite right in not delivering a decision that would clearly be against the expectations of the population of the country concerned. However, the end result is that up to the present day there is no right to dissolve one's marriage under the Convention. *Johnston* has never been overruled.

The right to divorce is, of course, quite an extreme example. Because family rights are developed by the ECtHR on an unsystematic case-by-case basis, the level of protection that is actually attained in various fields of family law is also quite uneven. It varies from the lowest common denominator in respect of divorce (it is quite plausible that *Johnston* would now

[29] See above n 26, para 55.

[30] It was suggested that the court might have preferred to go further in the protection of parent–children relationships, than in the protection of non-marital sexual relationships. See Johnson (1995).

[31] Mahoney (1998) has stressed that 'the Court (and the Commission) should be careful not to allow that machinery to be used so as to enable disappointed opponents of some policy to obtain a victory in Strasbourg that they have been unable to obtain in the elective and democratic forum in their own country'.

be decided differently, however) to one of a high degree, as in the most recent cases with respect to the rights of post-operative transsexuals.[32] However, the average of a 'narrow and traditional' concept of the family as developed in ECtHR case law was rightly summarised by McGlynn (2001).

4 European Charter: Still No Right to Divorce

The Charter of Fundamental Rights of the European Union[33] is important for our enquiry because it is alleged to represent 'a fully up-to-date *Ius Commune Europaeum* of human rights protection in Europe'.[34] The purpose of the Charter is 'to strengthen the protection of fundamental rights in the light of the changes in society, social progress, and scientific and technological developments by making those rights more visible in the Charter'. Therefore, in contrast to the 52-year-old Convention upon which it is built, the Charter could reasonably be expected to reflect the current level of the existing shared values. At least with respect to family rights however, almost all of these expectations have remained unjustified.

Article 9 of the Charter has the same meaning and scope as the corresponding Article 8 of the ECHR (Gijzen, 2001). According to Article 53 of the Charter, if the articles of the Charter coincide with those of the ECHR, they should be given the same interpretation. That means that they should also be interpreted in the light of the case law of the ECtHR (Lenaerts and de Smijter, 2001). However, if Community law provides more extensive protection, the Charter should be interpreted in the light of this law (Gijzen, 2001). That means that the level of protection may not drop below the level of protection guaranteed by the ECHR and the relevant case law, but it may be higher.

The right to marry under Article 9 of the Charter contains some promising alterations compared to the corresponding Article 12 of the Convention. But still, surprisingly enough, Article 9 has failed to incorporate the right to dissolve a marriage. We do not know whether this was a deliberate omission or simply an oversight. Anyhow, the introduction of this right would not have been superfluous, because Malta is waiting on the candidates' list.[35] Does this mean that the right to dissolve a marriage is still not a part of Community law?

---

[32] See eg the recent cases *Goodwin v the United Kingdom* and *I v the United Kingdom*, where the ECtHR finally acknowledged that the refusal to provide legal recognition to the new gender identity of post-operative transsexuals violates both Art 8 and Art 12 of the Convention. See respectively: *Goodwin v the United Kingdom*, Decision of 11 July 2002, and *I v the United Kingdom*, Decision of 11 July 2002, http://hudoc.echr.coe.int/hudoc/ViewRoot. asp?Item=0&Action=Html&X=713160219&Notice=0&Noticemode=&RelatedMode=1.

[33] [2000] OJ C364/1.

[34] The EU Charter of the Fundamental Rights—Some Reflections on its External Dimension (2001) Editorial, *Maastricht Journal of European and Comparative Law* 1: 3.

[35] Since respect for human rights is a precondition of acceding to the EU, the recognition of the right to divorce as a human right protected under EU law would put pressure on Malta to amend its legislation.

The aforementioned example shows that the Charter, at least in relation to family rights, is largely based on the same 'common ground' as the case law of both courts (McGlynn, 2001: 598). The European institutions have hardly gone any further than the vague text of the Convention, and have not even sufficiently reflected the achievements of the case law of the European courts. That might have happened not because of unwillingness.[36] A more plausible reason could be the same conservative–progressive divide that has so often precluded both European courts from going beyond the common ground. Because of this divide a higher level may simply not have been politically feasible. It is probably still true to some extent that 'the Community, when attempting to draw a list of human rights, would necessarily take a minimalist approach and be able to agree only on the lowest common denominator of such rights' (Neuwahl and Rosas, 1995: 16).

5 No Shared Values, No Common Expectations?

The case of the right to dissolve one's marriage shows that no shared values could be delineated both from the case law of the ECtHR and from EC law. The problem is that certain values, including the right to divorce, cannot acquire the status of values that are shared throughout the Union, precisely because of the differing ideas thereon within Europe.

This ideological controversy means that when the European Court has to make a value judgement, it has no 'standard that enables it to prefer one system to another, so that it cannot do much more than check whether the national authorities' decision was a reasonable one'.[37] In the *Handyside* case the ECtHR acknowledged that 'it is not possible to find in the domestic laws of the various Contracting States a uniform European conception of morals'.[38]

The conclusion that may be drawn is that if the drafters of the *Principles of European Family Law* would build their *Principles* upon the shared European family values, the *Principle's* level of modernity would tend to be unsatisfactorily low. The drafters of the *Principles* should of course invoke the shared values in every case when their level is fixed at a more acceptable level, but this might not often be the case.

CONCLUSION: WHY SHOULD THE PRINCIPLES OF EUROPEAN FAMILY LAW BE PROGRESSIVE?

The last issue I wish to address by way of conclusion is why the principles of European family law ought, in my opinion, to be progressive. The need

[36] The unsuitability of the minimalist approach to the development of EU human rights protection law is clearly shown by Neuwahl and Rosas 1995: 58–63.

[37] In respect of the ECHR, see Sapienza (1991), cited in Brems (2001) 361.

[38] *Handyside v the United Kingdom*, Judgment of 7 December 1976, Series A, no 24, para 48.

to determine the designated level of the modernity of the principles beforehand has to do with the progressive–conservative divide within Europe, reflected in the national family laws. If family law is built upon conservative values, it is often rather restrictive. This means that the population groups representing minority values are also subjected to the restrictions of that law, although they do not share its underlying convictions.[39] That entails certain problems, even if these predominant values are majority ones and therefore have democratic legitimation. Therefore these minorities often have the feeling that their minority rights are being infringed[40] in an undemocratic manner and their expectations regarding modernisation are being persistently frustrated. The different family values sometimes clash when it comes to reforming family law. The Irish and Italian divorce referendums are good illustrations of such clashes. If the predominant values are modern ones, this mostly results in a permissive family law that leaves room for every cultural group to arrange its family life in its own way.[41] That is the main advantage of permissive law over restrictive law in the context of ideological controversy. This is the most important reason why, in my view, the principles of European family law should be progressive and possibly absorb the most modern solutions reached in various European countries. McGlynn (2000: 241) was perfectly right when arguing that harmonised family law has to be *'utopian'* and *'libertarian'*. Whether or not the Commission on European Family Law will adopt the same attitude will become clear in the near future.[42]

Because the principles are not intended to be binding, and are deemed to serve only as models, such high-standard principles will be no more of a threat to the national cultures and national sovereignty than a good comparative law survey. The national reports, written by authoritative national experts, will provide a reliable picture of the state of affairs in the particular area of family law. The rules selected for the high-standard principles will underscore the highest achievements reached in Europe. Both will save the national governments, the courts and the European institutions a great

[39] A good example is the first Irish divorce referendum in 1986, when 63.5 per cent of the electorate voted against the introduction of divorce and 36.5 per cent voted in favour (James, 1997). As divorce is not compulsory, the result of the referendum meant that the majority of the Irish population denied the minority the right to dissolve their marriage, and imposed its view even upon the non-Catholic part of the population (about 8 per cent), as it does not share the Catholic notion of the indissolubility of marriage.

[40] See eg the *Dudgeon* case (1981), where the ECtHR acknowledged that the Northern Irish criminal prohibition of private consensual homosexual acts violated the rights of homosexuals protected under Art 8 of the Convention. *Dudgeon v the United Kingdom*, Judgment of 22 October 1981, Series A, no 45, para 60.

[41] The conservative wing can of course have ideological difficulties in accepting a permissive law. For instance, the Dutch law making marriage a possibility for homosexual couples is the most recent illustration of this.

[42] The questionnaire on the grounds for divorce and maintenance between the ex spouses, the issues chosen for the first set of the principles, must be completed by 15 Sept 2002, thereafter the General Report will be drawn up and the actual work on the principles will subsequently commence.

deal of time and money. At the same time they will give the promoters of the modernisation of domestic family laws some additional moral support.

An important precondition for such high-standard principles is that they would not be deemed to become binding law. I fully agree that 'moral and political reforms must be initiated from within each culture' (Holleman, 1987: 211) and cannot be forced from outside.[43] Any attempts to 'emancipate' parts of the European population through the enforcement of binding libertarian principles should be condemned as being paternalistic, disrespectful and doomed to failure in any democratic society. The task of high-standard principles should only be to highlight and to make more transparent the achievements in the legal solutions to family law problems, which have already been attained in different parts of Europe or have been elaborated by the drafters. It is for the national and the EU legislators to decide what they are prepared to adopt and what not.

REFERENCES

Alston, P (ed) (1999) *The EU and Human Rights* (Oxford, Oxford University Press).

An-Na'im, A *et al* (eds) (1995) *Human Rights and Religious Values: An Uneasy Relationship?* (Amsterdam, Editions Rodopi).

Berman, H (1983) *Law and Revolution: The Formation of the Western Legal Tradition* (Cambridge, Mass and London, Harvard University Press).

Boele-Woelki, K (2002) 'Comparative Research-Based Drafting of Principles of European Family Law' in M Faure and J Smits (eds), *Towards a European Ius Commune in Legal Education and Research* (Antwerp, Intersentia).

Bradley, D (1996) *Family Law and Political Culture: Scandinavian Laws in Comparative Perspective* (London, Sweet and Maxwell).

Brems, E (2001) *Human Rights: Universality and Diversity* (The Hague, Martinus Nijhoff Publishers).

Carozza, P (1998) 'Propter Honoris Respectum: Uses and Misuses of Comparative Law in International Human Rights: Some Reflections of the Jurisprudence of the European Court of Human Rights' *Notre Dame Law Review* 73: 1231–32.

Collins, H (1995) 'European Private Law and the Cultural Identity of States' *European Review of Private Law* 5: 363.

De Groot, GR (1995) 'Op Weg Naar een Europees Personen—en Familierecht' *Ars Aequi 1.*

---

[43] Collins (1995) 363 rightly concludes that the 'particular measures of harmonisation of European private law would pose no challenge to a worthwhile conception of the cultural identity and diversity of Member States. ... this can happen only ... when the proposed measures of harmonisation seek to replace basic institutional arrangements or rules representing a symbolic endorsement of particular moral ideals'.

Denissenko, M, Zuanna, GD and Guerra, D (1999) 'Sexual Behaviour and Attitudes of Students in the Moscow State University' *European Journal of Population* 15: 294.

Dillon, M (1993) *Debating Divorce: Moral Conflict in Ireland* (Kentucky, University Press of Kentucky).

Freeman, M (2001) 'Is a Political Science of Human Rights Possible?' *Netherlands Quarterly of Human Rights* 2: 134.

Gijzen, M (2001) 'The Charter: A Milestone for Social Protection in Europe?' *Maastricht Journal of European and Comparative Law* 1: 57.

Glendon, MA (1989) *The Transformation of Family Law* (Chicago and London, University of Chicago Press).

Hastrup, K (2001) *Legal Cultures and Human Rights: The Challenge of Diversity* (The Hague, Kluwer Law International).

Holleman, WL (1987) *The Human Rights Movement: Western Values and Theological Perspectives* (New York, Praeger).

Hondius, E (1993) *Naar een Europees Burgerlijk Recht, Preadvies Vereniging Burgerlijk recht* (Lelystad, Vermande).

James, C (1997) 'Ireland Welcomes Divorce: The 1995 Irish Divorce Referendum and The Family (Divorce) Act of 1996' *Duke Journal of Comparative and International Law* 8.

Johnson, N (1995) 'Recent Developments: The Breadth of Family Law Review Under the European Convention on Human Rights' *Harvard International Law Journal* 36: 513.

Kymlicka, W (1995) *Multicultural Citizenship: A Liberal Theory of Minority Rights* (New York, Oxford University Press).

Legrand, P (1999) *Fragments on Law as Culture* (Deventer, WEJ Tjeenk Willink).

Lenaerts, K and de Smijter, E (2001) 'A "Bill of Rights" for the European Union' *Common Market Law Reviews* 38: 296.

Liefbroer, A (2002) 'Het Gezinsideaal: Van Traditioneel naar Modern' *Demos* 18: 8.

Mahoney, P (1998) 'Marvellous Richness of Diversity or Invidious Cultural Relativism?' *Human Rights Law Journal* 1: 3.

McGlynn, C (2000) 'A Family Law for the European Union' in J Shaw (ed), *Social Law and Policy in an Evolving European Union* (Oxford, Hart Publishing).

—— (2001) 'Families and the European Union Charter of Fundamental Rights: Progressive Change or Entrenching the Status Quo?' *European Law Review* 26: 587–93.

Müller-Freienfels, W (1968–69) 'The Unification of Family Law' *American Journal of Comparative Law* 16.

Neuwahl, N and Rosas, A (1995) *The European Union and Human Rights* (The Hague, Martinus Nijhoff Publishers).

Oliveira, G de (2002) 'A European Family Law? Play it Again, and Again ... Europe!' *A Civil Code for Europe* (Coimbra, Coimbra Editora).

Örücü, E (1999) *Critical Comparative Law: Considering Paradoxes for Legal Systems in Transition* (Deventer, Kluwer).

Pintens, W and Vanwinckelen, K (2001) *Casebook: European Family Law* (Leuven, Leuven University Press).

Rothenbacher, F (1998) 'Social Change in Europe and its Impact on Family Structures' in J Eekelaar and N Thandabutu (eds), *The Changing Family. International Perspectives on the Family and Family Law* (Oxford, Hart Publishing).

Sapienza, R (1991) 'Sul Margine d'Apprezzamento Statale nel Sistema della Convenzione Europea dei Diritti de'Uomo' *Rivista di Diritto Internazionale*: 605–06.

Von Bogdandy, A (2000) 'The European Union as a Human Rights Organisation? Human Rights and the Core of the European Union' *Common Market Law Reviews* 3: 1317.

Willekens, H (1997) 'Explaining Two Hundred Years of Family Law in Western Europe' in H Willekens (ed), *Het Gezinsrecht in de Sociale Wetenschappen* (S-Gravenhage, Vuga Uitgeverij BV).

Zimmermann, R (1998) 'Roman Law and European Legal Unity' in A Hartkamp *et al* (eds), *Towards a European Civil Code* (Nijmegen, Ars Aequi Libri).

18

Family Law and Family Values in Portugal

MARIA JOÃO ROMÃO CARREIRO VAZ TOMÉ

INTRODUCTION

T HIS VOLUME PRESENTS from a range of countries and perspectives the view that we live in an era of change and controversy with respect to many kinds of values, including our values concerning family life.[1] The family has been subject to conflicting trends of privatisation and public concern and intervention. As a result, diverse paradigms have developed to describe the moral values that should underpin our family law (Cahn, 1997: 228).

It could be said that family law mirrors the fragmentation of family ideology. In this final chapter we look to the Portuguese example to examine the relationship between law and values at a time of change. In Portugal no significant consensus has emerged about the direction of the most recent family law reforms in Portugal. The issue is that of choice between competing moral principles. There are two competing visions of the family: one grounded in the longing for the stability usually associated with a two-parent heterosexual family, and another based on a recognition of the many recent changes in family form and structure. The apparent tension between legal rules and family representations has resulted in attacks on the *lato sensu* family law reforms.

Even using the term 'family values' as if it were an easy expression capable of firm meaning, is problematic.[2] In this context, to be clear, the term

---

[1] 'It is widely accepted that significant changes occurred in family behaviour in western societies during the last quarter of the twentieth century' (Eekelaar, ch 1, this volume). 'Changing family structures (or perhaps more accurately, the acknowledgement of changed structures) and emerging technologies are influencing the definition of 'parenthood' in both law and society' (Shapiro, ch 5, this volume).

[2] '...to reconsider the meaning of "family values", the consent or lack of it as to what are the "family values"; are these common for cultures or culture dependent; permanent or changing over time' (Fuszara and Kurczewski, ch 3, this volume). 'Family law is deeply rooted in cultural and ideological values, and these values are not homogeneous even within each particular European country' (Antokolskaia, ch 17, this volume).

'family values' is used to refer to a set of socially and culturally based expectations of the family. But the term 'family values' has also become a rallying cry against the development of new family forms. It is associated with the belief that there is some consensus as to what the family values are, and that these are deemed to be threatened.

It is very important to study family law in its social, cultural and historical context. The relationship between social and cultural concepts and law is suggested in the creation and interpretation of legal rules (Fineman, 1993: 387). The legal developments treated in this chapter are of course but an aspect of the fact that society itself is in a state of flux. The links between family, society and law are at stake.

Portuguese family law is characterised by the predominance of mandatory norms and by its institutionalism. The legal system reflects a favourable view of the family as an institution. It is held that the place for law for the family is within the familial institution. Older than the state, it is considered to be a natural entity which precedes the law, and within it resides an intimate, complex and difficult to rationalise set of regulations (Pereira Coelho and Oliveira, 2001: 163, 165–9; Lobo Xavier, 2001). In regulating family relationships, many legislatures limit themselves to recognise the 'law' that lives and is constantly constituted within the family as an institution. Because the constitutional right to form and be part of a family is a right to liberty, which is assigned in view of the family institution, it is translated into an institutional right.[3] Portuguese marriage law is also characterised by the co-existence of state law and canon law. Finally, it is also defined by its permeability to social changes and its connection with other human sciences.

It is crucial to acknowledge that the law is only one of the institutions that create norms in society. Law cannot guide where other constitutive philosophies will not follow. In spite of its 'constitutive' function, family law has not yet promoted the reshaping of wider social perceptions of the nature and value of familial relationships.

Most debate about the family typically assumes certain standard configurations and places family members in roles, which reflect an assumed division of family labour into complementary specialisations. The component's roles are perceived as making necessary but differentiated contributions to the whole (Fineman, 1993).

A consideration of individuals' roles within the family focuses attention on the specific functions assigned to the institution by society. The traditional family role divisions have significant implications for the organisation of

---

[3] In fact, according to the Constitution (Art 36 (1)), every citizen has the right to contract a marriage. It is submitted that this is either more than a mere fundamental right or simultaneously a real institutional right, for marriage is an institution constitutionally protected. Ie, marriage is viewed as an institution whose existence and essential structure is guaranteed by the Constitution. Thus the legislature is not allowed either to abolish marriage or to change its constitutive elements or 'essential nucleus' (see Pereira Coelho, 2001: 27–8).

Portuguese society. The creation of family roles is related to what are considered to be essential social functions for the institution, for example there are many implications derived from the fact that the nuclear family has functioned as the location of dependency (Fineman, 1993).

In fact, within the family there are socially and culturally assigned caretakers for these dependencies (typically women). These caretakers need economic and societal resources to fulfil their caretaking tasks. Caretaking responsibilities then go on to create dependency in the caretaker—the need of some social structure to provide the means to care for others. In a nuclear family, the caretaker herself, as wife and mother, is dependent on the wage-earning husband to provide for her so that she can fulfil her tasks. Given current social realities, needing extra structures, this model is no longer by itself capable of doing what it is intended to do (Fineman, 1993).

HISTORICAL BACKGROUND

Historically, the Portuguese family has been a gendered institution. It has been valorised as an institution for its perceived role in reproducing and transmitting norms of social behaviour to all its members. It continues to be gendered in its operations and expectations. In addition the complementary roles of husband–father, wife–mother and child–adult are formulated in the context of the relationship between the state and the family. Dependency, culturally assigned to the family, is privatised. Neither the state nor the market directly contribute to or assist in the necessary caretaking—that is done in the privacy of the family. The burdens of economic support and caretaking are allocated within the family based on the perceived family roles its members play. This assignment of burdens within the family operates in an inherently unequal manner; the uncompensated tasks of caretaking resting with women while men pursue careers that provide economically for the family but also enhance their individual career and, as a rule, their earning capacity is not reduced by marriage (Fineman, 1995a: 2187–88; Eekelaar and Maclean, 1994: 7).

Family law can be found in Book 4 of the Civil Code. This code was enacted in 1966 and its chief amendment was in 1977. In fact, until 1977 the patriarchal principle was the main principle in family law and the husband was the head of the family. Equality between husband and wife was introduced in 1977 (Art 1671(1), Civil Code). Family ideology is now focused on equality, reflecting co-operation between men and women appreciative both of financial support and of domestic work and caring—without regard to who did what! Family law does not provide for gendered division of tasks and recognises on an equal footing the role of breadwinner and of work in the home (Art 1676(1), Civil Code) (Pereira Coelho, 2001: 24; Vaz Tomé, 1997: 174). The great symbolic turning point came in 1977, when the husband was deposed as 'head of the family'. The reform of the Civil Code eliminated most of the restrictions on a married woman's right to contract, to sue and be sued, to hold property in her own name, and to carry on a trade or business without the consent of the husband, among other things.

Family law came a long way in the 20th century. In the 19th century some people believed the idea that wives were naturally dependent upon their husbands as firmly as the idea that children are naturally dependent upon their parents is believed now. The state was expected to bolster the husband's power over his wife whenever it was threatened (Olsen, 1985: 847). Some people believed that by empowering the head of the family— the husband and father—to act for the family and to settle intra-family disputes, the state could avoid intervening in the family. Domestic violence was discovered and largely forgotten (Rose, 1987: 55). Of transsexualism we knew nothing and homosexuals were more likely to find their own way. Quasi-marital relationships were denied legal status. There was little child law. There was no law of adoption, no child welfare system. The law placed full responsibility on the mother rather than the father for bringing about the undesirable situation of illegitimacy.

THE NORMATIVE FRAMEWORK

1 The Constitution

Marriage and the family enjoy the special protection of the state. The Constitution also guarantees the protection of the private sphere of marriage and the family from interference by the state. According to the Constitution, men and women are considered as equal (Art 13), as are husbands and wives, and it renders unlawful any discrimination against individuals on the ground of sex. It also settles the right of each individual to the free development of his or her personality. The state must remove the economic and social obstacles that prevent the full development of the human being and the effective participation of all workers in the political, economic and social organisation of the country.

The impact of the Portuguese Constitution of 1976 was profound for family law. Many traditional family law norms have been found to be inconsistent with the values contained in the new Constitution. At the constitutional level, one must emphasise the principles established in Articles 36, 67, 68 and 69 of the Portuguese Constitution.[4]

The principles adopted in Article 36 are very relevant. Firstly, every citizen has the right to constitute a family and to contract a marriage in conditions of full equality. Secondly, the requirements and effects of marriage

---

[4] The original version of the Constitution dates from 1976. It was revised in 1982, 1989, 1992 and 1997. In regard to those constitutional principles, see Pereira Coelho (1986) 63ff.

and of its dissolution by death or divorce are regulated by civil law, regardless of its form (Roman Catholic or civil). Thirdly, spouses have equal rights and duties in relation to civil and political capacity and regarding the upbringing and education of their children. Further, children born out of wedlock cannot be discriminated against on that ground. In addition, parents have the right and duty to educate and raise their children. Sixthly, children shall not be separated from their parents except on the ground of their failure to accomplish their fundamental obligations to them and only then by means of a judicial decision. Finally, adoption is regulated and protected by law.

According to Article 67(1), 'The family, being a fundamental element of society, has the right to the protection of the society and of the State.' In accordance with Article 68, which provides for the special value of motherhood and fatherhood, fathers and mothers have the right to equal protection 'in the accomplishment of their irreplaceable roles towards their children'. Article 69 states that children are entitled to the same protection, namely against the abuse of family authority.

It can be said that there is a fundamental right to marry. The legal recognition of marriage is considered as a basic human right. The fact that the Constitution places both marriage and family under the special protection of the state arguably supports impediments to marriage to the extent that they are 'protective' of the institution. Every citizen has the inalienable right to work (Art 58(1)) and, when deprived of the necessary means to live, has the right to social assistance (Art 63(1) (4)). Workers are guaranteed a livelihood in case of misfortune, sickness, disability (Art 63(4)) and involuntary unemployment (Art 59(1) (e)).

2 Family Law

The technical–legal concept of family is found in Article 1576 of the Civil Code. It considers as sources of legal family the relationships of marriage, parenthood, affinity and adoption. Under a legal approach, the family is composed of a group of individuals but is not itself a legal person. Taking into account the interests of the individuals, their autonomy and independence, the law has eliminated most references to the family's interest or good (Lobo Xavier, 2001: 1394). However, this does not mean that in some cases the law ignores it as holder of its own interests as different from the individual interests of the members of the group.

(a) Marriage

A choice between a civil and a Roman Catholic marriage is allowed, since the Portuguese legislature has established the so-called optional civil marriage (Art 1587(1), Civil Code). Same-sex marriage was not usually conceptualised as the subject of a marriage prohibition, but rather as outside the scope of marriage altogether. Marriage between persons of the same sex was considered to be non-existent. In fact, there is an express statutory definition of marriage as the legal union of a man and a woman (Art 1577: 'the contract between two persons of opposite sex who intend to constitute a family by living in full community of life, according to the rules provided by the Civil Code').

Rights, duties, responsibilities, and the discretion of husband and wife during marriage are based on the main feature that spouses are considered as two independent persons with equal rights and duties. Husband and wife shall support each other and jointly safeguard the interests of the family. This policy is an expression of the idea that the spouses are equal and that necessary decisions concerning family life should be reached together (Art 1671(2), Civil Code). Spousal independence and equality are envisioned as existing within a framework of co-operation.

(i) Personal rights and duties of the spouses The Civil Code deals elaborately with the personal relationship of husband and wife and, in particular, with the family decision-making process. The personal effects of marriage are governed by the principle of the equality of the spouses and of their joint right to control family life (Art 1671, Civil Code). The spouses are bound by mutual respect, loyalty, cohabitation, co-operation and assistance (Art 1672).

The spouses have been made equally responsible for family support and have been given an equal say in choosing a place of residence, raising their children and managing community property. The spouses together assure the moral and material direction of the family. There was an attempt to establish an egalitarian model (Art 1671(2), Civil Code) (Lobo Xavier, 2001; Vaz Tomé, 1997: 132).

In order to offer equal rights to both spouses the law establishes that each spouse retains his or her birth name and gives them the option of taking the other spouse's name, except where he or she has kept a former spouse's name, which is allowed in case of widowhood, where, if it is so declared at the celebration of the new marriage, it may be retained even after the second marriage (Arts 1677 and 1677-A, Civil Code). Upon divorce, a spouse may resume his or her birth name or the name he or she bore upon *entering* the marriage, but an ex-spouse can be restrained from using the other spouse's name after divorce in certain circumstances. In fact, keeping the ex-spouse's name requires his or her permission or a judicial authorisation (Art 1677-B(1)). There is the social custom of women taking their husband's surname upon marriage, which is widely followed. In conclusion, concerning the surname of a spouse, the accepted view is that he or she assumes his or her spouse's surname upon marriage only if he or she wishes to and that a divorced spouse can retain his or her former spouse's surname if he or she so wishes. The last original surname of a child is normally the surname of the child's father. The parents of a child have a choice—the surname entered in the register of births may be that of the father, the mother or a combination of both (Art 1875).

The model of housewife-and-maintenance marriage was replaced by the idea of marriage as a partnership of spouses pursuing their chosen occupations, activities or professions (Art 1677-D, Civil Code) and arranging their home life by common accord. Marriage is seen as a community of life in which the partners work out their own roles in consultation with, and having regard to, the interests of each other and the family (Art 1671(2)). The spouses are mutually obliged adequately to maintain the family by their work and property. If the running of the household is left to one spouse, that spouse as a rule fulfils his or her duty to contribute to the support of the family through work by managing the household. In many cases the law stresses the separate personalities of the family members rather than the unitary aspect of the family. Equality (Art 1671) has replaced hierarchy (Vaz Tomé, 1997: 129ff). The law has abandoned its former express or implicit stereotyping of sex roles within marriage and has moved toward a new model in which there is no fixed pattern of role distribution.

(ii) Property rights and duties of the spouses The transformation of the ideologies of marriage expressed in Portuguese law is a highly visible response to changes in the economic and social roles of women and in ideas about married life. The principle of equality of the spouses also governs the property effects of the marriage. There is also the principle of autonomy, whereby these effects depend, in general, on the marital property regime chosen by the spouses in a prenuptial agreement (Art 1698, Civil Code) or on the subsidiary marital property system which is the community of acquired property regime (Art 1717). The parties cannot only choose one of the three regimes established in the Civil Code—community of acquests, general community property and separate property (Arts 1721ff)—but they can also choose other property rules leading to the creation of a different property regime.[5]

The community of acquests property regime excludes all property acquired before marriage, and all property acquired thereafter by gift or inheritance (Art 1722(1), Civil Code). Regarding property management, there is the principle of autonomous management of separate property and joint management of community property with the exception of acts concerning ordinary management where separate management is the rule (Art 1678(1), (2) and (3)). That part of the community property represented by a spouse's earnings remains subject to the separate management of that spouse unless or until they are invested or converted into other assets (Art

---

[5] However, there are some legal restrictions. In fact, some issues cannot be governed by a prenuptial agreement (Art 1699(1), Civil Code); some rules apply irrespective of the marital property regime (eg Arts 1680, 1682(3), 1682-A(2) and 1682-B); there is a case where the general community property regime cannot be chosen by the spouses (Art 1699(2)); there are situations where the separate property regime is mandatory (Art 1720).

1678(2)(a)). Each spouse has exclusive powers to deal with his or her separate property (Art 1678(1)), that is, all property brought into the marriage or acquired thereafter by gift or inheritance.

(b) Parental Authority (Parental Responsibility)

Both the mother and father have equal rights to custody of their child during the marriage (Art 1901(1), Civil Code). Parental custody comprises custody of the child (physical custody) and custody of the child's finances (financial custody). The law concerning parents and children provides that mothers and fathers shall exercise their authority (responsibility) jointly (Art 1901(2)). Parents are obliged to protect the child's safety, health and morals, and to furnish him or her with care, supervision and education (Arts 1878 and 1885ff). Both parents have the right to administer and receive the income from their children's property (Art 1878). Parental power (responsibility) over the child's person and property is to be exercised by both parents (Art 1878(1)). Both parents can act as the child's legal representative (Arts 1878 and 1881). The law establishes mutual duties of parents and children to assist and respect each other (Art 1874). The law also provides for participation by a child in decisions regarding his or her education and upbringing, and in relevant family issues (Art 1878(2)). It can be said that it admonished parents to take into consideration the child's aptitudes and needs for independent responsibility at various stages of development.

The Constitution eliminated on equal protection grounds various rules which discriminated against illegitimate children solely because they were born out of wedlock. The parent and child relationship extends equally to every child and to every parent, regardless of the marital status of the parents. The parent–child relationship is what gives rise to legal duties, rights and obligations (Arts 1874ff, Civil Code). There is an equal sharing of parental rights and obligations (Art 1901(1)). At the same time, there is a trend toward diminution of the rights of both the mother and father, as children are increasingly treated as individuals with rights of their own.

The dominant image of the ongoing family in the Portuguese Civil Code is that of a community in which husbands and wives work out their own roles, parents exercise their authority (responsibility) in the interests of their children, and all family members collaborate with and assist one another in accordance with their abilities.

(c) Divorce

Divorce by mutual agreement is the preferred form of divorce. The spouses do not need to make known the cause (Art 1775(2), Civil Code). They can apply for divorce by mutual consent at any time in the Civil Registry Office (Arts 1775ff). The spouses shall meet the following requirements: they shall have agreed upon alimony, child custody and support and the family home

(Art 1775(2)). The Civil Registry officer can refuse his or her approval and the granting of the divorce if the agreements do not sufficiently protect the interests of the children or those of one of the spouses. In keeping with the central place given to divorce by mutual consent, the spouses are authorised, at any time before the judgment is rendered, to transform a fault action (or any other type of divorce suit) into a divorce based on agreement.

The idea of marital fault still plays a significant role in divorce, and court decisions continue to provide glimpses of what judges believe spouses are entitled to expect from each other. Fault divorce is available on the ground of 'serious or repeated violation of the duties and obligations of marriage, rendering the continuation of life in common intolerable' (Art 1779, Civil Code).

No-fault grounds were added to traditional grounds. No-fault divorce is available on the grounds of three consecutive years of de facto separation (Arts 1781(a) and 1782, Civil Code), one year of de facto separation if the defendant does not oppose to the divorce (Art 1781(b)), two years of absence without news of the absent spouse (Arts 1781(d) and 1783) or disturbance of mental faculties of the other spouse for three years (Art 1781(c)).[6]

(i) Effects of divorce Marriage is dissolved by divorce. What property is divided on divorce depends on the marital property regime chosen by the spouses. According to the subsidiary marital property regime, only community property is divisible and separate property is set aside to the party who owns it.

Under fault-based divorce, the consideration of one spouse as the sole or mainly guilty party for the divorce may have several property effects. On the one hand, if the spouses were married under the general community property regime, that spouse cannot receive more property assets than he or she would receive should they have been married under the community property of acquests regime (Art 1790, Civil Code). On the other hand, that spouse loses certain benefits, which were awarded by the innocent or less guilty spouse, or by a third party, if these were granted by taking into account marriage as either an act or status (Art 1791). The law alludes to benefits already received or to be received by the guilty spouse and encompasses both *inter vivos* and *mortis causa* gifts. Finally, he or she may be deprived of alimony (Art 2016). The spouse who obtains the divorce can also seek damages for reparation of the moral prejudice caused by the dissolution of the marriage (Art 1792(1)).

Alimony is awarded primarily according to the need of the dependent spouse and the ability of the other to pay (Arts 2004(1) and 2016(3), Civil

---

[6] Before 1998 no-fault divorce was available on the ground of six consecutive years of de facto separation, four years of absence without news of the absent spouse, and disturbance of mental faculties of the other spouse for six years. In this case, the court had the power to deny the divorce if it assumed that the divorce decree would very likely aggravate the mental faculties of the defendant.

Code), taking into account their situation at the time of divorce (Art 2016; Vaz Tomé, 1997: 308ff). While several years ago it was common to find an alimony award for a homemaker spouse until her death or remarriage, the trend now is toward shorter awards. A long-term marriage is no longer a guarantee of long-term maintenance. Although some courts do not try to equalise the standard of living in the determination of needs and resources, it is a factor along with age of the parties, length of the marriage, prospective earning capacity, property owned, fault, the health of the spouses, the time already devoted or which they will have to devote to the upbringing of the children, their professional qualifications, their existing economic entitlements, and their wealth, in income as well as capital, after the liquidation of the matrimonial regime (Art 2016(3); Vaz Tomé, 1997: 327ff).

Under the Civil Code an order for spousal maintenance ceases to have effect upon the death of either the person being maintained or the person who is liable to make the maintenance payments (Art 2013(10)(a), Civil Code), the incapacity of the obligor to pay (Art 2013(1)(b)), the disappearance of the need of the obligee (Art 2013(1)(b)), the remarriage of the party being maintained (Art 2019) or his or her immoral behaviour (Art 2019). Traditionally a spousal maintenance order did not automatically cease to have effect upon the commencement of a de facto relationship by the party being maintained. It was debated whether a de facto relationship extinguishes the alimony obligation due to the disappearance of the obligee's need (Art 2013(1)(b)) or rather to his or her immoral behaviour (Art 2019; Vaz Tomé, 1997: 375ff). The alimony payment is modifiable upon a change of circumstances (Art 2012).

In Portugal, ways have had to be found to depart from the ordinary rules of marital property where the family home is at stake and minor children reside with one parent. Judges have discretionary power to award possession of a rented home to one of the spouses, regardless of whose name is on the lease, in the light of the social and family interests involved, with compensation where appropriate to the other spouse (Art 84 RAU[7]). In the case of a home owned by both husband and wife, the judge, in liquidating the marital regime, may award the dwelling to one of them and compensation to the other (Art 1793, Civil Code). Even where one spouse owns the home, the non-owner may be awarded possession by way of a forced lease, with rent to be fixed by the judge, if a minor child or children reside with the non-owner spouse (Art 1793).

As far as child custody and support are concerned (Arts 1905 and 1906, Civil Code) it is up to the court to make the final decision.[8] The court may award custody according to the 'best interests of the child'. There is now a

[7] Ie the Legal Regime of the Urban Lease.
[8] The spouses can agree upon these issues, but their agreement is always subject to the court's approval.

legislative preference for joint custody. There is a legal presumption that it is in the best interests of the child to be in the parents' joint custody, which can be rebutted by the parents' lack of agreement and a justified court decision. Joint custody after divorce is now the rule and not the exception. In general, the court will not determine whether the wish of the parents to exercise joint custody actually meets the best interests of the child in any given case or whether another arrangement may be better. Should the parents fail to file a motion for a court ruling, joint custody will automatically continue to be effective after divorce. This legislative change was the result of the divorced fathers' lobbying. To say that joint custody is generally in the best interests of a child is questionable. This solution disadvantages women, since they are the primary caretakers. There is no real social change in the marital role division and fathers have not assumed a more active parental role in the ongoing family. In addition, where the parents have permanent disputes, continuous recourse to the courts will not be in the child's best interest.

Custody can be granted to both parents or to one of them.[9] However, a very close relationship must be preserved between the child and the non-custodial parent. As a general rule a non-residential parent has a right to visit his or her child. Restrictions on or denial of visitation may be proper if visitation would endanger the child's health and welfare.

Divorce does not have any effect on the parents' obligation to support their children. Biological parents have a primary obligation to support their children even if the parent did not intend to become a parent. The spouse with whom the children do not habitually reside remains bound to contribute to their maintenance and upbringing in proportion to his or her resources and to those of the other parent. The law allows for a child to be supported through higher education (Art 1880, Civil Code). The amounts awarded are often less than needed for the child's maintenance; some child support orders are never paid, and others are paid sporadically.

3 Inheritance Law

All surviving spouses, whether married under a community property or a separate property regime, are heirs. If the predeceasing spouse owned separate property, his or her estate includes such property as well as his or her half of the community property. Thus, the rights supplementing the survivor's right to his or her own half of the community can be quite significant.

The surviving spouse's position in Portuguese inheritance law makes clear the weakening of blood relationships and the intense protection of the

[9] Where safety, health, moral upbringing or education is at risk, the minor's custody can be given to a third party or to an establishment for education or assistance. See Arts 1905(2), 1907, 1918 and 1919, Civil Code.

marital family. The position of the surviving spouse in inheritance law has been criticised. He or she is an intestate heir and also a required heir. The surviving spouse has therefore an indefeasible share and is placed in the same position of supremacy over the deceased's descendants and ascendants (Art 2157, Civil Code).

4 Social Security Law (Especially Old-Age Pension Law and Survivor Pension Law)

The Portuguese Constitution (Art 6-3) establishes the principle that every citizen has the right to social security.[10] Portugal is a breadwinner state. Because of the dominant breadwinner principle, married women were excluded from most social security benefits and married men were granted additional benefits in order to support their spouses. The familial ideology celebrates the division of labour between husband and wife. The husband is viewed as the head of the household, and it is his duty to provide for the members of his family through full-time employment. The duties of the wife are to make a good home and provide care for the members of her family. The unit of benefit is supposedly the family, and minimum benefits and pay

[10] The insurance technique, the discovery of actuarial calculations and the development of mutualities contributed to the success of compulsory social insurance, which was for the first time adopted in Germany by Bismarck's law of 15 June 1883, and soon spread all over Europe. This system of protection had a great deal of influence all over the world. Under a legal approach, those schemes were essentially compulsory insurance based on the insured individuals' remuneration, relating to those whose social value was represented by their paid employment. The compulsory nature of social insurance was possible only because of state intervention. It was progressively affirmed due to the strong influence of socialist and state intervention doctrines that were supported by the Catholic Church doctrine. Social security is the result of a tendency that has progressively become more widespread: the socialisation of risks. There has been a shift from family, professional, associative or contractual solidarity as a guarantee to compensate damages likely to cause situations of need, to a national solidarity. The American idea of social work contributed to the development of the idea of social security. The Beveridge Report of 1942 introduced a modern social security system to the UK in a universal scheme, which was unified from an administrative and management point of view. It was also committed to cover all social risks and, in principle, based on a unified system of contributions among all community members. Social protection's extension to the entire population has been a characteristic of the modern systems' evolution after the Second World War. According to the insurance approach, the right to social security remains connected to paid employment. It is enforced within employment structures. Notwithstanding their differences, this is the case in most Western European social security systems. These systems have evolved towards universal coverage, as it is morally and politically very hard to exclude groups from protection. According to the universal approach, the link to paid employment is irrelevant. Here the concern is for the protection of the whole national population against either all social risks or some of them.

It can be stated that there are two different types of claims. Claims through paid employment tend to give benefits relative to earned income and give workers a standard of living comparable to that of their working life. Claims made by individuals as members of the society irrespective of their employment status tend to give benefits on the basis of a social minimum. Consequently, social security offers either the guarantee of an employment-related income or the guarantee of a social minimum. However, there is a tendency towards a structural unification where the two strategies of social security overlap.

embody the notion of the family wage. Entitlement is in practice differentiated between husband and wife. Eligibility is based on breadwinner status and the principle of maintenance. Accordingly, most wives' rights to benefits are derived from their status as dependants within the family and their husbands' entitlements. As a result, married women may lack individual entitlement to benefits. The family or household is to a certain extent the unit of social insurance contributions and taxation.

Societal notions of the role of the family are of vital importance in shaping social security law developments. Some of the present day debate about the future of the family reflects an increasing dissatisfaction with traditional assumptions about the family and its role embodied in social security law. Many of these assumptions underlie the principles of social security law as they are presently applied in Portugal. It is within this context that we should examine the inconsistency with which homemaking services are treated in Portuguese law (Oldham, 1995: 270).

The issue is of major significance to the vast majority of women whose employment-market activities are prejudicially affected by social patterns of child rearing and current divisions of paid and unpaid labour within the family. In many ways we conceptualise 'the family' as a single unit rather than as a group of individuals where there is a division of paid and unpaid labour. Under an approach that regards the family as a group of individuals, however, the division of paid and unpaid labour takes on a different complexion, since the best interests of the unit clash with the best interests of certain individuals within the unit. From an individualist perspective the traditional division of paid and unpaid both adversely affects the employment-market prospects and achievements of homemakers (Oldham, 1995: 270–1).

A major difficulty is the problem of what can be called the 'invisibility' of homemaking. Industrialisation saw the 'separation of home and workplace', while industrial and post-industrial capitalism observed the assignment of functions previously undertaken by or within families in respect of welfare, education and recreation. As a result modern families are viewed as more 'privatised', in the sense of more isolated, than they were in earlier societies. Thus homemaking can be described as 'invisible', because it is both carried on in the intimate and relatively isolated zone of the household and important productive functions that families still fulfil are hidden. In addition, the rendering of homemaker services is economically 'invisible'. Finally, homemaking can be described as legally 'invisible' because housework takes place in the 'private' sphere of family life.

Empirical research confirms that resources are not all shared equally within families. Quite apart from the absence of adequate day-care facilities, for many women it may be more economical to stay at home to look after the children until they reach school age. Even after that time, labour market participation by working mothers is limited: most full-time employers

assume that 'someone' is at home during at least part of the day to undertake primary responsibility for children. While not working, a housewife
suffers depreciation in employment-market value. There is a state interest
in promoting the welfare of future citizens and the performance of the
important social function of child-raising should not result in economic disadvantage (Oldham, 1995: 281–2). These factors have combined with ever-
increasing patterns of family breakdown, unsatisfactory financial settlements
and inadequate enforcement measures, to intensify the phenomenon termed
as the 'feminisation of poverty'.

The Portuguese social security system primarily bases eligibility on market place earnings, with some additional recognition of marriage. The result
is that, aside from forgoing earnings during the marriage, the stay-at-home
or secondary career partner (still typically the mother) accrues only a lesser, typically derivative (from the husband's), pension entitlement on retirement. Indeed, some recent thinkers challenge even the derivative benefits
now available to widows, wives and some divorced ex-spouses. If reason
were to guide the legislature, social security law—based as it is on the
income stream of future generations—would view the raising of children as
the primary (or at least an alternative) contribution on which eligibility
would be based (Krause and Meyer, 2002: 109).

(a) The Retirement Pension Right

Women's absence from the labour market in order to attend to family
responsibilities and lower wages produce direct and significant effects in the
long term upon their retirement pensions. Women's participation in the
workforce provides access not only to present income, but also to retirement benefits. This means that women will usually have lower retirement
incomes than men and appropriate adjustments are not made in the event
of marriage breakdown. Women do not receive equal benefits to men and
there is no division of benefits upon divorce.

(b) The Survival Pension Right

The survival pension right is triggered by the worker's death regardless of
age or cause: an occurrence upon which the law presumes that surviving
'relatives' are in need. 'Relatives' are those individuals who were presumed
by law to be dependent on the worker. The concept of family taken into
account for the purposes of the relevant survivors in the social security system and in the civil service social security system is broader than that of
marriage with its consanguinity and affinity ties. In fact, the social security system also acknowledges supporting relationships similar to familial
or quasi-familial relationships. Hence benefits were available to individuals
who lived with the deceased worker and were supported by him or her.

Individuals who are either legally separated or divorced will be entitled
to the survival pension only if they are receiving alimony at the time of the

beneficiary's death, or if the court had found that the decedent lacks suffi-cient financial resources to pay alimony. As the spouse considered to be the sole or the primarily guilty party in the divorce has no right to alimony (Art 2016(2), Civil Code) he or she, therefore, is not entitled to a survival pen-sion right.[11] In fact, requiring that the ex-spouse be receiving alimony in order to receive the survival pension improperly transfers the concept of fault into the social security system.

DISCREPANCIES BETWEEN FAMILY LAW AND FAMILY VALUES

It is very difficult to say whether family laws have changed due to changes in mores and people's beliefs or whether mores and people's beliefs have changed because of changes in family laws. It is most likely that both these phenomena have occurred (Pereira Coelho, 2001: 31).

1 Family Law

(a) The Concept of Family

The law has recently been to some extent the most flexible of Portuguese normative institutions, offering the promise of more flexible models of the 'family' than many other normative systems. Alternative sexual behaviour has been afforded protection or explicit quasi-family status.[12] Nevertheless, it is not just the law that confers status on the nuclear family.

(b) From Institutionalism to Individualism

Especially in the second half of the 20th century, the law began to endorse changes in the family that reflected individualism and valued choice (Dolgin, 1997: 34; Voegeli, ch 2, this volume). In fact, family law treats marriage as primarily the concern of the individuals involved. In this respect, the law mirrors the heightened intensity and instability of relation-ships held together more by emotional than economic ties. To the extent that families deserve protection from the law, that protection increasingly attaches to individual family members and not to the family unit as an undi-vided and indivisible whole.

Recognising the trend in law and in society to view the family more as a collection of individuals than a community, it can be urged that presently, family law treats families as both a collection of individuals and a community. Although the legal system has shifted its focus from families to individuals,

---

[11] We notice the great role that alimony plays in social security law. As opposed to statuto-ry law of 1910, the concept of fault assumes, according to some authors, a relevant role in the alimony legal regime and, therefore, it has a great deal of influence in the ex-spouse's right to a survival pension. See Vaz Tomé (1997) 66.

[12] In spite of such legal changes, however, the concept of the nuclear family remains firm, in part due to the strong influence of certain extralegal institutions. See Fineman (1993): 389.

society still relies on families to play a crucial role in caring for the young, the aged, the sick, the severely disabled and the needy (Glendon, 1989: 306).

(c) From Hierarchy to Egalitarianism

Family law reformers probably expected that fathers would perform more household duties, as modern mothers spent more time and energy in the market place. According to this view spouses, fulfilling egalitarian impulses, would rework their relationship into a non-hierarchical form. The law considers both partners to a marriage to be equals. Both individuals are likely to think they are entitled to pursue careers outside the home. Both are expected to share domestic tasks. We speak of a marital 'partnership' and presume marriage to be an egalitarian relationship (Fineman, 1998). The legal system reflects theses altered aspirations in laws that reject the traditional characterisation of the family as a hierarchical role differentiated institution in which the legal identities and abilities of husband and wife merged under notions of marital unity (*ibid*).

This approach to family reform influenced and informed the legal changes made during the past several decades—the refashioning of the 'egalitarian family'. Reformers assumed that sharing could and would happen. With the egalitarian aim established in law, women would be free to develop their careers and men would be unconstrained in choosing nurturing over other activities. In fact, marriage is characterised as a partnership between equals. Each makes contributions to the relationship, which, although they may be different in kind, are of equal value. Each spouse is considered capable of providing and caring for her or him and any children are shared responsibilities. The ideal is of spouses voluntarily joined and interdependent—separate yet united (Fineman, 1993: 396).

The concept of the marital partnership has also had implications for parental roles. Most state legal schemes have fashioned the generic category of 'parenthood' from the previously differentiated roles of 'mother' and 'father'. Many legal schemes express a preference for joint custody or shared parenting, as each parent is presumed indifferently involved and essential to a child's upbringing. This egalitarian reconstruction of the family concept was initially undertaken largely in response to women resisting their historically assigned roles as wives and mothers in the family. At the level of legal doctrine, these efforts have been extremely successful in implementing the idea of an egalitarian family. Family law language is remarkably gender neutral. As a result of reform movements of the 1970s and onwards, certain aspects of the law reflect a gender-neutral family ideal. In substantive terms, dependency is not assumed to be the justification for allocation of marital wealth to women; rather it is the contribution they have made to the family that justifies their partnership share at dissolution. The whole way in which marriage is discussed at divorce has change substantially in the past few decades (Fineman, 1993: 397).

The egalitarian family is imposed on marital units, and it generates tensions insofar as one goal to be attained by the partners is equality in the market place. Equality as an ideal has developed in a society that rewards and values market work. Family work is to be 'managed' so that women are free to develop their careers. Attempts to achieve equality in the public sphere, particularly in the market, however, leave the two-parent family as an institution potentially without available caretakers (Fineman, 1995a: 2208).

The solution for the potential dilemma that there will be no caretaker in the egalitarian family has been to 'share' caretaking. Nevertheless, sharing is not taking place. Little has changed in terms of who does domestic labour, and this is typically true regardless of whether or not both partners work. Where it is necessary to compromise one spouse's career for caretaking, economic incentives guide the choice between spouses. Continuing market inequalities typically ensure that when there is a need for a family member to accommodate caretaking by forgoing market time, the competent caretaker will be the lower earner, usually the woman. In addition, centuries of social and cultural conditioning shape the way women understand and exercise their 'choices' in defining their family role. The role assigned to the family—to care for dependants—mandates two parents and some form of role division. Therefore, the family will assume the gendered and unequal form almost inevitably (Fineman, 1995a: 2209–10).

Changes in law do not reflect 'real' changes, nor can they compel such changes. Gender divisions persist. There are neither lessening workloads nor new and 'egalitarian' divisions of labour within households. Women continue to bear the costs associated with the caretaking tasks that they typically perform. Even where both parties are working, most housework is done by women. These labours have material consequences that are uncompensated within the family. If such labour remains invisible, the fact that it goes uncompensated is endorsed. This result is supported by extra-legal norms and, given the cultural and market structures built and dependent upon the fundamental unequal division of family labour, the pattern is going to be very difficult to alter (Fineman, 1995a: 2199–200; 1993: 397–8).

Although the rules of the law may incorporate notions of equality, these norms are countered by other rules, which do not embody such notions (Ingleby, 1993: 355). Not only is women's work within the household unpaid and undervalued, but to a large extent their work in the market place is also perceived as secondary to that of men. Because of their 'dual role', many women work in poorly paid sectors of the employment market, in jobs for which they are overqualified, or in part-time jobs (Oldham, 1995: 283). There is clearly a need to enhance the viability of market employment for women. Suggestions aimed at achieving this objective have included increased efforts towards full implementation of equal opportunities legislation, better provision of public or publicly subsidised child care facilities, greater flexibility as to working hours, job-sharing by both parents and the encouragement of participation in child care and other household tasks by fathers (*ibid* 299). We still see that in the main in the marriage with minor children one spouse takes on primary responsibility for the raising of the children, thereby sacrificing earnings and career prospects, so that the other is free to build a career. Society has not kept pace with law—and the family continues to operate as a role-defined institution, allowing for and justifying persistent patterns of gender inequality in the larger Portuguese society (Fineman, 1993: 397).

(d) Divorce

The major divorce law reforms of the last and this century have all encountered opposition. Spouses are presently allowed to claim a divorce by mutual consent in the Civil Registry Office without any judicial control, at any time—even immediately after the marriage ceremony—and having only one conference. This reform was intended to reserve judicial intervention to cases where divergent interests are involved and to avoid useless and stigmatising procedures for the divorcing spouses. In addition it makes the couple responsible for their divorce, and it contributes to the privatisation and self-regulation of the family. Finally, it would reduce costs to both the spouses and the state. Many people insist on the need for safeguards—both of the interests of vulnerable members of the family and of the public interest in upholding the institution of marriage.

There is a belief that, if divorce were made harder to obtain, the rate would be reduced. While it would not seem a sensible policy for a state to provide incentives for couples to divorce, making the legal process of divorce more difficult seems unlikely to reach the desired outcome. Those who argue for harder divorce seem to have an exaggerated view of the power of the law to control people's domestic living arrangements. Such a view presupposes that the difficulty of escape keeps people married. It also presupposes that the difficulty of divorce is governed by the complexity of the legal rules. Divorce is always difficult in a social and emotional sense for adults and children and there is no reason to think that, in general, people do not think hard and struggle with alternatives before taking legal action. We also know from the countries where divorce is not permitted, that people are well practised in finding ways of reordering their domestic life, whatever the law says (Richards, 1995: 17).

The rise in divorce is associated with the development of companionate marriage. Expectations for marriage have risen as have the range of functions it is expected to fulfil. In the divorce area, there has been some rewriting of family law already in an attempt to reflect more 'contemporary' notions about the family. In considering the rules governing marriage and divorce, it is no longer clear what constitutes appropriate family behaviour—who has acted as a 'good' wife and mother or husband and father, fulfilling the well-defined roles in the family. In fact, it is no longer clear that these are even appropriate questions for the legal system to ask. The laws governing divorce have added to normative assessments that took into account conduct through consideration of 'fault' a system of default rules, such as no-fault divorce, divorce by mutual consent and preferences for joint custody, making the process more administrative than judgemental (Fineman, 1993: 396).

These may appear powerful justifications for removing questions of conduct from the law governing marital status, but it is clear that changes to no-fault divorce law have not removed notions of fault from divorcing parties. Since the law is not the only source of the rules that people apply in their relationships, it should not be assumed that legal changes are sufficient to change the attitudes of divorcees (Ingleby, 1993: 56).

Legal regulation of family creation and dissolution has moved away from insistence on marriage as the exclusive source of family ties. The adoption of no-fault grounds for divorce has eliminated the legal recognition of marriage as a lifelong commitment, and the dismantling of the distinction between marital and non-marital children has abolished the role of marriage as a defining element in parental (and particularly paternal) relationships (Carbone, 1996: 272).

Notwithstanding the pessimism about the future of marriage and even of the family and concern about the rise of single-parent families, in Portugal most marriages are only terminated by death; and most children live in households formed by their two married parents. The law sometimes seems little concerned about the rights and duties of the members of functioning families (Cretney, 1998: 155).

(e) De Facto Union: A New Form of Family?

Law now regulates the living-together of unmarried couples[13]. *Cum grano salis*, to a certain extent, cohabitants are now seen as equivalent to married couples. Thus the legal status of cohabitants is to some degree shaped by the vision of marriage. However, cohabitation is not totally assimilated to marriage. This assimilation has regard to the protection of the family home, labour law, social security law, tax law, adoption and lease law.

The growth of a law of cohabitation is clearly a response to the upsurge in alternative living arrangements and the perceived need to do justice between such partners (Freeman, 1997: 330). Law 135/99 of 28 August considered as a de facto union any relationship similar to the marital one (*tori, mensae et habitationis*), that is, any relationship established between a man and a woman who live for at least two years like spouses. This statute protected the family home and the social benefits derived from the social security beneficiary's death. If cohabitants buy an asset together, they will

[13] Like in Spain, before 1999 only some effects of the de facto union were regulated by law in a fragmentary and dispersed way. See Picontó Novales (ch 13, this volume).

be subject to the regime of joint-ownership rather than to a community property regime.

In the case of separation, ordinary rules are not applied where the family home or common residence is at stake. Where there is no agreement of the partners upon the transmission of the lease contract, judges have a discretionary power to award possession of a rented home to one of the partners, regardless of whose name is on the lease, in the light of the interests involved, with compensation where appropriate to the other partner (Art 84 RAU). In the case of a home owned by both partners, the judge may award the dwelling to one and compensation to the other (Art 1793, Civil Code). Even where one partner owns the home alone, the non-owner may be awarded possession by way of a forced lease, with rent to be fixed by the judge, if a minor child or children reside with the non-owner partner or the interests of the other partner justify it (Art 1793). Where cohabitation had lasted for two years, upon the death of the partner whose name is on the lease, possession of a rented home is granted to the other partner, in the light of the interests involved (Art 85(1)(e) RAU).

Law 7/2001, of 11 May, revoked Law 135/99 and protected the de facto union between people of either different or the same sex, that is, the legal situation of two individuals, irrespective of their sex, that live in a de facto union for more than two years. In fact, the law recognises same-sex couples in the same way as heterosexual non-married couples for a number of purposes. However, as opposed to heterosexual couples, same-sex couples are not allowed to adopt.

The struggle over the meaning of marriage is specially reflected in the demand for marriage of gays and lesbians. The law tried to deal with the gay rights challenge to the traditional heterosexual marriage (Krause and Meyer, 2002: 109).[14] Because current sexual and associational lifestyles differ so much, the law does not deal with them as though they all were role-divided, procreative marriage. Marriage has to a certain extent legally become just one lifestyle choice among many. It is probable that in many cases cohabitation is being transformed from a prelude to marriage to its alternative (*ibid*: 107). Since the de facto union was not legally assimilated to marriage, the law of marriage shall not be applied either directly or by analogy to that union (Lobo Xavier, 2001: 9ff).[15] Until very recently it was assumed that the legislature should not regulate cohabitation and that it was very unlikely cohabitants wanted it ('Les concubins se passent de la loi, la loi se désinteresse d'eux').

---

[14] It is interesting to note that the Bulgarian Constitution expressly forbids same-sex marriages. See Naoumova (ch 16, this volume).

[15] The importance of marking clear differences between the de facto union and marriage is underlined. As opposed to other countries like Canada, in Portugal the visibility of atypical family forms has not yet brought the application of family law into sharp focus, the legal family has not been systematically and dogmatically challenged and reconceptualised and, same-sex marriage was not legalised (see Glennon, ch 10, this volume). As in many countries that have now introduced legislation about same-sex relationships, Portuguese law is the result of lobbying by gay and lesbian rights groups (see Cottier, ch 11, this volume).

The fact that marriage is now demographically of less significance than it was before does not mean that marriage has lost its considerable legal importance. There are still many more married couples than unmarried couples. Neither of the partners in a relationship outside marriage is automatically entitled to the legal rights stemming from the status of marriage (Cretney, 2000: 10).[16] It is true that legislation sometimes gave rights to those who have lived together as husband and wife.

Although surviving cohabitants are not included among the heirs to a decedent's estate, a cohabitant is entitled to claim maintenance from the estate of a person by whom he or she was being supported (Art 2020, Civil Code) in case cohabitation had lasted for over two years and if he or she cannot obtain support from his or her relatives who are legally obliged to provide it. Judicial decisions did not sanction cohabitation's dissolution itself but rather the tort that caused it. Both the testamentary obligation (Art 2156) and the principle according to which a cohabitant still married is prevented from making donations to his or her partner prohibit *inter vivos* and *mortis causa* gifts between cohabitants (Arts 953 and 2196).

With regard to the establishment of maternity, the law does not distinguish between children born in and out of wedlock (Arts 1796(1) and 1803ff, Civil Code). If the mother was living in a de facto union during the legal period of conception, the paternity of her partner is presumed (Arts 1871(1)(c)). Unmarried parents can obtain joint custody if they live together with the child and want to assume jointly parental responsibility (Art 1911(3)). They shall declare their wish of exercising joint custody at the civil registrar (Art 1911(3)). The requirement of an official declaration of custody ensures that joint custody cannot become effective without the consent of one parent.

In public law areas, where family membership is at stake, the family is envisioned as an economic, rather than a legal, entity. Therefore, marriage-like cohabitation was legally considered. It is said that the ascendance of individual choice increasingly appears to have limits of its own. While a dominant theme of family policy debates in the closing decades of the last century was the need for family law to accommodate the reality of unconventional family life, an emerging theme in the opening of the new century is the need to define the limits of that accommodation. Family in the 21st century will not be solely a matter of personal choice; instead family must ultimately be defined by modern consensus about what is essentially good and special about that relation (Krause and Meyer, 2002: 116–8).

(f) People who Live Under a 'Common Economy' (Law 6/2001, 11 May)

Others who are not couples but are in defined 'common economy relationships' have been granted a more limited set of rights and obligations under

---

[16] As in Spain, in Portugal cohabitation is no longer considered as immoral and is increasingly viewed as another way of living as a couple (see Picontó Novales, ch 13, this volume).

some laws.[17] Through the enlargement of the circle of relationships recognised by law, regulation has been extended to groups of people sharing habitation.

According to the law, the concept of a 'common economy relationship' is applied where people live in community of table and home for more than two years and have established a life in common as far as mutual help and sharing of resources are concerned (Art 2(1)). It may be constituted by people either linked or not by family ties, by people of the same or of different sex, by two or more people. At least one of the members has to be 18 years old (Art 2(2)). The law also protects the situation of two individuals of different sexes who do not have sexual relationships, as well as those situations of three or more individuals who share the same space and share the living costs. It is not necessary that people share their incomes and resources; it is sufficient that they live in a community of mutual help where they contribute to the living expenses. These are situations that are not restricted to the community of economy, but also have regard to the share of material, sentimental, social and human recourses among other things. They are protected in labour law, tax law, protection of the common residence and transmission of the lease contract upon the death of the tenant member.

2 Family Values

The legal notion of family or quasi-family relationships does not correspond to social reality (Pereira Coelho and Oliveira, 2001: 27–28). According to the law (Art 1576), which considers as family relationships only those resulting from the sources referred to above, the de facto union is not a family relationship but rather a quasi-family relationship. This is merely a legal–technical concept of family. However, Portuguese law takes into account larger and less technical notions of the family, which are valid within certain domains or for certain effects. Thus, social security law uses the concept of 'family aggregate', which is also composed by the individual who is linked by a de facto union to the beneficiary and it is urged that a broad concept of family, which encompasses the de facto union, should also be accepted in lease law.

Critics of individualism often argue that expanding the definition of family to potentially to include any voluntary association of individuals who wish to see themselves as a family dilutes the meaning of family and endangers the continued vitality of the institution. People seem to doubt the value of families which do not conform to the 'traditional' norms and are

---

[17] Some view the legal acknowledgement of these relationships as a significant step in moving away from the sexual relationship as the key determinant of 'family'. See Graycar (2000): 737ff.

inclined to equate personal responsibility with the marital family model. There are concerns about laws and policies that exalt individual freedoms over those values of commitment and responsibility that bind individuals to each other and the belief that non-conforming families threaten these values (Woodhouse, 1996: 573; Eekelaar, ch 1, this volume).[18]

As the nature of inter-dependence between families and outside support systems changes, private law dealing with domestic relations tends increasingly to connect with a broad range of public laws and programmes affecting the family (Glendon, 1989: 294). The ability of families to carry out the tasks for which society relies on them, however, has been dramatically altered by changes in family structure, in the labour force participation of women, and in the nature of dependency itself. The modern two-earner family with children, and the single-parent family in particular, must rely more on outside support systems for dealing with their dependent members than the homemaker–breadwinner household, which has now become atypical. And while the pool of available caretakers within the family has been shrinking, the composition of the group in need of care has altered to include far fewer children and far more disabled and elderly people than it did before (*ibid* 307).

(a) The Concept of Family

Some societal acceptance of same-sex preferences and support privileges in quasi-marital relationships and the use of non-traditional forms of reproduction are mostly seen as evidence of a breakdown in Portuguese morality. Others prefer to view these changes as an accommodation of the new society to the voices of pluralism and inclusiveness, which, in turn, promotes a new cultural vibrancy. There is an obvious lack of consensus (Prennetta, 2000: 459).[19]

Cum grano salis, it can be said that the social and cultural concept of family is about husbands and wives and the children they produce. The core of husband and wife, with or without children, seems to qualify in all definitions. Many people consider this reproductive family to represent the 'natural' form of the family and some argue that the reproductive family should be viewed as an exclusive vision of the family in terms of

[18] With respect to the concept of individualism in Swedish family law, see Schiratzki (ch 8, this volume).

[19] Although some people invoke the impossibility of defining the family irrespective of the space–time and social–cultural context, Portuguese society has institutionalised the concept of the marriage-based family. It is looked at as the only legitimate institution of family law. It is viewed as the basic unit of society and the location for the individual's self-development and socialisation. It accomplishes educational and affective functions, and provides economic support for its members (see Mazzotta, ch 12, this volume). Like Switzerland, but unlike France, Norway or Great Britain, Portugal does not belong to the countries where marriage and birth of children are disconnected (see Cottier, ch 11, this volume).

policy and law (Fineman, 1999: 1208).[20] Divorce, promiscuity, homosexuality, reproductive technology and cultural changes have significantly altered the Portuguese legal view of the marital unit, and its foundation for the family. However, even though marriage may have become more flexible due to divorce legislation, 'lasting marriage is the goal and, even as the divorce statistics increase, remains the norm for most people' (Kohm, 2002: 106).

In spite of alternative visions and nonconforming behaviour, the culturally normative family remains intact: the heterosexual married couple and their biological children. Our cultural conception of the family as an entity is built around the married couple. This basic family relationship continues to be considered as presumptively appropriate and as the essential family connection (Fineman, 1995a: 2198). In fact, in Portuguese society, only one form of intimate entity has been so venerated in the culture as to become institutionalised as the model of intimacy. Historically only the nuclear family has been protected and promoted by cultural institutions. The reverence for the nuclear family is almost coercive, with the society defining and securing for the nuclear family a privileged position in regard to the ordering of intimacy (Fineman, 1993: 388–9). Contemporary Portuguese social policies concerning the family are rooted in historical patriarchal structures. These concepts continue to influence the ways in which society constructs the family (*ibid*: 1418).

Things have changed. Domestic arrangements that do not conform to the family unit are on the rise. More and more individuals are living alone than in past decades. Divorce rates are increasing,[21] and single motherhood is on the rise.[22] Couples choose not to become parents in larger numbers than prior generations.[23] Furthermore, even in conforming families (married with children), the traditional roles have broken down. Many women work outside the home either in a full- or part-time capacity, and some are as deeply

---

[20] It is said that the common experience of mankind has shown that the marriage-based family deserves preferred legal status precisely because it is the best forum for providing all of the contributions to children and to society that are offered only in part by other relationships. The law can serve as a powerful messenger in holding up to society a standard which the collective voice of a people approves as the ideal for all. Of course the law must take into account existing realities, but in doing so, must not detract from its message about what is ideal by substituting other relationships for marriage or setting up other institutions which serve to compete with marriage and which are treated as equivalent to marriage as the foundation of the society (Duncan, 2001: 78). Marriage is not merely a custom or a tradition; it is a way of life, the foundation of civilisation. Thus the family is wrongly assumed to be unchanging, an essential institution, natural in form and function—the repository for dependency (see Fineman, 2001: 1418).

[21] In 1999, the divorce rate (26 per cent) was higher than in 1997 (21.2 per cent) (Comissão para a Igualdade e para os Direitos das Mulheres, 2001. *Situação das Mulheres*, p 86).

[22] In 1999, the rate of monoparental families was 10.6 per cent (Comissão para a Igualdade e para os Direitos das Mulheres, 2001. *Situação das Mulheres*, p 86).

[23] In 1999, the birth rate was 1.5 per cent (Comissão para a Igualdade e para os Direitos das Mulheres, 2001. *Situação das Mulheres*, p 92).

committed to career and job advancement as their husbands.[24] The number of persons marrying is also in decline. The median age for marriage has risen.[25] The increase in civil marriage[26] is connected with the rise in the number of second and subsequent marriages. But it also masks a change in the understanding of marriage: there has been a cultural shift in which marriage is seen more as a terminable contract rather than a lifelong commitment. Cohabitation is no more stable than marriage, and is probably less so. Cohabitations tend to be short-lived, after which they either break up or are transformed into marriages. People are having children outside both marriage and cohabitation. Although the law does not distinguish births within a stable cohabitation from those to single and unpartnered women, there are big differences. There has been a decrease in the proportion of households filling the 'traditional' structure of a couple with dependent children.

Women's rejection of the hierarchical family, the dissolution of the conceptual lines between the domestic or 'private' sphere and the market/political or 'public' sphere, and the increased participation of women in the workforce (with their consequential shouldering of dual responsibilities) challenge the vitality of the nuclear family. Both social policy and some legal regulations seem to ignore these changes with their continued resort to the nuclear family unit without introducing the adequate adaptations (Fineman, 1995a: 2183–84).[27]

Legal regulation of each of these different relations and processes has emerged at different times and in relation to different concerns. They have

[24] At this point it is interesting to point out that in 1999, 44.9 per cent of women were participating in the labour market. Moreover, the percentage of employed women with part-time jobs was 16.3 per cent compared to 6.2 per cent for men. Furthermore, women also earn less than the similarly situated men. In 1998, their remuneration was 76.7 per cent of men's. Finally, in 1999, the female unemployment rate was 5.0 per cent and the male rate was 3.2 per cent. In addition, 83.7 per cent of these women had a full-time job. Women work mainly in agriculture, traditional industries and domestic service (Comissão para a Igualdade e para os Direitos das Mulheres, 2001. *Situação das Mulheres*, pp 71ff; see also Fineman, 1995a: 2188–89). It can be stated that women's employment rate in Portugal is one of the highest in the European Union.

[25] In 1999, the average age in first marriage was 25.6 years for women and 27.3 for men. See Comissão para a Igualdade e para os Direitos das Mulheres, 2001. *Situação das Mulheres*, p 86.

[26] In 1999, the rate of civil marriage was 33.5 per cent (Comissão para a Igualdade e para os Direitos das Mulheres, 2001. *Situação das Mulheres*, p 85).

[27] The current challenges to the concept of the family to a large extent merely reformulate and update basic assumptions about intimacy—changing some aspects of the old family concept to accommodate new family or quasi-family forms. Specifically, they retain the centrality of sexual affiliation to the organisation and understanding of intimacy. The nuclear family as natural is assumed (Fineman, 1993: 393). The substance of one set of challenges is the argument that non-traditional entities should be accepted as 'families', because they perform the same function of fulfilling the emotional and material needs of their members. Intimate relationships are analogised to the nuclear family, combining functional and symbolic appeals in arguments for legal and social recognition (*ibid* 393).

Analogy arguments accept the appropriateness of the marriage institution, which is entitled to a prevailed position within law and society. They assert that the designation of 'family' should encompass more, different and non-traditional relationships—the non-traditional should be entitled to privileged status also (Fineman, 1993: 394). Furthermore, the belief that defined their terms differently. They do not operate according to a single division of 'public' and 'private'—spaces, activities and relations, which are within the scope of regulation for one purpose, are outside it for another. There is a lack of harmony between some branches of the law. Rather than conferring a false unity upon the diversity of legal regulation, analysis should treat this diversity as a clue to the social intelligibility of the law (Rose, 1987: 55). Furthermore, law does not exist in isolation from other regulatory systems. Law here should be seen in an extended sense, as all those interdictions, urgings, interventions, techniques and evaluations that seek to shape events towards desired ends. Legal mechanisms need to be relocated within this far wider field of regulatory mechanisms ranging from taxation, through welfare to the design of domestic space (*ibid*: 55).[28]

(b) Divorce

The trend towards facilitating the procedures of divorce—which accompanies the deinstitutionalisation of marriage, the privatisation and self-regulation of

it is marriage that constitutes the core affiliation is evident in the debate on alternative families. Proposed alternatives are analogised to it in its formalised form—marriage. Legal recognition of these alternatives is justified by reference to their similarity to heterosexual marriage in regard to the assumed emotional and economic functions. This analogy accepts the nuclear family as an institution that appropriately structures the discourse about alternative intimate entities (*ibid*: 3940).

A different type of challenge to the nuclear family confronts some of the foundational concepts that justify the contemporary preference for the nuclear family. The sentimental designation of the nuclear family as a refuge from the cruel world has become hard for some to maintain when social movements such as feminist and child advocacy have brought to light the very real potential of exploitative and abusive behaviour within families. These arguments tear the veil of 'privacy' from the nuclear family revealing that it fails to perform the social and psychological functions that were the justification for its privileged position. Ultimately, such arguments call into question the whole concept of the nuclear family as a legally privileged unit as a form of social organisation. The arguments focus on the individuals within families, affording the entity no independent deference per se (Fineman, 1993: 395).

Other legal systems have attempted answers by broadening the definition of marriage to encompass transsexuals, by creating new forms of relationship recognised by law such as homosexual registered partnerships, by giving a legal status to heterosexual cohabiting couples through legislation. In such answers marriage remains the model to which other relationships aspire (O'Donovan, 1993: 84).

[28] Some state-created background rules shape and reinforce social roles by assigning power and responsibility within the family. These background rules are not usually thought of as state intervention, but they implicate the state in the prescribed family roles. The content of family roles has changed (Olsen, 1985: 848–9). Today the state's role in reinforcing economic dependency is still significant. Although state laws no longer require women to perform unpaid work for their husbands as part of the marriage contract, as in previous centuries, some laws still provide a significant economic incentive for domestic labour to remain unpaid. An additional basis for women's economic dependency is low pay (*ibid*: 851). In addition, to view the husband and wife as the basic family unit may be unrealistic in a society with a divorce rate increasing and never-married motherhood on the rise (Fineman, 1995a: 2202). If the never-married or divorced mother devotes her time to market work in order to support her child no one will be available to perform her caretaker role. If she fulfils her culturally assigned obligations by sacrificing her career to bear the burdens of dependency, as a single or divorced mother without a wage earner to support her, she will starve unless she asks for support to the state. In any event her family has not dealt with its dependencies privately (*ibid*: 2209).

the family—has been widely criticised (Lobo Xavier, 2001: 2ff). In addition, it is submitted that the 'divorce without a judge' or administrative divorce could bring about a new sort of post-divorce case and the loss of the guarantees that are assured by the legal process. It is urged that modern divorce law and practice have resulted in a sort of legitimisation of polygamy by way of legalising multiple, successive marriages or relationships of persons who have continuing legal, financial and social ties to prior partners and children (Krause and Meyer, 2002: 1023).

CONCLUSION

The emergence of different legal quasi-family relationships cannot be considered as a sign of the decline of the nuclear family. It is not inevitably an attempt to redefine the family to allow greater individual choice in determining one's own family form. Rather it shows the development of a new morality that is beginning to inform family law and is focused on connection, care, and commitment to other family members, but also contains problematic notions of choice.

The new morality embodied in family and quasi-family law is grounded in caring, commitment and fairness. It continues to recognise the existence of obligations between family members. The trend in family law, even if toward personal autonomy, is still toward conceptualising individuals within a familial form. Although there is a movement toward increasing personal autonomy, this autonomy is still sought within the context of the family. Individuals continue to want a familial relationship; they simply want more control over the terms of that relationship. This movement toward personal autonomy is nevertheless a movement toward relationships, not away from them (Cahn, 1997: 270–1). The rights of individuals are placed within the contexts of community, equality and commitment.

Moral discourse about the family has shifted, not disappeared. Newly developing concerns about fairness, equity and caregiving fit within the conventional definition of 'moral' concerns. There should be a willingness in family law to recognise dependencies within the family. The new ideology is based on fairness and equality both within and among families. This standard is able to recognise and consider the dependencies within the family. The so-called new morality focuses on nurturing relationships.

Family may well be reconceived in its details or particular configurations, but as an essential institution it remains secure. Society's task in formulating family law in the years ahead will be to articulate its own family values (values of responsibility and care), not merely to accept those proffered by history or contemporary individual choice. The family that will emerge will be one defined overwhelmingly by a consensus over what human intimacy and commitment is valuable (Krause and Meyer, 2002: 119–120). Strengthening families requires rebuilding not only a sense of commitment but also an infrastructure of jobs, housing, public health, schools and community services that make it possible for individuals to form families, raise healthy children, and care for their sick and elderly members (Woodhouse, 1996: 580).

It can be said that laws governing familial relationships have not developed in line with the norms governing behaviour in society at large. There is a disjunction between the culturally dominant definition of the family and the empirical and normative reality of the institution (Cardia Vonèche and Bastard, ch 6, this volume). The application of norms of equality to the family has not significantly altered the reality of gendered allocation of work within it. Changing hierarchical relationships between spouses into relationships of equal status has not shifted responsibility for caretaking. Women continue to care for dependants, but also to work outside the home. The trend is toward statutory equality between the sexes. Whether equality in the law equates to true equality in practice remains to be seen.

Family behaviour does not exactly correspond to the set of legal norms. The laws affecting families and the patterns of behaviour that constitute the social institution of the family are not aligned. Families and marriage are viewed as pre-legal institutions. There is a contrast between the homogeneity of the concept of family that underlies some legal and social regulations and the diversity of social reality. The family model assumed by social policies—a married heterosexual couple with children, and a male breadwinner—is far from corresponding to the multiplicity of family models that actually co-exist in our society. In certain cases, apart from the nuclear family, the concept of family in Portuguese law is also used to describe other primary living units in which the care and upbringing of children takes place.

The starting point for the dependants' social security system is their typical need for support rather than their own contributions. This is justified in the children's case, since an autonomous contribution can neither exist nor be demanded and, therefore, their exclusion from the support creditors' domain is not possible. It is, however, questionable where there is an autonomous contribution that has a socially recognised value, like homemaking. This contribution is not taken into account in the exclusively indirect social security of the housewife and mother. In fact, her housework is the only reason for her dependency on her husband's social security through her right to support. Her right to support connects her contribution with the social security system.

An analysis of the gender system emphasises the ways in which men, able to be 'ideal workers' to a far greater extent than women, reap most benefits. While empirical information refutes the general applicability of the traditional ideal of a male who, as head of the household, provides economically for his wife and children, legal and political thinkers often consider the attachment of a legal responsibility for providing for women and children to men as the panacea for many social ills (Fineman, 1998: 93).

There are numerous instances where we notice the limited power of law, on its own, to advance or retard broad social changes in the area of family life. But we must not unduly minimise its potential to influence social trends. Law performs an important societal function when it disciplines transformations and transitions in society, imposing conceptual order (Lobo Xavier, forthcoming).[29] The law does not resolve many issues like the role of the family in the provision of economic support, the interaction between the family and the state and the normative legal and social functions of the family, and the reconstitution of the typical gendered division of domestic labour (Glennon, ch 10, this volume).[30]

We must begin to think of family policy in terms of the functions we want the family to perform, in a way that is responsive to emerging realities. We should establish a system able to reflect the functions society should protect and encourage (Fineman, 1995a: 2203; 1995b: 227ff).

We should not continue to describe the family as a mere 'unit of consumption', since it ignores the important productive roles it plays. Housework contributes to the labour power of the wage earner by the production of use values necessary for the wage earner's subsistence and it also plays an important part in the larger economy in the reproduction of labour (the rearing and socialisation of the next generation of labour). Little attention has been paid to the important welfare functions, which are still carried on within families, in terms of care of the sick, elderly and disabled (Oldham, 1995: 274–75; Lobo Xavier, 2001: 1400ff).

Some people continue to insist that families can only be built upon the foundation of a marital tie. Others emphasise the biological connection and minimise the importance of legal relationships in favour of kinship structures that form affiliations transcending current formal definitions of the family. For others, the preference is for an affective family, a unit composed of those with whom we choose to connect but who may not be 'related' to us by either blood or marriage. Family affiliations are expressed in different kinds of affiliation acts. Some are sexually based, as with marriage. Some are forged biologically, as through parenthood. Others are more relational, such as those based on nurturing or caretaking or those developed through affection and acceptance of interdependence (Fineman, 1995a: 2190–91).

---

[29] It is said that the relationship between legal rules and social norms is complex and dynamic, as the law may act to incorporate developing social norms, or to strengthen a weakening social norm, or to withdraw support from an outdated or unacceptable norm (Maclean, 2000: 2). Moreover, it is frequently very difficult to know whether the 'law' is attempting to impose behavioural patterns or reacting to societal norms (Eekelaar and Maclean, 1994: 7).

[30] As far as elderly people are concerned, inter-generational relations have been supported by social ('taking care in the older years') and legal norms and the relationship between the state and the family has been largely neglected (Todorova, ch 15, this volume). Political debates have not yet focused on the role family plays in caring for the elderly (Van Houtte and Breda, ch 14, this volume). To a certain extent, the obligations of the greater society to children, disabled and elderly people are not sufficiently developed (Shapiro, ch 5, this volume).

Within the variety of extra-legal cultural and social systems that shape our beliefs about families there are two core concepts that predominate and affect law. The first is that family has a 'natural' form—the nuclear family. This natural family predates the state and is also viewed as a complement to the state. The second concept is that of the private family—a unit entitled to protection from the state. Ideally the private family raises children and cares for the ill, the needy and the dependent without demanding public resources to do so. But according to the private family responsibility for dependency, society directs dependency[31] away from the state and privatises it (Fineman, 1995a: 2205; Lobo Xavier, 2001: 1400ff).

The result is the continuation of gender inequality. The tasks assigned to the private family mandate that costs associated with dependency be allocated among family members, and this allocation is gendered. Our perception of the family as a social institution facilitates the continuation of gendered role divisions and frustrates the egalitarian ideal.

REFERENCES

Cahn, NR (1997) 'Review Essay: The Moral Complexities of Family Law' *Stanford Law Review* 50.

Carbone, J (1996) 'Symposium: Ethics, Public Policy, and the Future of the Family: Morality, Public Property and the Family: The Role of Marriage and the Public/Private Divide' *Santa Clara Law Review* 36.

Cretney, SM (2000) *Family Law* (London, Sweet & Maxwell).

—— (1998) *Law, Law Reform and the Family* (Oxford, Oxford University Press).

Dolgin, JL (1997) *Defining the Family, Law, Technology, and Reproduction in an Uneasy Age, 1997* (New York and London, New York University Press).

Duncan, WC (2001) '"Don't Ever Take a Fence Down": The "Functional" Definition of Family—Displacing Marriage in Family Law' *Journal of Law and Family Studies* 3.

---

[31] It is important to distinguish between various forms of dependency. One is the natural dependency. It is natural in that it results from the status and situation of being a child and often accompanies ageing, illness or disability. This type of dependency is developmental in nature. Dependency will always be with us as a society and as individuals. The second, complementary form of dependency, however, is more problematic for policymakers. Those who care for natural dependants are often themselves dependent—a derivative dependency that stems from their roles as caretakers and the need for resources that their duties generate. This type of dependency is not natural, nor is it universal. It is socially defined and assigned, and that assignment is gendered (Fineman, 1995a: 2206). '[W]illingness to apply the balance between work and family responsibilities in a "fair" way, given the continuous emphasis on the provision of child-care by the mother' (Eekelaar, ch 1, this volume). In fact, the downside of traditional marriage is that one partner—typically the woman—has sacrificed earnings and career to raise children and, on divorce, has little property and limited employment prospects (Krause and Meyer, 2002: 102).

Eekelaar, J and Maclean, M (1994) 'Introduction' in J Eekelaar and M Maclean (eds), *A Reader on Family Law* (Oxford, Oxford University Press).

Fineman, M (1993) 'Our Sacred Institution: The Ideal of the Family in American Law and Society' *Virginia Law Review* 2.

—— (1995a) 'Masking Dependency: The Political Role of Family Rhetoric' *Virginia Law Review* 81.

—— (1995b) *The Neutered Mother, the Sexual Family and Other Twentieth Century Tragedies* (New York and London, Routledge).

—— (1998) 'Symposium: The Inevitability of Dependency and the Politics of Subsidy' *Stanford Law and Policy Review* 9.

—— (1999) 'Symposium: Privacy and the Family: Panel III What Place for Family Privacy?' *George Washington Law Review* 67.

—— (2001) 'Symposium: Contract and Care' *Chicago–Kent Law Review* 76.

Freeman, M (1997) 'Family Values and Family Justice' *Current Legal Problems* 50.

Glendon, MA (1989) *The Transformation of Family Law, State, Law, and Family in the United States and Western Europe* (Chicago and London, The University of Chicago Press).

Graycar, R (2000) 'Family Law: Law Reform by Frozen Chook: Family Law Reform for the New Millennium?' *Melbourne University Law Review* 24.

Ingleby, R (1993) *Family Law and Society* (Sydney, Butterworths).

Kohm, LM (2002) 'How Will the Proliferation and Recognition of Domestic Partnerships Affect Marriage' *Journal of Law and Family Studies* 4.

Krause, HD and Meyer DD (2002) 'American Law in a Time of Global Interdependence' US National Reports to the XVITH International Congress of Comparative Law, Section II, 'What Family for the 21st Century?' *American Journal of Comparative Law* 50.

Lobo Xavier, R (2001) 'Novas Sobre a União "More Uxorio" em Portugal' *Estudos Dedicados ao Prof. Doutor Mário Júlio de Almeida Costa* (Lisbon: Universidade Católica Portuguesa).

—— (forthcoming) 'Família: Da Crise à Desregulamentação'.

Maclean, M (2000). 'Introduction' in M Maclean (ed), *Making Law for Families* (Oxford, Hart Publishing).

O'Donovan, K (1993) 'Marriage: A Sacred or Profane Love Machine?' *Feminist Legal Studies* 1.

Oldham, M (1995) 'Homemaker Services and the Law' in A Bainham, D Pearl and R Pickford (eds), *Frontiers of Family Law* (Chichester, Wiley).

Olsen, FE (1985) 'The Myth of State Intervention in the Family' *Journal of Law Reform* 18: 4.

Pereira Coelho, F (1986) *Curso de Direito da Família* (Coimbra, University of Coimbra).

—— (2001) 'Casamento e Divórcio no Ensino de Manuel de Andrade e na Legislação Actual' *Boletim da Faculdade de Direito* (Coimbra, University of Coimbra).

Pereira Coelho, F and Oliveira, G (2001) *Curso de Direito da Família*, vol 1, *Introdução-Direito Matrimonial* (Coimbra, Coimbra Editora).

Prennetta, JP Jr (2000) book review 'Family Values and the New Society: Dilemmas of the 21st Century by George P Smith, II Connecticut: Praeger, 1998' *Journal of Contemporary Health Law and Policy* 16.

Richards, MPM (1995) 'Private Worlds and Public Intentions—the Role of the State at Divorce' in A Bainham, D Pearl and R Pickford (eds), *Frontiers of Family Law* (Chichester, Wiley).

Rose, N (1987) 'Beyond the Public/Private Distinction' *Journal of Law and Society* 14.

Vaz Tomé, MJ (1997) *O Direito à Pensão de Reforma enquanto Bem Comum do Casal* (Coimbra, Coimbra Editora).

Woodhouse, BB (1996) 'Symposium: "It All Depends on What You Mean by Home": Toward a Communitarian Theory of the "Nontraditional" Family' *Utah Law Review* 569.